Mega-events and social change

MANCHESTER
1824

Manchester University Press

Globalizing Sport Studies

Series editor: **John Horne, Professor of Sport and Sociology, University of Central Lancashire, UK**

Public interest in sport studies continues to grow throughout the world. This series brings together the latest work in the field and acts as a global knowledge hub for interdisciplinary work in sport studies. While promoting work across disciplines, the series focuses on social scientific and cultural studies of sport. It brings together the most innovative scholarly empirical and theoretical work, from within the UK and internationally.

Books previously published in this series by Bloomsbury Academic:

Global Media Sport: Flows, Forms and Futures
David Rowe

Japanese Women and Sport: Beyond Baseball and Sumo
Robin Kietlinski

Sport for Development and Peace: A Critical Sociology
Simon Darnell

Globalizing Cricket: Englishness, Empire and Identity
Dominic Malcolm

Global Boxing
Kath Woodward

Sport and Social Movements: From the Local to the Global
Jean Harvey, John Horne, Parissa Safai, Simon Darnell and Sebastien
Courchesne-O'Neill

Football Italia: Italian Football in an Age of Globalization
Mark Doidge

Books previously published in this series by Manchester University Press:

The Greening of Golf: Sport, Globalization and the Environment
Brad Millington and Brian Wilson

Sport and Technology: An Actor-Network Theory Perspective
Roslyn Kerr

Sport in the Black Atlantic: Cricket, Canada and the Caribbean Diaspora
Janelle Joseph

Localizing Global Sport for Development
Iain Lindsey, Tess Kay, Ruth Jeanes and Davies Banda

Mega-events and social change

Spectacle, legacy and public culture

Maurice Roche

Manchester University Press

Published by Manchester University Press
Altrincham Street, Manchester M1 7JA
www.manchesteruniversitypress.co.uk

British Library Cataloguing-in-Publication Data
A catalogue record for this book is available from the British Library

Library of Congress Cataloging-in-Publication Data applied for

ISBN   978 1 5261 1708 3   hardback

First published 2017

Typeset in 10.25 on 14.5 pt MinionPro-Regular
by Toppan Best-set Premedia Limited
Printed in Great Britain
by CPI Group (UK) Ltd, Croydon CR0 4YY

*For my fine young grandson, Hector Roche (born 13 October 2014),
for whom Life is now the 'great event'*

Contents

Tables

Globalizing Sport Studies series editor's preface

There is now a considerable amount of expertise nationally and internationally in the social scientific and cultural analysis of sport in relation to the economy and society more generally. Contemporary research topics, such as sport and social justice, science and technology and sport, global social movements and sport, sports mega-events, sports participation and engagement and the role of sport in social development, suggest that sport and social relations need to be understood in non-Western developing economies, as well as European, North American and other advanced capitalist societies.

The series *Globalizing Sport Studies* is thus in line with a massive growth of academic expertise, research output and public interest in sport worldwide. At the same time, it seeks to use the latest developments in technology and the economics of publishing to reflect the most innovative research into sport in society currently underway in the world. The series is multi-disciplinary, although primarily based on the social-sciences and cultural-studies approaches to sport.

The broad aims of the series are to: *act* as a knowledge hub for social-scientific and cultural-studies research in sport, including, but not exclusively, anthropological, economic, geographic, historical, political science and sociological studies; *contribute* to the expanding field of research on sport in society in the United Kingdom and internationally by focusing on sport at regional, national and international levels; *create* a series for both senior and more junior researchers that will become synonymous with cutting-edge research, scholarly opportunities and academic development; *promote* innovative discipline-based, multi-, inter- and trans-disciplinary theoretical and methodological approaches to researching sport in society; *provide* an English-language outlet for high-quality non-English writing on sport in society; and *publish* broad overviews, original empirical research studies and classic studies from non-English sources.

When the *Globalizing Sport Studies* series began I approached several authors including Maurice Roche to see if they were interested in contributing to it. It is a great pleasure therefore to see the publication of *Mega-events and social change*. In this volume Maurice Roche offers what might be seen as the sequel to his pioneering work on mega-events, *Mega-events and Modernity*, first published in 2000. *Mega-events and social change* in many ways surpasses that earlier volume and offers sociology, as well as the emerging fields of event, critical event, and mega-event studies, a more comprehensive, theoretically sustained, and sophisticated contribution. By focusing on change across three modalities – mass communications media, cities and urban environments, and global cultures – the book offers the most valuable overview of mega-events and social change published to date.

As Roche notes, since his earlier book was published, new issues have arisen that contour the social and cultural contexts for the hosting of mega-events. He refers to these as features of 'secondary-phase modernisation', including the technological changes brought about by the digital revolution, the global ecological crisis and the development of complex globalisation processes. These issues help shape the contradictory tensions underpinning mega-events in the twenty-first century, between their continued expansion, growth and apparent popularity on one hand and the development of greater risks and vulnerability on the other.

In September 2016, for example, the rising costs of hosting the Olympic and Paralympic Games in Tokyo in 2020 were announced by an expert panel, and Rome's city council voted against supporting a bid for the 2024 Games. Both developments indicate ways in which a disenchantment with (sports) mega-events is growing. This disenchantment is not news to those – academics, researchers and journalists – who have been arguing for some time that there are difficulties with the hosting of mega-events as they are currently organised. Yet the attractiveness of, and expansion in, hosting the Olympics and other sports mega-events has been underpinned by several social developments – technological, economic and political – that Roche addresses in this book. Sports mega-events now have a global audience as a result of technological innovation in mass communication, especially the development of satellite television. The related formation of a sport–media–business alliance transformed sports mega-events and professional sport generally in the late twentieth century. The idea of packaging, via the tri-partite model of sponsorship rights, exclusive broadcasting rights and merchandising, attracted sponsors of the Olympics through the association with sports and the vast global audience exposure that the events achieve. Similarly, interest in hosting sports mega-events has grown as they have become seen as valuable promotional opportunities for cities and regions. Hence in an era when 'world-class city' status is still seen as a vital asset in attracting and often redirecting flows of capital, investment and people, the fame and celebrity thought to accompany being one of a small number of, say, Olympic host cities, remains a heady brew.

Mega-events and social change sets out to engage event studies and other scholars in debates about the sociological and contextual aspects of mega-events. It provides an updated, renewed and developed analysis from a leading figure in the field that takes into account the latest writing on the subject. It sets the bar high and will serve as a benchmark for all future work on mega-events.

John Horne, Preston and Edinburgh, 2017

Acknowledgements

This book has been brewing for over a decade, and various people, whether wittingly or not, have helped me with the work which has led to its production. Recording my thanks for this here is not intended to burden them with any responsibility for the ideas and views it contains. My interest in the study of 'mega-events', including in their sport, cultural and heritage aspects, has been helped, over the years, by Mike Robinson, Ian Henry, John Horne, Garry Whannel, Alan Tomlinson, Vassil Girginov, Peter Millward and Paul Jones in the UK, and also by Liana Giorgi in Vienna, Ning Wang and Zhonghua Guo (in China (Guangzhou)), Sammy Chiu (Hong Kong) and Roger Lyn and Chia-Ling Lai (Taiwan (Taipei)). Work on the study of 'culture', including its media and public policy aspects, has been helped, over the years, by exchanges with my local colleagues Jackie Harrison, Bridgette Wessels and Peter Jackson (Sheffield University) and also with Nick Stevenson (Nottingham University) and Philip Schlesinger (Glasgow University). My longstanding interest in the socio-historical analysis of macro social change is present in this book as in my previous books. I want to record, albeit very belatedly, that this interest was first sparked by Ernest Gellner, who was my teacher, mentor and colleague at the LSE in the 1960s and 1970s. In more recent decades it has been stimulated by various sociological and social-policy colleagues including Gerard Delanty and Bob Deacon, and John Urry, who sadly died in 2016 and who will be long remembered.

Opportunities to develop, present and debate some of the book's ideas and themes about mega-events and social change in the last decade or more have been provided by invitations to speak at various conferences and symposia. In this context I would like to thank the following organisations for their support: the International Olympic Committee (Lausanne), the World Leisure Association (Kuala Lumpur conference), the European Commission (symposia in

Vienna and Bologna), the Soros Foundation (symposia in Belgrade, Kiev, Sofia, Tblisi and Nis), the Feltrinelli Foundation (Milan), the Chinese Association of Museums (Taipei), the Foundation of the Hellenic World (Athens), the International Centre for Olympic Studies (London, Ontario), the Baptist University Faculty of Social Sciences (Hong Kong), Sun-Yat Sen University (Guangzhou), the National Taipei University of Education and National Taiwan University (Taipei), and Leuven University (Leuven), among others. In the UK opportunities and support have been provided by the British Library (London), the Academy of Social Sciences (London), the British Sociology Association (symposium in London), the Political Studies Association (conferences in Manchester and Liverpool), Birkbeck College (London), Goldsmiths University College (London), Birmingham University and the University of East London, among others. In addition a dialogue with the Milanese publisher and academic Federica Olivares in recent years provided stimulus and encouragement for the work involved in the production of this book. In relation to the book's publication process I must, of course, thank Manchester University Press, and particularly Tom Dark, Alun Richards and John Banks, for the professionalism and dedication of their work on this project.

Chapters 2 and 3 on media issues expand very considerably on some embryonic ideas originally published in a Spanish collection on mega-events ('Megaeventos y cambios comunicativos. El complejo mediatico-deportivo en la era de Internet' pages 117–34, in Ramon Llopis Goig (ed.), *Megaeventos Deportivos: perspectivas científicas y studios de caso*, Editorial UOC, Barcelona, 2012). Chapter 7 on mega-events in China is a modified version of a discussion published in a Brazilian collection on mega-events, 'Megaevento, cicades e regioes no mundo', pages 156–94, in Ricardo Freitas, Flavio Lins and Maria Carmo (eds) *Megaeventos, comunicacão e cidade*, Editora CRV, Curitiba, Brazil, 2016).

Finally, for their support on this book project I would like to thank my wife Jan for her patience, and also my family, Helen, Steve, Liz and little Hector Roche, for just 'being there'.

Introduction

Book Introductions should aim to answer three main questions, namely, why the book has been written (and thus relatedly why it might possibly be of interest to readers), what it is about and how its concerns and contents will be addressed and organised. In this Introduction I will address these three questions.

Rationales

The rationales for writing this book are at once personal, practical and intellectual. Hopefully the latter two rationales in particular also provide reasons why the book may be of interest to people concerned with the study of mega-events and events more generally, so I will begin with them. Firstly, on the practical front the field of mega-events, together with its hinterland of the world of less-than-mega cultural and sporting events in general, has developed and grown in various significant ways since the turn of the millennium. In recent times events have also become much more visible in policy terms, in media discourse and in public awareness than they were in previous decades. However, at the same time as they seem to be becoming more important to us than they have ever been, they are also becoming, in some cases and in some aspects, more criticised than ever before. We increasingly make mega-events part of our lives at the same time as becoming witnesses to the possibility that some of them might not have much of a future. There are significant problems both at the level of particular events and at the level of mega-event organisers. At the level of particular events the transmission of good practice within the world of mega-events remains weak and unreliable. For instance, in spite of the rise of public concern for mega-event legacies or long-term impacts, the 2014 Sochi Winter Olympics had a negative impact on its region within Russia's eastern Black Sea coast and Caucasus mountains; the planning of the 2015 Expo in Milan made little clear, agreed and effective provision for an urban legacy; and the planning of the 2016 Rio Olympics suffered from a range of important and preventable political, economic and ecological problems.[1]

Beyond the level of particular events, further problems of a serious and even existentially threatening kind have arisen in recent times at the level of a number of mega-event owner organisations. FIFA (the Fédération International des Football Association) in soccer and in athletics the IAAF (the International Amateur Athletics Federation) have long been suspected of having become mired in various forms of corruption.[2] In 2015 and early 2016 these charges were definitively revealed to have substance, and the two organisations are now facing profound challenges to reform themselves in order to restore their international legitimacy and credibility. Academic perspectives on social realities can become complacent in their theoretical, empirical and moral orthodoxies and prejudgements, particularly in the social sciences, whether they are of a mainstream or of a critical kind. However when realities change, and also when they become challenging and even paradoxical, as is currently the case in the field of mega-events, then we need to be willing to renew our understanding of these changing realities and to be open to the new issues they raise.

Secondly, a rationale for this book lies in the developments on the academic fields of event studies in general and mega-event studies in particular. In the late twentieth century the academic literatures in these areas were arbitrary and patchy in their coverage and, to the extent that they did so at all, they tended to value information over understanding, and to accumulate knowledge slowly. However in recent years, and related to the practical changes and growth in events briefly noted above, this situation has changed a lot. Event-related literature both for academic teaching and for research purposes has begun to grow considerably. To a great extent this acceleration has been driven, particularly in Britain, by the growth of university courses and qualifications in the professional and practical field of event management, and thus by the growth of demand for intellectual resources from both teachers and students in this field. Thankfully, however, the new literature has not been restricted exclusively to management-oriented work serving professional and practical interests. It has also included discussions and studies embodying broader interests in the social contexts and politics of events. These have included contributions in allied areas such as event studies, event policy (studies), critical event studies and the critical political economy of mega-events.[3] This book aims to make a contribution to contemporary interests in these fields, not least in re-emphasising the relevance of sociological and related inter-disciplinary perspectives for the understanding of events and mega-events.

Finally, on the personal front a decade had passed since I had published a study of mega-events, *Mega-events and modernity: Olympics and Expos in the growth of global culture* (Roche 2000). This was the product of various lines of sociological and socio-historical work I had undertaken in the late 1980s and 1990s. While I continued to work on mega-events in the 2000s I also rebalanced my sociological interests to allow for the development of a project of work on the socio-historical and contemporary aspects of Europe. This resulted in a study of the socio-historical grounds of the European social formation (Roche 2010a), arguing for the possibility of a sociology of Europe. Work on this project remains ongoing (in spite of the 2016 British vote to 'Brexit' the EU, indeed because of it), and it also informs some of the analysis underlying this present book. At the time that it was published my mega-event book achieved what I had hoped for it, namely to make a contribution to the field of mega-events studies. However, in spite of this (or, perhaps better, because of it) as time went by and as major social changes began to make themselves felt in society in the first decade of the new century it became clear that it was increasingly necessary to update, renew and develop my earlier analysis, hence the present book.

Subject matter

We can now turn from rationales for the book, the 'why?' question, to address the 'what?' question, that is, the nature of its subject matter. As the title signals, the book is concerned with 'mega-events' and 'social change', and particularly with the sociological challenges involved in attempting to understand the former in relation to the latter. Chapter 1 explores the nature of each of these topics further in general terms, and the implications of these discussions are applied and illustrated in more detailed studies of mega-events in the body of the book. My perspective on the nature of social change is introduced later in the Introduction, when we also consider the overall nature of the book's discussion and argument. However first we need to consider what mega-events are.

I conceptualise mega-events, in this book as in my earlier book, in broadly sociological terms and thus as being multi-dimensional. As such particular cases of mega-events are always potentially empirically fluid and variable along a number of axes, and they can have characteristics which, while they may be retrospectively comprehensible, were (whether by design or accident) unpredictable at the time. Some key sources of such variability among mega-events are, for instance, dimensional axes running from self-conscious modernity to the incorporation of tradition, from the national level to the international and global levels, from city-based localisation to the dis-location of becoming media events, from short-term to long-term impacts and so on (see Roche 2000, pp. 8–10, ch. 1 passim, also ch. 8 passim). The implications of such an understanding of mega-events, in this book as in my previous book, are that we should recognise the risks of theoretical hubris if we aspire to some sort of social scientific omniscience about mega-events. The view taken here is that while the analysis of mega-events does need to be theoretically informed and to involve a systematic understanding of their contexts, none the less it also needs to remain open to their potential empirical fluidity and variability. The apparent predictability of many aspects of mega-events can be misleading; mega-events always have the capacity to surprise us and show us something new about our social world.

Given mega-events' multi-dimensionality and their empirically variable character, we should be cautious and careful about prematurely fixing their features whether theoretically or methodologically. Nevertheless, for the purposes of this Introduction a rough and provisional definition of mega-events is relevant at this point, and the definition I offered of them in my earlier book on mega-events remains useful. That is: '"Mega-events" are large-scale cultural (including commercial and sporting) events which have a dramatic character, mass popular appeal and international significance' (Roche 2000, p. 1). In my earlier study I located mega-events like Olympic Games and International Expos as 'the most visible and spectacular examples of a dense social eco-system and social calendar of public events in modern societies' (Roche 2000, p. 3). I suggested that the wider field of public events can also be analysed as including (at least) 'special', 'hallmark' and 'community' types of events (Roche 2000, p. 4, table 1.3). In this framework mega-events can be distinguished in terms of the global and international nature and scale of their target visitor markets and of the media interest in them. In complete contrast community events are organised to address local visitor markets and local television and press. Intermediary between the global and local levels are hallmark events (like national sport championships), and special events (like world regional sports events or single-sector events like Formula 1 Grand Prix motoring competitions). Hallmark events, which can have a role in identifying a nation, principally operate at the national level of visitor markets and media interest, whereas special events can address and be influential in both national and international-level visitor markets and media.

Event planners and managers might feel obliged to proclaim that an event is a mega-event when they bid and plan for it ahead of time. However the empirical variability of particular events suggests that researchers and analysts may be better advised to recognise the inherently provisional nature of such claims and to wait for the 'delivery' of an event and its outcomes before concurring that an event actually qualifies for this status. Relatedly the roughness of the public-event categorisation given above indicates that, in particular cases, mega-event characteristics sometimes my well be significantly shared with event cases in the non-mega-event categories, particularly 'special events'. Given the growth and diversification of such events and event categories in recent years it may well be useful, for both theoretical and empirical purposes, to explicitly broaden the field of mega-event studies to take account of second-order mega-events as well as the first-order mega-events which it currently addresses, and to make the border between them more permeable.

An interesting step in this direction has been made in a contribution to mega-event studies recently by Martin Muller (Muller 2015a).[4] Building on previous definitional discussions, including those noted above in my earlier work, Muller proposes a new more empirically based approach to determining whether or not an event can be judged to have had the scale and character of a 'mega-event'. He recognises that such events must be understood as being multi-dimensional and focuses on four aspects, namely tourism, the media, finance and urban legacy. Muller specifies these respectively in terms of events' visitor attractiveness, the reach of the audience reach of the media, event-related cost and transformative impacts, and he suggests that they can be usefully measured, respectively, with reference to (ticketed) visitor numbers, the value of broadcast rights, total costs and the proportion of the total budget taken up by urban capital and infrastructure spending. Muller argues that the value of using his multi-indicator approach is attested to in his application of it to a range of large-scale events in the 2010–13 period.

This analysis generates a hierarchy among these events which is intuitively credible (for instance, the 2012 London Olympics is confirmed as being the largest in Muller's sample of cases). It also suggests that the category of mega-events needs to be understood in a flexible way in the contemporary period, and that it is realistic to broaden it beyond the classic (and first-order) mega-event genres (i.e. Olympics and Expos, see Roche 2000). The FIFA World Cup soccer championships have long been viewed as being 'mega-events, and also other large-scale events can be argued to have elements of a mega-event character. Muller's analysis suggests that the mega-events in the 2010–13 period which he is concerned with should be understood to include not only the 2012 London Olympics and the 2010 Shanghai Expo but also the 2010 FIFA World Cup soccer championship in South Africa, the 2012 UEFA European Nations soccer championship shared by the Ukraine and Poland, the 2010 Asian Games in Guangzhou and the 2010 Winter Olympics in Vancouver. Given this, in my view in the field of mega-event studies it is becoming useful, even necessary, to distinguish more clearly and consistently between first-order and second-order mega-events, and there is an increasing need to devote more research attention to the latter group. That said, in spite of this counsel of perfection the present book will mainly (although not exclusively) focus on the classic first-order genres of the Summer Olympic Games and Expos as exemplars of mega-events. Finally, we can note that Muller's analysis draws attention to the category of 'major events' which lie in the hinterland of the category of mega-events. An implication to be drawn from this might be that the links between mega-event studies and the hinterland of general event studies could benefit from being better recognised and cultivated in research and scholarship.

Analytic approach

Finally, there is the 'how' question, namely the issue of how I plan to understand, address and discuss mega-events. In this book, as in my previous work, my general approach to mega-events is to see them as products of a combinations of collective agency and structural factors. They are events which, initially at least, need to be seen as products of their times and places. As far as their times go, they can be usefully interpreted as particular reflections and refractions of the broader and deeper structural dynamics affecting their social contexts. And as far as their places go they can also be usefully interpreted, given their changing structural contexts, as projects by host communities to mark and symbolise collective identities and to influence the longer-term nature of urban environments. It is on the basis of these general understandings of mega-events as reflections and refractions of social contexts, and as marking and influencing projects, that I aim to explore the book's general theme of the relationship between mega-events and social change in the contemporary period. At this point it is relevant to introduce some of the ideas about social change which will be discussed in more detail later in Chapter 1. They contribute to the rationale for this book and also provide its conceptual and theoretical framework.

In my earlier study of mega-events (Roche 2000) I was, of course, concerned throughout with the topic of macro-social changes, and this analysis provides a basis on which to build in this present book. Where it is appropriate, I will refer to this and other aspects of that earlier study during the course of my discussion here. It is fair to say that the main social changes I was concerned to relate mega-events to in the earlier book, particularly in the socio-historical chapters making up its first part, were those associated with the main historical phase of the modernisation process, namely those of industrialisation and nation-state-building, particularly in the West. However, contemporary twenty-first-century macro-social changes are different from these first-phase modernisation processes, and thus they pose different problems of interpretation in relation to the mega-events they contextualise.

The contemporary changes (which I refer to as secondary-phase modernisation, see Chapter 1) include the digital revolution, the global ecological crisis and qualitatively new and more complex forms of globalisation.[5] Respectively these refer to (1) the rise and worldwide social diffusion and permeation of digitally based information and communication technologies; (2) environmentally destructive processes such as global warming together with greening policy responses requiring the pursuit of environmental conservation and energy sustainability at all levels from the global to the local and (3) the acceleration of economic globalisation and associated reactions such as world-regional geopolitical structuring (e.g. the re-emergence of China) and 'civilisational' cultural conflicts (e.g. the re-emergence of Islam). These are deep and transformative macro-structural processes with both positive and negative impacts and implications for contemporary societies. It is conceivable that their progression might be capable of being channelled, with their positive impacts being encouraged, and their negative impacts being slowed. However the essentially adaptive character of such responses by nation-states recognises that, even if there was the will to do so, it is hard to imagine how these macro dynamics might be halted or reversed. In particular it is inconceivable that they might be influenced in such ways either in the short term or by forms of policy and action organised only at national and urban levels. For mega-event producers operating at the level of host nations and host cities, and within medium-term time frames, such changes present themselves as the given conditions in which they must design and deliver their event projects.

Since around the turn of the new millennium mega-events as particular types of social process have begun to change qualitatively compared with mega-events in the twentieth century. The perspective taken in this book focuses on this contemporary period, but, as noted above, in other respects it develops further the approach of my earlier book. That is, without implying any mechanical determinism, the approach understands the collective agency exemplified in mega-events to reflect and refract the social contexts of their time. So in order to understand changes within the mega-event world we need to go beyond it and to explore the changing social contexts of events which lie in the deeper macro-structural changes indicated above. Given this perspective we can make the reasonable assumption that mega-events will continue to change further as we go forward in the twenty-first century, reflecting the continuing influences of their changing social contexts. To illustrate this we can point to three particular mega-event changes. These concern (1) the socio-technical nature of their mediatisation, (2) the ideological framing and content of their messages and also (3) their geopolitical location. The perspective taken in this book is that each of these reflects deeper social structural changes and poses major challenges in policy and practice to mega-event owners and producers, and also to social movements and host publics associated with them. Later in the book we need to consider in greater detail each of these ways in which mega-events, as social phenomena and social processes, are changing, and also how such changes at the level of mega-events relate to deeper changes in their social contexts. So both levels and types of change, both within the mega-event world and in its wider social context, should be briefly introduced here.

Mega-event change and contextual social change

Firstly, in the contemporary period we have witnessed *qualitative changes in event mediation.*[6] In the second half of the twentieth century sport mega-events like the Olympics increasingly became accessible to mass public participation around the world by being televised as 'live' events. They also came to depend organisationally on income from the sale of live television rights. However the mass diffusion of internet access around the world in the early years of the twenty-first century is effectively a profoundly transformative and irreversible process, as transformative and irreversible as all previous 'media revolutions' have been (for instance such as those associated with the rise of radio in the interwar period and the rise of television in the early postwar period). It is beginning to qualitatively change the conditions of mediation of mega-events, whether for good or for ill. This is so both for sport mega-events like the Olympics and also for cultural mega-events like World Expos but particularly for the former.

Secondly, in the contemporary period we have witnessed a *greening of mega-events* and their messages.[7] Traditionally mega-events have been legitimated in relation to a number of key ideologies, particularly internationalist, host-nationalist and commercial ideologies. In addition they have been used as vehicles of communication of these ideologies from elite groups to mass publics. In the contemporary period, because of the apparently inexorable growth of the global ecological crisis, together with publics' awareness and concern about this, an additional ideology has tended to be added to this set of legitimations and communications, namely that of environmentalism. To frame and promote mega-events in 'green' terms of sustainability and conservations is no doubt undertaken for defensive as well as for progressive reasons. That is, it is done in the bidding and preparation phases to pre-empt and deflect public unease and media criticism of large-scale projects. Because of their scale and uniqueness from the host city's perspective, they can inevitably carry a certain degree of risk of wasting public financial resources as well as urban resources of land, buildings and infrastructures. In addition the 'greening' of mega-events can be undertaken for more progressive reasons to promote ecological values and models both at event-time and also, in the post-event period, as event-legacies, including such visible green legacies as major urban parks and public spaces.

Finally, in the contemporary period we have witnessed geopolitical changes affecting *event location*.[8] From their creation in the late nineteenth century and through the twentieth century the first-order mega-event genres tended to be staged almost exclusively in nations of the West. However in recent years a trend seems to have got under way which tends to undermine this de facto Western monopoly. In addition this situation shows no signs of being reversible. The probable new future of mega-events is that, whether for good or ill, staging them will increasingly be shared with non-Western powers and world regions.

Book structure and contents

The three sets of changes within the contemporary world of mega-events help to contribute to the paradox we noted earlier in outlining the rationale for this book, namely that of mega-events' increasing popularity and yet the simultaneous vulnerability and riskiness which threaten their future. Thus they will provide us with a thematic structure for the studies in the chapters which follow. The book is organised into three main parts together with a general introductory chapter (Chapter 1) on the relationship between mega-events and contemporary social change which elaborates on the book's thematic structure. The parts that follow are concerned respectively with the three sets of mega-event and contextual changes, namely those concerned with the media aspects (Part I), the urban and the ecological aspects (Part II), and the locational and geopolitical aspects of contemporary mega-events (Part III) introduced earlier. It goes without saying that these changes are too large and complicated to be addressed in a comprehensive and exhaustive way in this book. Thus the discussion inevitably has an exploratory and provisional character which is aimed at reanimating the interest of event studies and mega-event-studies scholars and researchers in the sociological and contextual aspects of mega-events.

Chapter 1 outlines a framework for interpreting contemporary macro-structural social change and applies it in general terms to media, urban and locational mega-event issues. This framework of perspectives and ideas is then used and applied in the three parts. Part I consists of two chapters on media-related aspects of contemporary mega-events, particularly sports mega-events, in the context of the wider social impacts of the digital revolution. Chapter 2 reviews the established symbiosis between the old media complex based around television, the challenges posed to this by the rise of the new media complex based around the internet, and the search for a new basis of co-existence between old and new media in the sport mega-event field. Chapter 3 explores the problems that so-called internet piracy causes for sport mega-events, states' policy responses to this and mega-event organisations' search for a new symbiosis between events and the media.

Part II consists of three chapters on urban and environmental aspects of mega-events, in a period of rapid urbanisation in many parts of the world and also of ecological crisis. Chapter 4 outlines how mega-events can be understood as being material as well as performative spectacles which are physically 'embedded' in cities as legacies, not only for the short term but also for the long term. Thus the chapter is concerned with the association of mega-events with the construction of iconic and legacy-oriented buildings, infrastructures and places which are often 'bequeathed' as potentially positive inheritances to their host cities in the post-event period. However it also includes more negative aspects and impacts including those relating to the high security requirements (and thus security spectacles and security legacies) involved in staging mega-events in the contemporary period. With this as a background Chapter 5 focuses on the Olympic Games genre of mega-events and on their *place-making* urban impacts and legacies. By contrast Chapter 6 looks into mega-events' simultaneous record of creating new public spaces in modern cities, and it does so mainly with reference to the Expo event genre. The chapter highlights the association of contemporary mega-events with urban impacts and legacies which are both green and *space-making*, notably through their capacity either to create or to reanimate major urban parks and green public spaces in host cities.

Finally, Part III consists of two chapters reflecting on the contemporary global shift in mega-event locations and the wider context of this, notably in relation to the social dynamics of what I refer to as complex globalisation and the changing geopolitical relations between the West and non-Western world regions. This part does not aim to provide exhaustive and systematic coverage of these large and complicated contextual issues. Rather it aims to take advantage of some highly visible recent developments in the world of mega-events in very different and contrasting Western and non-Western contexts, to illustrate and reflect on them. Thus Chapter 7 focuses on the main non-Western region of East Asia, and specifically on its core, the People's Republic of China. It looks into China's economic development, its associated new and massive urbanisation processes, and the associated staging of a number of first- and second-order mega-events by Chinese cities. By contrast Chapter 8 focuses on a traditional and familiar Western mega-event host city, namely London, looking in particular at the 2012 Olympics event, and its concern to create legacies particularly involving urban regeneration.

Notes

1 Planning for Brazil's 2016 Rio Olympics mega-event was long dogged by a series of apparently intractable problems, including those of water pollution (creating health risks for rowing and sailing competitors), inadequate security (for both competitors and visitors) and inadequate transport systems. In addition the event had the misfortune to coincide with a major political crisis in Brazil involving the suspension of President Dilma Rousseff, and also with a major health crisis which is of international significance involving the spread of the zika virus (see for instance Butler 2016b and Attaran 2016).

2 On the problems of FIFA and the IAAF (at least, as they stood in 2015–16) see for instance Apuzzo et al. 2015, BBC 2015b, Gibson 2015f and 2016, and Ingle 2016. For a critical sociologically informed analysis of FIFA as a flawed organisation by a social researcher with long experience studying it see Alan Tomlinson (Tomlinson 2014), and see the recent critical discussion of the organisation by the economist Andrew Zimbalist (Zimbalist 2015). Also see comments on FIFA in the final section of Chapter 1 later.

3 On event studies see Getz 2012, Bowdin et al. 2010 and the contributions to Page and Connell 2012; on event policy studies see Foley et al. 2012; on critical event studies see Rojek 2013 and Spracklen and Lamond 2016; and on the critical study of mega-events (including critical political economy approaches) see the contributions to

Horne and Manzenreiter 2006, Tomlinson and Young 2006b, Hayes and Karamichas 2012b, Lamond and Platt 2016 and Gruneau and Horne 2016b.
4 For a recent alternative engagement with the definition of mega-events see also Sprackler and Lamond 2016, ch. 4.
5 References relating to the three sets of changes introduced here are given in Chapter 1 and its notes.
6 On media changes see Chapters 1 and 2, and associated notes.
7 On urban and 'green' changes see Chapters 1 and 6, and associated notes.
8 On locational and geopolitical changes see Chapters 1 and 7, and associated notes.

1

Mega-events and macro-social change

In the Introduction we observed that in recent times, and certainly since the turn of the century, mega-events have been changing in notable ways from the way they were in the mid- and late twentieth century. This book aims to look into these important new trends, to document them in a range of cases and also to explore their contexts and motivations particularly in relation to deeper vectors of social change. In the Introduction we noted three main changes in particular. Firstly, as with so many aspects of contemporary culture and society, sport mega-events in particular, notably the Olympics, have become not only media events but also digital media events. As such they have increasingly been experienced by publics using a repertoire of new as well as old media, that is internet-enabled tablets and mobile phones as well as old twentieth-century media like radio and television. Secondly, contemporary mega-events are increasingly pursued and staged by cities with an explicit interest in their potential to have long-term positive effects or legacies. Unlike those of most twentieth-century mega-events, these long-term effects are not only the subjects of explicit aspiration and planning, but also they invariably give a priority to green legacies relating to ecological sustainability and the promotion of the relevance of the natural world for life in cities. Thirdly, contemporary mega-events are increasingly being staged outside of their traditional nineteenth-century and twentieth-century locations in the West (particularly Europe and North America). There has been what appears to be a permanent global shift in mega-event locations in which the 'Global South' (particularly Africa and South America) and the East (particularly the Middle East and the Far East) now share the hosting of mega-events with the West.

These three changes in contemporary-era mega-events as compared with those of preceding eras are illustrated in the various case studies which make up the body of this book. However to begin with, in this chapter, it is first necessary to set the scene for later discussions with some observations about relevant aspects of late twentieth-century and contemporary social change. The book aims to take a generally sociological and socio-historical approach to the understanding of mega-events which interprets them as being, among other things, performances which reflect (and refract) more general forces and vectors of macro-social change, and which as such are often accredited with some power to influence or catalyse wider social changes, particularly in their host cities.

This chapter, then, firstly aims to introduce and outline a sociological framework of ideas and terms of reference for exploring these deeper and broader contexts of social change relevant to the understanding of contemporary mega-events. This is addressed in the first section of the chapter. Secondly, it aims to initially indicate how this analysis of social change generally applies to the three changes in mega-events we are concerned with. This discussion is developed in the remaining three sections of the chapter which are concerned with issues connected with media change (second section), urban change (third section) and global change (fourth section). Each of these three sections introduces framework ideas and themes in the analysis of relevant aspects of contemporary mega-events which are then taken further in the more detailed discussions in the corresponding chapter in the three main arts of the book.

Contextualising mega-events: western modernisation

To understand mega-events sociologically and socio-historically we need to outline a provisional understanding of the general social contexts in the West (Europe and North America) within which they were created, in which they have become institutionalised, which they can be interpreted to reflect and symbolise, and in which they are currently changing both in the West and in the wider world. Any such understanding needs to involve a conception both of the long-term processes of modernisation which have shaped Western society since at least the nineteenth century and also of the distinctive features of modernisation and social change in the contemporary late modern period both in the West and in the wider world order. Such issues of macro-social structure and change are inevitably complex matters which, equally inevitably, require some simplification if they are to be made manageable for the purposes of understanding the deep social contexts of mega-events.

Thus Table 1.1 provides a schematic representation of a range of social changes associated with modernisation processes particularly in Western societies from the mid-nineteenth century through to the present. The schema in

Table 1.1 Western modernisation, nineteenth to twenty-first century: a schematic representation of long-term macro-social change

Key societal dimensions and dynamics	'Primary-phase' modernisation 1850–1970	'Secondary-phase' modernisation 1970 to present
Techno-economic	*Industrialisation* Industrial capitalism; mechanisation, electrification and factory production; intensified marketisation and exploitation of domestic mass labour, of colonial resources and of nature	*Post-industrialism* Science- and technology-based capitalism (via digital age internet, automation and robotics etc.); service, information and knowledge-based industries; worldwide mass transport and telecoms infrastructures
Political-economic	*Nation-state-building* National industrial capitalist economies; internationalism via competitive empires; state taxation and the building of warfare states and welfare states	*Globalisation* Global capitalism, with complex international economic interdependencies and inequalities; rise of neoliberal ideology; world regionality; weak global governance; 'glocal' adaptations and local protectionist reactions
Cultural-economic	*Mass culture* Mass marketing and mass consumption; mass communications via succession of old media (publishing, press, radio, television); mass sport and mass tourism	*De-massified culture* Co-existence of mass with individualised consumption, and of old with new (digital age) media; rising awareness of importance of cultural industries (e.g. marketing, media, sport, tourism etc.)

Table 1.1 Western modernisation, nineteenth to twenty-first century: a schematic representation of long-term macro-social change (Continued)

Key societal dimensions and dynamics	'Primary-phase' modernisation 1850–1970	'Secondary-phase' modernisation 1970 to present
Political-cultural	*Nationalist identities and public culture* Official ethno-national monoculturalism and legitimated xenophobia; colonial and Imperial ideologies and practices; rise of public cultural institutions (e.g. museums etc.); rise of mass state-based primary and secondary schooling and cultural reproduction	*Cosmopolitan identities and public culture* Human rights and individualism; postcolonialism and post-imperialism; de facto multiculturalism and cosmopolitanism and varieties of localist/anti-global reactions to this; growth of adapted 'quasi-public' cultural institutions and cultural policy (regulation of cultural economy etc.); rise of mass tertiary education (cultural production and reproduction)
'Civilisational' worldview (humanity–Nature relationship)	*Mastery over nature* Dominance of economic (and related) progress ideologies; unsustainable over-exploitation of natural environments and resources by combinations of main primary-phase modernisation dynamics (above)	*Conservation of nature* Crisis-driven rise of green and conservationist ('neo-progress') ideologies; belated public recognition of humanity's ecological limits and conditions; weak attempts to promote sustainable economy and society nationally and internationally

this Table makes the conventional sociological assumption that, from a theoretical point of view, social systems can be analysed as being composed of at least three relatively autonomous dimensions, namely the economic, the political and the cultural (the domains respectively of capital, work and exchange; power and authority; and meanings, values and communication). And it adds the dimensions of technology, as the domain of equipment, material power and capability, used to reproduce humans' embodied existence, and to make and remake environments and to interact with nature in so doing. In order to understand social change it suggests that particular types of social dynamics and transformative capabilities are historically found in the social fields created by the combination of at least two dimensions, namely techno-economic, political economic, cultural economic and political-cultural fields, and also in an ideological aspect of the technology dimension which can be referred to as the civilisational worldview concerning the relationship of humans with nature.[1]

The political economic field and also, relatedly, the techno-economic field have periodically played leading roles in major social change, notably, given the centrality of the development of capitalism to Western and later global society, in the era of modernisation. This is argued for both by (uncritical) (neo-) liberal economic modernisation and development theory and also by critical political-economy perspectives both in general terms and also in the special area of the analysis of mega-events. However the schema presented here does not require that these dynamics must always be seen to have this primacy, intellectual strategies which risk over-simplification and omniscience. Rather the schema is intended to be open to the complexities and surprises of real socio-historical change. Thus it is open to the possibility that one or more of the remaining dynamic fields (namely political-cultural, cultural-economic and techno-cultural (civilisation worldview) dynamics) can play a leading role.

This openness and rejection of omniscience is particularly necessary in understanding the volatility and complexities of macro-social change in the contemporary period. In the early twenty-first century the rise of the global internet, the ecological crisis and the march of a re-energised trans-national capitalism are arguably combining to create a complex condition of 'runaway globalisation' (for instance see Giddens 2002). This emerging multi-dimensional social condition threatens to undermine the cultures, environments and economies of all established national societies, even so-called superpowers, and it seriously challenges humanity's capacity to politically regulate it and to culturally adapt to it. The mega-events staged in the contemporary period cannot be understood, in relation to their deep social contexts, in terms which are limited to those of the field and dynamics of political economy, even with the addition of the field and dynamics of the techno-economy. In addition account needs to be taken of the dynamics of the political-cultural, cultural economic and techno-cultural fields, one or more of which could in principle, if social reality indicated it, be assessed as taking a leading role among the dynamics driving macro social change.

The schema points to the dominant role in Western modernisation of industrialisation and capitalism and also the building of monocultural national
warfare and welfare states. These techno-economic and political economic
dynamics led the development of a modern societal model which also involved
mass culture; nationalist identities and public culture; and a techno-culture (or
civilisational worldview) which was pervasive both within and between national
societies (Roche 2010a, chs 4, 5 and 6). This latter involved a belief in 'progress'
and in humanity's capacity and even duty to achieve it by empowering itself
through the project of dominating and exploiting nature.[2] However in recent
generations this version of modernisation and the modern societal model has
begun to co-exist and conflict with, and to a certain extent to give way to, a
significantly different one. This has suggested that it is appropriate to envisage
the long-term macro-social changes involved in Western modernisation as
having at least two main phases. We can refer to these as being primary and
secondary phases and roughly date them respectively from the mid-nineteenth
century to the late twentieth (1850–1970) and the late twentieth century to the
early twenty-first (1970 to present). In Table 1.1 the phases and differences
between the social models they involve are indicated by columns 2 and 3.

Reasons and causes for the phase-shift from primary to secondary were
related to the working out of the logics of first-phase dynamics. These involved
the creation of unintended consequences which acted as negative feedbacks and
were self-limiting processes in relation to primary-phase dynamics. This is not
the place to explore this aspect of the causes of phase-shift in detail. However
an example can be given in the case of the overall impact of the full set of modernisation dynamics involved in the techno-culture or civilisational worldview.
The primary-phase ideology that humanity's exploitation of nature was part of
a project of progress which could be sustained indefinitely had, by the late
twentieth century, turned out to be a self-serving delusion. What is more it
turned out to be reflexively self-defeating since the project tends to degrade
humanity's planetary life conditions and thus undermines its own possibility as
a project. To attempt to counter the ecological crisis has required new forms of
ecological political mobilisation and policy-making among elites and publics at
all levels from the global to the local. The crisis and the responses to it, caused
and motivated by primary-phase dynamics, clearly mark the end of one phase
of modernisation and the beginning of another.

The changes leading to the emergence of the new secondary-phase societal
model can be roughly dated from the oil price increases and the associated crises
of Western capitalist economies of the 1970s, and it also involved the related

rise of neoliberal ideology in the 1980s. The 1990s witnessed the emergence of digital technologies and new media, the beginnings of an international recognition of and response to the global ecological crisis, the collapse of the Soviet Union's and Eastern European communist alternative to capitalism, and the rise of Eastern (East Asian) capitalism (the latter initially in its 'Asian Tiger' form in Taiwan and South Korea and in the city-states of Hong Kong and Singapore followed by the portentous emergence of mainland China as a hybrid 'communist-capitalist' global economic superpower).[3]

The new social model which is emerging in the secondary phase of modernisation at both the nation-state level and the international/global level of social organisation involves the development of a post-industrial and digitally based techno-economy; a complex and digitally enhanced 'runaway' form of globalisation and global capitalism involving the dominance of neoliberal ideology, structural inequalities and world regionality; a de-massified and individualised consumption-based cultural economy qualitatively empowered by the internet and digital media; a political culture in which ideals of trans-national human rights, multiculturalism and cosmopolitanism have a new degree of relevance for individuals and publics (as a source both of identities and of conflicts); and in which the dominant techno-cultural ideology (or civilisational worldview) is increasingly coming to be based on the green values involved in recognition of the need for the conservation of nature and for sustainability in the economy and in social life more broadly.

On the basis of this analysis, then, instabilities and social changes observable in the contemporary period within and between national societies in the West can be usefully interpreted as local manifestations of the continuing overlap and transitory tensions between the declining primary-phase social model and the emerging secondary-phase model. The schema presented in Table 1.1 is angled towards representing modernisation dynamics and phases in the West and in a West-centred world order. However, although non-Western world regions' experiences of modernisation processes are not explicitly addressed in the Table, the terms of reference are of use for understanding them. The volatility of social affairs in 'developing' and 'emerging' societies in many world regions outside of the West in the contemporary period can also be usefully interpreted in terms of tensions between primary-phase and secondary-phase models of modernity. However in these regions the underlying dynamics and transformative processes, unlike in the West, are connected with the simultaneous underlying development of some elements of the primary-phase social model in parallel with an overlay of elements of the secondary-phase social model. The distinct complexities of such parallel and overlapping developments are exacerbated by the digitally accelerated pace at which they are being undertaken and (particularly in China's and India's cases) the historically unprecedented scale of the populations involved in and affected by them.

The West currently remains dominant in the global political economic and techno-economic fields and thus also in geo-political fields and other related cultural fields. Thus the contemporary modernisation (both primary and secondary) of non-Western world regions is generally being undertaken as a process of integration of states in these regions to greater or lesser extents into a West-defined and West-dominated global social complex. However in our times such forms of regional development and global integration can evidently be fraught, violent and incoherent processes, involving forms both of traditionalistic reaction (e.g. Islamic fundamentalism) and also of progress-based resistance (e.g. Brazilian democratic protest movements). In addition, given the historically portentous fact of the rise of China, they are consistent with the possibility that a general global shift is under way in the twenty-first century away in the global complex and world order, away from a West-centred version and towards a more multi-polar version.[4]

The staging of mega-events every few years has been an effectively continuous process since the mid-nineteenth century through to the present, interrupted only by the two twentieth-century world wars. Over the course of this time the particular events themselves, the evolution of the event genres and the evolution of international organisations controlling them all occurred against the background of the social contexts provided by the primary and secondary phases of modernisation outlined here. While fully recognising mega-events' character as testimonies to social agency (at least the agency of political, economic and professional elites and also in various ways of mass publics) we can also recognise that they can be analysed as being to one extent or another modernising projects and as such reflections and refractions of their times and of the modernising and socially changing societies which created them. In addition to reflecting their social contexts they can also be said to symbolise these contexts, and in many cases also to act as catalysts helping to change some elements particularly of the urban contexts in which they were staged.

In the primary phase of Western modernisation Expo events in particular, and also Olympic events, albeit more indirectly, can be usefully analysed as reflecting various local aspects of the industrial capitalism, nation-state-building and national identity-building, mass culture and nature-mastery worldview associated with the general primary-phase social model (Roche 2000, part 1).

This was the general line of argument of the historical half of my previous book *Mega-events and modernity*. Comparable with this argument the present book proposes that, while recognising the social agency involved, this same kind of reflective relationship can be argued to exist in respect of mega-events staged in the secondary phase of modernisation, and particularly in the contemporary period of the last two decades. In the contemporary period mega-events continue to reflect primary-phase social dynamics because, on the one hand, in the West, they remain important albeit declining factors in the dominant social model and, on the other hand, in non-Western emerging and developing societies, primary-phase modernisation continues to be pursued. However, as we have suggested earlier, in our times mega-events themselves have begun to change. So in this book I suggest that to understand these changes it is necessary to understand the new social contexts and dynamics, namely those of secondary-phase modernisation, which they arguably reflect and refract.

The three key mega-event changes are those of the impact of digital and new media on the mediatisation of mega-events, the turn to long-term legacy and green urban policy rationales for the staging of mega-events and the global shift of mega-event locations to include non-Western as well as Western societies. Each of these three changes can be said to reflect aspects of the new second-phase social model. In the following sections this argument is outlined as a prelude to looking into the three changes in greater detail in the chapters in the three parts which make up the main body of this book.

Social change and mega-events 1: media change

In this section we outline a general conception of the social nature and inter-relationships of various types of media, how they have changed over the course of Western modernisation and how they have provided important deep social contexts for developments in the field of mega-events. This situation, particularly the shift from media like radio and television, which we can refer to as old media, to new media related to the rise of the internet, is more structurally important for sport mega-events like the Olympic Games than it is for Expos. So we will focus on the former event genre both here and in Part I where Chapters 2 and 3 respectively explore positive and negative aspects of the new relationships which are emerging beween mega-events and media in the contemporary new media environment.[5] The introductory discussions in this section and also in the later chapters draw generally on the understanding of the macro-social changes involved in Western modernization which were outlined in the previous section, particularly those connected with media-relevant aspects of the techno-economic and cultural economic dynamics (see Table 1.1).

Before considering the relationships between the old media, the new media and mega-events more directly it is worthwhile stepping back for a moment to gain some historical and macro-sociological perspective on these phenomena. In the course of searching for such a perspective, and generally when thinking about the nature of media and their relationship with society, we can sometimes overlook the importance of a very familiar and everyday phenomenon. This phenomenon is that of speech and oral communication, particularly in an oral language system which is well known and respected within a given community. In my view this medium of communication, namely everyday spoken language, needs to be understood as foundational and all other media systems and technologies are essentially secondary to it, however much they have changed and developed over the generations.[6] Particular secondary media and their particular messages may be held to influence what and how people experience and think, but that influence is exercised only though people's everyday social lives and the speech this necessarily involves, not least their conversations about their (secondary) media experiences. This foundational mediatisation of the social world is as relevant for understanding people's experiences and uses of the new media in our times as it has been (and still remains) for the old media.

Media and Western modernisation

Media in premodernity and early modernity in Europe

Most premodern civilisations came to be mediatised to a certain extent by the development of writing and reading, at least among social elites. This scribal form of literate culture is also true for medieval Europe. However in Europe the invention of printing and the dissemination of printed texts by the new publishing industry based on it from the fifteenth century onwards meant that within a few centuries literacy became much more widespread, and ultimately became all-pervasive. This mass diffusion was a result of a number of additional major long-term social structural transformative processes, including the development of capitalism and ultimately of industrialisation and the associated urbanisation of populations.[7] However, in the sixteenth century, the 'long revolution' towards a literate culture in early modernity was also the result of a cultural dynamic, namely the civil war in European Christianity associated with the Protestant

Reformation. Protestantism emphasised the religious importance for the stand-ing and salvation of every individual Christian believer of reading the word of God in the sacred book of the Bible. The mass take-up of this version of Chris-tianity in northern and western Europe created historically unprecedented cul-tural conditions and dynamics. These significantly helped to promote the popular diffusion of literate skills, the development of printing and creation of a book industry and market, and the continent-wide creation of a public sphere of religious and secular debate and inquiry, the intellectual peaks of which we know as the seventeenth- and eighteenth-century European Enlightenment period.

Thus European societies entered the period of early modernisation on the basis of an evolving media system which was essentially multi-media at a foun-dational level. That is, it was for increasing proportions of European societies simultaneously both oral and literate, and of course it remains so in our times. Generations of social reformers and activists from the nineteenth century onwards fought long and hard, and continue to do so, to ensure that their gov-ernments respect this interpretation of modern society and thus achieve near-universal literacy through publicly funded education systems. This foundational (and constitutional) multi-mediaticity should be borne in mind when we con-sider the processes of media development associated with Western modernisa-tion from the nineteenth century onwards.

Primary-phase modernisation phase and the old media

European and North American societies in this period witnessed, adopted and were deeply influenced by a series of technologically, militarily and commer-cially driven additions to the their existing multi-media communication envi-ronments. These processes created the distinctively modern mass media communication environment people became familiar with over the course of the twentieth century. The periodic additional media can be analytically visual-ised initially as layers within an existing multi-media system. The foundational oral-literate multi-media layers were progressively added to by a series of other layers. Initially, in the late nineteenth century there was the extension of book-oriented literacy into new fields because of the rise of the popular press and magazine industries. As we know this was followed in the twentieth century by a series of science-based media technology breakthroughs including film and radio from the 1920s and television from the 1950s and 1960s. By the late twen-tieth century modern societies are characterised by mass public access to and competences in a fairly diverse multi-media environment or complex consisting (from the perspective both of every socialised individual and also of every society as an organized system) of layers of oracy, literacy, radio, film and television.

Of course the metaphor of layers is far too limited to adequately characterise the history of the modern multi-media complex whether in general or in the case of particular societies. It is too passive to do justice to the changing and often conflictual relationships of status and power between media industries and communities of communicators representing the various non-oral media. For instance the rise of radio was seen as an existential threat to the press and was resisted by the latter, and in its turn the rise of television was seen a threat to all of the other media of communication and resisted by them. The threats were perceived to be not just to film (as we noted earlier) and to radio but also to literacy per se (appearing to herald 'the death of the book') and indeed even to the exercise of oracy and conversation themselves (given television's require-ment for being watched more or less in domestic silence).[8]

At different periods and in different societies various types of modus vivendi and co-existence have been achieved among the media in the modern multi-media complex. However this has usually involved an acquiescence of most of the various media forms and technologies in the social and cultural dominance of one of their number. This has been the case in relation to the dominance of television in the 'television age' which it can be suggested ran from the 1950s and 1960s through to the 1990s and beyond. The subsequent media age, namely the digital age, has been developing since the 1990s and digitally based new media, particularly the internet, can now be said to dominate in the new multi-media complex.

Secondary-phase modernisation and the advent of new media

In this period of overlap between contemporary society's new and older versions of the multi-media complex, digital media's effects on television are complicated (see for instance Table 1.2). New media (and new media corporations, products and demand) have significantly displaced old media, particularly television, in terms of power and visibility in the overall media (and wider) economy. However, in other respects, for instance in terms of media content, television and the internet could be said to have entered a period of creative mutual interaction with internet and user-generated material enlivening television broadcasting and with the internet providing resources for television viewers to deepen and supplement their interests in television content off-screen. How this period of overlap will ultimately work out, for television and its organisation as an industry – whether positively (with television retained as a media enclave within the new media's communication environment) or negatively (with the collapse of television corporations and broadcast networks) – is currently unclear.

Media, sport events and Western modernisation

Symbioses between media and sport during modernisation

The brief account in the preceding discussion of the changing nature of the multi-media complex in modern society, particularly the periodic shifts in the dominant technology and industry, provides a basis for understanding some of the major influences on mega-events and their changes throughout the modernisation process from the late nineteenth century through to the present. This is particularly so in relation to major sport events and their hinterland in the mass interest which has developed in sport culture in modern societies. Various media have been instrumental at various periods for commercial reasons in promoting the development of this mass sport culture and its peak moments in major events such as the Olympic Games through sponsorship and mass communication. We can envisage this as a series of synergistic relationships in what we can refer to as the evolving 'media–sport symbiosis'.[9] The media–sport symbiosis evolved in three main stages in Western society, and at each stage professional mass spectator sport became intimately connected with the media industry which was dominant at the time.

Firstly, in the initial period of the development of mass sport from the 1880s through to the First World War, sport culture and its events came to be linked with the mass press industry. A notable example of this is the link between the early development of the French sport newspaper *L'Auto* (precursor of today's *L'Equipe*) and the legendary annual cycling event, the Tour de France. The leaders of *L'Auto* created the event in 1903 to boost the newspaper's circulation, and they were very successful in doing so. Over a century later the media–sport link remains in the case of the Tour. The event continues to be organised, along with many other cycle races inside and outside of France, by a unit of the media group (EPA, Editions Phillipe Armaury) which also owns *L'Equipe*.[10]

The second and third stages were dominated respectively by the rise of mass radio and later mass television. By the late 1920s the broadcasting of sport events, news and information became an important programme element in the new medium, and helped to popularise it. A notable example here was the linkage in Britain between the newly founded BBC media organisation and its broadcasting of nationally significant annual sport events like the Football Association Cup Finals from Wembley Stadium, the Grand National steeplechase horse race from Liverpool and the Lawn Tennis Championships from Wimbledon. This process was repeated across Western societies in relation to television when it became the dominant media industry in the multi-media complex whether in public-sector-based or private-sector-based forms from the 1950s and 1960s onwards. In the British case the BBC added television coverage of major sport events to its radio coverage, and this process, initially at least, enabled both the broadcaster and the relevant sport organisations to establish themselves firmly as major national cultural institutions in postwar Britain.[11]

The form of media–sport symbioses, then, has changed over time in relation to changes in the nature of the multi-media complex prevailing in the wider society in any given period. This provides relevant background for recognising the potential significance of the current shift in the complex from one dominated by what is now the old media technology and industry of television to one which is increasingly dominated by the 'new media' including the internet. It also indicates that in considering this shift we need to bear a number of aspects of media–sport symbiosis in mind, particularly those relating to finance, consumer markets and fan experience. Firstly, in relation to the *financial aspect*, media organisations have traditionally seen it as being in their own interests, not least as part of their brand-promotion and marketing strategies, to fund sports organisations and events through sponsorship and in other ways. This aspect of the media–sport linkage may have begun a century or so ago at a relatively low level in the example of *L'Equipe* and the Tour de France, but evidently over time it has evolved to become big business, as in the example of the contemporary affair between English Premier League soccer and Sky television. Secondly, there is the *consumer market aspect*. Media audiences and sport audiences have undoubtedly always overlapped to a certain extent. However the systematic linkages which have developed between media organisations and sport organisations enables the market reach of both sides of the partnership to be extended as the process of overlapping and reciprocal recognition between them proceeds as the partnership develops.

Finally, there is the *sport fan experience aspect*. Fans are a particular kind of cultural consumer with a special degree of emotional identification and loyalty to particular clubs and players. This status is developed in the core experience of being a spectator at sport events. But it also involves participating in whatever the media environment might be which surrounds events at particular times. Evidently this is very different experientially and in term of interaction and communication within the sport culture depending on the media environment prevailing at the time. It is one thing to experience sport in a media environment which is restricted to being that of pre-event and post-event press coverage. It is something entirely different not to be present at the event but none the less to experience the event live via media. And evidently live broadcasting has taken two completely different forms. On the one hand initially there was only radio broadcasting. This imposes the sensory restriction on listeners of exclusive reliance on a commentator's descriptions and interpretations which require them to use their imagination to give meaning to the event. On the other hand later the live televising of sport events enabled viewers to watch the action and to imagine that, therefore, they could participate in the event more deeply and even in ways comparable to those of spectators present in the stadia.

The nature of the multi-media complex influences the nature of sport culture at the time of events, whether people are present at them or not, and also in the pre- and post-event periods. Evidently this has changed qualitatively over the last century or more, becoming more differentiated as time has gone on, from a combination of oracy and press literacy to the contemporary combination not only of oracy and press literacy but also of the coverage and experiential possibilities offered both by live radio and television broadcasting. Currently the new media, particularly people's uses of the internet, are beginning to change the prevailing multi-media complex again and to affect the nature of the media–sport symbiosis in all of its aspects. In what follows we can look into some concrete aspects and examples of both the prevailing media–sport symbiosis and the potential changes implied in it by the increasing presence and dominance of the new media in the multi-media complex more widely.

Mega events and new media in the digital age: The potential for media–sport symbioses in secondary-phase modernisation

A high degree of symbiosis has evolved over the past two generations in the relationship between the Olympic movement and its mega-events on the one hand and the old media industry of television on the other. The maintenance of the vitality and growth of this symbiosis has to be a matter of great strategic importance for sport mega-event owners like the International Olympic Committee (IOC). However as we have noted above our period is marked by a range of social changes and by social, cultural and political reactions and adaptations to them, including in the worlds of media and of mega-events. In recent decades the television age communication environment has begun to be overshadowed by the emergence of the distinctive communication environment of the digital age and the mass take-up of new media. So the question we will consider in Chapters 2 and 3 is how this is affecting the prevailing media–sport modus vivendi which has been long-established between television and the Olympics.

Of course these changes are on such a epochal, global and structural scale that it would be over-optimistic and hubristic to expect that such a question could be settled in any definitive way at the present time. The question must remain an open one for as long a period of time as the digital age takes to emerge to full dominance, and for as long as the current period of its overlap with the television age persists. However in this sub-section we can begin to look into the question, albeit in a necessarily limited, exploratory and speculative spirit, by setting the new scene with some observations about the new media. In Part I we then consider some of their positive implications for recent Olympic mega-events (Chapter 2) and some implications and possibilities which are more potentially negative for major sport events like the Olympics (Chapter 3).

To begin with, we need a snapshot of the current situation of the coming of the digital age and its overlaps and relationships with the television age. Table 1.2 summarises some relevant information about the global growth of the internet, the key new media technology of the digital age, across the main regions of the world. Given its apparent ubiquity and familiarity in our present social world it is sobering to recall just how recent this technology is and how rapid its rise has been in terms of historical time. It began to be socially influential initially in the West from the mid-1990s, a mere two decades ago, and Table 1.2 presents its remarkable growth between 2000 and 2014. It also presents information about current public use of television to contribute an impression of the prevailing nature of the general multi-media environment in different world regions.

Table 1.2 maps out the massive global growth in internet users from 2000 to 2014, and also allows us to see something about the nature of the current overlap between digital and televisual media technologies and environments. The 'penetration' of the internet into the homes and lives of people in the West in 2014 has begun to approach the levels of near-universality which were achieved decades ago in the postwar period by television, and before that by radio. However they remain low in non-Western world regions at between a third and a half of the population. Nevertheless the rate of growth of internet use in the West has been relatively rapid, multiplying three times over the 2000–14 period in North America and five times in Europe over the same period. And even

Table 1.2 The digital age (1): the mix of old and new media use in the secondary phase of modernisation

World regions[1] (using Olympic categories)	Internet users in 2000 (millions)	Internet users in 2014 (millions)	Internet penetration 2014 (% population)	Television penetration 2014(% of people watchingTV/video daily in key world regional nations)	
				TV	*Net-based TV*[2]
North America	108	310	87.7	75	24
Europe	105	582	70.5	80	17
Asia	114	1,386	34.7	66	33
Middle East and Africa	4.7	408	30.0	85	9
Latin America	18	320	52.3	82	26
Oceania	7.6	26.7	72.9	79	18

Sources: IWS 2014 and TNS 2014
Notes
1 The key nations used here for each world region are USA (North America), UK (Europe), China (Asia), South Africa (Middle East and Africa), Brazil (Latin America and the Caribbean) and Australia (Oceania).
2 Viewing of internet-based TV or video daily via digital age devices, namely PCs, mobiles or tablet computers.

though internet penetration remains relatively low in the developing countries of non-Western world regions it is unlikely to remain so for very much longer since its growth rates in these regions are very high. Internet penetration has multiplied tenfold in the 2000–14 period in both the Asia region and the Middle East and African region, and by many times more than that in the same period in the Latin American region. The fact that internet penetration rates remain so low in these regions indicates the existence of an international media divide not only in terms of the internet but more broadly in terms of telecommunications infrastructures. It also indicates that a major potential continues to exist for much further growth of the internet, reinforcing its status at the core of the newly emerging global multi-media communication environment.

The information about audiences for television summarised in Table 1.2 also enables us to recognise the persistence, in spite of the advent of the early digital age, of what some commentators refer to as people's 'love affair with television'. It remains a very popular cultural and social form in all societies in the modern era.[12] Television penetration rates (when measured by the percentage of people watching daily) remain high in all world regions. However evidently processes of 'media convergence' are beginning to get under way in various respects in the new communication environment of the digital age. Television systems and sets are becoming based on digital technology, and television screens are increasingly becoming 'smart' and capable of operating as internet screens. In addition as Table 1.2 indicates (column 5), currently relatively small proportions of television watchers are beginning to access television programme contents through the use of digital devices such as personal computers (PCs), tablet computers and internet-enabled (Third Generation, 3G) mobile phones. We will follow up this sketch of the changing social context of old and new media in Western and non-Western world regions in more detail in the chapters which make up Part I of the book. There we can explore the growing problems faced by the prevailing symbiosis between the old media and mass sport culture with its focus on the production and consumption of major events, and also the possible emergence of different forms of media–sport symbiosis in the emerging new media environment.

Social change and mega-events 2: urban change

Mega-events have always been urban events as well as media events. As such they have both reflected and affected the social character and changes of the cities which hosted them. In particular they have often left behind special and publicly valued places (e.g. museums or stadia) and spaces (e.g. major urban parks), albeit in an ad hoc way. This 'urban legacy' aspect of mega-events has become more of an explicit and planned characteristic over the last two decades, and we explore it in more depth and detail in relation to event-legacy places and spaces in the chapters in Part II of this book. To prepare for this in this section we introduce the urban and legacy aspects of mega-events by relating them to the general schema of macro-social change outlined in the first section above.

All of the great social dynamics of the 'primary phase of modernisation' in the West (i.e. the techno-economic, political-economic, cultural-economic, political-cultural and civilisational dynamics such as industrialisation, nation-state-building and so on) were associated with, and given material and tangible form in, a series of waves of city-building, creation of urban places and spaces, and associated processes of urbanisation.[13] The types of buildings and zones, and allied urban institutions and organisations, involved in the urban embodiment of each of the main social dynamics are schematically indicated in Table 1.3.

Table 1.3 Western urbanisation, nineteenth to twenty-first century: a schematic representation of the embodiment of long-term macro-social change in cities

Primary-phase modernisation and city-building (mid nineteenth to late twentieth century)		Secondary-phase modernisation and urban regeneration (late twentieth to early tenty-first century)	
Societal dimensions and dynamics	*Urban places, spaces and institutions*	*Societal dimensions and dynamics*	*Urban places, spaces and institutions*
Techno-economic *Industrialisation and capitalism*	*Buildings & zones for* e.g. Factory production Finance and trading; rail hubs and hotels; class-based housing quarters	*Techno-economic* *Post-industrialism and capitalism*	*Buildings and zones for* e.g. Service economy Knowledge and digital economy; international transport (airports, rail hubs)
Political-economic *Nation-state-building*	*Buildings and zones for* e.g. State government and administration (in capitals); law and policing; urban Infrastructures (e.g. public transport, energy etc.); Imperial governance (in capitals)	*Political-economic* *Globalisation and glocalisation*	*Buildings and zones for* e.g. Multinational corporations; higher education; global inter-city competition and links
Cultural-economic *The mass consumer culture economy*	*Buildings and zones for* Elite and mass shopping; mass media (press, radio and TV, especially in capitals); mass sport (stadia); nations' interests in staging periodic temporary mega-events in major cities	*Cultural-economic* *De-massified or individualised consumer cultural economy*	Buildings and zones for Elite and mass shopping; leisure and entertainment; heritage and tourism; states' and cities' interests in staging periodic temporary mega-events

Table 1.3 Western urbanisation, nineteenth to twenty-first century: a schematic representation of the embodiment of long-term macro-social change in cities (Continued)

Primary-phase modernisation and city-building (mid nineteenth to late twentieth century)		Secondary-phase modernisation and urban regeneration (late twentieth to early tenty-first century)	
Societal dimensions and dynamics	*Urban places, spaces and institutions*	*Societal dimensions and dynamics*	*Urban places, spaces and institutions*
Politico-cultural *Nationalist monocultural ideology, identity promotion and public culture*	*Buildings and zones for* e.g. Schooling Exhibition and archive (art galleries, museums, libraries); mass public assemblies and parades; nations' interests in staging periodic temporary mega-events in major cities (often using public parks)	*Politico-cultural:* *Glocal multicultural and cosmopolitan Ideology, identity promotion and public culture*	*Buildings and zones for:* e.g. Ethnic & migrant housing and cultural quarters; Cultural co-existence and encounter (via public spaces e.g. parks, and via recurrent public events and festivals); states' and cities' interests in staging periodic temporary mega-events (often using public parks)
Civilisational worldview *Nature-mastery and progress*	*Buildings and zones used to symbolise this* e.g. Botanical gardens Zoos; parks	*Civilisational worldview* *Nature-conservation and 'neo-progress'*	*Buildings and zones reinterpreted to symbolise this* e.g. Botanical gardens, zoos and parks

As part of the primary modernisation process mass migrations occurred throughout the West from the country to the city (and also from the country in Europe to the city in America). And, in spite of the persistence of social deprivation, urban populations and national economies both set out on very long-term growth trajectories. National societies in America and Europe were transformed from being mainly agriculturally based to being mainly city-dwelling. As part of this, many of the major Western cities we are familiar with in modern America and Europe were either qualitatively expanded or created ex nihilo particularly in industrial regions in the nineteenth century. These cities rapidly acquired the specialised urban spaces and places which political leaders and power elites deemed to be appropriate for the operation, decoration and celebration of their political power, for the organisation of industry and trade, for the housing and control of the masses, for mass entertainment and recreation and so on. In this process modern institutions such as the factory and the parliamentary assembly, the school and the prison, the housing complex and the park, were first given visible spatial and material form through urban architecture and design.

The secondary phase of modernisation in the West, as we saw earlier, has been under way since at least the geopolitical upheaval of the oil crisis in the mid-1970s. It involves the increasingly prominent and influential dynamics of post-industrialism, globalisation, cosmopolitanism and environmentalism. Cities in the West which had originally been designed to support capitalistic industrialisation were now afflicted with processes of de-industrialisation and capital flight. They faced the challenge to renew or regenerate themselves as potential economic hubs in a new post-industrial economic environment. They needed to reuse polluted ex-industrial urban zones or port facilities for various social purposes including the new economy of the cultural industries of exhibitions, entertainment and tourism. In both economic and communicational contexts they were becoming local ('glocal') hubs of the emerging worldwide inter-city and international circuits and networks which the term 'globalisation' began to be used to refer to in the 1990s. One significant aspect of globalisation is an increase in international flows of economic migrants, particularly to cities. Thus Western cities have become significantly more ethnically diverse and face new challenges of cultural integration. Cities in the secondary phase of modernisation have also faced challenges posed by the environmental indifference and degradation associated with the primary phase. They need to envisage and also to actively promote green values such as sustainability across the full range of urban policy areas (e.g. in relation to energy supply, mass transport services, waste disposal, housing etc.).

These phases of modernisation and the often troubled processes of transition between them provide significant resources and rationales for the staging of mega-events; and understanding them also provides intellectual resources for the sociological and contextual analysis of mega-events. In Table 1.3 mega-events are seen as urban and cultural policies and thus as elements in the cultural-economic and political-cultural fields of social dynamics. However, in contemporary times they are increasingly seen as having the potential to have an influence within all of the other dynamics. In the primary phase of Western modernisation in the late nineteeth century and early and mid-twentieth century mega-events were created as part of the material embodiment of that phase in primary urbanisation. So Expos in particular allowed ideologies and values associated with societal modernisation dynamics (industrialisation and nation state-building, nationalism and imperialism, and nature-exploitation) to be celebrated and propagated within the host nation and also internationally. On the other hand, within the host city, besides providing a local amplification of these ideologies and values, they also provided a popular platform for social experimentation and communication about possibilities in the fields of urban architecture, infrastructure, planning and lifestyle.

In the secondary phase of modernisation Western cities have used the staging of mega-events to reflect and mark, and to model and promote, some of the new ideas and attitudes which are required to face the many challenges posed by the advent of secondary modernisation (see Table 1.3). Thus they have been used to promote host cities' post-industrial economic sectors, including cultural industries such as tourism; to promote host nations' and host cities' 'soft power', including their recognition and connectedness in trans-national (international and global) geopolitical terms and contexts; to promote cultural integration and multicultural values in the host nation and city; and to model and communicate pro-ecological values and practices. In the contemporary period mega-event projects often involve plans to create long-term legacies relating to these kinds of uses.

In the chapters in Part 2, particularly Chapters 4 and 5, we explore the often spectacular architecture as well as the functional buildings and zones which Expo and Olympic mega-events have frequently left as their urban legacies, and which they are increasingly required to do both by international mega-event organisations and also by urban elites and planners. An important urban use of mega-events in this context is the final one mentioned in our list above, namely to model and communicate pro-ecological values and practices. This can be referred to as a 'greening' of the mega-event in order to contribute towards the 'greening' of the host city. Such projects relate to the civilisational dynamic in modernisation processes and they are the focus of the discussion in Chapter 6. The remaining comments in this section are concerned with providing some relevant background for this aspect of one of the book's arguments about changes in the character of mega-events. This is the argument that, unlike mega-events staged in the primary phase of modernisation, those staged in the contemporary secondary phase are invariably tasked with communicating and contributing to short and long-term green projects in their host cities.

Cities, progress and nature: mega-events and green urbanism

In our earlier discussions of the macro-social changes of Western modernisation and its associated urbanisation processes we suggested that a 'civilisational worldview' underpinned the primary phase in all of the major Western societies This derived from various sources, including Enlightenment ideas and (paradoxically) the experience of effective European empire-building around the world due to the military advantages conferred by scientific and technological developments. In the early nineteenth century the transformative experience of Europe's industrial revolution was added to a conceptual concoction which came to be known through the influential idea and ideal of progress.[14] Implicit in this idea was the notion that nature was a realm of reality and of resources distinct from humankind, but fortunately readily accessible to them. This notion meant that humans could and should 'master' and use nature, whether in the form of the growth of scientific knowledge, the increase of technological power, the exploration of the planet, the exploitation of the planet's material, energy, food and other resources, or all of these processes combined. The worldview of progress, with its underlying mastery-of-nature notion, not only underpinned the general societal dynamics of modernisation such as industrialisation and nation-state building, but did so particularly at the level of primary-phase urbanisation and city-building. The hubris of modernity's nature-mastery worldview and its commitment to unlimited urbanisation and industrialisation have led to the contemporary global ecological crisis.[15] In this crisis ironically it is humanity which is now being inexorably mastered and endangered by forces of nature. Responding to this the green imperatives of ecological sustainability have become pervasive in contemporary politics and policy-making (albeit to different degrees, for varying motives and with varying degrees of effectiveness) at all levels from the global to the local and including, importantly in this context, the urban.[16]

Evidently, whether in the ancient, medieval or modern worlds, cities have always substituted varying versions of an artificial and patriarchal 'man-made' (thus, 'un-natural') environment in place of a natural environment.[17] This has been taken to a qualitatively new level in the modern era in the apparently inexorable diffusion and acceleration of urbanisation processes both within societies and across the planet.[18] In the primary phase, particularly in the twentieth century, Western urbanisation came to tangibly and visibly instantiate the worldview of progress as mastery of nature, with their burial of fertile land under the 'concrete jungles' of their buildings and roads, and with their canalisation and bridging of rivers. Later in the primary phase and particularly in the secondary phase of modernisation and urbanisation the city's ecological damage and its challenge to nature was further symbolically represented in the mushrooming of 'sky-scraper' buildings in central city areas.

When Western societies were simultaneously nation-building and city-building in the primary phase of modernisation, the city's progress worldview and its challenge to nature were promoted through a series of modern urban cultural innovations which operated to disguise the ecologically damaging aspects of the city. These innovative urban cultural institutions included some which were directly concerned to display and advance knowledge about and control of nature, namely botanical gardens and zoological gardens. In the midst of the 'man-made' city, in their different ontological spheres and in their different ways, these cultural institutions organised and publicly presented versions of progress, that is versions of modernity's new and evolving abilities to master nature's flora and fauna. Later, in the secondary phase, the purpose of these kinds of institutions and their challenge to nature would come to be significantly reinterpreted in more pro-nature ecological or green ways as sites and organisation for the conservation rather than mastery of Nature.

In the primary phase of modernisation and urbanisation, then, the city–nature relationship was already recognised as being an oppositional one. And this led to the creative development of some characteristic urban cultural and environmentally relevant institutions, places and spaces. These include botanical gardens, zoos, museums, art galleries together with the valued spaces in which they were often located, namely urban parks. In Chapter 6 we explore one further city-originated cultural institution, namely Expo mega-events. We will look at Expos in relation to these early (proto-) versions of the greening of urban policy, and indeed as being themselves embryonic proto-green urban policies to the degree that they involved the renewal or creation of urban parks and public space. In the secondary phase of Western modernisation and urbanisation, in the contemporary period, there has been an change in mega-events towards explicitly seeing them as green projects. In Chapter 6 we explore this analysis in some detail in the case of Expos, understood both as short-term urban performances and as generators of long-term urban legacies.

Social change and mega-events 3: global change

The strategy in the sociological approach to mega-events developed in this book is to focus on some key changes within the world of mega-events in the contemporary period and to understand these in relation to deeper and broader contextual themes in the long-term macro-social changes involved in Western modernisation. Mega-events and their changes can be usefully understood as reflecting, symbolising and influencing these deeper contexts. The latter were summarised in the first section (above) as involving interconnected changes in modern societies' techno-economic, political-economic, cultural-economic, political-cultural and civilisational dimensions. As we have noted, the media-related and city-related changes in the world of mega-events we have introduced so far can be understood, at least in the first instance, as relating respectively to the techno-economic changes involved in the digital revolution and to the civilisational worldview changes involved in the global ecological crisis, particularly policy responses to it at the urban level. Each of these relationships between changes in events and their contexts is explored in more detail in the main body of the book.

We can now turn to the final mega-event change we are concerned with, namely that involving a global shift in event locations from mainly Western host cities and nations to a more shared pattern between Western and non-Western sites. As in the preceding discussions of mega-event changes, the strategy will be to relate this process to underlying dynamics of macro-social change, to introduce the main terms of reference here and to explore the issues in greater detail later (in Part III). In this case, at least in the first instance, the dynamics concern the political economic dimension of the modern social order, especially those commonly associated with globalisation. This section, then, is divided into two main parts. The first part introduces general aspects of globalisation and also of capitalism which contemporary mega-events can be said to reflect and refract, and to mark and influence. These aspects include neoliberalism and 'glocalisation'. The second part introduces the global shift in mega-event locations which has been evident in the early twenty-first century. Both sets of issues, together with their interrelationships, are explored later in greater detail in the chapters which make up Part III of the book.

Globalisation, capitalism and mega-events

Globalisation is commonly understood to refer largely to an economic process, mainly involving the extension of the capitalist economic system around the world. And, at least when the process was first recognised and commented on, it was also assumed to have a relatively standardising character. However to be useful in our analysis of mega-events globalisation needs to be understood in more nuanced ways, that is in terms of a conception I refer to as 'complex globalisation'.[19] Firstly I aim to emphasise, as against the economistic version, that globalisation has an intrinsically multidimensional character (that is that it also involves political, cultural and technological societal dimensions and dynamics). Thus secondly, as against the standardising version, I aim to emphasise globalisation's intrinsically complex character.

Complex globalisation 1: globalisation and neoliberalism

Globalisation emerged from the mid-1990s as an increasingly well-recognised phenomenon, much-commented upon in social-scientific discourses as well as public discourses.[20] Throughout the twentieth century the Soviet communist political-economic and geopolitical system had been the only substantial alternative to the dominance of Western industrial capitalism as a way of organising modern national and international economies. With the collapse of Soviet communism in 1989–90 the way was open for American and European versions of production and consumption, technology and finance, to infiltrate and influence national economies worldwide and to increasingly enable them to become integrated into an evolving and semi-autonomous 'global' unitary system, particularly in what we have referred to earlier as the secondary phase of Western modernisation.

In the secondary phase this roughly coincided with the significantly ideological phenomenon of a rise and influence of the radically pro-capitalist (pro-free market, pro-individualist and anti-statist) worldview referred to as 'neoliberalism'.[21] In the late twentieth century and contemporary period this has been politically influential as an ideology not only in the West but also beyond, particularly in 'developing' societies. However neoliberalism's ideological presence and influence are no guide at all to its cognitive worth as an analysis of economic and social reality. Fundamental weaknesses are its sociologically unrealistic abstraction of economic processes from social contexts and also its normative conflation of economic analysis with ideological wishful thinking. In addition, the alleged universalism of its conceptual repertoire (for instance economic rationality, the logic of markets etc.) implied an apolitical and uni-form vision of the potential of the modern world order (and thus of the process of globalisation), namely that it could be (or could be made to be) a great singular and stateless market.

Ironically the weaknesses of such right-wing neoliberal perspectives on the nature of capitalism and economic globalisation can also be shared, albeit perhaps unwittingly, by social researchers of a very different or 'critical' political persuasion, including contemporary analysts of mega-events and of events in general.[22] Representatives of both camps can view mega-events in ways which overemphasise their economic aspects and generally overly standardise their nature and impacts. Thus mega-events can be seen by each camp as being instruments for promoting market-based economic growth and capital accumulation, whether in a benign way (from a neoliberal and mainstream economy perspective) or in a malign way (from a critical political economic perspective).[23] In my view misrepresentation problems can arise for both camps from their theoretically influenced tendencies to over-simplify the complex realities of globalisation and, in the course of this, to de-contextualise and overemphasise the economic dimension (the 'hidden hand of the market', the 'logic of capital' etc.).

From my theoretical perspective on the social contexts and changes involved in modernisation (see the discussion in the first section of this chapter) globalisation needs to be understood more historically and empirically as being intrinsically complex and multi-dimensional (see also Roche 2006b and Urry 2003). Relatedly, contemporary capitalism needs to be understood as being capable of taking a variety of hybrid forms dependent on the political, cultural and technological contexts it infiltrates and within which it becomes embedded.[24] It is from this general perspective that the account and analysis of mega-events is undertaken in this book.

Thus second-phase modernisation, as we have seen in the earlier discussion, in its globalising and capitalistic aspects, needs to be understood as being at the very least a *political* economic process, rather than a purely economistic process. Also, in that analysis, globalisation-relevant processes are evidently multi-dimensional and are present in other societal dimensions and dynamics, such as those concerned with technology, culture and ideology. In addition in the West ascendant secondary-phase institutions and processes have overlapped with, and continue to co-exist in tension with, declining primary-phase versions For instance in spite of a 'logic of convergence' among Western economies nevertheless national governments and national cultures evidently retain much influence over economies which enables them to sustain important nationally distinctive characteristics. This is not least in terms of the persisting variations among them which they have been able to sustain in terms of welfare and tax policies and which social-policy analysts recognise as a range of hybrid types of 'welfare capitalism'.[25] Nationally based differences can also generate a variety of types of neo-colonial relationships between relatively wealthy Western countries (internally undergoing secondary-phase modernisation) and non-Western developing countries (internally undergoing various combinations of accelerated primary-phase and secondary-phase forms of modernization). These types constitute a further range of hybrid systems of capitalist political economy and as such they contribute to the multi-form character of contemporary global capitalism. Furthermore the real diversity of the political economic and social contexts in which various forms of global capitalism are embedded has become highly visible in recent times. This is clear in the growth in the early twenty-first century of such hybrid emerging society socio-economic formations as China's 'communist capitalism', East Asian 'Confucian welfare capitalism' and Arab Gulf states' 'Islamic capitalism' among others.[26]

Complex globalisation 2: glocalisation and cultural differentiation

Complex globalisation is interconnected with the media and urban changes affecting mega-events which were introduced in earlier sections. On the one hand the rise of the internet adds a globally integrative technological and cultural-communicative dynamic to the core economic integrative processes which enhance their effectiveness in production, consumer and financial contexts. On the other hand cities' imperatives to redefine and regenerate themselves in post-industrial and cultural economy terms pushes them to integrate themselves into the global economy both through infrastructures which tend to standardise them (e.g. the uniformity and predictability of international airports) and also in what we can refer to as glocalising ways, for instance through touristically relevant cultural developments (e.g. local heritage exhibitions and festivals which are marketed internationally as well as nationally) which tend to culturally differentiate them.

Cultural differentiation can have an ambiguous character. Some of these kinds of processes are elements of what is required for cities and localities to establish place-recognition and to be successful in international tourism markets. Thus some forms of local identity-assertion and/or renewal and of differentiation can operate in explicitly pro-global rather than anti-global ways. In the context of such a complex-globalisation perspective we can refer to processes of local differentiation at all levels below the global (particularly of the pro-global kind, but including also those of the apparently 'anti-global' kind, see below) as being forms of glocalisation.[27] In Part III of the book we are concerned with globalisation in the sense of the global integration-by-differentiation, or glocalisation, at the level of cities. In Chapter 7 this is illustrated with reference to some of the major Chinese cities, and in Chapter 8 it is illustrated with reference to London as both a national capital city but also as a world city or global city. In addition in discussing these cities and their mega-event projects later we are also concerned with a higher level of organisation and differentiation within world society, higher even than that of the nation-state level, namely that relating to geographic and socio-historical regions of world society such as Europe and the Far East. So the mega-events discussed in this chapter are understood to represent globalising influences both at the level of their host cities and also at the level of China as an objective core of East Asia understood as a world region. Similarly the mega-events discussed in Chapter 8 are seen to represent globalising influences operating in London which in turn are understood not only as a national capital but also as a standard-bearer of the West and the European world region.

Finally, in relation to the issue of globalisation's cultural and political differentiation effects, it is relevant to note that the core economic processes involved in globalisation can readily generate anti-global reactions in the political and cultural spheres of societies affected by them, both in long-affected (i.e. Western) and in newly affected (i.e. emerging and developing) societies. This adds to contemporary globalisation's intrinsic complexity. These reactions can involve the reassertion or renewal of political and cultural identities and differences, from the international level (e.g. common languages, civilisations, world religions or ethnicities) to the community level, but particularly at the level of nation-states and cities. None the less anti-global politically and culturally reactive processes exist only because of the forces of globalisation, and indeed they themselves can be organised at a global level. In this and other ways they register the presence and significance of globalisation. Thus, in terms of my complex globalisation perspective, globalisation needs to be understood as encompassing these reactive and differentiating political and cultural aspects as well as the integrative techno-economic aspects.[28]

The worldwide spread of complex globalisation since the late twentieth century accelerated notably in the early twenty-first century, not least because of the diffusion of technological empowerment related to digitisation and the internet. This has had a range of implications for mega-events, some of them of a rather ambiguous kind. The latter include developments in the social roles of mega-events as transient glocal hubs and vehicles (whether understood as representing cities, nations or world regions) simultaneously (1) for the dissemination of the virtues (such as they are) of the pursuit of capitalist economic growth (and, to a more limited extent also of neoliberal ideology), and green limits–to–growth ecological ideology, and (2b) for displays of the achievement of commonalities and also for the legitimation of differences connected with modernity and the modernisation process. Complex globalisation in general reconfigures the multiple societal dimensions of the economy, polity, culture and technology by means of new flows or global shifts of people, capital and information through new network linkages within and beyond territorial nation-states. Contemporary mega-events reflect and mark such global shift processes, and we explore and illustrate them in the discussions and case studies in the body of this book. For the moment we can introduce these themes by focusing on a particularly visible aspect of the relationship between contemporary mega-events and globalisation, namely the global shift in their spatial locations away from the traditional Western monopoly towards patterns of event distribution which are more inclusive of non-Western locations.

The twenty-first-century global shift in mega-event locations

Mega-events have always tended to reflect and mark the times in which they are produced. This is as true of the contemporary twenty-first-century 'editions' of the Expo and Olympic genres discussed in this book as it was of the original editions in the late nineteenth century and the institutionalised editions of much of the twentieth century.[29] However throughout most of these generations mega-events remained unchanged in one important respect. That is they were created and staged in the West, and they largely continued to be staged there throughout the twentieth century. This situation had reflected the political, cultural and economic lead in development and modernisation which the West built up over this period of time.

Mega-event locations: a long-term end to Western monopoly?

However, the situation relating to mega-event locations has changed in the first decade or so of the twenty-first century. Table 1.4 illustrates this change in relation to the three leading genres of mega-event, namely the Olympics, the FIFA football World Cup competition and World Expos. Table 1.4 indicates that the distribution of the hosting of these events in the contemporary period has now become much more equally balanced between Western countries and countries outside of the West. This shift in part represents explicit policy developments

Table 1.4 The global shift in mega-event locations from the late twentieth to the early twenty-first century

Periods	Mega-events	West	Non-West	
			Developed	*'Emerging'*
1980–2000	*Summer Olympics*	1984 Los Angeles 1992 Barcelona 1996 Atlanta 2000 Sydney	1980 Moscow 1988 Seoul	
	FIFA Football World Cup	1982 Spain 1990 Italy 1994 USA 1998 France		1986 Mexico
	Expos	(1984 Knoxville) (1985 N. Orleans) (1986 Vancouver) (1988 Brisbane) 1992 Seville (1998 Lisbon) 2000 Hanover	(1985 Tsukuba) (1993 Daejon)	
2000–2022	*Summer Olympics*	2004 Athens 2012 London	*2020 Tokyo*	2008 Beijing 2016 Rio de Janeiro
	FIFA Football World Cup	2006 Germany	2002 Japan and South Korea *2018 Russia*	2010 South Africa 2014 Brazil *2022 Qatar*
	Expos	(2008 Zaragoza) 2015 Milan	(2005 Aichi) (2012 Yeosu)	2010 Shanghai *2022 Dubai*

Sources: See the websites of the IOC (www.olympics.org/); of the BIE (www.bie-paris.org/); and of FIFA (www.fifa.com)
Note: Parentheses indicate second-order Expos; italics indicate future events.

within mega-event 'owner' organisations as in the case of FIFA. More generally it represents such organisations' active adaptations to the power of wider globalising forces relayed to them from their multinational corporate sponsors, their partner media companies and their potential host nations and cities. We need to consider whether this is likely to be a temporary or a long-term trend.

The concept of the West used in Table 1.4 includes the countries of North America and Europe, together with the largely Western-settler country of Australia. The residual category of non-Western countries used in the Table is divided between Developed and Emerging types. For the purposes of constructing this

Table the developed type is taken to include Russia and Japan which had each become industrialised by the interwar period in the early twentieth century together with South Korea which industrialised rapidly from the 1980s. Also for the purposes of the Table the emerging type is taken to include Mexico, Brazil, China, South Africa, and the Gulf states of Qatar and the United Arab Emirates. Although each of these societies contains large low-income sectors their economies have all been growing considerably and rapidly in recent years in spite of periodic problems and temporary reverses. To refer to the change from a West-centric to a more shared distribution of mega-event locations between the West and the non-West as a global shift implies that it is not a short-term phenomenon and that it is likely to persist in the long term in the twenty-first century. The grounds for this assumption are economists' projections about world economic growth through to 2050 and the increasingly prominent economic position 'emerging' societies will occupy in the global economy. This position was originally proposed in 2001 by economic analyst Jim O'Neill and his colleagues for what they identified as the BRIC group of high-population (about three billion in total) and high-growth non-Western emerging countries (namely Brazil, Russia, India and China, a group to which South Africa was added later, hence BRICS).[30] O'Neill subsequently modified his analysis to include an additional group of large and high-growth non-Western countries, namely the MINT group (Mexico, Indonesia, Nigeria and Turkey).[31] In the later analyses as in the earlier ones the projection is that the West's economies as a whole (e.g. the G7 group, i.e. US, Canada, UK, Germany, France and Italy, together with Japan) are likely to be overshadowed by around 2040 by non-Western emerging economies (e.g. by the BRIC group, which, as a counterweight to G7, formed itself into an official international organisation in 2009-10 and now runs an international development bank).[32] These changes would ultimately require that the West-originated and dominated institutions of global governance of the international economy (particularly the International Monetary Fund and the World Bank) would need to be reorganised to reflect the new countervailing aggregate power, even dominance, of non-Western countries.

Actual developments in the international economy since the millennium and new long-term projections have generally confirmed this kind of analysis, albeit with some caveats. The caveats relate to the pace of Western relative decline probably being slower than the original BRIC analysis implied, and the pace of BRIC growth being slower and more variable than predicted. Also, realistically, the West is likely to long retain considerable (even if no longer dominant) economic power in a non-West-dominated global economy and international order more generally.[33] However given that a long-term global shift in economics and geopolitics is under way in favour of leading non-Western countries this is likely to be reflected in the field of mega-event locations. So the global shift which is observable in the world of mega-events is also likely to be a long-term one.

Governments in emerging societies are likely to be motivated to bid to stage mega-events for the same sort of reasons that Western societies were originally motivated to do so, for instance to reflect and mark their 'progress' and their (at least) first-phase modernisation, not only for their own citizens but also in the eyes of the international community of nations. In addition, although mega-events can be risky projects for developing and emerging societies in terms of such possibilities as waste and corruption, they can also offer the possibility of more substantial and longer-term developmental influences and legacies, not least in relation to host cities. An important case in this respect is that of South Korea, whose capital city, Seoul, staged the Summer Olympic Games in 1988, and we can take a brief look at it at this point.

A premonition of the 'global shift' of mega-events: the case of South Korea and its 1988 Olympics

In the course of their seminal sociological study of the mediation of the Seoul Olympics James Larson and Heung-Soo Park assess this mega-event as having had two normatively positive catalytic influences, one economic and one political (Larson and Park 1993). The economic influence was the impetus the Games gave to the electronics sector of the South Korean economy, and thereby ultimately to national economic growth and social development. The political influence was the impetus it can be argued to have given to the process of democratisation and thus to national political development.[34]

Politically South Korea had been run by undemocratic, corrupt and repressive military dictators since the end of the Korean war in the 1950s. The Olympic Games was a prestige project initiated by one of them (President Hee) and carried through by two others (Presidents Chun and Roh). Although popular worldwide, the Games event was not popular with the Korean public because of its association with the unpopular President Chun. A national political crisis built up in which the people (workers, students and the new middle class) could exert pressure on the government by threatening chaos during the Olympic event 'when the world would be watching'. This public pressure culminated in Chun's resignation shortly before the Games. Roh took over as a provisional leader offering democratic Presidential elections after the Games. He was elected President, and although he turned out to be as corrupt as his predecessors,

Larson and Park observe that the Olympics indicated a 'delegitimation … of military dictatorship' and some progress on the way to a more liberal and democratic polity in South Korea (Larson and Park 1993, p. 245).

In terms of the economic influence Larson and Park suggest that the event 'gave impetus to the development of several broadcast-specific technologies' (1993, p. 145) produced by new Korean electronics industries, which in turn can be shown to have fuelled the growth of Korean electronics exports. This industry now represents the country's leading export industry, having been developed in the 1980s in preparation for the Olympic event and overtaking the previous leading export sector, textiles, in 1988, the year of the Games (p. 145). They observe that 'Analysts have attributed such growth to publicity associated with the Olympics and the promotion of technological growth in electronics and telecommunications necessitated by the Olympics' (p. 145). Generally Larson and Park argue that South Korea used the Olympic event 'to enter the Information Age' (p. 143). That is, what had previously been a largely agriculturally based economy was able to use the mega-event as a springboard to leap into a dynamic and technologically led version of industrialisation. In the pre-event phase, 1980 to 1988, bidding for and preparing for the Olympics, South Korea advanced from 28th to 16th position among the world's economies ranked in terms of personal incomes or GDP per capita.[35] This beginning of its 'Asian Tiger' economic phase resulted in a doubling of Koreans' incomes (GDP per capita) within a decade following the Olympics, and a further doubling by the early twenty-first century (O'Neill 2013, p. 29, figure 3).

Arguably the Seoul Olympics anticipated the recent global shift in mega-events to non-Western locations by a number of decades. South Korea could be said to have benefited both politically and economically from its Olympic project and its aftermaths. While there seems to be a good deal of substance in the claim of economic benefits, the event's beneficial political influence remains ambiguous. In spite of its positive democratic associations the fact remains that the Seoul Olympics project was decided on, bid for, built by and staged by largely authoritarian political regimes. The ambiguous nature of the economic and political impacts of mega-events and their claimed benefits is a problem for all host countries. But this is particularly so given the contemporary global shift in mega-event locations to more of a more shared distribution between Western and non-Western countries in the staging of mega-events. Non-Western societies, whether developed like Russia or emerging like China, have problematic political records in terms of the rule of law, democracy and human rights, whatever their nominal claims to adhere to such values.[36]

This qualitatively new and probably permanent situation of global shift in the location of mega-events means that basic political and ethical questions about the selection of mega-event hosts, the way they prepare and stage events, and the purposes they use them for will need to be inscribed to a new degree in the processes of monitoring, reporting, researching and assessing mega-events. This sets new ethical and organisational challenges for mega-event owner organisations like the IOC, and also for the international networks and movements of sport and cultural authorities and professionals together with interested media and publics that these organisations are supposed to represent. We note possible risks and problems of locating mega-events in authoritarian states in the case of the mediation of China's Beijing Olympics 2008 and Russia's Sochi Olympics 2014 later in Chapter 4. Risks are beginning to arise again, for instance, in relation to the planning and staging of the FIFA World Cup in Russia in 2018 and in Qatar in 2022, each of which has generated much debate in Western media and publics.[37]

As regards social change and mega-event organisation problems, this chapter has introduced social changes in the media, urban and global contexts underlying both the staging of particular mega-events and also the operations of the organisations which attempt to legitimate and control them. The scale and pace of change in these three areas has been considerable in our contemporary period and is the subject of the discussions in the three parts of his book. These changes have in turn increased the vulnerability both of particular mega-events and also of mega-event organisations to risks and problems. The conviction that we need to step back and renew our understanding of the underlying social changes and of their implications for mega-events is part of the rationale for engaging in the exploratory studies which make up this book. In this context it is worth concluding this Introduction by briefly observing the pressing nature of some of the problems mega-event organisations currently face particularly in the sphere of sport.

Given the scale and pace of professional sport's international mediatisation and commercialisation in recent decades (see Chapters 2 and 3) it is perhaps comprehensible why sport mega-event organisations like the IOC, FIFA, the IAAF and others have become vulnerable to corruption and to questionable and unaccountable processes of selection of event hosts. The IOC experienced this in the 1990s. Although the international public and media criticism of this played a role in delegitimising IOC inaction, it took the power of legal and financial pressure in the USA from Congress, the FBI, NBC television, and corporate sponsors to get the IOC to publicly acknowledge and address the problem. Nevertheless it finally did reform and improve its self-regulation around 2000 under the incoming Presidency of Jacques Rogge (see the account in Roche 2000, ch. 7), and arguably it continues to do so under the current President (Thomas Bach, see the IOC's Agenda 2020, IOC 2014a). However unfortunately FIFA remains tainted by corruption and by questionable and unaccountable event-host selection processes.

FIFA's problems are of very long standing, having developed particularly under the 24-year FIFA Presidencies of the Brazilian Jão Havelange (1974–98) and the 17-year Presidencies of his Swiss protégé Joseph Blatter. They culminated in 2015 with, on the one hand, a crisis within the organisation (FIFA's attempted suppression and distortion of an investigation, by its own ethics committee, into the selection of Russia and Qatar as 2018 and 2022 hosts respectively), and, on the other hand, a crisis over the Presidency (initially over the re-election of Blatter, see Gibson 2015b) which was followed almost immediately by Blatter's announcement of his 'resignation' (although he nominally retained his post until 2016). In spite of the volume of criticism of this lamentable situation in the international media, until recently there was little reason to assume that it would improve in the near future. FIFA had not yet faced the powerful US legal and financial forces which the IOC had faced in the 1990s. Since the traditional and contemporary cultural and economic base of world football was and remains Europe and its political headquarters is in Switzerland, it has been assumed that FIFA was less exposed than the IOC was to pressure from US sources. However recently this situation appears to be beginning to change.

US governments and the FBI have long had interests in investigating corruption involving FIFA officials representing North America (CONCACAF, the Confederation of North, Central American and Caribbean Association Football). In a dramatic move in May 2015 the FBI issued arrest warrants for eight CONCACAF-related FIFA officials, including the confederation's president Jeffrey Webb and its ex-president Jack Warner. They happened to be attending FIFA in Switzerland and were detained by the Swiss police in order to be extradited to the USA on FBI arrest warrants. In the USA they face prosecution on charges which, according to the *New York Times*, include 'racketeering, wire fraud and money laundering conspiracy' (see Apuzzo et al. 2015). In addition Blatter has been cited and investigated by the Swiss police for corruption and FIFA's revived ethics committee has excluded him from any future role in football administration. In principle this is (or ought to be) a powerful stimulus to the much-needed reform of FIFA which, among many others, FIFA's main commercial sponsors have jointly called for (see BBC 2015b). However at the time of writing it remains an open question whether FIFA is capable of organising and carrying through an IOC-type reform process.

Conclusion

In this chapter we have introduced the three main areas within twenty-first-century mega-event studies which the three main parts of this book aim to address, namely relating to contemporary developments in mega-events' media, urban and global aspects and the deeper macro-social contexts and dynamics which underlie and condition them. In terms of the latter we have outlined a conception of the social world as comprising a set of macro-social dimensions together with a conception of long-term macro-social change which includes a multi-phasic conception of modernisation, an understanding of globalisation as intrinsically structurally complex and a conception of 'really existing' capitalism as unavoidably hybridised and embedded in a range of social contexts. The theoretical perspective on mega-events taken in this book, then, is an inquiring sociological one, namely that they may be most usefully interpreted and understood as being potentially socially influential reflections, refractions, and symbolic markers of these underlying social conditions.

Notes

1 My perspective on the multi-dimensional nature of modern social formations and on modernisation processes of change (for instance as in Roche 1992, 2000 and 2010a) has been influenced by both classical and postwar sociological analysis and social theory, in the former case particularly Max Weber and in the latter case a range of figures (including Talcott Parsons, Ernest Gellner, Jürgen Habermas, Emmanuel Wallerstein, Anthony Giddens and Manuel Castells). In the contemporary period the notion of modernisation is less invoked in the analysis of Western societies than it has been in the past, the idea that Western societies have become postmodern has become more fashionable and modernisation is more debated in relation to the development of non-Western societies. The notion of globalisation (seen as a multi-dimensional social process and not from an exclusively economic or neoliberal perspective, e.g. Beck 2000, Held et al. 2000 Scholte 2005, Urry 2003) can encompass the analysis of formations and dynamics in both Western and non-Western societies. Since the millennium it has significantly overtaken and subsumed the notion of modernisation. I recognise this particularly in the discussion of the nature and basis of the global shift in mega-events (see section four below and Chapter 7). However in my view, when appropriately reinterpreted in terms of phases, as indicated here, modernisation remains analytically useful and provides a way of grasping the complexity, interconnections and dynamics of contemporary social formations in both Western and non-Western societies.

2 On the idea of 'progress' see the discussion in Chapter 6 and also note 8 there, and note 14 in this chapter.

3 See for instance Guthrie 2006, Dicken 2015 and Held et al. 2000.

4 See for instance Dicken 2015 passim and also Roche 2010a, ch. 7, also ch. 1.

5 To help explain this focus on media aspects of Olympics rather than Expos some background points and issues should be indicated here. The advent of the old broadcasting media of radio and particularly television opened the way for the live coverage of sport events and for what I refer to later as the media–sport symbiosis which has been of great relevance for the development of sport mega-events like the Olympic Games. Expos, as mainly exhibitionary rather than performance events, have not been affected in the same way by the rise of the old media and particularly television. Thus there is no comparable symbiosis between this kind of mega-event and the media which might, in turn, be threatened and changed by the rise of the internet. Consequently there is much less to investigate and discuss in the field of Expo–media relations as compared with Olympic–media relations. However this situation might be changing. As exhibitions Expos have a structural resemblance to museums and art galleries, and indeed can be seen as transient proto-versions of these institutions. Since contemporary museums and art galleries are beginning to adapt to the digital age and to incorporate the internet in their display presentation, their marketing and publicity and their booking systems (e.g. see IMLS 2008, Arup 2013, Nemo 2013, also Hastac 2012), a comparison with the situation in the equivalent operations of contemporary Expos could in principle be an interesting topic for future Expo-related media research. Another non-sporting cultural genre which, however, has a performative and event-based character rather than an exhibitionary character, is that of the music festival. As a live event the music festival is potentially comparable with sport, and can also be organised on a large (international and second-order mega-event) scale. Like Expos and museums and unlike sport events, music festivals never developed a symbiosis with television in the pre-digital era. However with the advent of the digital age and online streaming of live (in addition to archived) television coverage, music festivals, comparably with sport culture and its events, are beginning to adapt themselves positively to the internet and to develop something of a new symbiosis with it (e.g. Reidy 2016).

6 See for instance Roche 2014 on ordinary language analysis. My approach to the fundamental importance of both orality and literacy in more recent times has been influenced considerably by the notable work of the British anthropologist Jack Goody. See for instance his study of literacy's epochal civilisational influence, 'The domestications of the savage mind' (Goody 1977), and also his seminal paper with the literary historian Ian Watt on 'The consequences of literacy' (Goody and Watt 1975).

7 See for instance Vincent 2000 on the social history of mass literacy in Europe, also the seminal work of the cultural sociologist and social historian Raymond Williams on 'the long revolution' in culture which popular literacy helped to promote in Britain (Williams 1961). Also see Goody and Watt 1975.

8 See for instance Asa Briggs and Peter Burke's social history of the media 'from Gutenberg to the Internet' (Briggs and Burke 2009), and also Everett Rogers's classic study of the history of media technologies and the recurrence of the social process of diffusion of innovation (Rogers 2003).

9 The media sport literature contains various ways of referring to what I am referring to as a symbiosis. For instance, David Rowe, a leading writer in the field, refers to the relationship as 'an unholy trinity', see Rowe 2004a, and also his edited collection Rowe 2004b.

10 On the history of the Tour de France cycle race see for instance Wheatcroft 2007.

11 On the social history of the relationship between television and sport in Britain see Whannel 1992.

12 For contemporary international data see TNS 2014 and Kohli 2014. For a classic sociological discussion on television as a popular cultural form, from the earlier years of the television age, see Raymond Williams's discussion in Williams 1974.

13 On the long history of Western urbanisation from premodern periods through early and then industrial modernisation, see Mumford 1966, Tilly 1994 and Rabb and Rotberg 1981. On contemporary global urbanisation across the developing world see UNDESA 2014. In the premodern era the vast majority of people in all societies lived and made their living in the countryside and not in towns and cities. The growth of urbanisation is a long-term worldwide process which characterises the modern era simultaneously with other trends such as globalisation. The proportion of the world's (growing) population which lives in cities has been rising inexorably since the beginning of industrialisation in eighteenth-century Europe. By 2014 this proportion had reached 54 per cent, and this is projected to grow to 66 per cent by 2050 (see UNDESA 2014). Apart from the general urbanisation of people which is associated with modernisation and globalisation, social theorists have also pointed to other types of related urbanisation processes, particularly the urbanisation of capital in the contemporary global capitalist economy (see for instance Harvey 1985). On other relevant aspects of sub-global-scale local (e.g. urban) social and political processes associated with globalisation see social theoretical discussions of 'glocalisation' (e.g. Brenner 2004) and 'glurbanisation' (e.g. Jessop and Sum 2000, Bercht 2013).

14 On the idea of progress (together with its relationship to Nature, including human nature) see Pollard 1971 and Nisbet 1980.

15 The World Wildlife Fund (WWF) documents this contemporary global ecological crisis (i.e. the ongoing record of global warming, species extinctions, loss of biodiversity, atmospheric pollution, oceanic pollution etc. generated by human activity around the world) in its annual reports, see for instance WWF et al. 2014. The reality of the crisis, particularly global warming, has been recognised in international policy-making, albeit with little positive effect, for a number of decades. The recent (2015) UN-backed Paris Agreement aims at limiting global warming and is to be implemented from 2016–17 onwards. It embodies a more urgent and committed recognition of the crisis by the world's nations and appears to promise a more effective response to it (e.g. see EC 2015 and C2ES 2015 for summaries and resources relating to the Treaty).

16 The contemporary ecological crisis and the consequent imperative for pro-environmental green policies at all levels are evidently large issues which justify more extensive explorations and discussions than can be provided in this book. (For a discussion of the relationship between a pro-environment worldview and citizenship, including the rights of future generations, see Roche 1992, pp. 52–3 and p. 243). However my discussion in this chapter in particular assumes that the crisis, and the need for policy responses to it, provides an important background problematic which is deeply influential on contemporary urban policy-making in all world regions, including policy-making relating to urban mega-events. On this aspect see comments on the modern mastery-of-nature worldview in Chapter 6 below.

17 On cities in ancient and medieval society and changing premodern versions of the contrast between man-made and natural environments see classic discussions in Mumford 1966 and Pirenne 1969. For more recent discussions see, respectively Smith 2003 and Tilly 1994.

18 See note 12 above.

19 On complex globalisation see Roche 2006b and 2010a, ch. 1, also Urry 2003.

20 On globalisation generally see also Held et al. 2000 and Scholte 2005, For both moderate and critical sociological interpretations of the process see for instance Lechner and Boli 2005 (a world culture perspective) and Wallerstein 2004 (a world-system perspective).

21 On neoliberalism in general see Davies 2014 and Brenner at al. 2010. On neoliberalism in relation to mega-events see Gruneau and Horne 2016a, Darnell and Millington 2016, Eisenhauer et al. 2014, and Parnell and Robinson 2012.

22 For instance contributors to Gruneau and Horne 2016b, also Rojek 2013.

23 Neoliberal economists can be boosters for events, but they can also be severe critics of events which result in the economic failures associated with waste, corruption and the construction of white elephants, e.g. Zimbalist 2015.

24 See the discussion and references in Roche 2010a, ch. 6.

25 See note 23.

26 On Chinese capitalism and globalisation see for instance Guthrie 2006. On various other contemporary forms of what has been referred to as 'state capitalism' see McDonald and Lemco 2015.

27 On glocalisation, as the influences of globalisation on local social levels and processes, see Brenner 2004. My usage of the idea also shares the spirit of the wider interpretation of glocal social processes with particular reference to cities which is associated with Bob Jessop's neologism 'glurbanisation' which has been applied in the understanding of Chinese experiences of urbanisation by Jessop and Sum 2000 (in relation to Hong Kong) and Bercht 2013 (in relation to Guangzhou).

28 On anti-Olympic protests see for instance Lenskyj 2000 and Giulianotti et al. 2015.

29 See Roche 2000, chs 2, 3 and passim.

30 See O'Neill 2001, and also Wilson and Purushothaman 2003.

31 See O'Neill 2013, ch. 3, also 2011.

32 On BRICS as an international grouping rather than as an economic abstraction see BBC 2014, also see The BRICS Post website, http://thebricpost.com/, and discussions in Lo and Hiscock 2014.

33 See McRae 2015, Ward/HSBC 2011, and CEBR 2014.

34 See Larson and Park 1993, pp. 143–5, and pp. 166–8; also Roche 2000, pp. 148–9 and pp. 185–7.

35 See WB 2014 which gives information on the ranking of the most affluent countries in the world as indicated by GDP (World Bank statistics, formated by Classora).

36 See for instance World Audit's annual 'democracy audit' which assesses countries and ranks them in terms of their possession of a range of indicators of democracy in four 'divisions' from division 1 which is the most democratic to division 4 which is the most undemocratic and authoritarian. In the most recent audit Russia and China are allocated to division 4 at rank 121st and 131st respectively among the countries of the world (World Audit 2015). See also the *Economist* magazine's 'Democracy Index 2014' which undertakes a similar task, and allocates Russia and China to the category of 'authoritarian regime' ranking them 132nd and 144th respectively (EIU 2015).

37 For additional reports and analysis relating to the corruption problems currently facing FIFA and the IAAF see the Introduction, note [2].

I

Mega-events and media change

2

Mega-events and mediatisation: between old and new media

The social history of mega-events such as Olympic Games and Expos over the course of the modern period reveals how much they have been altered by and have adapted to changing social contexts during the last century or more (Roche 2000). However social change 'does not sleep'. It is evidently dynamically present in the social world of our current late modern period, and it will influence the nature and production of mega-events as we move forward in the twenty-first century. To approach an understanding of mega-events in relation to their changing contexts we outlined a relevant sociological concept of contemporary macro-social change in Chapter 1.[1] There it was suggested that contemporary social structural change includes such globalistion-relevant dynamics and vectors as the global shifts and geopolitics involved in the new multi-polar world order which is currently emerging, particularly with the rise of China to economic and political superpower status, and also the gathering storm of the planet's ecological crisis.[2] Structural social changes on this massive scale inevitably carry implications of change for mega-events, for the nations which host them and for the collective forms of festive culture and cultural citizenship associated with staging them. In this part of the book we are concerned with other changes which were also introduced in Chapter 1 and are arguably of an equally revolutionary and influential kind. These concern changes in the contemporary technologies, social institutions and cultural forms of the media of information and communication.

Our period is now one which is caught between on the one hand the social institutions and influences of the old media, particularly television, and, on the other the rapidly diffusing presence of the new media, the information and communication equipment and environments based on digital technologies. Understanding media contexts is a vital element in the sociology of mega-events and in understanding not only the past and current nature of mega-events as

social phenomena and as cultural movements but also their changes and possible futures. We have already noted this general idea in passing when considering the importance for mega-events of the rise and influence of mass television
(Chapter 1). Even before it had become effectively universal in the US in the
1950s and in Europe in the 1960s this period was being referred to as the television age. An interesting illustration of the common usage of this concept here
is that of a legendary figure in the birth and growth of America's film industry
from the 1920s to the 1950s, namely Samuel Goldwyn, founder of the MGM
film corporation. Towards the end of his life he recognised the scale of the
coming media transformation caused by the ineluctable spread of television into
people's homes. And he recognised the challenges this would pose to his own
industry and its distribution system based on networks of theatres located in
the urban public sphere. In an essay on 'Hollywood in the television age' written
in 1949 he had the vision to recognise that the film industry would need to adapt
to the coming dominance of the television industry rather than try to out-
compete it, and also that the future of much of the film industry would ultimately be in making films for television (Goldwyn 1949).

The coming of the television age inevitably carried major implications for
another form of cultural industry, namely mega-events. As we touched on in
the previous chapter, the rise of a television-age media environment was positive
for the Olympics and other major sport events and it accelerated their development. However, at the same time, it tended to undermine the cultural relevance
of Expos. In this chapter we look further into these changes in the social and
media contexts of mega-events, particularly with reference to sport events and
the Olympic Games.

In the 1960s the Canadian media analyst Marshall McLuhan famously
claimed that the social impact of television would be to produce a 'global village'
(McLuhan and Powers 1989). He was wrong about this, at least in the short
term. Rather for most of its modern history the advent of mass television, as in
earlier generations with the advent of the mass press, has generated numerous
'national villages'. In these villages people have been the targets of one-way
message transmission from centralised communication systems located in
capital cities or their provincial satellites. Like 'villagers' in the public square,
national citizens have been convened as an imagined collective by what media
studies analysts refer to as national and international media events. The seminal
study of this phenomenon by Daniel Dayan and Elihu Katz sees it as involving
television coverage of cultural and political events which are deemed to be
particularly important such as 'contests, conquests and coronations' (Dayan and

Katz 1992, p. 1).[3] They further characterised media events as being perceived by publics as being semi-obligatory to watch and to remember, and in watching them citizens typically understand themselves as being 'witnesses to history' (Dayan and Katz 1992).[4] The parallel and related development of mass national and international sport and their related events, in the way they have been mediated initially by the mass press and then by mass television, can be said to have contributed to the tradition of 'media events' and thus to the formation of national villages and national cultural identities. However over the last three decades television broadcasts of the Olympics and the football World Cup can be said to have developed in two ways.

Firstly, they have extended their geographic reach far beyond national audiences to audiences worldwide. Secondly, they have increasingly co-existed in both positive and negative ways with the emerging new media environment which has emerged since the 1990s. In relation to the first of these points we are familiar with the idea that Olympic television broadcasts tend to stimulate nationalism, particularly in the host nation. In addition live television coverage began to reach around the world when satellite television technology became available from the time of the Seoul Olympics 1988 (Larson and Park 1993).[5] Since that time it can be speculated that Olympic television has also begun to cultivate a limited form of internationalism and cultural cosmopolitanism by creating transient but recurrent experiences of a global village, at least in this particular sector of popular culture.[6] In relation to the second point about television's co-existence with new media both in general and in the context of mega-events a number of observations should be made. Earlier we noted the idea that in the history of media and their social implications there are periodic structural shifts which are commonly referred to as being from one media age to another. Just as this was recognised for the television age by (among many others) the film industry leader Sam Goldwyn, so something similar can be said about the idea of a digital age. This now-common expression has recently been used by new media corporation leaders who have achieved a similar status to that which was achieved in a previous generation by Goldwyn in the film industry. In 2013 Eric Schmidt and Jared Cohen, founders of the giant and globally influential internet browser company Google, published a book *The new digital age*. Their recognition of the scale of the potential social impact of this shift from one media 'age' to another is indicated in their subtitle *Reshaping the future of people, nations and business* (Schmidt and Cohen 2013).

The potential impacts of the digital age of the internet and new media on the old established media forms and industries like television are ambiguous and uncertain both in general and in relation to mega-events. On the one hand the present and future dynamism of the internet and its multi-media and interactive aspects and uses can be argued to ultimately threaten the very existence of single-media and one-way transmissive organisations like television corporations, just as television once appeared to threaten the very existence of the film industry. We return to consider this general cultural threat issue later, in Chapter 3. On the other hand this new medium is already globally extended in dense communication networks. And as such, and at least for the current period, it is consistent with, and can technically carry, enhance and deepen the new global reach of the 'old' television medium in terms of media-events and sport mega-events.

A relatively recent example in the context of mega-events which illustrates both the vast scale of the televisual mediation of the Olympics and also the potentially positive relations between the old medium and the new media is the 2008 Beijing Olympics. In terms of the scale of the global reach of Olympic television it is estimated that the opening ceremony was watched simultaneously by 1.4 billion people around the world (IOC 2009). In addition what was also noticeable about mediation aspects of this particular Olympic event was that it was possible to portray it not only as a television event of practically unique scale but also as being, simultaneously, 'the first truly digital Games' (IOC 2009). In this case old and new media seemed to operate in parallel, and in their different but complementary ways they each served exceptionally large worldwide audiences and networks of media users. In terms of the internet aspect, the main organisations involved in staging the event, including the television broadcasters, made huge amounts of information and hours of event coverage available to the public. A breakdown of the number of individuals accessing Olympic information and/or images in the internet was not made available at the time. But the fact that 8.2 billion internet page views were recorded suggests that it was likely to be in the hundreds of millions (IOC 2009). Of course there were also other more negative aspects of both the internet coverage and its relationship to the television coverage. And we consider these more negative aspects of the mediation of the Beijing Olympics in the following chapter. For the moment these large audience and user numbers, which relate to both the 'old media' form of television and also to the new media form of the internet, are a good indication of the global scale and nature of sport mega-event genres like the Olympics. They also remind us that we need to recognise and address the underlying processes of mediatisation which makes this global scale possible, and which through wider media technology and media age changes, change the conditions and character of the production and consumption of mega-events as cultural performances.

So far we have seen that a major process of development and change in the media and its social role is under way in our times. The new media context of the internet is emerging alongside of the mainstream old media context of television, and both are providing mass public access to our social world in general, and also to sport mega-events like the Olympic Games in particular. These two very different media systems currently seem to be operating in a parallel, even a complementary, way. But the discussion in this and the following chapter suggests that we need to consider the possibility that this situation will not endure. Rather it could be replaced over time by more potentially competitive and conflictual relationships as internet use and the diffusion of digital communication systems continue on their apparently inexorable worldwide growth paths.

Each of these possibilities, both the benign and the conflictual, the complementary and the threatening, testifies to dynamics in the general relationship in the contemporary period between media and society, and between media change and social change, dynamics which have been referred to in the field of media studies using the term 'mediatisation'.[7] Mediatisation needs to be better understood and researched in general, and also in particular when we aim to understand the current social situation and significance of mega-events together with the possible challenges and futures they face. Unfortunately research into media aspects of mega-events is still its infancy. There have only been a limited number of social-scientific studies of Olympic mediation in the old media regime of mass broadcast television.[8] These are far too few in relation to its social significance as part of the emergence of a global level of social and cultural organisation in our times. And, perhaps predictably, there are as yet no substantial or systematic studies, on a relevant scale, of the mediation of the Olympics in the changed context created by the rise of the new media.

This chapter aims to make a small contribution to this field from a sociological perspective by reflecting on some of the wider contexts and issues relating to the rationale for studies in this field, and also on the directions they might take. The discussion is divided into two main sections. The first is concerned with the changing nature of the media and wider social contexts in which the relationship between the Olympics and media has developed. On this basis it then looks at the symbiotic relationship which developed and continues to endure between the Olympics and the old media, particularly television. The second section introduces the changing social context involved in the growth of new media, together with the potential for the growth of positive relations between the Olympics and the new media. The discussion of the new media's positive possibilities, together also with its negative possibilities, for the Olympics and major sport events is taken further in the following chapter.

Mega-events and old media: the symbiosis between the Olympics and television

In the preceding discussion it was suggested that the history of modern popular culture and of mega-events has been marked by a series of symbioses between dominant media technologies and industries on the one hand and sport on the other. To illustrate the issue of symbiosis and its relevance to the understanding of mega-events we can now focus on the relationship between the Olympics and television. In the preceding discussion it was also noted that media–sport symbiosis involved linkages in at least the three main spheres of consumer markets, spectator experiences and of course finance. In considering the relationship between Olympics and television in principle all three types of linkages are relevant.[9] However since they provide the material conditions for any other links to occur and also for reasons of space we focus here on finance links.

The growth of US television's interest in the Olympics 1960–96

The USA in the immediate postwar period experienced high employment rates and fairly continuous economic growth for over a generation, which enabled a large internal market of people with relatively high disposable incomes to be developed. The introduction of the new media technology of television into this market in the early 1950s led to its practically universal adoption by the 1960s. Given America's commitment to market capitalism and a minimal role for the state, the organisation of television was mainly commercial, funded by advertising, and came to be dominated by three large companies, CBS, ABC and NBC.[10] The linkage between television and advertising drove the development of a cross-continental consumer culture and this included mass interest in the televising of national sports like baseball and American football which had already been highly commercialised by this period. To serve the interest in the sport dimension of this evolving American media culture US media companies bought rights to broadcast Olympic Games from the rights holders, the International Olympic Committee (IOC).

Initially the sums involved were low. The US media corporation buying the rights to TV broadcasting could readily recoup their costs from income from advertisers for programming slots located within or near Olympic programming. So, albeit with the benefit of hindsight, it is clear that for at least the two decades of the 1960s and 1970s the prices paid for the North American rights to televise the Olympics indicated that the IOC was significantly undervaluing them as commercial assets. For instance CBS paid only $390,000 for the TV rights to the Rome Olympics of 1960.[11] Interestingly that was the only Olympics for which the European Broadcasting Union (EBU) ever paid more than the US networks for the rights to broadcast the Games in Europe (even if that was only a mere $660,000).

The EBU acts on behalf of many national 'public service' broadcasters in and around the European world region. In 1960 television was becoming more common in Western European households. The staging of an Olympic Games on the European continent meant that there was no time-zone problem for European viewers, thereby giving the EBU an interest in bidding for the live television rights. On the other hand, in the pre-satellite TV era US viewers had to wait for the video records of events at the Games to be flown across the Atlantic, considerably reducing the value of live television rights to US TV companies. Table 2.1 enables changes in payments to the IOC for TV rights by USA and European TV groups to be compared over the long-term in the period from 1960 through to 2012.

In the 1960s and 1970s competition between the three US major television networks for the North American regional rights to televise the Olympics began to increase, with ABC winning more often than the others at this time. However this competition led to a regular doubling or even trebling of the prices being paid every four years. By the time of the 1980 Moscow Olympics the price paid, this time by NBC, had risen to $72.3 million. By this time also the EBU and the IOC had settled into a longstanding informal understanding about keeping the European regional price of Olympic television to a minimum. So the EBU paid only $5.6 million, which was a small fraction of the comparable price charged to American television.

In the history of the escalation of television income to the IOC a significant point was reached in relation to the 1984 Olympics in Los Angeles (LA). Staging the event in the US increased the commercial value of televising it considerably, and ABC ended up trebling the sum that NBC had previously paid for the 1980 Moscow Games. However this evidently took ABC to its limits and it was never again able to acquire rights to broadcast an Olympic Games in North America;

Table 2.1 Olympic TV Income, 1960–2012: Summer Olympics, USA and Europe

Year	City	USA TV (US$ million)	Europe TV (US$ million)
1960	Rome	0.39 (CBS)	0.66 (EBU)
1964	Tokyo	1.50 (NBC)	no data
1968	Mexico City	4.50 (ABC)	1.00 (EBU)
1972	Munich	12.50 (ABC)	1.70 (EBU)
1976	Montreal	24.50 (ABC)	4.50 (EBU)
1980	Moscow	72.30 (NBC)	5.60 (EBU)
1984	Los Angeles	225.00 (ABC)	19.80 (EBU)
1988	Seoul	300.00 (NBC)	28.00 (EBU)
1992	Barcelona	416.00 (NBC)	90.00 (EBU)
1996	Atlanta	456.00 (NBC)	247.00 (EBU)
2000	Sydney	715.00 (NBC)	350.00 (EBU)
2004	Athens	793.50 (NBC)	394.00 (EBU)
2008	Beijing	893.00 (NBC)	443.40 (EBU)
2012	London (and Vancouver 2010)	2,200.00 (NBC)	746.00 (EBU)

Sources: Roche 2000, table 6.3, p. 183; Pena 2009, table 3

NBC has won every one of these competitions for TV rights since that time. At the 1984 LA Games ABC contributed the unprecedented sum of $225 million to the IOC's funds in order to acquire the North American rights. This together with the success of its newly introduced Olympic sponsorship system meant that the IOC was in a stronger position to make a contribution to the costs of staging the event. In addition the commercial and organisational expertise of the local Olympic organising committee meant that the LA Games achieved the unusual feat of making an operational surplus of revenue over costs, a surplus which could be ploughed back into the development of track and field and other Olympics sports in the US.[12]

The growth rate of income to the IOC from the sale of television broadcasting rights in North America since 1984 Games no longer amounts to a doubling or trebling every four years as it had done prior to 1984. However by the time that the Games returned to the US in 1996 at Atlanta the price NBC paid for the rights had reached $456 million, which was double the 1984 price albeit over the course of twelve years. Thus there has been a predictability about the fact of the long-term growth in the value of each successive Olympic Games event to US television networks. The rate of this growth has remained very substantial even as the scale of the sums involved, and thus of the income to available to support the Olympic movement's activities, has reached levels which would have been unimaginable in the 1960s.

The Olympics and television in the early twenty-first century: 1998–2012

In more recent years the IOC's fee income from US television for the North American rights has continued the same kind of relentless climb as we have seen in earlier decades. This long-term trend in the financial aspect of the Olympic sector in the modern media–sport symbiosis seems to be a strong one. In particular it has remained singularly unaffected by the historically unprecedented scale of the financial crisis and recession which hit the American and global economy in the 2008–11 period. Since the Sydney Olympics 2000 the value of individual Summer Games events has moved beyond half a billion dollars and on towards a billion dollars. By the time of the 2012 London Olympics the cost to the dominant US network NBC of the televising the Games had reached $1.2 billion (Greyser and Kogan 2013, table 1).

Table 2.2 is an IOC financial summary which usefully maps the Olympic sector of the modern media–sport symbiosis in the recent years of the contemporary period 1998-2012. It enables the picture of growth in the Olympic–television symbiosis which we have provided in the preceding discussions to be brought up to recent times. The IOC now auctions Olympic events as integrated sets of Winter and Summer Games, so the years in the Table relate, respectively, to Nagano and Sydney (1998 and 2000) Salt Lake City and Athens (2002 and 2004), Turin and Beijing (2006 and 208), and Vancouver and London (2010 and 2012). Also the Table reminds us that this media–sport symbiosis is a global and not just a Western phenomenon. It shows us the geographic and economic range of variation in the commercial valuations of the Olympic mega-event as television spectacle and programming. So it records the differential range of fee income from television companies in world regions which roughly relate to the Continental Associations which make up the Olympic organisational structure. The Continental Associations are Africa, America (North and South), Asia (including the Middle East), Europe and Oceania. The Table aims to indicate the traditional dominance of Western countries (North America and Europe, columns 2 and 3) in providing television income to the Olympic movement.

Table 2.2 Broadcast rights fees for Olympic events 1998–2012 (US$ million)

Winter and Summer Games	North America (USA and Canada)	Europe[1]	Asia	Oceania[2]	Central and South America[3]	Middle East and Africa	Total
1998 and 2000	1,124.0	422.1	208.0	64.9	14.2	11.9	1,845.1
2002 and 2004	1,397.4	514.0	232.6	54.3	20.8	12.9	2,232.0
2006 and 2008	1,579.0	578.4	274.0	79.7	34.0	24.9	2,570.0
2010 and 2012	2,154.0	848.0	575.0	126.0	206.0	41.0	3,850.0

Sources: IOC 2013d, also IOC 2012c

Notes

1 'Europe' here is more extensive than the EU, see www.eurolympic.org/.

2 'Oceania' here includes Australia, New Zealand and Pacific island nations.

3 'Central and South America' here includes the Caribbean.

However it also aims to indicate the extent to which the contribution from non-Western countries (in Asia, Oceania, Central and South America, and in Africa and the Middle East, columns 4–7), while continuing to be relatively minor, has none the less been growing significantly in recent years.

Growth in fee income from regions outside of North America and Europe has begun to accelerate as they develop economically and become further integrated into the processes of economic and cultural globalisation and begin to share more equally with the West in the staging of Olympic and other sport and cultural mega-events. This is particularly noticeable in the increases in fees paid between 2006–8 and 2010–12 from Asia and Central and South America, which are both world regions in which Olympics have recently been staged (i.e. Beijing 2008 and Rio de Janeiro 2016).[13] It still remains the case that, as we have seen already has long been the case, television income from the North American world region continues to be the largest single element in the IOC's television rights income, and indeed outweighs the income from all other world regions put together. However it would appear that in very recent years the balance in terms of contributions to the Olympic movement and its activities is beginning to change somewhat in favour of the non-North American regions.

The IOC retains 10 per cent of its income for its own expenses (including its headquarters building, library, archives and museum at Lausanne), and distributes the rest as follows. The bulk, around 50 per cent, goes to local Organising Committees of the Olympic Games (OCOGs) (IOC 2014b). These funds are assumed to cover up to 50 per cent of the directly event-related costs of any given Games event (with the remaining funding coming from non-IOC sources, namely the OCOG's own commercial sources and/or from public authorities in the host city and nation). The remaining 40 per cent is divided fairly equally between two main groups of recipients. On the one hand there are the 204 National Olympic Committees (NOCs, the main constituent elements of the worldwide Olympic movement) and also the Olympic Solidarity organisation (OS, which provides support to poorer NOCs in developing countries). On the other hand there are the International Sport Federations (IFs, the international governing bodies for each of the sports represented at Olympic Games). In addition minor payments are made: to international sport governance organisations (such as the World Anti-Doping Agency and the Court of Arbitration for Sport), to the recently established (in 2010) Youth Olympic Games and also to a reserve fund (the Olympic Foundation) for use in relation to discretionary culture, education and sport projects (and also in exceptional circumstances in relation to the costs involved in the non-staging of a Games event).

In this section we have been able to look into the financial aspect of the media–sport symbiosis in the case of one of the main producers of mega-events, namely the Olympic movement and its relationship- with the old medium of television. We have seen how the bulk of the activities of the IOC and the Olympic movement have long been heavily dependent on the income from the recurrent sale of television rights, and they have become increasingly so over time. This dependency is clearly evident in the contemporary situation where 73 per cent of IOC revenues in the 2009–12 period were derived from television rights sales as against only 18 per cent from their main (TOPS) commercial sponsorship scheme. We now need to consider how this situation might change given the rise of the new media.

Mega-events and new media: the potential for symbiosis between the Olympics and the internet

The development of personal computers developed and penetrated into people's households in the Western societies from the 1980s onwards. The gradual roll-out of high-capacity (optic fibre) broadband cable systems and networks to connect them provided the material infrastructure and communication capacity on which the first stage of the internet, with its Pandora's box of informational, interactive and open-ended uses, could be launched and grow from the mid-1990s onwards. We are currently in the second stage and the second decade of the digital age, which has seen a flowering of the new media. This has been stimulated and enabled by the existence and development potential of the internet, and also has had the feedback effect of promoting the global spread of the use of the internet. As indicated in Table 2.3, in the second decade the internet has experienced rapid worldwide growth and it is reasonable to assume that this trend is likely to continue, over the coming third decade (c. 2015–25), extending and consolidating the internet's presence and uses particularly in non-Western world regions.

This growth in the second decade of the digital age has been fuelled by the creation of a series of perceivedly useful internet-based and oriented devices and services. Table 2.3 contains some illustrations of some of the most popular of these new media (iPhones, Google, Facebook, YouTube, Twitter etc.). They have by now become part of the 'furniture of our lives', having so much brand recognition that it is sometimes difficult to recall the sheer *recency* of their creation. They represent some of the means by which increasing proportions of the planet's population have been enabled and motivated to access and use the internet in recent years. These examples of new media include 'smart' devices

Table 2.3 The digital age (2): new media products and services: global growth 2000–15

Examples	Year created	Users, value etc.
Smartphones		
Apple iPhone	2007	569 million units (2007–14)
Android phones	2008	1.5 billion units (2008–13)
Tablet computers		
Apple iPad	2010	c. 400 million units (2007–14)
Wireless networks		
WiFi Alliance	1999	–
Wifi Direct (P2P)	2008–9	2 billion devices and in 25 % of global homes (2013)
Browsers		**Monthly users in 2014 (millions)**
Google	2004 (PLC)	1.57 billion
Social media		
Facebook	2004	1.3 billion
YouTube	2005	373.26 million
Twitter	2006	284 million
Online Information		
Wikipedia	2001	500 million

Sources: On the growth of smartphones see Golson 2014 and Eastwood 2015; for all internet-related devices see Gartner 204. For other sources see the Note (below) and Statista 2015a, b, c, d, e, f, g
Note: Sources for the main items in column 1: Apple iPhone (Statista 2015a); Android phones (Statista 2015b); iPad (Statista 2015h); Google (Statista 2015f and 2015g) (i.e. in 2014 Google had 54 % penetration of the global internet market of 2.92 billion users); Facebook (Statista 2015c); Twitter (Statista 2015d); YouTube (Statista 2015e) (i.e. total for users in the world's 15 leading countries with highest numbers of users); Wikipedia (Wiki 2015c), WiFi Alliance and Wifi Direct (Wi-Fi 2015).

('smart' mobile phones and mobile tablet computers), network infrastructures (wireless networks), and online services (browser, social media and information services). Both individually and as a set they provide an informal illustration of some characteristic features of the emerging new digital age as a cultural and communication environment. For each of the items the Table indicates the relative recency of their creation (column 2) and also gives a rough indication of the trans-national/global scale or reach of their usage and popularity (column 3).

The dynamism of international demand for some of these individual types of product or service has helped to inflate the profits, brand valuations and stock-market valuations of some of the media technology companies noted in the Table. The Apple and Google corporations, for instance, currently generate annual net profits of around $39.5 billion and $14.4 billion respectively (Neate 2015). And in 2015 the Apple corporation became the first American corporation (or indeed corporation of any nation) which has been seriously assessed as having a stock-market value in the region of $1 trillion. As far as Apple goes, this leading situation has been generated not only by the recognition of the distinctive innovativeness, technical quality, design aesthetics and utility of its devices within its domestic market in the US but also by the company's marketing success in converting this brand recognition into sales internationally, and particularly in the massive and growing consumer market which is emerging in contemporary China, among its new urban middle class.[14]

The development of co-existence between the Olympics and the internet

In previous media ages in the modern West, in the age of the press, and later the age of television, media industries had often been allowed to warp into systems of oligopoly or quasi-monopoly in national markets dominated by 'media monster' organisations sometimes owned or run by 'media moguls'.[15] From this kind of position of general market dominance media companies were often interested in buying into dominance in the media-sport market, including acquiring television rights to major sport events like the Olympics. We noted two leading examples of this kind of television age tendency earlier, namely NBC's persistent and successful drive to acquire the North American rights to televise successive Olympic Games, and the persistent and successful drive by Sky TV and its owner Rupert Murdoch to acquire the British rights to televise English Premier League (EPL) football matches. However the situation with the new media corporate monsters like Apple and Google seems to be different. They may be much bigger companies in terms of profits and valuations than old media television corporate monsters like NBC and Sky TV. And they may dominate particular national markets in the anglophone West in digital media markets to the same degree that leading television companies have dominated their televisual markets. But outside of the West, in regions where they also need to operate successfully, and thus in the global economy more generally, their positions are intrinsically more insecure. They can face market intelligence barriers, regulatory barriers or market barriers from the competition of singular or multiple 'national champion' corporations in the various different world regional and non-anglophone linguistic spheres in which they both choose to operate and need to operate.

The high visibility, high valuation and local market dominance of new media corporations like Apple and Google in principle suggests that they have more social power than television companies, at least in financial terms if not also in other cultural and political terms. However such power has not yet led them to challenge the leading television corporations for control either of nationally significant sport televisual programming in general or the televising of major international sport events like the Olympics in particular.[16] No doubt there are a range of reasons for this current apparent lack of interest in beginning to develop anything like the kind of media–sport symbiosis which had been developed by old media television with sport and the Olympics. However one of the reasons may well be that new media corporations, given their core linkages to the internet, operate with an understanding of the nature of communication media which stresses their individually tailorable and many-to-many interactive character. Such an internet-oriented understanding is essentially out of sympathy with television's one-to-many one-way broadcast logic in the media–sport field as in all of its fields and programming genres.

However, beyond this, it may be that new media corporations together with the communication environments they sustain operate in ways which are not just indifferent to mass television broadcasting of sport and Olympic events but which are actually undermining of them and damaging to them. We need to consider these more negative and conflictual possibilities in the following chapter. For the moment we can consider a more benign alternative, namely that the apparent indifference of the new media to the control of live sport event televisual content indicates at least a potential for some sort of peaceful co-existence between the old and new media in this field. Such a peaceful co-existence would seem to be what television, from its side of the media technology and industry field, would prefer to aspire to in respect of media sport. So, in relation to the Olympics, the mega-event owner, the IOC, and the main television rights purchasers, particularly NBC, have sought to incorporate new media elements and processes in the mediation of recent Olympic Games events, and we take a look at this in the next chapter.

Within the contemporary multi-media complex and environment, the old media of print, radio and television continue to co-exist and compete for people's attention. In that environment people remain highly oriented to television in general, and to spectacular televised sport events and sport mega-events in particular. As we have seen, in recent years the contemporary multi-media environment has become substantially more complicated with the emergence of the new media. The advent of the digital age is ambiguous in its implications for the old medium of television. It clearly dislodges television from its dominant position overseeing the media industry landscape, and to a lesser extent edges it away from the centre ground in that landscape. However in other respects, by reconstructing television on the basis of digital technology and providing new resources of popular and inexpensive user-generated video content, the digital age could be held to provide the conditions for a renaissance in the status and popularity of television, whether only as an enclave within the new media environment or as more of a partner in it. In this new situation television channels have multiplied and viewers are increasingly able to exercise choice and to time-delay, archive or otherwise personally tailor mainstream television programming. In addition the internet, with its capacity for video-streaming television programming, could be said to add to this apparent empowerment of television viewers, although the implications of these changes for television companies as programme creators and schedule managers are less clear.

Whether or not television is likely to be as reanimated as its viewers might be in the digital age it is clear that the internet has the capacity to empower people in ways which could not be imagined in the decades of television's dominance on the modern multi-media complex.[17] It offers users a massive new range of possible actions, interactions and experiences in fields such as producing and consuming, information-gathering and self-educating, entertainment-seeking, and communicating with individuals and network communities. These possibilities in turn have a number of positive and negative potentials as far as the social role and cultural experience of mega-events are concerned. In the following comments the focus is on the potential socio-cultural benefits; later we turn to consider some of the potential socio-cultural costs.

Arguably some of the internet's socio-cultural benefits lie in its ability to use and draw in new ways on older media forms and institutions, although some important problems for the future of these institutions also lurk within these inter-media relations. Besides television, then, the internet can also draw on the press and its main characteristics of news journalism, commentary and photography. In this respect the internet offers users unprecedented opportunities for new forms of inter-mediation, namely through creative personal tailoring and synthesising of contents from (among other sources) the two older media forms of both television and the press. Individual net-users, among other things, can increasingly co-produce their media contents and experiences by aggregating and editing for themselves combinations of pre-produced press, video and social networking contents and experiences. They can thereby effectively construct open-ended multi-media programmes capable of supplementing and enriching any televisual programming content of interest to them. In addition, importantly, they can do this on a mobile basis, including when engaged in on-site participation in the event.

These possibilities can be understood to have the potential to qualitatively transform the nature of people's experience of and engagement with any type or genre of televisual content, including the media and televisual contents and experiences relating to mega-events. In this context, and in a positive 'benefits' perspective, the media technology revolution represented by the advent of the internet already has the capacity in principle to massively enrich the experience of the sports fan, or of the cultural patriot or of the cultural cosmopolitan in their mediated experiences of international sport competitions such as the FIFA World Cup and the Olympic Games.

The IOC has been very aware for some time of the potential benefits as well as the potential downsides connected with the internet and new media in relation to its showcase Olympic events. The post-event marketing and media reports which it requires host city organisers to contribute to have begun to feature information about internet-related aspects of the Olympics since at least the Games of Sydney 2000. By the time of the Beijing Olympics in 2008 the IOC was willing to confidently proclaim the event as 'the first truly Digital Games' (IOC 2008, p. 24, and IOC 2009, p. 3). As we have already noted above in Tables 1.2 and 2.2, even though the digital age and its core technology of the internet are only two decades old, this communication environment remains distinctively wedded to continuous and sometimes qualitative change in terms of the diffusion of innovative new media technologies and their uses. Table 2.2 indicates the fact that social media systems, such as those of Facebook, YouTube and Twitter, and the popular mobile computing systems capable of animating them and diffusing their use globally, such as Apple's iPhone and iPad, had barely been created by the time of the Beijing Olympics. They were products of the second decade of the digital age.

So, whatever the IOC might have meant by describing the Beijing Olympics, and by implication all subsequent Olympics as being 'Digital Games', this meaning could not have included much of substance relating to the use of the set of transformative digital technologies and systems listed in Table 2.2. Rather, the appropriate recognition of the distinctive influence of this particular set could come only some years later. It came in relation to the 2012 London Olympics which the organising committee (LOCOG) and others described as the first 'social media Olympics'.[18] The advent of the 'social media' aspects of the internet, together with the devices and services necessary for this, generally helped to drive the massive global expansion and diffusion of the internet in the second decade of the digital age which was indicated across all world regions in Table 1.2. This expansion can be seen as being reflected over the same period in the expansion of the use by national and global publics of the internet as part of their engagement with successive Olympic Games events. Table 2.4 provides some information about Olympic-related internet traffic.[19] This indicates the scale and timing of the expansion of use of what we might refer to as the Olympic internet in the period 2000–14. The speed and scale of

Table 2.4 Olympics and the internet, 2000–14 (official Games websites)[1]

Olympic Games	Unique users	Page views
2000 Sydney	8.7 million	230 million
2002 Salt Lake City	3.0 million	325 million
2004 Athens	8.9 million BBC site 12.2 million NBC site	–
2006 Turin	4.3 million BBC site	–
	13.3 million NBC site	331 million
2008 Beijing	278 million	8.2 billion
2010 Vancouver	73.6 million	1.2 billion
2012 London	109 million LOCOG site 10.6 million IOC site	8.5 billion online, plus 1.1 billion on mobiles
2014 Sochi	305 million	1.4 billion

Sources: Sydney 2000 (IOC 2000); Salt Lake City 2002 (IOC 2002); Athens 2004 (IOC 2004); Turin 2006 (IOC 2006, Reuters 2006, FierceWireless 2010); Beijing 2008 (IOC 2008, IOC 2009, Carter and Sandomir 2008); Vancouver 2010 (FierceWireless 2010); London 2012 (IOC 2012c); Sochi 2014 (Kantar 2014, Kondolojy 2014b)
Note
1 'Official Games websites' refers to internet sites and services provided by one of more of the IOC, the host city OCOG, and/or the companies holding territorial Olympic TV rights. User and view figures relate to the 16-day duration of the Olympic Games event on these sites. The figure for Beijing unique users is the total of the following world-regional groups of users: 153 million China, 51 million Europe, 21 million Africa, Asia and the Middle East, 23 million Latin America (all in IOC 2009, p. 4), plus 30 million in North America (Carter and Sandomir 2008).

expansion in unique users of official Games websites at Winter Olympics, from the 3 million recorded at Salt Lake City in 2002 to the hundredfold increase to 305 million recorded at Sochi only twelve years later, was remarkable (see column 2). This rapid and global expansion can be expected to continue. In the medium term it is likely to consolidate the relevance of the role of the internet alongside that of television in the global mediation of the Olympic mega-event.

Another related indicator of the expansion of public interest in and use of the internet in relation to the Olympics in the second decade of the digital age is the number of views people make of the video-streams which are provided on the official Games sites. This has a particular relevance to the issue of the relationship between the internet and television in the mediation of the Olympics since, on the one hand, experientially video-streams have some of the quality of Olympic television programme content. However they are not live and thus allowing free access to them does not diminish the value of television companies' exclusive control of live Olympic broadcasting rights. The IOC has been monitoring this type of Olympic-related use of official Games internet sites since the time of the Beijing Olympics. The volumes of video-stream views at successive games are as follows: Beijing 628 million, Vancouver 272 million, London 1.5 billion online (plus 376.5 million on mobiles) and Sochi 1.4 billion.[20] Video-stream viewing of Olympic material is evidently occurring on a very large scale. It is also occurring on a rapidly increasing scale, as is indicated by the fact that the totals have more than doubled in the mere four years which elapsed between the Beijing and London Olympic events. Together with the trend of the data on unique users and page views in Table 2.3 this helps to confirm the possibility of a convergence in the medium term between the scale of the international public's uses of television and of its uses of the internet in experiencing and participating in Olympic Games events. This in turn suggests a possible basis for complementary and even symbiotic relationships to grow between the old and new media in this field.

The rise of the internet in the sphere of the Olympics and its mega-events is not only capable of operating in a benign way, let alone as part of any new kind of symbiosis, with the established mainstream televising of Olympic events. It is also capable of operating in more negative and damaging ways in relation to Olympic television. To return to the mediation of the Beijing Olympics for a moment, this was not only the first significantly 'Digital Games', it was also the first time that the IOC had developed and deployed a 'geo-blocking' media strategy. This is a strategy in which it defends the territorial exclusivity of the television rights it has sold to particular television companies by blocking the unauthorised use of broadcast imagery produced in one country being shown in another one. This and other problems are connected with the new importance of the internet both in the wider social and communication environment context and also in the sphere of the Olympics. We now need to look into these more problematic aspects of the relationship between the old media and the new media in the mediation of major sports and the Olympics Games, and also into the policy responses to them by relevant actors from sport and event organisers to governments.

Conclusion

In this chapter we have been concerned with exploring the early stages of structural change in the media–sport (Olympics) symbiosis from the television age to the digital age. On the media side this refers to changing versions of the prevailing multi-media complex, here from a television-dominated to an internet-dominated version. This in turn can be interpreted at least two ways, namely from the perspective of an interest either in the media production or in the media consumption dimensions of the complex. The discussion in this chapter has been mainly concerned with developments connected with the media production dimension. When we look into this situation further in the next chapter we will also need to take adequate account of the media-consumption dimension and users' experiences. including at recent and highly digitally influenced Summer Olympics games, namely those of Beijing 2008 and London 2012. So in the following chapter we look into these two important cases in terms of both their media production and consumption aspects. In addition we consider what they illustrate about both negative and positive aspects of the evolving relationship between television and the internet in the context of the mediation of the Olympic mega-event.

Notes

1 The period that I refer to in this chapter informally as late modern runs from the 1970s to the present. It corresponds to the period I refer to as the secondary phase of modernisation in Chapter 1 and elsewhere throughout this book.
2 These two vectors of social change are discussed later in Chapters 7 and 6 respectively.
3 It is worth noting that, although some of the phenomena they refer to as being 'media events' are not in themselves festive (for instance state funerals), nevertheless

generally media events tend to involve a degree of communal celebration and thus to involve 'festive viewing' (Dayan and Katz 1992, p. 1). An alternative to this socio-logically nuanced approach to these phenomena is that of an approach informed by a critical political-economy perspective which regards them as 'media spectacles' (see Kellner 2003a, 2003b, 2003c and 2004). Some links between these two approaches are briefly considered in Kellner 2010.

4 The 'witness to history' aspect of their book is seen in its subtitle, namely *The Live Broadcasting of History*.

5 On nationalist and internationalist aspects of Olympic television see Moragas et al. 1995.

6 On cosmopolitanism see Delanty 2009; on cosmopolitanism in the context of media, particularly in the field of news, see Robertson 2010; on internationalism and cosmopolitanism in the fields of sport culture and mediated sport see Roche 2000, ch. 7, 2006a and 2007. A politically as well as theoretically interesting mega-event case to consider in relation to these themes is that of the FIFA World Cup soccer event hosted by Germany in 2006. For an account see German Government 2006.

7 For recent discussions of mediatisation see Couldry 2014, Hepp 2013, Krotz 2009, 2014 and Lundby 2009. However in spite of the analytic attention currently being given by various networks of media sociologists and social scientists to the concept there remains a significant lack of agreement about its meanings and research impli-cations. In addition the main writers have not yet envisaged how it might be applied to the study of the media aspects of mega-events. Given this situation my use of the term in this chapter is intended to be provisional and pragmatic. It is grounded in concrete historical and contemporary examples and illustrations intended to illumi-nate the concept's meaning and utility.

8 The (few) academic studies of the televising of the Olympics over the last two decades include those of Larson and Park 1993 on the Seoul Olympics 1988, Moragas et al. 1995 on the Barcelona Olympics 1992, Billings 2008 on the Turin Winter Olympics 2006 and a collection edited by Qing and Richeri eds. 2012 on Beijing 2008. Also see the review of the early studies in Roche 2000, ch. 6.

9 On the financial symbiosis see the discussion in this section, also Roche 2000, pp. 182–4. On changing aspects of the mediation of the Olympics as a consumer brand and also as a spectator experience see Chapter 3 later.

10 The acronym brand-names of these television companies stand for Columbia Broad-casting System (CBS), American Broadcasting Company (ABC) and National Broadcasting Company Universal (NBC).

11 See Table 2.4 for this information for 1960 and also for comparisons between pay-ments for TV rights by USA and European TV groups from 1960 through to 2012. Sums in dollars are US dollars throughout the book unless otherwise stated.

12 On the success of the 1984 LA Olympics as a commercial project see the account by the main organiser Peter Ueberroth (Ueberroth 1985).

13 See the information on NBC and London 2012 in Chapter 4 below

14 By 2014 the use of the internet in China had grown rapidly to 557 million mobile internet users and 649 million 'netizens' (Millward 2015).

15 For a socio-historical overview of the various media ages and the role of the oli-gopolistic power of particular media technologies and organisations in these, in the particular societal case of the UK, see Curran and Seaton 2010. For a contemporary 'media mogul' see information on Rupert Murdoch in IOC 2014b.

16 However for some qualifications of this picture see the references to the telecom company BT and the internet company YouTube/(Google) in the following chapter and their interests in sport video (Chapter 3).

17 See for instance Manuel Castells's notable sociological account of the rise of the internet (Castells 2002). He reminds us how the original visions and versions of the internet were an ambivalent and potentially conflictual combination of individual libertarianism and a 'free-for-all' system on the one hand and of the power of the state (particularly the US military) and corporations on the other (ibid., chs 1, 2 and passim).

18 See for instance Sweney 2012; we return to this case later in Chapter 3.

19 For information on the sources used to construct Table 2.4 see the Sources and Notes section of the table.

20 Video-stream views for the Olympics are a sub-group of 'page views'. Thus, although they are large numbers they tend to be lower than the numbers for page views which they help to compose. Information on video-steam views for the Olympics 2008–10 can be found in the following sources: Beijing 2008 (IOC 2008, IOC 2009, Carter and Sandomir 2008); Vancouver 2010 (FierceWireless 2010); London 2012 (IOC 2012c); Sochi 2014 (Kantar 2014, Kondolojy 2014b).

The digital age, media sport and mega-events: piracy and symbiosis in the cultural industries

What are the implications of the digital age and new media for media sport and the mediation of sport mega-events like the Olympics? We began to address this question in the preceding chapter and in this one we explore it further. Whereas the previous chapter focused more on the internet's positive implications, in this one we are more concerned with the threat and realities of the internet's negative implications. However we return to consider the more positive implications and the possibilities for a new symbiosis between television and the new media in the context of the Olympics towards the end of the chapter.

The discussion in this chapter is organised in four main stages. The first stage is concerned with general problems in the cultural industries connected with the rise of the internet, such as criticisms of cultural parasitism and piracy. The second stage focuses on the latter problem in particular and looks at recent governmental policies and practices which aim to address and curb internet piracy in both the US and the UK. The third stage is concerned with problems of internet piracy in the field of media sport and the related field of major sport events like the Olympic Games and also high-profile and high-value football matches. It looks at efforts to contest internet piracy in the main codes of football, namely in American football (particularly in relation to the annual Super Bowl game) and in soccer (particularly the competitions organised by the English Premier League). This section also considers the problem of internet piracy in the context of the Olympic Games, and 'hard' and 'soft' approaches by the IOC in its efforts to address the problem. Finally, the fourth stage of the discussion returns to consider issues relating to the nature of the current co-existence between television and the internet-based media in the context of the Olympics, and the possibilities for a new symbiosis in this area.

The internet, cultural industry problems and government policies

In Chapter 2 it was useful to be able to set our focus on the media sport and mega-event aspects in a broad context of social change connected with the pervasive social influence of digitisation and the new media. In the second decade of the digital age the growth of this influence has occurred rapidly and in a largely unregulated manner. The process has been largely driven by the market-based dynamics which have arisen between powerful new digital-age corporations and the global currents of mass public internet use and consumer demand they service. However, within their limitations, Western governments at national and EU level have attempted to guide and manage these developments on the basis of interpretations of the public interest. Since the internet has developed for many in the West as an apparent realm of freedom this has usually involved much public debate and occasionally some controversy between defenders of such freedom and proponents of the legitimacy of, and the need for, legal regulation.

Governments have been challenged to find new balances between freedom and regulation in relation to the media. In terms of regulation they have tended to take a dualistic approach, attempting to maximise socially positive aspects and to minimise negative aspects. The potentially positive aspects of the growth and pervasive influence of the internet include such developments as: an extension of the public sphere (increased communicative space both for freedom of expression and for public accessibility and accountability of democratic governments and state systems); increased efficiency and effectiveness of organisational and inter-personal communication; and the creation of many new fields and forms of industry and employment. The negative aspects include: increased threats to the legal order and the state from terrorist and criminal organisations; new possibilities for the surveillance of citizens and for state and corporate intrusion into their privacy; the disruption, and in some cases destruction, of pre-digital industries and forms of employment; and the increased potential for the illegal infringement or theft of 'intellectual property' referred to as 'internet piracy' (see below).

We are particularly concerned with policies relating to the final two points on this list, and they are inter-connected and influential in the field of the contemporary cultural industries. The category of 'cultural industries' can be defined in various ways.[1] For our purposes in this section it includes the production, distribution and consumption of performances, products and services in fields such as music, film, press, magazines, book publishing, television and also in such television-related sectors as media sport and Olympic television. These industries and their organisations create value, profits and employment on the basis of the exclusive possession of 'intellectual property' (IP); and thus they need to defend these rights if they are to operate sustainably and to thrive on this basis. General governmental policies have begun to be developed to mini-mise what is commonly referred to as internet piracy and its threat to IP rights protection in the cultural industries. It is useful to take a brief look at some examples of these later since they provide the context for the anti-piracy policies and activities of media sport organisations and mega-event organisations which we then need to go on to consider. However first we need to outline what inter-net piracy implies and illustrate how its implications can be disruptive and even destructive for cultural industries. In this context we can briefly look into the industries of the press, popular music and television.

Internet parasitism and piracy

Internet piracy is the rather lurid metaphor often used to refer to what in law is typically referred to as the illegal process of online copyright infringement.[2] This refers to the copying of any kind of cultural content (particularly musical, televised or film-based audio-visual content) without authorisation or payment and distributing it through the internet whether on a publisher, fee or friendship basis. The concept applies on the one hand to internet users who access or download such material and also internet companies who enable them to do so. Internet piracy is claimed to threaten the market conditions and financial basis of organised media production, including that of the television industry. As we will see later in some detail, it undoubtedly threatens television companies' (exclusivity-based) interest in and coverage of live sport and cultural events, and thus their often substantial financial contribution particularly to sport events and sport organisations (BBC News 2007 and Justia 2010).[3] Internet parasitism is a term which can be used to refer to legal practices of online aggregation of various kinds of information. In a press industry context this practice is claimed to threaten the market conditions and financial basis of organised journalism and newspaper production, and thus to threaten, among other things, print-media interest in and coverage of sport and cultural events.[4] We can briefly consider each them in turn, with an emphasis on the latter process given the strategic importance of the media (television)–sport symbiosis we have already touched on.

The internet has cultivated an unprecedented openness in the availability of information and audio-visual entertainment products to people in contemporary societies. Arguably it has also cultivated a common culture of interest and usage of this medium among people which assumes that these kinds of things are naturally occurring, naturally plentiful, costless to produce and free to access.[5] However such common assumptions completely misrepresent the nature of information and audio-visual entertainment products, as they have developed in complex modern capitalist societies. In any society such things need to be understood as the products of human activity (and thus not as naturally occurring etc.). But particularly in modern societies they need to be understood rather as culture and not nature, and as cultural products. In such societies cultural products are typically produced by the work of people operating in differentiated cultural professions, state cultural administrations and bureaucracies, and also in profit-seeking cultural industries serving mass consumer markets.[6]

The problematic impacts of the internet and its use to access and redistribute cultural products on a free-for-all basis have become evident in recent years. The new capabilities include the re-presentation of information and images created in a variety of contexts by internet aggregation services; file-sharing on peer-to-peer social networking sites such as those operated by companies like Facebook and YouTube, and audio- and video-streaming services (e.g. BitTorrent systems, see later). The internet's free-for-all culture can operate to undermine the financial bases of industries which are built largely on the mass sales either of mediated performance experiences (film and music) or of physical objects carrying cultural meanings (videotapes, DVDs, CDs and newspapers). The internet's threatening impacts on the film industry[7] have been much debated and resisted by the industry in recent years.[8] The same sorts of problematic impacts have been particularly felt in the cultural industries of the press and popular music[9] and also in the strategic cultural industry of television, including its sub-sector of media sport and the mediation of sport mega-events.

As we have noted in the case of the Olympics and EPL soccer, mega-event organisers and professional sports organisation in general derive substantial income from the sale of rights to exclusive television broadcasting of events. Organisations like the EPL use this income in part to finance the training and development of new cohorts of players. To the extent that internet piracy threatens these income streams it also threatens this sport training and development process in a way which is comparable to a certain extent with the problems currently being experienced both in the press industry and also in the popular music industry. With this in mind we can now consider the general problems faced by particular cultural industries and their implications for media sport and sport mega-events, in relation first to the press, and then in relation to music and television.

The press industry, aggregation and quasi-piracy or parasitism

The expressions quasi-piracy and parasitism are colourful ways of referring to the negative implications of internet operations such as online news aggregation. Such operations are made possible by the advanced development, application and use of contemporary internet search engines and browsers, and formally they are not illegal. In the case of the press, newspapers' own websites have often been difficult to monetise by charging readers for access, and thus they have tended to be provided on a free access basis. In recent times online aggregative news services have grown up which take stories and content from newspaper news coverage and also from newspaper websites.[10] In so doing aggregators effectively also take (the interest and time of) newspapers' readers. In doing this they ultimately also threaten to take the advertisers who would have previously paid press organisations for spaces in their newspapers or websites in which to place advertisements to communicate with their readers. Companies and advertising agencies are increasingly switching their advertising expenditures away from the press to pay internet-based aggregators and other such companies for the right to locate their messages and images directly on non-press internet sites (OECD 2010; also Elgan 2012).

The income for press industry companies can derive from various sources including the largesse of wealthy proprietors and cross-subsidy from within multi-media conglomerates' operations. But traditionally it derives from two main sources: on the one hand from readers paying the price charged for possession of the physical newspaper and on the other hand from advertisers paying for space in the pages of the newspaper for the display of messages from themselves and their clients. Press readership has been in long-term decline in most developed countries, and the effect of the internet's access to alternative online information and news sources has hastened this. The migration of advertising from physical newspapers and magazines to the internet is accelerating this decline. The future for the traditional press in general does not look as if it is likely to be a very positive one.

From the perspective of the press industry, internet browser and aggregator companies can seem 'parasitic', that is as being at least morally if not legally questionable. In addition, as parasites they can pose an existential threat to their hosts. The threat to the operation of newspapers, of course, carries major potentially negative consequence for the training of journalists and to the organisation and operation of journalistic functions in contemporary societies. This, in turn, is of great importance to the maintenance of democratic politics and public spheres.[11]

The music industry and internet piracy

Like other cultural industries the financial basis of the music industry traditionally depended on revenue from the sale of cultural performances, meanings and experiences to consumer markets, in this case by means of the sale of physical objects carrying cultural meanings (from vinyl records to compact discs (CDs). This revenue-stream provided for profits and returns on capital investment. But it also provided funding sources for investment in the identification and development of new artists and for the potential to acquire incomes on a long-term basis which would attract people to specialise in the processes of musical production and performance. The internet has made it possible for consumers to acquire the cultural products of this industry without making any contribution to its costs of production, a scenario which threatens to undermine the whole financial basis of this industry and the variety of cultural performers, performances and works that it sustains. Without being fatalistic it is nevertheless unrealistic to suppose that the further development of people's use of the internet in this way can simply be halted, for instance by national or international regulation, at least not in the short term.

From a worldwide music industry perspective, then, there is an urgent current need to explore the possibility that some compensation for the decline of revenue from record and CD sales can be achieved from internet sources. To what extent and in what ways can internet use be monetised? To what extent can internet users be persuaded or coerced to pay for downloading music, and to what extent can advertisers be attracted to pay for advertising slots on relevant websites? Currently these issues remain open and disquieting questions for people in the music industry. In the meantime artists in music are adapting to the impact of the internet which depresses their income from record and CD sales. They are increasing their (non-mediated) live performance activities together with the ticket prices and thus income from these performances. The internet can then be used in a way which, from the artists' perspective, is more controlled and complementary. It need not be a threatening free-for-all;

rather it can be used for the purposes of loss-leader-type advertising and image-projection.

The television industry, internet piracy and media sport

The impact of the new media on the junior partner in the traditional inter-media complex, namely the press, in supporting the mediation of mega-events may eventually turn out to be less important than its impact on the senior partner, television. The threat to the press from parasitic online news aggregation services is a threat from activities which are within the law. However television, particularly live television sport, is threatened by online activities which are widely defined in developed countries to be illegal, and are commonly referred to as 'internet piracy'. As we have noted earlier, the powerful cultural hybrid of media sport emerged in, and a result of, the mass television era. Governing bodies in the major popular sports took a lead in creating this symbiosis between mass sport and mass television. Their gambles paid off in most cases. They have generally thrived and thus been able to invest heavily in the production of national and international sport mega-events. They have been able to charge premium prices to media companies for the sale of sport television rights and associated intellectual property rights on an exclusive basis. However given the media technology revolution led by the internet, the media tide may now be turning.

Internet piracy is particularly consequential for the live televising of sport games and contests in which the outcome is essentially unknown and the process of achieving a known outcome is thus a dramatic and compelling viewing experience. Television companies pay a premium to sport and event governing bodies for the rights to be the exclusive providers of television programming covering major sport events. Internet piracy involves such things as accessing and rerouting sport event coverage from audiences in one nation where it might have been paid for to distribution for audiences in other nations where it might not have been. It can involve copying and distributing conventional television coverage of sport events on a slightly delayed near-live basis. Also it can involve the unauthorised capturing, uploading and distributing of elements of event performances by spectators present at the event using mobile equipment.

As the second decade of the twenty-first century progresses it is possible that internet piracy will begin to undermine the exclusivity of the television rights to national- and international-level sport and its events which have been traditionally been purchased at such high cost by media companies. If this scenario of effectively non-exclusive (ultimately free-for-all) sport event coverage was ever to develop significantly then the prices achievable from television companies for this kind of programming content could decline substantially. In turn, if this was to happen then the income available for the original sport television rights holders, namely the sport and mega-event governing bodies and event producers such as the IOC and governing bodies in professional football, would also begin to collapse, since this source typically constitutes the biggest single component of their income.

Internet piracy and state regulation

In the second decade of the digital age, as we noted earlier, governments in the West are increasingly attempting to catch up with the rapid changes occurring in the communication environment which are both led and symbolised by the rise of the internet. They seek to stimulate and guide the positive aspects, including those relating to the development of the knowledge-based and creativity-based economy. And they seek to minimise and manage the negative aspects, particularly internet piracy's disruptive and threatening effects both on traditional industries and also on cultural industries based significantly on intellectual property (IP) and its associated rights (IPR). The US has taken a leading position in the development, organisation and global promulgation of the internet, and also it has a large and long-established professional sport and media-sport sector. Thus US government anti-piracy policies and practices in general and in the media sport field are particularly worth noting, and we will emphasise them in the following discussion.[12] However developments in Europe both at EU and national level are also worth noting.[13] In what follows we will look in particular at the UK which, in recent times, has been taking a notably aggressive position against internet piracy in general and also in the media sport field.[14] First we outline the general anti-piracy regulatory positions in the UK and the US. Then in the following sub-section we look at how actions against piracy by governments and sport organisations have progressed in fields of media sport relevant to the staging and televising of major sport events, particularly those of professional football and the Olympics.

UK government regulation of internet piracy

In the UK the legal protection of intellectual property has long existed in various forms in technological, artistic and commercial fields and these were brought together in law in 1988 by the Copyright, Designs and Patent Act. However this was effectively in the pre-digital era and by the second decade of the digital age UK law was long overdue for updating to address the new challenges posed by the internet and the new media technologies allied to it. In the closing years of the New Labour series of UK governments (1997–2010) an official report on 'Digital Britain' was undertaken and published. Among other things this identified the pressing need for future governments to take a strategic approach to the development of access for all UK citizens to digital information and communication devices and resources by means of the creation of nationwide broadband and wireless systems. It envisaged giving the national telecoms regulatory agency (Ofcom) new powers to promote 'Digital Britain', for instance in monitoring the roll-out of the national digitisation project (to make fast broadband cable systems available to all), and also to operate a new digitally aware defence for IP rights.

On the basis of this report in 2010 a new law was passed, namely the Digital Economy Act. This created significant new penalties to sanction and deter internet users from accessing and downloading material which would infringe content-owners' IP rights. For individuals these penalties included ultimately the threat of their devices being temporarily disconnected from the internet and for internet companies they included the blocking of offending websites. These new regulatory powers were seen as controversial not only by some internet users but also by the UK-based group of internet service provider (ISP) companies which would be implicated in the enforcement of them. Thus the implementation of the Act has been considerably delayed. This was initially because of legal appeals, which ultimately failed, by some of the ISPs against the Act. Subsequently it was due to the lengthy, but ultimately successful, attempt by the telecoms authority Ofcom to negotiate a voluntary form of implementation of the Act's anti-piracy code with the ISPs and with the involvement of the IP rights-holding content providers. This process resulted in 2014 in a 'Creative Content UK' 'alert programme' jointly administered by Ofcom and the ISPs with the support of the IP rights holders which began in late 2015.

The 2010 Act's provisions against internet piracy have been effectively been divided into two different approaches which we can refer to as 'hard' and 'soft'. The soft approach is directed against the small-scale and possibly ill-informed activities (of admittedly significant numbers (Curtis 2014)) of individual internet users. The hard approach is directed against large-scale and organised piracy or the enabling of it. In terms of individual internet users the new system involves a series of warning letters sent to them if they were infringing IP rights.

The original Act envisaged ISPs being required to provide assistance to IP rights holders in taking civil actions against such users. However this aspect has been shelved (although not removed from the legislation). The new 'Creative Content UK' programme is essentially understood as a public education process rather than a disciplinary process. However In terms of internet companies found to be illegally infringing IP, the UK group of ISPs agreed to participate in a much harder approach of the issuing of warnings and 'takedown' notices to offenders, and ultimately in the blocking of websites. So far the latter approach has been backed by the EU's legal regime (Woollacott 2014) and has resulted in the blocking of more than a hundred pirate websites (TF 2015). This latter approach sets the scene for, and is politically and legally consistent with, a significant recent development in combating internet piracy in media sport in the UK which we will come to later (for instance see Curtis 2014).

US government regulation of internet piracy

As we have seen, US new media and internet companies played a leading role in creating the new technological and communicational dynamics of the second decade of the digital age, together with their potential for piracy and its problems. Its active cultural industries lobbies, together with its policy-makers and legislators, have followed along somewhat more closely than their European counterparts. In 2008 they combined to get a significant act passed into law, namely the PRO-IP Act, concerned with 'Prioritizing Resources and Organization for Intellectual Property'.

Among other things this Act considerably increased the power of US Federal government departments and agencies to defend IP rights by enabling them to take what are effectively pre-judicial policing-type action against alleged internet pirate individuals and companies. In particular the Act provided the legal basis for an annual series of anti-piracy campaigns called Operation in Our Sites (OIOS). OIOS is run by a US Federal Government agency called National Intellectual Property Rights Coordination Center (NIPRCC). This was originally created in 2000; however it has evidently been reanimated since the passage of the PRO-IP Act. NIPRCC primarily works with the Department of Justice (DOJ) and Department of Immigration and Customs Enforcement (ICE) and also a range of other relevant US Federal agencies. In addition it co-ordinates with foreign governments and policing forces like Interpol, Europol and the governments of Canada and Mexico. NIPRCC's OIOS campaigns began in 2010 and they were (and are) against internet piracy and IP infringements in the fields of music, film and other cultural and entertainment industries. To give them further effectiveness and public legitimacy the campaigns typically include actions against counterfeit drugs and goods with fake trademarks. The authorities' most common action is 'domain name seizure', in which a website becomes the property of the US government, visitors to site are informed about this fact and the site is otherwise closed. Between 2010 and 2014 the OIOS campaigns have involved the seizure of over 2,500 sites (Taylor and Camayd 2014).

The apparent effectiveness and public toleration of the PRO-IP Act and of the OIOS campaigns may have emboldened US policy-makers to try to go further along these lines. In 2011 they gathered cross-party support for two bills (referred to by the acronyms SOPA and PIPA) which aimed to strengthen further the legal protection of IP rights and the penalties for internet piracy. However leading internet companies such as Google and Wikipedia helped to promote a public campaign against these bills on the grounds that they amounted to an unwarranted extension of state censorship powers and threatened some of the basic rights and liberties of US citizens. This generated sufficient visible and vocal public criticism of the bills to convince the legislators to shelve them in 2012. However the PRO-IP Act remains on the statute book, the NIPRCC remains in place to enforce it and OIOS-type campaigns and website seizures and closures continue. So, in spite of the public defeat of SOPA and PIPA the US state retains active and practical interests in defending IP rights and the cultural and knowledge-based economy dependent on them, and in doing so by means of an aggressive regulatory stance towards internet piracy. This stance extends into the fields of media sport and related sport mega-events, as we note next.

Contesting internet piracy in media sport and mega-events

In the second decade of the digital age the global extension of the internet and the permeation of its allied complex of new media technologies into everyday life has gathered pace, along with the combination of social benefits and problems associated with these developments. In the previous section we noted the emergence of the problem of internet piracy and also how governments in the UK and the US have been beginning to attempt to exercise some regulation in relation to this problem. These general developments provide the context for, and find an echo in, related issues in the fields of media sport and sport mega-events in the same time period. In this final stage in the discussion we focus on these fields firstly in relation to the two main codes of professional football, namely American football and soccer, and secondly in relation to the Olympics.

Professional American football in the US and professional Association football ('soccer') in most of the rest of the world, particularly Europe and Latin
America, are each among the most popular single sports in the world. Soccer
is much the more popular game worldwide, but each of them regularly generates
major sport events in national league finals and international competitions.
These peak at 'mega-event' level every four years in the FIFA World Cup competition and at near-mega-event level annually in the American Super Bowl
game. So it is relevant to consider them in the context of a discussion concerned
with major events like the Olympics against the background of the social changes
generated by the contemporary structural change in the media environment
from a television-dominated form to an internet-dominated form.

Sport fans in general have much to gain from the engaging characteristics of
internet and new media in terms of the new worlds of information, sociability
and emotionality offered by media sport in the digital age. We noted this in the
second section in relation to the Olympics and the same also goes for the mass
publics involved in the sport cultures of the main codes of football. However
we have also seen how the Olympics, since the 1980s, entered into a symbiotic
relationship with television not just in terms of audiences' and fans' experiences
but also financially. Over the course of the last generation television companies
have consistently been willing to pay premium prices to sport organisations like
the IOC for what are effectively temporary IP rights, namely the rights to
televise the IOC's sport events. The high value of such rights reflects the fact
that, on the one hand, the events televised are live and in addition are guaranteed
to be dramatic because they have intrinsically uncertain outcomes. On the other
hand, the high prices also reflect the economic scarcity value of live event broadcasts. That is, the broadcasts belong 'exclusively' to a single broadcaster and,
because of this scarcity value, the latter can 'monetise' them by restricting access
to event broadcasts to audiences who have paid to watch them and by selling
presence in and around the programme content of the broadcast to advertisers.
The kind of financial symbiosis involving the construction of scarcity value
which we earlier saw to exist between the Olympics and particularly US television (Chapter 2) has also long existed for the two main codes of professional
football. For instance in the UK the English Premier League's (EPL's) massive
growth in wealth and international status since its formation in the early 1990s
has been largely due to the regular financial infusions its clubs receive from the
recurrent sale of the EPL's television rights, often on a near-monopoly basis to
the Sky TV corporation (Roche 2000, ch. 5, pp. 167–81; see also the discussions
of EPL later in this chapter).

Such a television-based financial symbiosis and business model enables sport event owners such as the IOC and the EPL to be effective event- and IP-generating organisations and to have international recognition and status consequent on this. However from what we have seen of the nature of internet piracy in the discussion so far, it is evident that, whether sooner or later, it has the capacity to seriously disrupt and undermine such professional sport business models and thus to threaten the operation and even existence of the sports organisations per se. As was suggested in the previous section, media sport is as much exposed to these kinds of threats from internet piracy as are other cultural and entertainment industries such as the music and film industries. Of course professional sport organisations, like organisations in other cultural industries, have an instinct for self-preservation, and so they have come to be very conscious of these threats in recent times. Thus the NFL, IOC and EPL have each either supported or actively organised anti-internet-piracy actions in the media sport field, and we will look into these further in the following discussion.

However, as we saw earlier at the level of general anti-piracy actions by governments, internet piracy comes in various forms. Actions to address these forms can be different, and arguably they need to be so if they are to have some degree of effectiveness, credibility and public legitimacy. For instance the nature of the threat posed by individuals seeking to acquire pirated broadcasts of sport events for personal and inter-personal use, even if it is done en masse, is of a different order from that of internet companies which make such broadcasts available on a large scale, aware of the IP infringement involved and for profit. While a 'hard' regulatory strategy might be appropriate for the latter type of piracy, arguably 'softer' approaches, aimed at educating the public about relevant laws and their rationales, and also informing them about alternative legal ways of accessing and experiencing media sport events, are more appropriate for the former type of piracy.

In the field of media sport such mixed approaches to engagement with and regulation of the problems posed by different types of internet piracy are more probably more evident in the case of the IOC and its attempts to protect its Olympic events from piracy. By contrast the EPL has tended to take a harder approach in its anti-piracy activities, albeit with varied results. We look into each of these cases in the following discussion of attempts to counter internet piracy in media sport. This proceeds in two stages. The first stage is concerned with piracy issues in the two main codes of football, beginning with a brief look at American football, and moving on to a lengthier look at soccer in the example of the English Premier League. The second stage is concerned with piracy issues in relation to the Olympics, both in general and also in relation to the cases of the Beijing 2008 and London 2012 mega-events.

Contesting internet piracy in media football

American football and internet piracy: the Super Bowl

The Super Bowl is the most important annual event in the American code of football. It is understood (at least within the US) as a world championship since it is a game between the two top clubs representing what were traditionally the two main organisations of American football, namely the National Football League (NFL) and the American Football League (AFL). These are now absorbed as separate 'conferences' within the NFL. The game always takes place in winter early in the New Year, and always on a Sunday, which allows the whole weekend to be experienced as a nationally significant holiday. The television broadcasts of the game, together with the star-studded entertainment which is programmed during the halftime break, constitute a spectacular show and media event. The broadcasts regularly attract very large audiences within the US (e.g. 112.2 million in 2014, over a third of the US population), and in addition they also attract notable audiences around the world (e.g. 160 million in 2014) (O'Connell 2014 and Both 2015). The game also attracts large numbers of internet users to communicate about the event (e.g. 50 million unique users in 2014 (Kissell 2015)).

The NFL football authorities, over the last decade, have tried to avoid giving any single media company a monopoly of the right to broadcast the event. Instead they have tended to cycle the annual right to make the broadcast around three of the leading American TV companies, NBC, CBS and Fox. None the less this right remains highly valuable to the media companies for periodically attracting mass audiences and wealthy advertisers, and they are prepared to pay premium prices to secure this right. Inevitably the attractiveness of the live broadcasting of this major sport event stimulates a demand for free access to it among minority sections of the public who either cannot afford the subscription to the relevant channel or the other possible payment methods, or who choose not to afford them. This demand, in turn, stimulates numerous pirate companies to provide free video-stream access to the game, monetising their operation through advertising.

The annual OIOS campaigns against internet piracy run by the US Federal authorities since 2010, which we noted earlier, recognises the high national interest in and profile of the Super Bowl event. And they regularly feature elements involving action against piracy involving unauthorised video-streaming of the event. These are undertaken in collaboration with NBC and the NFL, the relevant stakeholders in the IP of Super Bowl. For instance, in relation to the 2014 Super Bowl, in an action co-ordinated with the NFL, the US government agencies of the HSI and OSIO closed down over five thousand websites and seized counterfeit NFL merchandise worth over $21.6 million (ICE 2014). The website domain name seizures in this media sport field, as in all others, are an example of regulatory actions which have a dual character, with both hard and soft aspects. No doubt from the perspective of the owners of presumptively pirate video-streaming sites they are experienced as hard, intrusive and punitive state actions. However, from the perspective of individuals trying to access pirated content, they are not punitive and have a much softer character, presenting themselves as effectively being exercises in public education about the US polity's interest in intellectual property rights, and its willingness to defend them. The situation is less clear in other polities in relation to the regulation of internet piracy in the fields of media sport in general and of media football in particular. We can illustrate and consider some of the comparisons with the US by taking a look next at anti-piracy actions in professional soccer in the UK.

Soccer and internet piracy: the English Premier League

In the USA anti-internet piracy actions in the field of media sport and particularly the field of media football, are on a significant scale and have been led by the state. However, by comparison, in the UK the problem has been engaged with, but it has been approached differently and more inconsistently. In Britain the policy lead has been taken by civil society, or at least the market sector of it. This has occurred within a supportive legal and governmental context which, as we saw earlier, has slowly begun to develop since the enactment of the Digital Economy Act in 2010. The most publicly visible and arguably the most socially significant actions have been undertaken in recent years by the English Premier League (EPL).

As noted earlier the EPL has grown greatly since the early 1990s, and its constituent clubs have benefited greatly financially, from the periodic sale of the rights for live broadcasting of its matches, in particular, in relation to broadcasts within the UK, to its long-term television partner Sky UK TV. This company, previously known as BSkyB, was founded and remains controlled by the controversial Australian-American media mogul Rupert Murdoch. Sky's recurrent acquisition of EPL's broadcast rights in a succession of three- or four-year contracts over two decades has been on a temporary but exclusive and usually monopolistic basis. However, in recent years, in response to pressure from EU Single Market competition authorities, EPL's monopolistic arrangements with Sky have begun to be eroded. Competitor television companies, currently British Telecom (BT), have begun to be able to acquire a minor share of EPL games, although this also remains on an exclusive basis which BT customers pay to access.

The value of these deals to the television companies, and their willingness to pay EPL premium prices, has continued to balloon over the years. In the most recent deal, in 2015 for the three football seasons of 2016–17 to 2018–19, Sky and BT were willing to pay EPL the unprecedented sums of £4.18 billion ($5.05 billion) and £960 million ($1.202 billion) respectively for the live broadcasting rights to major and minor packages of games (126 matches for Sky and 42 matches for BT per season). Besides the television rights for broadcasting within the UK the EPL was also able to sell rights to broadcast in overseas territories around the world for the same three-year period for around £3.36 billion ($4.42 billion). This took the overall value of the deal to the EPL to over £8.5 billion ($11.16 billion) (Gibson 2015). This ballooning of the value of exclusive live televised football has occurred in spite of the rise of the internet communication environment and the associated escalation of the risks of internet piracy poses to these investments. The increased risks that piracy might burst media sport's financial balloons helps to explain the recent and current motivation behind sport authorities like the EPL and, as we see later, the IOC, in their activities to try to control it.[15]

In EPL's case two such actions are particularly are worth noting, even if only one of them resulted in success and thus is likely to have some sort of impact. These actions involved taking two notable internet companies, namely YouTube and FirstRow, to court in order to get the legal system to order them to desist giving free public access to videos of all or parts of EPL matches. In the first action, which was ultimately unsuccessful, EPL joined with a group of other cultural industry companies including other sports organisations and led by the major US entertainment conglomerate Viacom.[16] In 2007 the group brought the action against YouTube, a globally leading video-sharing site, and its parent company Google, in the US court system. EPL's case against YouTube was that the latter 'knowingly misappropriated' EPL's intellectual property. That is, its case was that YouTube allowed and promoted video footage of EPL matches to be viewed and shared on its site without recognising EPL's rights over this material and without paying EPL any compensation costs.

The case dragged on through the legal process for a number of years and ultimately failed in 2013 for two reasons. Firstly, it had been prosecuted as a class action jointly between sport media companies and entertainment media companies of various kinds. However the court's judgement was that there were not sufficient commonalities of interests to justify seeing these complainants and their complaints as a class. Secondly, the complainants had claimed that YouTube colluded with the people who uploaded EPL video clips to its site in their knowing infringement of EPL's IP rights. The court's judgement was that that YouTube did not know and could not reasonably be expected to know what the motivation of its uploaders was, and thus it did not collude in any knowingly illegal action.

Finally it could be argued that EPL's action was not well-considered or well-targeted from the very beginning. The prime threat from internet piracy in the field of media sport is in the area of long-format live or near-live videos of whole matches. Giving the public free or inexpensive access to this directly threatens the scarcity value of exclusive rights to live broadcasting. However EPL's case was intrinsically weak in respect of this issue, since YouTube imposes a cap on the duration of uploaded video clips. The kind of short-format clips of parts of EPL matches which were uploadable to YouTube's service might have been argued to infringe upon and threaten EPL's ownership of and trade in clips of post-event edited 'highlights'. But this is a relatively marginal aspect of its media-sport interests. For instance the price paid by BBC television to acquire the EPL's highlights packages in the most recent deal for 2016–19 was only £204 million ($268.29 million), a small fraction of the prices paid for the rights to produce live broadcasts of whole EPL matches. Even if EPL and its associates had been successful in their action against YouTube it would not have given EPL much protection against the main threats that internet piracy poses to the professional football industry it organises.

However the second of EPL's legal actions was pursued through the British court system.[17] It was better targeted and in 2013 it resulted in successful judgement in favour of EPL and its co-complainant group of professional sport organisations (which included the European football governing body UEFA, the Professional Golf Association and the Rugby Football Union). The action was ultimately directed against the internet company FirstRow by means of placing a legal requirement on all of the British-based internet service providers (ISPs, namely BT, Virgin Media, Sky, Talk Talk, Be and O2) to block access to First-Row's website.

FirstRow is a company specialising in enabling users worldwide to have free access to video-streams in many sports but particularly including professional soccer. It is based in the Netherlands but operates in English, serves users in the US, Europe and elsewhere, and generates income from advertisers mainly based in the US and UK. Although it is a relatively small company financially (valued at $5.8 million), its reach to publics around the world is considerable, since it gets 679,000 daily views and 5.4 million daily page views and is ranked in the top two thousand most visited sites on the internet in terms of traffic (URLRate 2014). An important issue for EPL, and for the court, was that the free services of FirstRow were being made available to the public in the commercial contexts of UK sports bars, as a way of increasing bar revenues while avoiding paying fees to the EPL's broadcast rights-holding partners, Sky and BT.

FirstRow operates as an aggregator, gathering together information about and links to many video-streams of sports events from various sources including user-generated sources which in turn can include pirated material. It then provides simple connecting links and presentational frames for the video-streams it aggregates. Although FirstRow claims not to directly hold and host pirated material on its website it enables users to readily find and freely access such material. The judgement of the court was that FirstRow profits from facilitating public access to infringing (pirated) content, and thus the UK ISPs implicated in the case were legally required to take action to block the site.

This follows similar actions in the US which, as part of OIOS campaigns, have blocked access to FirstRow's main website and its proxy websites. The blocking mechanism in the US case is a notice to site-users about the illegality of the site and the US authorities' seizure of it. The UK authorities cannot seize domain names in this way, not least because the company continues to operate as a legal entity, albeit in a foreign country. After the conclusion of the case FirstRow continued to operate its site. However now it presents users, particularly those making pirated video available within FirstRow's system, with some very clear and serious warnings, namely: 'If you are from UK or USA you are NOT allowed to use this site' and 'If you add pirated streams we WILL give your IP address to authorities' (FirstRow 2015; see also note 17).

Time will tell whether this version of the site-blocking of pirated media-sport content will have much effect on the attitudes and behaviours of individual British internet users. However it is reasonable to assume that it is likely to deter the use of FirstRow's services by commercial sport bars in the UK, since ISPs

can now accumulate evidence of their use of a blocked site, and they risk prosecution by EPL and other such rights holders for participating in the public
communication of pirated material. From considering contemporary anti-
internet piracy actions in the media-sport worlds of American football and
Association football we can now turn to look at this issue in the context of the
Olympics in recent times.

Contesting internet piracy in the Olympics in the digital age

Earlier we noted how, over time, the IOC has come to be heavily financially
dependent on income from the sale of rights to broadcast the Olympic Games
live (e.g. Table 2.1). This was not a particularly risky strategy during the television age. But as the digital age has developed, and as we have seen with other
sectors of media sport like professional football, such dependence evidently
carries intrinsic risks. In particular internet piracy in the forms of unauthorised
video-sharing and video-streaming threatens the scarcity value of live broadcasts and thus threatens to deflate the income derivable from selling them. The
logic of this situation supplies the motivation for sport authorities to engage in
both short-term and long-term actions to contest internet piracy in order to
defend their traditional and lucrative partnerships with television broadcasters.

General governmental attempts to control internet piracy, as we saw earlier,
can recognise at least two types and levels of piracy, namely on the one hand
individual-level small-scale downloading and/or accessing of pirated material
for personal and inter-personal use, and on the other hand internet-company-
level large-scale hosting of pirated material, or organising of public access to it,
for commercial gain. In addition governmental policies can either take a punitive (or hard) approach, or a public educational (or soft) approach to these types
of piracy. More commonly, they can take some combination of the two
approaches. Like these governmental approaches the strategy which the IOC
has evolved to counter internet piracy in the field of the Olympics also recognises the differences between the main types and scale of piracy, and it engages
in actions to counter them which could be characterised as a combined or
dualistic approach, using both hard and soft strategies and tactics.

In this section we are particularly concerned with the approaches to counter-
ing internet 'piracy' which have been undertaken by the IOC and related organisations in the context of recent Olympic Games events. The focus is on what I
am referring to as the 'digital age', namely c. 1995–2015, particularly the second
decade (c. 2005–15). In this latter period the problem of internet piracy has

accelerated on the basis of the period's radically innovative new communication environment, in which the internet and the new media have been empowered and have become not only deeply entrenched and influential in the countries of the developed West, but also extensively used worldwide including in developing countries (see Tables 1.2 and also 2.3).

Origins of the IOC's hard approach to internet piracy

The hard aspect of the IOC's activities against internet piracy has built on its rigorous approach, in the pre-digital period, to protecting the commercial value of its main symbol or trademark, namely that of the five intertwined Olympic rings representing the continents and world regions. In the early 1980s the IOC developed a programme (the TOPS programme) for its main corporate sponsors which guaranteed a limited group the exclusive right to associate their brands, products or services with the Olympics through use of the symbol in advertising. The corollary of the creation of artificial scarcity value in relation to this piece of intellectual property has been the recurrent need to take legal action against companies which use the symbol without authority and without paying the IOC.

The IOC has an unusual degree of international diplomatic status and recognition. Thus in 1981 it was able to achieve an international treaty under the auspices of the United Nation's World Intellectual Property Organisation (WIPO). This, the Nairobi Treaty, created international legal protection for the Olympic symbol, and it initially involved over twenty states, a number which has grown to over fifty states currently (WIPO 2015b).[18] In addition since the 1990s the IOC has required nations hosting Olympic Game to create special time-limited national legal IP protection for Olympic-related material, including both the Olympic symbol and also local Olympic event symbols and trademarks relating to the particular Games event being hosted. This was in part to counter the rise of the indirect and parasitic version of IP infringement or piracy referred to as 'ambush marketing'. This occurs when corporations which have no contractual relationship either with the IOC, through the TOPs programme, or with the local OCOG host, none the less find ways of alluding to, and thus associating themselves with, the Olympic event and its symbols. The Australian government passed a law protecting Olympic symbols, trademarks and copyright in 1996 during the preparation of the Sydney Olympics 2000. Although the event performed satisfactorily for TOPS sponsors and local sponsors, ambush marketing was in evidence and needed to be contested. The IOC had been conscious of the need to address this kind of problem since the Nairobi Treaty. But the experience at Sydney confirmed the need for an organised and vigilant approach within a strong legal framework. And since that time both the IOC and the local OCOGs have been proactive in policing and enforcing such laws in host nations.

A recent example is that of the London 2012 Olympics where the legal frameworks were formidable. The UK had already created an Olympic law protecting the IOC's IP in its symbol in 1995 to support the failed bids by the city of Manchester to stage the Olympics. After London had won the right to stage the Games in 2005 a further law, referring to the London dimension and also to the Paralympic Games which was to be linked to the 2012 event, was created in 2006. This was strengthened further in 2011 when the main pre-event Olympic organisations, namely the Olympic Delivery Agency (ODA) along with the London Games organisers (LOCOG), were given legal authority to police the enforcement of IP and other relevant laws in the Olympic areas. Implicitly and in theory the main targets of such IP protection are large corporations seeking to add to their existing brand recognition and profits by means of an unauthorised association with the Olympics. However in practice, given the IOC's and their partner OCOGs' recurrent willingness to threaten legal proceedings against infringers and fearing the consequent reputational damage this would cause them, large corporations now tend to avoid ambush marketing in relation to the Olympics. Rather, as in London, it is small and local businesses, such as shops and street traders, which tend to take the risks, either intentionally or out of ignorance of the law. At the London Olympics 896 cases of infringements of the Olympic laws by such businesses were recorded, and compliance with the laws was achieved in most cases by the threat of legal action rather than the need to realise the threat (DCMS 2012a). Understandably this caused a lot of media and public debate and criticism in the UK about LOCOG acting in a heavy-handed way. However, this publicity in itself could be assumed to have helped to spread public awareness of the Olympic IP laws further and added to their deterrence effect.

If the Sydney 2000 Games marked a step-up for the IOC's 'hard' approach to IP protection in terms of the need to counter ambush marketing, it was also an important turning point for its awareness of and approach to internet piracy. For the first time the IOC commissioned digital-age companies with the technical knowledge and capability to monitor the whole of the internet to identify and assist with the prosecution of infringements of its IP rights on the internet. According to one report in those very early days of the digital age at least thirty violators were caught (Bellaby 2000). One of the key monitoring companies used at Sydney, the UK-based NetResult, was also used in the IOC's anti-piracy monitoring system for the Salt Lake City Olympics in 2002.[19] The IOC has continued to strengthen and institutionalise its sophisticated internet monitoring capabilities in order to take punitive enforcement actions to defend its IP rights for every Olympic Games since that time.

Developments in the IOC's approach to internet piracy

The IOC has developed its internet infringement-monitoring capabilities considerably since the Sydney 2000 Olympics in order to support its hard approach to anti-piracy policy. However it has needed to do so given the general acceleration in internet piracy due to the growth of the internet and the increasing empowerment and interconnectedness of the new media alternatives to television in the second decade of the digital age (c. 2005–15). Its hard approach continued throughout the period of these developments and through to the most recent Olympics. At the 2014 Sochi Olympics the IOC supported its major television rights-holder NBC, now in collaboration with internet-based video-streaming and video-sharing sites YouTube and justin.tv, in anti-piracy activities. Between them they managed to get 45,000 illegally posted videos or pirate streams stopped, that is taken down or prosecuted. Twenty thousand of these were identified and filtered out for the IOC and NBC from its own site by YouTube in the USA, twenty thousand were stopped from similar sites in Russia and in addition a further five thousand illegal streams of live Games competitions were stopped (Bauder 2014).

An important reference point in the development of the 'hard' aspects of the IOC's approach in the second decade of the digital age was the Beijing Olympics in 2008, which the IOC recognised as 'the first truly digital Olympics' (IOC 2008).[20] For the IOC to have brought the Olympics to China, an authoritarian political regime encompassing a massive and rapidly burgeoning capitalist market economy, had been an internationally controversial and debated issue. Although China's 2008 Games were ultimately largely a success in sporting and presentational terms, various political controversies circled around their preparation and performance. Some of these, of course, related to China's state-controlled media environment. Whatever China's pre-event indications, it was always improbable that this environment would be significantly opened up and freed up for the Games. Nevertheless some of the government's censorship and banning system relating to the internet (the so-called 'Golden Shield' system) was slightly and temporarily relaxed to accommodate journalists and foreigners. Access was permitted to the websites of some human rights organisations and Western media like the BBC's Chinese-language service, although only in Olympic areas in Beijing and only for the duration of the Games (Branigan 2008). Although the proportion of the Chinese population with access to the internet in 2008 was relatively low in comparative world terms, the absolute numbers were very large. Of these around 153 million of China's 'netizens' watched legal online streams of Games (IOC 2008). In addition, as part of its soft strategy, the IOC also provided a large amount of coverage which was available in legal online streams (see later).

However while this provision may have dampened the appetite in China and elsewhere for access to pirated material on the internet, it by no means eradicated it, and the demand remained substantial throughout the duration of the Games (Biao 2008; TF 2008). One episode is interesting to note in this context. A few days after the impressive and much-watched Opening Ceremony of the 2008 Olympics an internet site (TorrentFreak) which monitors and comments on legal and non-legal online video-streaming reported that 'even though it was free to watch on TV all around the world ... over a million people have already downloaded the opening ceremony via BitTorrent' (TF 2008). The IOC seems to have registered this report and responded to it. To understand the nature of its response it is first necessary to give some information about BitTorrent.

BitTorrent is a system for enabling data-heavy files, like audio and video files, to be rapidly communicated on a free peer-to-peer file-sharing basis. It has been held to be responsible for a large amount of internet piracy at both the personal and small-scale levels and also at the company and large-scale level. At the former level although the scale of piracy is small the aggregate numbers of people involved are significant. For instance in the US in 2011 over two hundred thousand internet users were sued by music industry rights-holders for using BitTorrent services to share audio files on a free basis with each other, thereby damaging revenues to the industry and incomes to the musicians (Kiss 2011). At the company and large-scale level BitTorrent services which index and link to peer-to-peer networks freely sharing music, film, television, and sport television have been claimed to be very damaging to the IP rights and revenues of those industries around the world, and they have been successfully prosecuted on this basis in many jurisdictions, particularly in the West. One of the most extensive and popular of such BitTorrent tracker services, which is notorious for being explicitly committed for ideological as well as financial reasons to internet piracy, is the (originally) Swedish-based company The Pirate Bay (TPB).

By the time of the Beijing Olympics TPB had already become highly controversial in Sweden. In 2006 it had been raided by the police and had its servers seized for breach of copyright. From that time a case was built by Swedish authorities against TPB's founders and operators which led to their trial and sentencing in 2009–10 (Kiss 2009). In 2008 the IOC evidently decided to try to make a public and symbolic gesture against the infringement of its IP in video clips and coverage of the opening ceremony of its Games by focusing on TPB company. It requested the assistance of the Swedish government in blocking TPB's activities in helping to distribute Beijing Olympic video. This was not immediately successful in that the Swedish government merely passed on the IOC's request to the Swedish police (Ustinet 2008; IOC 2008). However it was sufficient to provoke one of the company's co-founders, Peter Sunde, into responding with a threat. He was reported as saying 'We were going to ignore the Olympics, but now we're loading our cannons. Our weapons of mass distribution are pointed towards China' (TF 2008). Later, in 2009, together with three other co-founders of TPB, Sunde was to be heavily fined and sentenced to jail in Sweden. He managed to evade Swedish law until 2014 when he was finally caught and was forced to serve eight months (Goldberg and Larsson 2014).

Nonetheless the relative success of state actions against TPB's founders and operators like Sunde has done little to stem the flow of BitTorrent-based internet piracy. Back-up copies of TPB's systems have usually been ready to become operational whenever actions have been taken to close it down. (Although by 2015 it is now suggested that, as a result of governmental actions against the company, TPB is finally 'struggling to stay afloat' (Kamen 2015).) In addition the IOC's action at the time of the Beijing Olympics in this particular case was not notably successful since TPB continued to operate and Olympic videos remained online and available for mass access. However during the Beijing Olympics the IOC employed the British-based internet monitoring company Friend MTS to identify unauthorised Olympic video material and automatically issue legal takedown notices, and this was evidently successful in some cases, for instance that of the US sport video-streaming company ItsGameTime.tv (Kafka 2008). The IOC notes that its 'Beijing 2008 Internet Monitoring Programme used technology based on fingerprinting technology, combined with sophisticated web crawling techniques, to prevent, track and take action against the upload of unauthorised Olympic content' (IOC 2008, p. 133).

Overall the IOC concluded that for the Beijing 2008 Olympics 'The total effect of the [its] anti-piracy campaign succeeded in containing online infringement of Olympic video to minimal levels. Traffic to pirated footage was vastly outweighed by traffic to legitimate footage on official IOC partner platforms' (IOC 2008, p. 133). Consistently with this, since the Beijing Olympics, in spite of the persistence of the problem of internet piracy, it is arguable that the IOC's anti-piracy activities, both hard and soft, have had some tangible effect in controlling it. By the recent 2014 Sochi Olympics the IOC estimated the proportion of people watching the Games by illegal and pirated means to be as low as 2 per cent (Bauder 2014). We now need to look a little further into the soft aspects of the IOC's anti-piracy approach.

The IOC's soft approach to internet piracy

The onset of the digital age of the ubiquitous internet, and its associated multi-platform new media communication environment, has posed fundamental challenges to the IOC. Evidently, as we have seen, there is the challenge of piracy and the various problems, including importantly financial threats, which it generates. However in addition an organisation like the IOC (together, it should be added, with its media partner organisations like NBC in the USA and the BBC in the UK) remains influenced by traditions and practices deriving from pre-digital periods. So it also faces a less definable familiarity problem. That is it has a lack of experience and understanding in relation not only to the new media environment but also to its users. While the latter are doubtless from all age-groups, young people are a particularly significant user-group since they are growing up as 'digital natives', knowing only the new internet-based media environment.

The soft aspect of the IOC's media strategy in the digital age, particularly post-Beijing, is best seen not only as addressing the piracy problem but also as simultaneously addressing the familiarity problem. Since the Beijing Olympics the IOC, in collaboration with its partner media organisations, has been developing interests and capabilities in monitoring the public's uses of television and internet-enabled devices during Olympic Games. In the following section we need to look further into these inquiries. This is not least because they raise the important possibility that a new symbiosis between television and the Olympics together with the internet might be developing and replacing the traditional symbiosis discussed earlier between television and the Olympics. If there is any substance in this possibility this would provide a new basis on which the Olympic movement might rethink itself as a potentially familiar part of the development of the digital age rather than always fated to be distinct from it and unfamiliar with it. The soft aspects of the IOC's approach to the internet, then, involve activities which on the one hand are intended to help prevent piracy arising in the first place and also on the other hand contribute to the IOC's familiarisation with the internet and with its potential utility for Olympic movement purposes. These activities include promoting public education about the history and values of the Olympics, associating the Olympics in positive and accessible ways with popular social media companies such as YouTube, and offering attractive internet-based alternatives of its own, notably an online television service which it planned to launch in late 2016. We can look at these latter two actions next.

At the Beijing Olympics in 2008, as part of its 'hard' anti-piracy policy the IOC managed to get the co-operation of the YouTube video-sharing platform to use its internal monitoring system to help with the takedown of video material which infringed the IOC's IP rights, and this co-operation has continued through subsequent Olympics. This approach contrasts with the conflict which existed at this time, as we have seen earlier, between YouTube and another leading media-sport organisation, namely the EPL. The EPL was determined to view YouTube (unsuccessfully as it turned out) as part of the problem of piracy rather than as part of a potential solution to that problem. A major contributor to the spirit of co-operation between the IOC and YouTube without doubt was the IOC's decision to launch an official Beijing Olympics channel on YouTube (IOC 2008; Sweney 2008). This was a channel which made Olympic highlights, news and clips freely available in 78 territories. However the territories were limited to places in Asia, the Middle East and Africa where the IOC might have sold broadcast television rights but had not sold any rights to provide the Olympics in an online video-on-demand form. It was thus intended to complement and not compete with television and it may have contributed to reducing people's demand in these territories to access the Olympics online through pirate means and sites. During the Olympics the channel had 21 million video views with 40 per cent of the traffic coming from India and South Korea (IOC 2008).

The IOC's interests, both in reducing the demand for internet piracy in a 'soft' way by offering legal alternatives and also in familiarising itself with how YouTube and other social media might be useful for Olympic movement purposes, continued in succeeding years. Thus, immediately following their limited experiment with the YouTube Beijing Olympics channel in 2008, the IOC created a new office concerned with social media in 2009. In the same year it invited Martin Sorrell, the head of WSL, one of the world's largest advertising companies, to address and advise them about the relevance of social media for their media operations and also on the possibility for an online Olympic channel. Sorrell encouraged the IOC to envisage moving away from its traditional television-centred perspective and towards a greater presence online, including a permanent online Olympic channel. However to make such a strategic shift it would need to recognise and design programming to serve the distinctive motivations of sports fans. This was particularly true of young sports fans, and their special level of commitment to consuming and 'playing' with video material relevant to their interests. Drawing on US examples Sorrell suggested that the IOC might be able to 'monetise' such a channel by using fans' willingness to pay a channel subscription for access to such things as archive footage (AP 2009b).

Although the IOC has evidently had an interest in evolving its media strategy beyond the polarity between its traditional pro-television and anti-internet piracy characteristics, it has taken some time to do so. Since Beijing it has continued to offer historic Olympic footage on its YouTube channel. And a further step was taken at the London 2012 Olympics when the IOC added the vitally important category of live video-streaming of events to its YouTube channel programming, freely available in Asia and Africa. The channel provided 2,700 hours of broadcast coverage and 59.5 million video-streams were delivered to users; 34.5 million of those were live streams (IOC 2012c, p. 26). Recently the IOC announced a further significant step in the evolution of its media strategy, namely the creation of a new digital TV channel which it planned to launch in late 2016. This was decided as part of the IOC's Olympic Agenda 2020 policy review process.[21] The channel is planned to cost $600 million over the first seven years, it will be based in Madrid and will be available worldwide and on a year-round basis. It will cover all Olympic sports, carry archive footage, cover some international sport events and it will be particularly aimed at promoting Olympic sport interest and understanding among young people worldwide. This final and most recent case of IOC media policy seems to exemplify both the soft preventative approach to anti-internet piracy and also that the IOC is making some progress in relation to the challenge of overcoming its lack of familiarity with the media environment of the digital age. Finally we need to take a step back from the contemporary problem of internet piracy and the IOC's responses to it, to consider the nature of the current co-existence and the potential symbiosis between television and the internet in the field of the mediation of Olympic mega-events.

Towards a new symbiosis between Olympic television and digital media?

The second decade of the digital age (2005–15) witnessed ongoing technological, organisational and behavioural changes in the communication environment which have further challenged the status, nature and role of mainstream television systems. These changes and challenges have been reflected at all levels in television but particularly in the televising of the world's biggest events, notable among them the Summer Olympics of Beijing 2008 and London 2012 and, to a somewhat lesser extent, the Winter Olympics of Turin 2006, Vancouver 2010 and Sochi 2014. In this section we look particularly at this situation in relation to the case of the US.

As we have seen earlier, the recurrent winner of the IOC's auction for the US TV rights in recent decades has been the NBC corporation. Its reliable willingness to pay premium prices for the rights has been strategically important in the financing and empowering of the IOC and the Olympic movement in this period. In the midst of the rise and popularisation of internet-based television and video NBC has supported the IOC in its anti-piracy strategies and policies both of the defensive or hard kind and also of the more proactive and preventative soft kind. Policies of both kinds, but particularly of the latter kind, are more likely to be effective to the extent to which the evolving communication environment is one in which television and digital media could at least be assumed to be capable of co-existing rather than endlessly threatening each other. An interesting question to pursue here is whether something more than mere co-existence might be conceivable. In the field of media sport at least, might a new symbiosis between them be possible? In what follows we take a look at this possibility. To inform that discussion, in Table 3.1 we begin by mapping out the US audiences achieved on the one hand for NBC's prime-time Olympic television broadcasts and on the other hand for NBC's internet-based television services, comparing them over the course of the recent series of Olympics (listed above).

The table indicates a number of things. Firstly there is the persistently high degree of online reach and popularity of Olympic Games events in the US, which regularly attract the attention of between half and two-thirds of the nation's population (column four). Secondly there are the audiences for the carefully packaged mid-evening prime-time Olympic 'shows' characteristic of American TV's approach to the event (columns two and three). Allowing for a slight decline in relation to the Sochi 2014 event (for which there may be particular historic-political reasons), opening-night and average-night audiences for Olympic Games broadcasts have remained buoyant. If anything, in the case of the Summer Games, they have been growing at record levels. Finally this enduring general strength of interest among US audiences for Olympic television has co-existed with a massive and continuous growth in the numbers of people legally accessing live coverage by means of NBC's internet-based video

Table 3.1 The 'media Olympics' in the second decade of the digital age: prime-time TV audiences and digital users in the USA, 2006–14

Olympic Games: year and city	Prime-time TV audiences (millions)		Total American viewers (of some portion of TV coverage) (millions)	Digital audiences (unique users of NBC's Olympic website) (millions)
	Opening Ceremonies	*Nightly averages*		
2006 Turin	21.6	20.9	184.0	13.0
2008 Beijing	34.2	27.7	211.0	30.0
2010 Vancouver	26.4	24.5	190.0	46.0
2012 London	40.7	31.1	219.4	57.1
2014 Sochi	25.9	21.4	151.0	61.8

Sources: de Moraes 2014; Baker and Adegoke 2012, Bookman 2014 and James 2012, Nielsen 2008, Futterman and Schechner 2008, Kondolojy 2012, Carter and Sandomir 2008, Collins 2012a, 2012b, FierceWireless 2010

services (column five). The situation mapped out in the case of the US in Table 3.1 would seem to be one in which, at the very least, public uses of television and the internet to access Olympic mega-events in the contemporary period seem to be capable of co-existing with each other. Whether it is credible to interpret this situation in stronger terms, as being one of potential symbiosis, calls for more searching types of studies and analyses to which we can now turn.

The mediation of the Olympics in the second decade of the digital age

The 2008 Beijing Olympics: the 'first Digital Games'

As we noted in Chapter 2, and also as Table 3.1 indicates, the mediation of the Beijing Olympics involved both the mass viewing of mainstream television broadcasting of the Olympics and also lower but still very substantial levels of public access of internet-based Olympic information and video imagery online. The old and new media appear to have operated in a complementary way in this case. The IOC regarded the Beijing Olympics as 'the first truly Digital Games' in the sense that it was the first to present 'a worldwide offering of the Olympic Games being broadcast on internet and mobile platforms'. In addition to the internet-based services of the official TV rights–holders, the IOC launched its own temporary internet channel called 'Beijing 2008' which was available on the YouTube platform (a platform which is now owned by Google). The overall experience of the Olympic mediation process at Beijing seems to have been viewed as a positive one by the IOC. Thus it concluded that 'with online plat-forms ... it is now realistic to broadcast and consume each and every moment of the Games, not just on-demand but live'. And 'a multi-platform offering through TV, the internet and on mobile devices, far from cannibalising ratings, was, on the contrary, not only complementary, but indeed enhanced, TV ratings' (IOC 2009, p. 3, also IOC 2008 ch. 3). The IOC's Director of Media and Market-ing for Beijing, Timo Lumme, observed that 'The Beijing Games proved that online broadcast has been complementary to television ratings, with record figures across both platforms' (quoted in IWGA 2008).

The 2012 London Olympics: the 'first Social Media Games'

As we have seen earlier, a new wave of new media internet-based devices (mobile smartphones and tablets) and services (e.g. Facebook, YouTube and Twitter) enabled social media to rapidly bloom as a global cultural phenomenon in the second decade of the digital age (c. 2005–15). These were not significantly present at the time of the Beijing Olympics in 2008; however, a mere four years later, by the time of the London Olympics in 2012, this situation had completely changed. This new communicative environment encouraged the IOC and par-ticularly the London Games organisers (LOCOG) and Olympic TV rights-holders like NBC and the BBC to develop special Olympic services for social media and also to monitor people's Olympic-relevant use of these and other social media services and systems.

Table 2.3 presents some of the high levels of unique users (109 million for the LOCOG site) and page views (8.5 billion for all Games sites) which were recorded for official Games websites and services, and earlier we also noted the unprecedented level of video-stream views which was achieved (overall 1,876.5 billion). LOCOG had anticipated that people would make a lot of use of mobile devices (smartphones and tablets) to access Games information and images and to exchange views about them. Nevertheless these platforms, including 376.5 million video-stream views accessed on them, took up a far higher percentage (60 per cent) of all interactions between the public and LOCOG sites and services than LOCOG had planned for (Sweney 2012). Outside of official websites the theme of the Olympics was highly visible on Twitter and Facebook during the course of the Games, including in relation to the accounts that IOC and LOCOG created on these platforms. Twitter registered 150 million Olympic-related tweets (Gilbert 2012) and Facebook recorded 49 million Olympic-related users and 100 million Olympic-related 'likes' (Balfour 2012; Miah 2014).

In this context we need to consider the probability that the owners and viewers of television sets are also owners and users of internet devices. So, from their experiential perspective, in a period of change and overlap between old and new media, the ideas both of co-existence and symbiosis in the field of media sport/(media Olympics) refer, among other things, to people's interest in and ability to combine and switch between television viewing and internet use. We look into this issue next.

Emerging patterns of media sport and mega-event consumption: recent Olympic Games

Since the Beijing Olympics in 2008 NBC's internal market research unit has carried out various kinds of monitoring and interview-based studies of the US audiences for Olympic television. Nodding in the direction of the fact that the corporation paid the IOC around $1billion for the American TV rights to each of the Beijing 2008 and London 2012 Games, the head of the NBC unit, Alan Wurtzel, refers to these investigations as 'The Billion Dollar Lab'.[22] This is because the events offer special opportunities to study the nature of and changes in people's simultaneous and cross-referring uses of multiple media.

To put the studies into context, some background media and corporate changes between Beijing and Vancouver on the one hand and London and Sochi on the other should be noted. Firstly, in addition to television and personal computers (PCs) with internet access, the US public had little or no access to 'smart' (internet-enabled) mobile phones and to mobile internet-enabled tablet computers at the time of Beijing, although they had limited access to smart-phones by the time of the 2010 Vancouver Winter Games. However this situation radically changed in the short time which elapsed between these events and the events of London and Sochi. By the time of the latter events smart phones and tablet computers had become common among the US public, and they added qualitatively to the media complexity and choices they already faced, given the longstanding roles of television and PC-based internet in people's lives.

Secondly, at the time of Beijing and Vancouver NBC's strategy for presenting Olympic Games was heavily orientated, as it had always traditionally been, towards presenting it through television broadcasts. Very little provision was made for the NBC's subscribers to access live coverage by means of video-streams on the NBC's internet services of the two weeks of competitions making up the Games. Arguably NBC was overly concerned at this time with two kinds of threat from internet-based video-streaming. On the one hand it feared that people's legal use of its own digital services would 'cannibalise' their interest in using its television services (and thus reduce their exposure to the Olympic programme-related communications which advertisers and sponsors were willing to pay NBC premium prices for). On the other hand it also feared the possibility of internet piracy of its internet streams. Thus it tended to view the relationship between television and digital media mainly in zero-sum terms. However before the London Games NBC changed its Olympic presentation strategy to a much more digital-friendly and additive approach, namely one of 'television plus digital media'. So, for both the London and Sochi Games, in addition to the packaged prime-time Olympic TV shows and daily television coverage, NBC made available extensive live-streaming coverage of all of the Games competitions to its subscribers on its internet-based services.[23]

The studies of NBC viewers and internet users by Wurtzel's unit over the course of the Beijing and Vancouver Olympics indicated that the fear of digital use cannibalising television viewing was based on a misunderstanding of how people operated in the emerging multi-media environment.[24] Rather the findings indicated that television remains the dominant medium in people's experience of the Olympics. However people used the various other platforms and screens of their digital new media devices alongside their televisions to complement and extend their television viewing experiences. If people who only watch television are compared with those who watch television and also use digital media, it might be assumed (for instance on the 'cannibalism' assumption) that the latter would watch less television than the former. In fact the information for Beijing and Vancouver was rather that viewers and users using both actually watched *more* television than the television-only group.

This research no doubt contributed to NBC's change to a more digital-friendly strategy by the time of the London 2012 Olympics. The unit's studies of US audiences of the London event confirmed what had been found in the earlier studies. Indeed they amplified them, finding that multi-media users watched *much* more television than television-only viewers, namely 5.5 hours per day as compared with 3 hours per day (reported in Chozick 2012). In addition NBC's prime-time Olympic television shows faced a 'tape-delay' problem because of the time differences between the US and both London and Sochi. This meant that the crucial live quality of uncertainty of outcome which motivates viewers of sport events was often missing for US audiences, as results were known before the Olympic show. This might have been reasonably assumed to reduce the US public's reliance on television to satisfy its interest in the Olympic competitions and to increase its reliance on accessing digital video-streaming, whether of the legal or illegal kinds, to reconnect with the live experience. However, as Table 3.1 indicates, this situation may well have stimulated expansions of legal digital use at both London and Sochi, and simultaneously television audiences grew to record levels in relation to London, and remained relatively strong in relation to Sochi. Public interest in the prime-time television version of events was not only not damaged by the availability of live digital streaming but on the contrary was compatible with and even stimulated by the latter.

This general picture was confirmed in the case of the mediation of the London 2012 Olympics by audience monitoring undertaken by the BBC as the official Olympic media rights-holder and host broadcaster for the UK. This monitoring indicated that the British public was both interested in and capable of managing a considerable range of choice in terms of the BBC's coverage of the Olympic event (O'Riordan 2012). This involved coverage of every Olympic sport from every one of the Olympic venues by means of 24 video-streams. O'Riordan comments that BBC 'data clearly shows people moving across streams to check out a whole host of different events'. For people as viewers or users this could often occur over the course of a whole day. This typically involved the use of a home- or work-based computer during the working day, a home-based television set in the evening and mobile devices in the hours around midnight. In addition mobile devices would be typically used during the course of the whole day as 'second screens' to provide access to some of the alternatives available among the 24 video-streams on offer.

The London 2012 Olympics was generally regarded as being a success on a number of fronts, from its organisation to its role as a catalyst for urban regeneration (as we discuss later, see Chapter 8). One of these fronts was its mediation both in terms of the content of its programming as a television spectacle and also in terms of its proto-symbiotic combination of television-based and internet-based mass-communication operations and services

Conclusion

In this and the previous chapter we explored the rapidly changing and pervasively influential media environment in the general field of media sport and its major events, and in the allied field of sport mega-events like the Olympics. In the previous chapter we reviewed the symbiotic relationship which developed in the television age between the Olympics and television, together with the nature of the disruptive changes involved in that relationship given the emergence of internet and the digital age. In this chapter we have taken that discussion further by engaging with both negative and positive implications of the new media environment in relation to sport events and the Olympics. On the negative front we looked into the issue of internet piracy and the threats it poses to IP-based creative and cultural institutions and industries both in general and also at the level of media sport and Olympic television. Given this context we looked at the substantial and ongoing struggles to defend IP rights and to counter internet piracy which are being undertaken both at the general state level in the West and also particularly in the fields of media sport and the Olympics.

In the case of the Olympic movement it was noted that the IOC and its television company partners have begun to develop a dualistic 'hard' and 'soft' strategy since the Beijing Olympics in 2008. The hard approach continues the monitoring, warning and prosecuting activities undertaken against piracy developed since the Sydney Olympics 2000 against both the large scale of pirate (and piracy-enabling) companies, and also at the small (but mass) scale of individual users. This hard approach can be effective, but given the nature and growth of the internet, this effectiveness is limited and increasingly of a symbolic kind. It was clearly in need of supplementation by a different kind of strategy aimed at distracting mass publics from piracy and removing their need for it by improving the quantity and quality of internet-based television coverage of Olympic Games from official and legally available sources. Although this soft strategy is still in its early stages there are indications that it is making some progress. As the new media environment of the digital age develops, extends and permeates further into the modern social world, so the potential might grow for new forms of media sport and Olympic–television symbioses to be developed. Time will tell. Whatever the practical outcome the explorations undertaken in Part I have indicated the considerable social significance of these new media and cultural dynamics in the relationship between mega-events, and social change. Hopefully also these discussions have indicated why and how the study of new media dynamics might now be more firmly located than it typically has been in the field of contemporary mega-event studies and its inter-disciplinary research interests.

Notes

1 On the category of 'cultural industries' see Hesmondhalgh 2005. A broader and more inclusive view of the category is taken in Roche 2010a, pp. 207–11, and for a perspective emphasising the relevance of IP see EU 2013.

2 On internet piracy, or online copyright infringements, from an international regulatory perspective see Panethiere 2005 and UNESCO 2010, also Kretschmer 2005 and
   Allen 2010; also the UK government's Digital Economy Act 2010, which attempts to
   control piracy in the UK (UK 2010, also BBC News 2009 and Merrick 2009). For
   relevant sociological insights into net users (i.e. the pirates, or at least the pirates'
   'fellow travellers') see Mattelart 2009 and Yar 2007.
3 On media companies' financial contributions to sport organisations in general see
   the discussion of media sport and Olympic television in Roche 2000, ch. 6, also
   Chapter 3 above, and the discussions in sections two and three later in this chapter.
4 Media mogul Rupert Murdoch has taken a critical stance in relation to internet
   parasitism on behalf of his (largely traditionally based old media) media companies
   vis-à-vis a major new media company, the giant internet search engine corporation
   Google. He claims that internet browsers in general and Google in particular effectively steal the news that his organisations produce without authorisation or compensation. In 2009 he announced that he was considering removing his organisations
   from Google's and other browsers' listings to pressure them to pay for his content
   (see Tryhorn and Johnson 2009). Also see note 11.
5 On the origins of this 'free-for-all' culture in earlier stages in the history of the
   internet see Castells 2002 and also Wessels 2009.
6 On cultural industries and the new media see Hesmondhalgh 2005, ch. 7, also TERA
   2010.
7 On the internet's threat to the film industry see, for instance, RocSearch 2007,
   Verkaik 2010, Strauss 2013 and Lodderhose 2014.
8 For internet impacts on the entertainment industry see Barnett 2010; for general
   impacts across all of the main media industries see for instance Kung et al. 2008,
   Clark 2010. For sociological perspectives on the internet's impacts on the cultural
   industries see Levine 2011 and di Maggio 2014a and 2014b, and for an economic
   perspective see Ji and Waterman 2013.
9 On the internet's difficult relationship with and implications for the press see for
   instance OECD 2010, and for the music industry see for instance Dolata 2011.
10 For instance online news aggregator sites like The Huffington Post.
11 In this context it is relevant to observe that, in 2015, after much public criticism for
   alleged abuses of its monopoly position in the European browser market and under
   the pressure of anti-monopoly action from the EU, Google announced a major new
   co-operative venture with leading elements of the European press and broadcast
   industries. The project aims to develop ideas and internet products to enable high-
   quality journalism to be sustainable in the digital age, and Google plans to back it
   with €150 million of funding over three years (Martinson 2015).
12 On USA anti-piracy law see Department of Justice 2009. On the shelving, after public
   controversy, of the more recent PIPA and SOPA proposals to strengthen anti-piracy
   laws see Williams 2012.
13 On EU-level law and policy relating to IP protection against piracy and other
   infringements see TERA 2010 and EU 2013; and on the approach taken by the
   European Court of Justice against internet piracy see for instance Jackson 2013. On
   French and German governments' thinking about anti-piracy policies see for
   instance Horten 2013 and Tiffen 2012 respectively.
14 On UK anti-piracy laws see UK Gov 2010.
15 The scale of the piracy problem facing UK sport authorities including EPL in recent
   years is indicated by a statement made by a representative of the internet monitoring

company NetResult, which some of them use to combat it. In an interview with the BBC the representative claimed that over the preceding two years eighty thousand illegal streams were identified. It appears that they were readily removed by means of warnings and without recourse to the full legal process (Izundu 2010).

16 On the EPL's case with other plaintiff sport and entertainment organisations against YouTube in the USA's legal system see for instance BBC News 2007a, Justia 2010, and Gibson 2013.

17 On the EPL's case with other plaintiff sport organizations against FirstRow in the UK's legal system see for instance Neal 2013, Nixon 2013 and Smith and Wooden 2013.

18 It is worth noting that a number of leading countries like USA, UK and China are not signatories to the Nairobi Treaty. However these countries commit to compliance with IOC Charter rules and requirements when they bid to host Olympic Games, and also when they stage them.

19 NetResult is now part of the Thomson Reuter company, a North American media and information group.

20 Along with the IOC, the EBU also saw the Beijing Olympics as the first 'digital Games' (EBU quoted in Goggin 2013, p. 26).

21 On the IOC's planned online television channel see IOC 2014a, also Spangler 2014 and Donner 2014.

22 See Wurtzel 2012; Wurtzel and Fulgoni 2012; see also de Moraes 2014; Chozick 2012

23 On NBC's new positive approach to online live-streaming since 2012 see de Moraes 2014 and Bookman 2014.

24 See note 22.

II

Mega-events, legacy and urban change

4

Embedding mega-events: staging spectacles in changing cities

The idea that mega-events can be seen as spectacles refers to the impressive large-scale and unique sets of performances associated with them. This spectacle aspect needs to be understood in contextual terms. It is inter-connected with other types of performance aspects which are contained within mega-events and which help to structure and characterise them as cultural productions and collective experiences. These other performance genres particularly include that of festival, and also, in the case of the Olympics, those of ritual and game or competition.[1] However all of these performance aspects of mega-events, including the spectacle-oriented performance aspect, need a material-cultural setting to be possible. Just as the art of drama needs the physical setting of a theatre containing (at the very least) a stage for the actors and seating for the spectacting public, so mega-events as performances need something comparable, albeit on a bigger scale and in more complex forms (for instance see Hiller 2012).

Elsewhere in my analysis of 'Mega-events and modernity' (Roche 2000, ch. 5) I suggested that a mega-event's main site should be seen as analogous both to a theatre and also to a touristic theme park, albeit a temporary version of each. The 'theme park' analogy is particularly relevant for the main site of a World Expo, which, in the largest category of Expo, typically contains many differently designed pavilions representing the participating nations. And it is relevant also for understanding the main site of an Olympic Games, with its large-scale Olympic stadium and the various functional buildings and venues, such as swimming and diving centres, indoor cycling centres and so on, which are needed to stage the various sport competitions making up the Games event. Many of the pavilions contained within Expo theme parks can be impressive, or 'spectacular' in their own right, and this goes also for some of the main buildings contained within Olympic theme parks. This secondary material-related type of spectacle can be said to add to the primary performance-related understanding of events as being spectacles, which refers to the idea that they are perceived as impressive sequences of actions and performances at the time of the event.

In the post-event period, what might be said to remain of either of these types of spectacle, how might they be capable of leaving a legacy? If the mega-event was sufficiently impressive as a performative spectacle it might well remain as a collective memory. Thus it might become part of the ongoing public identity of an ex-host city and nation, and part of the narrative or story about themselves that ex-host cities and nations recurrently tell both later generations and also visitors. In addition some of the key buildings, places and spaces of the original theme parks may also remain physically. And if they were originally perceived, at event-time, as having a materially spectacular character, they may be able to go on exerting such an effect on publics who encounter them in post-event periods. This possible contribution of the material spectacle of the event to its post-event legacy is more likely to happen if some of the mega-event's original buildings or structures were designed with that in mind, that is if they were designed as distinctively creative pieces of architecture.

In this and the following chapters in Part II we explore some aspects of these material characteristics of mega-events, investigating how spectacular architecture needs to be contextualised and embedded in relation to various *unspectacular* aspects of the event. These aspects include temporal features of the event as a long-term process involving a pre-event policy-making and site-building phase, and a post-event legacy phase. They also include structural and spatial aspects of the original event theme park which may not be spectacular but which, none the less, may possibly be publicly valued at event-time and, particularly, in the post-event period. For the purposes of our discussion these can be divided into two main types. On the one hand there are material urban legacies of the functional and place-making type (as in the perceivably useful architecture of cultural and sporting buildings and complexes). On the other hand there are also physical urban legacies of a non-material or space-making type, as in the landscape architecture of new or renewed urban parks together with the recreational (or, more emphatically expressed, re-creational) green spaces that contribute to the quality of the environment and urban life in former host cities.

We engage with these differing kinds of mega-event material and non-material urban legacies in the following chapters, focusing mainly on the place-making type in Chapter 5 (on the urban legacies of Olympics), and on the space-making type in Chapter 6 (on the urban legacies of Expos). In this chapter we first need to set the scene for these later discussions, so this chapter proceeds in two stages. Firstly, the discussion is concerned with the nature of the material spectacles connected with mega-events. Secondly, it takes a step back to consider the macro-social changes involved in the long-term modernisation process, which are reflected in cities and thus determine the urban conditions in which mega-events are staged and to which they both respond and contribute.

In the first section we begin by recognising and exploring the importance of the 'material spectacle' aspect of mega-events throughout their history over the course of the modernisation process. In particular, in our times, since at least the turn of the millennium worldwide processes of making and remaking cities have generally involved the marking of central city areas by means of the construction of distinctive landmark buildings, and sometimes spectacular buildings, whether financed from public or from corporate sources. A substantial profession of internationally oriented and internationally recognised architects and celebrity architects (commonly referred to as 'starchitects') has developed to service these demands.[2] Mega-events have participated in these processes. They have often been marked by the commissioning and construction of iconic buildings and structures from internationally known architects which have been intended to contribute particularly to events' performative spectacle aspects at event-time, and also more generally to their host cities in the post-event period. In the course of this we recognise that each mega-event is a unique project which inevitably carries its own risks, whether of a financial, touristic, security or other nature. Thus they always have the potential to turn into 'negative spectacles', and often these have involved the excessive costs and/or post-event disuse of the iconic architecture which was originally intended to celebrate them.[3]

Next, in order to be able to gain a perspective on events' material spectacle aspects we take a step back from these fairly immediate and tangible concerns to take account of the wider social and urban contexts in which events can be said to be embedded. These contexts are varied. On the one hand, they range from deep and long-term macro-level processes of social structural changes which have influenced the formation of cities in general and which have, thus, been reflected, at the more micro-level, in urban events in particular. We discuss these in the second section below. On the other hand they also include the changing policies of international mega-event movements and their leadership organisations. Long periods of indifference by these organisations to the long-term impacts of their events have given way, in the contemporary period, to an increasing interest in and control over such legacies. We discuss these in the third section. And we conclude that section and the chapter with a conceptualisation of some of the main types of long-term urban impacts of mega-events.

This discussion prepares the way for the subsequent engagement, in the following chapters, with historical overviews and contemporary-period case studies of the urban impacts and legacies of Olympic Games and of Expos.

Events and urban spectacle: architecture and host cities

Mega-events like Olympics and Expos evidently involve performative spectacle of various kinds. However every performance for a mass public needs to be situated in relation to physical constructions which can function as some kind of stage or a theatre. We can refer to this as a primary form of the embedding of performance spectacle within the event as a multi-dimensional process. Some of these constructions can be functional, but others can be designed to be impressive and to add the spectacle of the performance which they enable and frame. We can refer to these particular constructions as contributing material spectacle to the production and experience of the event. Also, in the post-event period, if these constructions are retained as permanent fixtures (as part of the event's legacy) we can refer to them as continuing to contribute the potential for material spectacle as well as collective memory to the urban landscape and to subsequent generations of urban publics.

If performative spectacle can be embedded in the physical constructions of the event site, including their material spectacle aspects, then the latter, reciprocally and in their turn, can also be understood as embedded in the social space and time of the event as a complex social process. Spatially they can be understood as being embedded, during the time-period of the event, in the operation of the event site as effectively a version of the theme park genre (Roche 2000, ch. 5). Later, in the post-event period, they can be understood as being embedded in the event impacts and legacies of the various urban development uses to which the event site is put. In the contemporary period these 'multi-theme park' urban-legacy impacts and uses of the event and its site increasingly include, among a number of others, those of visitor tourism and resident recreation.

In this chapter we are concerned with mega-events understood as these kinds of complex social processes, and particularly with their material spectacle and physical legacy aspects. Since their creation and institutionalisation in the nineteenth-century, Expo events always had a material spectacle aspect, and subsequently, over time, Olympic events also developed this kind of aspect, particularly over the last generation from the late twentieth century through to the early twenty-first. The early Expos also contributed 'physical legacies' of various kinds to the long-term development of central areas of their host cities, even if only in intermittent and unsystematic ways. Later, and particularly in recent times, both Expo and Olympic events have been designed to be both markers and catalysts of positive social change within their host cities. Their physical legacy aspects have typically been intended to contribute to a variety of urban policy uses and their material spectacle aspects have often been used in urban tourism and recreation contexts among others. The idea that mega-events might generally operate as markers and catalysts of positive social and urban developments is explored in more detail in the discussion in the following chapters. Of course, given human fallibility and the intrinsically complex and unpredictable character of international politics and economics, the various potential positivities of mega-events have not always worked out in reality as the organisers might have hoped and planned. We take note of aspects of this potentially 'negative spectacle' character of mega-events later in this chapter.

However in this chapter it is first necessary to map out and briefly survey the field we are concerned with here, namely that of the social history of relationships between changing cities and the material spectacle and physical legacy aspects of the mega-events they have periodically hosted. Apart from journalistic and case-specific accounts of these relationships, these topics have been relatively little studied in a systematic, comprehensive and comparative way by social scientists. This is particularly so for the material spectacle aspect and related physical legacy and urban development aspects, However there are some notable exceptions which are noted particularly in the studies of Olympics in relation to their host cities by Stephen Essex and Brian Chalkley among others,[4] and the studies of Expos in relation to their host cities by Javier Monclus among others (Monclus 2009; Greenhalgh 2011). Based on this work, the tables which follow (Tables 4.1 and 4.2) list some of the most notable material spectacles associated with mega-events, the former covering the period 1850–1970, the latter the period 1970–2020, and they enable us to survey developments in each of these periods.

Mega-events, material spectacles and host cities (1): 1850–1970

Table 4.1 aims to provide some historical information about the relation between, on the one hand, host cities and, on the other hand, mega-events and the material spectacles often associated with them for the 1850–1970 period. It identifies some notable constructions created for Expos and for Olympics,

Table 4.1 Mega-events, material spectacles and host cities (1): some event architecture which is now urban heritage, 1850–1970

Expos			Summer Olympics		
Year and city	Iconic construction (and urban heritage)	Internationally notable designers (and national designers)	Year and city	Iconic construction (and urban heritage)	Internationally notable designers (and national designers)
1851 London	Crystal Palace (1854–1936)	*Joseph Paxton*			
1873 Vienna	The Rotunda (1873–1937)	(Karl Freiherr von Hasenauer)			
1888 Barcelona	Columbus statue	(G. Buigas)			
1889 Paris	Eiffel Tower	*Gustav Eiffel*	1896 Athens	Pan-Athenaic Stadium	(A. Metaxas and E. Ziller)
1900 Paris	Grand Palais, Pont Alexandre III	(C. Girault et al.) (J. Resai and A. D'Alby)			
1901 Glasgow	Kelvingrove Art Gallery and Museum	*John Simpson* (and E. Milner Allan)	1912 Stockholm	Olympic Stadium	(T. Grut)
1924, London	Wembley Stadium (1924–2003)	*John Simpson* (and M. Ayrton)	1928 Amsterdam	Olympic Stadium	(J. Wils)

1929 Barcelona	Palau Nacional	(E. Cendoya and E. Cata)
	Olympic Stadium	(P. Domenech)
	German Pavilion	*Ludwig Mies van der Rohe*
1929 Seville	Plaza de España	(J.-C. Forestier)
1937 Paris	German Pavilion	*Albert Speer*
1951 London	Royal Festival Hall	(R. Matthews and L. Martin)
1958 Brussels	Atomium	(A. Waterken)
1962 Seattle	Pacific Science Center	*Minoru Yamasaki*
	Space Needle	(J. Graham Jnr)
1967 Montreal	Habitat 67,	*Moshe Safdie*
	Biosphere,	*Buckminster Fuller*
	West German Pavilion	*Frei Otto*
1936 Berlin	Olympic Stadium	(Werner March) & *Albert Speer*
1952 Helsinki	Olympic Stadium	(Y. Lindgren and T. Jantti)
1964, Tokyo	Olympic Indoor Arena	*Kenzo Tange*

Sources: On Expos see note 12 and BIE website (www.bie-paris.org). On Olympics see the IOC website (www.olympic.org) and www.worldstadiums.com/stadium_menu. For basic information on international architects see http://architect.architecture.sk/ and www.pritkerprize.com/. On Speer's building work see note 8

Note: Names of significant architects or starchitects are italicised mainly indicating those in particular which have remained as iconic features of the urban landscape of the cities that once hosted particular events, key event-derived elements of host cities' urban heritage. It also identifies some of the period's main material spectacle designers (the architects, engineers and sculptors) for each mega-event. Among these the table makes a provisional differentiation between those designers who came to have an international reputation (and thus who, like the events they worked on, came to the attention of a growing international public) and, by contrast, those whose reputation remained more restricted within the cultural public sphere of the nations which hosted the events.

As Table 4.1 indicates, in the 1850–1970 period Expo events compared with Olympic events tended to involve more notable architects and designers, and to leave behind more iconic constructions. Constructions for Olympic events have had a much greater profile in more recent times as we note in a moment (see Table 4.2 in relation to the 1970–2020 period). But significant Olympic-related creations in this earlier period include those of the notorious Nazi architect Albert Speer.[5] Speer redesigned the Berlin Olympic Stadium and its associated sport and public event complex for the 1936 Berlin Olympics. They also include work (namely the main Olympic indoor arena) by the noted Japanese architect Kenzo Tange for the 1964 Olympics in Tokyo. However in this early period Expos have had more of a tradition of leaving legacy constructions in their host cities.

The great international impact of the first modern Expo in London 1851 was largely due to the spectacular building in which it was contained, popularly referred to as the Crystal Palace. This had been designed by Joseph Paxton as a temporary construction for the Expo's central London site in Hyde Park.[6] However Paxton later reconceptualised the great structure as a permanent building and relocated it to a south London suburban parkland site at Sydenham, where it was installed as a permanent and popular public cultural, entertainment and recreational facility in 1854 (also see Chapter 6 later). Unfortunately after many decades of popularity and public use it was destroyed by a fire in 1936 and was not replaced. It is a sign of our contemporary times and of the new level of valuation of urban heritage (and in this case of urban event legacy) in these times that in the 2013–15 period, a major property development company seriously considered reconstructing the Crystal Palace on its original site at Sydenham, albeit with new retail, hotel and touristic functions as well as cultural and entertainment uses. Although the project failed it is perhaps even more a sign of our times that this company was Chinese.[7]

Perhaps the most spectacular construction for an Expo was, and remains, the 300-metre public viewing tower in Paris created by Gustav Eiffel and his company for the 1889 Paris Expo and popularly named after him (Harriss 1975). The Eiffel Tower is also the greatest example of a continuing physical legacy of an Expo. It has continued to function as a key element in Paris's set of urban heritage and tourist assets, and also as a globally recognised icon for the city. Other spectacular and iconic constructions originally created for Expos and with an enduring urban legacy and touristic significance include the original Wembley Stadium in London (designed by Sir John Simpson for the 1924-25 British Empire exhibition, but replaced with a new version in 2003); the Plaza de España in Seville (designed by Jean-Claude Forestier for the 1929 Seville Expo); the Royal Festival Hall in London (designed by Robert Matthews and Leslie Martin for the Expo-like Festival of Britain in 1951); the Atomium monument in Brussels (designed for the 1958 Brussels Expo by Andre Waterkeyn as a massive model of the atomic structure of the cell of an iron crystal); and the Space Needle tower in Seattle (designed by John Graham for the 1962 Seattle Expo).[8]

More minor contributions to Expos by notable designers which endure in host cities as Expo 'legacies' include works by Mies van der Rohe, Yamasaki, Safdie and Buckminster Fuller. Ludwig Mies van der Rohe, the hugely influential pioneer of modernism and functionalism in twentieth-century architecture, designed the temporary German pavilion at the 1929 Barcelona Expo. This was later re-created in 1986 as a permanent structure on the same site to memorialise the original creation. The architect Minoru Yamasaki is perhaps most known for having designed the original and iconic 'Twin Towers' World Trade Center buildings in New York city in 1970–71. As we know, the iconicity of these towers attracted the Al Qaeda Islamic jihadist group to target and destroy them in a major terrorist strike in 2001. This has had major consequences for driving mega-events to become negative 'security spectacles' which we discuss later in the chapter. One of Yamasaki's earliest pieces of work is the Pacific Science Center in Seattle, a building originally created for the 1962 Seattle Expo. The 1967 Montreal Expo featured impressive although relatively minor pieces of work by a number of creative designers who were later to become internationally notable. These included Moshe Safdie, who designed Habitat 67, an innovative model for urban housing; and Richard Buckminster Fuller, a pioneer and promoter of geodesic dome construction, who produced the monumental geodesic Biosphere. Notable architects have also been involved in Expos as designers of temporary national pavilions. Examples in relation to Germany include

Albert Speer (see above), who designed the imposing German pavilion for the 1937 Paris Expo; and Frei Otto, the designer of the West German pavilion for the 1967 Montreal Expo (who was later to be responsible for the Olympic Stadium and associated Park complex for the 1972 Munich Olympics).[9]

Mega-events, material spectacles and host cities (2): 1970–2020

Information about the more contemporary period of 1970–2020 is contained in Table 4.2. This is concerned with the same kind of relationships between iconic 'material spectacles' created for mega-events and their presence and role in host cities as Table 4.1. However we should note some significant differences between the periods. These concern, on the one hand, the material spectacle aspect and, on the other hand, the physical legacy aspect, and we can briefly look at each in turn.

In relation to the material spectacle aspect, in the preceding period even internationally known designers tended to be known mainly within the peer-group of designers and also to the national publics constituted as the readerships of newspapers aimed at the upper and middle classes. By contrast in the contemporary period events' material spectacle aspects often tend to be produced by designers who have been selected because of their special global reputation and celebrity status for international publics through the mass media. They can be referred to using the colloquialism 'starchitect'.[10] Mega-event sites in the contemporary period often tend to be physically marked by one or more spectacular, creative and iconic constructions which can be referred to as examples of 'starchitecture'.

This controversial term has come into common use in the media from the 1980s. The discursive usage followed the creation of a new level of international institutionalisation and professionalisation within the field of architecture in this period (an aspect of many pervasive globalisation processes) by means of the introduction of high-profile competitions and prizes for architecture. The most significant of these was the introduction from 1979 of the annual Pritzker Architecture Prize, which is regarded as having for architecture and design some of same kind of status as the Nobel Prize system has in other fields.[11] It is notable that many of the creators of iconic constructions for mega-events in the contemporary period, for instance Frei Otto, Norman Foster, Frank Gehry, Zaha Hadid, Herzog and de Meuron and Richard Rogers, who all have 'starchitect' celebrity status, have also all been Pritzker Prize-winners.[12]

Table 4.2 Mega-events, material spectacles and host cities (2): starchitecture in urban development and legacy projects, 1970–2020

Expos			Summer Olympics		
Year and city	Starchitecture	Starchitects (or designers)	Year and city	Starchitecture	Starchitects (or designers)
			1972 Munich	Olympic Stadium	*Frei Otto*
			1976 Montreal	Olympic Stadium	*Roger Taillebert*
1986 Vancouver	Science World	(Bruno Freschi)	1988 Seoul	Olympic Stadium	(Kim Swou-Geun)
1992 Seville	Alamillo Bridge	*Santiago Calatrava*	1992 Barcelona	Collserola Tower	*Norman Foster*
				Montjuic Tower	*Santiago Calatrava,*
				Olympic Village sculpture	*Frank Gehry*
1998 Lisbon	Vasco da Gama bridge	(Armando Rito)			
	Oriente station	*Santiago Calatrava*			
2000 London	Millennium Dome	*Richard Rogers*	2000 Sydney	Olympic Stadium	(HOK/Populous)
			2004 Athens	Olympic Stadium	*Santiago Calatrava*

Table 4.2 Mega-events, material spectacles and host cities (2): starchitecture in urban development and legacy projects, 1970–2020 (Continued)

	Expos		Summer Olympics		
Year and city	Starchitecture	Starchitects (or designers)	Year and city	Starchitecture	Starchitects (or designers)
2008 Zaragoza	Bridge Pavilion	*Zaha Hadid*	2008 Beijing	Olympic Stadium (Bird's Nest)	*Herzog & de Meuron*
2010 Shanghai	China National Pavilion	(He Jintang)	2012, London	Aquatic Centre	*Zaha Hadid*
				Orbit Tower	*Anish Kapoor*
				Olympic Stadium	(HOK/Populous)
2015 Milan	Expo Park	*Herzog & de Meuron*	2016 Rio de Janeiro	Museum of Tomorrow	*Santiago Calatrava*
2020 Dubai	Expo Masterplan	(HOK/Populous)	2020 Tokyo	Olympic Stadium	(Originally *Zaha Hadid*)[1]

Sources: On Expos see note 12 and BIE website (www.bie-paris.org). On Olympics see the IOC website (www.olympic.org) and www.worldstadiums. com/stadium_menu. For basic information on international architects see http://architect.architecture.sk/ and www.pritkerprize.com/

Notes: Names of significant architects or 'starchitects' are italicised

1 Hadid's plan for the Tokyo Olympic stadium proved to be highly controversial as well as expensive, which led to the Japanese government cancelling and replacing it in 2015 (e.g. see Gibson 2015d, 2015e).

In the contemporary period, as Table 4.2 indicates, mega-events have often enlisted 'starchitects' to provide them with an element of physical spectacle at event-time and also the possibility of some positive post-event legacy impacts, for instance as tourist attractions. In what follows, taking the winning of the Pritzker Prize as a guide, we note some of the most important works in this field. Norman Foster designed a major telecommunications tower for the 1992 Olympics in Barcelona. The tower is located in the Collserola hills and parkland in the west of the city, and also functions touristically as a public viewing platform. For the same Olympics Frank Gehry was commissioned to decorate the new Olympic Village area, near the old inner-city Barcelonetta fishing port, with a large-scale monumental sculpture of a fish. While this is not on the same scale as his spectacular art museum building in Bilbao, constructed in 1997, it has elements of the same effect in each case, namely to contribute to the identity and the touristic 'branding' of the host city. Zaha Hadid designed the 'Bridge Pavilion' for the Expo held in Zaragoza in 2008 and also the Aquatics centre which hosted swimming and diving for the 2012 London Olympics. Jacques Herzog and Pierre de Meuron were the lead designers for the main Olympic stadium, the iconic 'Bird's Nest' stadium, which was built for the 2008 Olympics in Beijing, and they were also the site designers for the 2015 Milan Expo.[13] Richard Rogers designed the vast iconic building (which was popularly known at the time as the Millennium Dome or simply The Dome) in London in 2000 which housed the Expo-like 'Millennium Experience' exhibition.[14]

Not all contemporary mega-event material spectacle designers who undoubtedly have starchitect status have won the Pritzker Prize. The most visible exception in this respect is Santiago Calatrava. Calatrava's constructions featured prominently at the Expos at Seville 1992 (a bridge) and Lisbon 1998 (a railway station), the Summer Olympics at Barcelona 1992 (a telecommunications tower) and Athens 2004 (the main Olympic stadium). He is also the designer of a museum for the 2016 Rio de Janeiro Olympics. Starchitects tend to lead architecture and design companies which operate at a global level, bidding for and delivering construction commissions across many countries and regions of the world. However, in addition, with or without starchitect leadership, internationally organised architecture and design companies have developed which specialise in the creation of constructions for events at all levels, including mega-events. These may often be functional but they may also have some material spectacle aspects. HOK/Populous is a good example of such a company, and it created impressive Olympic stadia as the focal points of the Summer Olympics

both at Sydney 2000 and at London 2012. It is also responsible for the site masterplan for the forthcoming Expo in Dubai in 2020.

Making a spectacle of themselves? Mega-events as negative spectacles

Focusing on mega-event urban legacies in the way that we have so far in this
chapter does not, of course, mean making unwarranted assumptions about
them, namely that their long-term impacts are always intentional and fully
understood, let alone that they are always positive. Evidently mega-events can
have various long-term unintended as well as intended impacts, and these can
often be at least publicly controversial and sometimes objectively negative in
various ways.[15] The notion that events can come to be seen by publics as deeply
problematic and negative spectacles includes the idea that they can be badly
managed and waste public resources and also that they can be inappropriately
concerned with security aspects, and we can take a look at each of these issues
in turn.

'White elephants' and 'the mega-event syndrome'

The most obvious sorts of mega-event risks include the following: the problems
associated with budget over-runs and generally excessive costs; the creation of
facilities complexes which are of excessive scale (the so-called 'gigantism' or
'monster' problem) and/or of little lasting value in terms of post-event use by
the host community (the so-called 'white elephant' problem and associated
problems of profligacy and waste); and human rights risks (for instance connected with coercive relocation of urban residents in order to clear space for
event-related developments and/or perceived event security needs). Each of
these sets of problems can create negative spectacles, including negative media
coverage, in both the short and long terms, relating to negative event legacies
connected with public debt, to visibly underused or even disused facilities and
even to public disassociation with and regret about the staging of the event.

Muller (2015c) has recently summed up some of these sorts of problems as
comprising 'the mega-event syndrome', a familiar pattern of problems which can
often affect the planning and delivery of mega-event projects. These include the
following: overpromising of benefits and underestimation of costs; the event
project's priorities overriding and distorting other urban planning priorities,
and even tending to be seen as a 'quick fix' for other major planning challenges;

risk-taking with public resources for developments which ultimately may mainly benefit private and elite interests; and the inappropriate creation of special legal regimens for events. Muller's recommendations are a mixture of the mild and the radical. The mild advice is that planners should do better what they already often claim that they try to do, namely bargain more with event-governing bodies, cap and earmark event-related public expenditures and seek independent expert project assessment. His more radical suggestion is that mega-events should not be tied in with large-scale urban developments. This advice would disconnect mega-events from the long-term legacy aspirations in which both mega-event owner organisations and candidate host cities have tended to be interested in the contemporary period. For this reason, and whether for good or ill, it is unlikely to be heeded.

Finally it is also worth noting the sometimes enigmatic and changing character of assessments of the social and other costs, benefits and legacies of mega-events as urban projects. Events which may have been judged negatively in terms of their short-term impacts may come to be evaluated differently and more positively from the perspective of hindsight and/or longitudinal research. The cases of the 1976 Montreal Olympics and the 2004 Athens Olympics are relevant in this context, and we will look into them further in the following chapter. However even where an event's long-term impacts may be judged to have been positive we should not assume that such impacts were fully envisaged and understood during the planning of the event. Rather it is recognised that event sites and facilities in the post-event period often need to be invested in and actively developed over the medium term, if they are to succeed in creating and sustaining long-term positive legacy effects within host cities.[16] And this may be in ways that could not be envisaged or planned in detail in the pre-event period. The medium-term aftermath of the London 2012 Olympics is relevant in this context, and we look into this case further later (in Chapter 8).

'Security spectacles'

Olympic Games can occasionally become negative spectacles, rather than the festivals and spectacles of sport that they aim to be, because of failures in their organisation of security for the athletes, administrators or spectators who participate in them. Notoriously this occurred in the cases of the 11 Israeli athletes and coaches and one German policeman who were murdered by Palestinian terrorists at the Munich Olympics in 1972. However a new era for security in many areas of life in Western societies, including mega-events, was created by the mass murder of nearly three thousand people in New York City by the Islamist jihadi terror organisation Al Qaeda on 11 September 2001 (9/11). The persistent post-9/11 terrorist threat particularly from jihadist groups, which since 2014 notably includes so-called Islamic State (IS), has been registered in a number of acts of mass murder including in Madrid 2004, London 2005, Paris 2015, Brussels 2016 and Orlando 2016. The impact of this on the Olympics from 2001 onwards has been to promote the post-9/11 'securitisation' of the Games events, that is to increase the priority which has had to be given to security.

Relatedly, this has led to a massive escalation in the costs allocated for security at and around the competition venues for both Winter and Summer Games events. For instance in the last Summer Games before 9/11, namely the 2000 Sydney Olympics, the organisers' overall expenditure on event security was $179.6 million, which works out as an average cost per athlete of $16,062. However in the first Summer Games after 9/11, namely the 2004 Athens Olympics, the comparable figures showed a near tenfold increase, that is $1,500 million overall and $142,897 per athlete. This trend was continued for Western Olympic events in the case of London's 2012 Games where the comparable figures were $1,997 million and $181,545 per athlete (Houlihan and Giulianotti 2012, table 1, p. 707). The figures for the intervening Olympic Games in Beijing in 2008 were even higher, and we look again at this case in a moment. This situation has led to a relatively recent growth of academic interest within an interdisciplinary sub-field of mega-event studies in mega-events' securitisation processes and their security-related aspects. This often takes a critical perspective which is summarised in the idea that Olympic events in significant ways have now become security games or security spectacles.[17] Before we explore this idea further it is worth pausing to reflect on two points.

Firstly, the mass murders by IS-related terrorists in Paris in 2015 (130 deaths) and Nice in 2016 (84 deaths) confirmed what has long been evident, namely that there are now real terrorist threats to crowds in consumer cultural zones and venues in Western cities, including sport events and stadia. Thus the threats to Olympic events, particularly in cities and locations in the West, are real and they clearly need to be countered by the construction of effective security systems. Secondly, even where there are no explicit threats to them such as from terrorist organisations, mega-events necessarily involve a major exercise in the arts of crowd management to ensure public safety within the venues and the overall event site. And failures in this area can, themselves, create human tragedies to rival those of major accidents and emergencies such as fire and the structural collapse of buildings. Mass deaths through crowd crushes occasionally occur at large sport events. In Britain in 1989, 96 Liverpool FC fans died, with 766 injured, at a soccer match at the Hillsborough stadium in Sheffield, South Yorkshire. This became a deeply negative spectacle burned into the national collective consciousness. It was extensively covered at the time by the national media, it has been recurrently memorialised and debated since and it has contributed to the development of stadia and event policy and regulation.[18]

Tragedies like this are a sobering reminder of the public safety risks that Olympic and Expo mega-events must run, even if, to date, they have been largely able to avoid them. In the context of our interest here in security aspects of mega-events what is also noteworthy about the Hillsborough tragedy is that it was almost entirely a product of human failures in the surveillance and management of one particular part of the crowd by the organisation entrusted with responsibility for this, namely the local South Yorkshire police force. An important implication here is that this issue of basic public safety for the mass crowds of people who throng mega-events like the Olympics, as with the issue of real threats from terrorist organisations, requires that high standards of crowd management and security services, including effective surveillance systems, are provided for the public. Furthermore, given the flow of visitors into host cities for Sumer Olympic events, and given also the tendency for host cities to programme some Olympic competition outside of the Olympic zone and around the city's streets and parks, the public safety demands on event-related security systems are unusually high and challenging.

The recent growth of academic interest in the area of mega-event security has developed descriptions of event cases together with more general concepts and research agendas. And since security systems necessarily infringe upon personal liberty and also can be expensive, for these and other related reasons much of this work has understandably taken a politically critical perspective. This is particularly comprehensible in reference to cases of Olympic events staged in largely authoritarian societies, as in the case of the Beijing Summer Olympics 2008 and the Sochi Winter Olympics 2014. These cases featured the full panoply of security systems and technologies, including comprehensive crowd surveillance and screening at venues, the visible militarisation both of the Olympic zone and also of the host city more generally, and even the monitoring and censorship of personal communications. As such they fully justified being conceptualised as examples of security games, security spectacles and military urbanism. However arguably these Games-time developments were more of a quantitative, scalar, increase on already-existing extensive and intrusive state-centred policing systems in the host societies. The more interesting, if more debatable, lines of analysis in contemporary mega-event security studies are those which suggest that the same kinds of concepts can be equally well applied to host cities in societies whose governments and publics understand them to be democratic and to value individual liberties and rights.

Security systems have an ambiguous character. In part they must aim for maximal visibility and symbolic communication to reassure publics and to 'harden' target areas to deter potential terrorists and criminals. For instance in addition to the presence of heavily armed troops and police various kinds of ground-to-air missile systems were on display in the vicinity of the Olympic stadiums during both the 2008 Beijing Games and 2012 London Games events. However, equally, part of their operations needs to be unobserved, as with various forms of intelligence gathering including communications monitoring. To refer to mega-events like Olympics as potential 'security spectacles' undoubtedly has meaning and application in relation to the former. But in my view it does not mean much or add much to our understanding in relation to the latter forms of securitisation of mega-events. In addition it is limited in the following way. The spectacular character of high-visibility security personnel and technologies displayed at Olympic mega-events has an intrinsic limit in terms of such things as the overriding festival and hedonistic character of the Olympic event overall as a complex spectacle. Organisers plan such events to achieve this character, and publics expect to experience this when participating in them. The spectacular, and indeed charismatic, character which is intrinsic to a mega-event, particularly the Olympics, could not be repeatedly overridden or distracted by the presentation and experience of the spectacular aspects of events' security apparatuses without risking their very existence as popular cultural institutions.

More credible is the emphasis in some mega-event security studies on the idea that people's encounter, at mega-events, with the event's security system is not so much an encounter with a security spectacle but rather that it is a normalising of the (precisely non-spectacular) presence of security systems in everyday urban life. In this it is arguably comparable with the normalisation of the intrusive screening systems which have become standardised in airports around the world in the management of public access to and public safety in international air travel. If security is becoming something of a spectacle at mega-events it would appear to be so in a secondary way to events' intrinsically spectacular character, and also in a way which readily converts into what is perceivable as normal and familiar both in event-based and in wider host-city environments.

Observations of the potentially spectacular and also the normalising character of the visible element of security systems at contemporary mega-events like
Olympics do indeed bear witness to the ongoing growth of the process of securitisation of mega-events in our times. However these observations do not, in
and of themselves, provide uncontestable grounds for critiquing these processes.
Up to a point they are normatively defensible in terms of event organisers' legal
and moral responsibilities for basic public safety including, in the current
context, death threats from demonstrably dangerous jihadist terror networks.
Mega-event security studies provide more substantial grounds for a critical
analysis of the securitisation process to the extent that they reveal its linkages
to state and corporate power.

Mega-events, particularly the Olympic Games, and the particular kind of
'security spectacle' they involve, provide influential global media sites as well as
local urban sites in the host nation for security-industry corporations to dem-
onstrate, display and effectively market their services and technologies. These
corporations can be generally linked to the security institutions and intelligence
resources of states, and in the case of major American corporations with the
unrivalled scale of US state intelligence and surveillance resources. During
mega-event projects such corporations are enrolled with host nations and cities
in public–private partnerships in the provision of particular events' security
systems. These partnerships can be interpreted as embodying a broad interpretation of the globally influential political economic ideology of neo-liberalism.[19]
The continued progress of such partnership versions of securitisation can thus
be said to implicate mega-events in the international reproduction and promotion of the global neo-liberal US-dominated international status quo.

Mega-event security studies aim to address this problematic among others.
An important and interesting contribution in this context is that of Minas
Samatas (2011) which provides a comparative study of security and surveillance
at the 2004 Athens Olympics and the 2008 Beijing Olympics. Samatas observes
that in the US post-9/11 a 'global homeland security industrial complex' involving mainly US corporations has expanded. The corporations which provided
security and surveillance systems for the Sydney 2000 Summer Olympics and
the Salt Lake City 2002 Winter Olympics were led by the Science Applications
International Corporation (SAIC), a large US government contractor and close
to many arms of the US government including the CIA, the FBI and the US
Defense Department. As a small and weak state Greece was pressured by an
international security advisory group involving the US, Germany and the UK
to accept SAIC as the provider of these services for the 2004 Athens Summer

Games and for more general use in the management of the city as a security legacy thereafter. SAIC designed a surveillance and security system involving among many other things creating a large CCTV network in the Olympic venues and in Athens more generally. Also during the Games the surveillance operation involved the blatant security spectacle of a highly visible airship on station over the city as an additional data-gathering resource. This system was referred to as C4I (Command, Control, Communication, Computer Integration) and SAIC subcontracted its development and delivery to the large German engineering company Siemens.

This SAIC/Siemens arrangement did not work out well for Greece, whether at the time of the Athens Olympics or later. It involved what was at the time the unprecedented level of expenditure of $1.5 billion on Games security costs, adding to the financial pressure of broader Games-related costs and debts and weakening Greece's ability to deal with its financial and economic problems during and after the 2008–10 global recession and the EU financial crisis related to it. In addition from 2004 Siemens tried to use its strategic position to bribe Greek government officials to win further government contracts. This scandal was legally and financially settled in favour of the new Greek government only in 2012. Finally the technical complexity of the C4I system software meant that in the course of the 2004 Olympics it 'crashed and became operationally useless' (Samatas 2011, p. 3353). In Samatas's view the Games' overriding security orientation drove the event and the host city in the direction of becoming an 'Olympic militarised fortress' and an 'Olympic panopticon' which was staffed by seventy thousand military and security personnel. In spite of all this Samatas's participant observation of the event suggested that the event 'was generally pleasant and offered many enjoyable moments and opportunities to visitors' (Samatas 2011, p. 3356). The balance that Athens managed to achieve between the Olympic security spectacle and the Olympic festival/spectacle was not replicated in the Beijing Games in 2008.

The expenditure on security at the Beijing Olympics has been calculated to have greatly exceeded even the increased post-9/11 figures we noted earlier for the Athens Games and also the 2012 London Games. Thus Beijing's total security expenditure was $6,500 million which works out as an expenditure per athlete of $607,022 (Houlihan and Giulianotti 2012, table 1, p. 707). During the 2008 Games the Olympic security spectacle in Beijing (e.g. 300,000 CCTV cameras, 100,000-strong anti-terrorist armed forces, 150,000 additional security personnel and 290,000 citizen security volunteers (Samatas 2011, pp. 3352–3)) tended to overwhelm the Olympic festival/spectacle. Samatas judges that the massive security effort 'made for a secure but sterile Games' (Samatas 2011, p. 3356). Prior to the event, by the turn of the millennium China's efforts to monitor, censor and control its citizens' access to and use of the internet (commonly referred to as 'the Great Firewall of China') were already ambitious and effective. In this context in the run-up to the 2008 Beijing Olympics China recognised that the Games provided them with a special opportunity to import Western security expertise and technology, evading America's economic sanctions in this sector, in order to help modernise its urban surveillance and policing systems given the rapid growth of its major cities. On their side members of the US security and surveillance-industrial complex were keen to enter and exploit China's large and growing market. Thus IBM, General Electric, Nortel and Cisco were among a group of US corporations which China was willing to use to help organise its surveillance and security for the Beijing Olympics. In turn they were able to use their work at this prestigious mega-event as a platform from which to promote their goods and services thereafter both within China and beyond.

Samatas's general analysis acknowledges that there are important local differences between Olympic host polities which must affect the nature and degree of securitisation at Olympic Games. Thus he found significant differences between Athens and Beijing, including in the social limits which were capable of being placed on the mega-event securitisation process and the security spectacle. No doubt these reflected differences between a small democratic nation and a large authoritarian one. That said, however, Samatas's general analysis of Olympic securitisation processes emphasises convergences and commonalities in these processes, in which the global and the 'glocal' dominate over the local, and he illustrates this in his juxtaposition and comparison of the cases of Athens and Beijing. Later we return to discuss other organisational and legacy aspects of these two Olympic Games mega-events which provide a basis for further comparisons of their similarities and differences (see Chapter 5 on the Athens Olympics and Chapter 7 on the Beijing Olympics).

Events and urban contexts: mega-events and host cities

Modernisation and embedding the spectacle: mega-events as theme parks

Earlier in this chapter we observed how the history of mega-events, from the long decades of the primary phase of modernisation in the late nineteenth century and much of the twentieth century, through to the secondary phase, was often marked by the creation of material spectacles. These take the form of especially impressive and distinctive iconic architecture (starchitecture) or other such iconic physical constructions. They help to provide the stage or theatre at event-time for the planned and unplanned spectacular performances which characterise much of the typical programmes of these events. Both the material and also the performative aspects of mega-events in their spectacle character reciprocally provide immanent event-time contexts for each other. Thus they can be said to be embedded in each other during event-time, and the whole spectacular ensemble can be referred to as a transient event theme park.[20] In addition, where the physical constructions are intended to be permanent, or at least to have a life beyond the event, we can view them as being re-embedded in the distinctive social space-time contexts of the post-event legacy uses and development of the event site.

In our period, in the secondary phase of modernisation and urbanisation, the field of mega-events and their post-event urban impacts and legacy uses and developments has become a potentially broad and complex one, possibly includ-ing social, economic, cultural, spatial, infrastructural and ecological dimensions among others, both within and beyond the original event site. In recognition of this, contemporary post-event sites and their development can be usefully regarded as open and inclusionary multi-theme legacy parks (rather than the closed and exclusionary type of (mono-) theme parks they may have been during event-time). In the chapters on mega-events in China and Britain later in Part III we explore some of these post-event multiple and varied thematic impacts. However, for the moment and for the purposes of this chapter, I will focus mainly on some of their impacts in generating what we can refer to as 'strategic urban spaces', which are among the material conditions underpinning urban public spheres.[21]

Event legacies: event movements and urban places and spaces

Background

The materially spectacular aspects of mega-events need to be understood in relation to their contexts. In the second section (above) we took an initial look at the idea that one important and overarching type of context is that of seeing the events as reflective of, embodying elements of and contributing to deeper and longer-term social changes which affect their host societies in general, but which particularly affect their host cities. This discussion indicates that mega-events need to be understood sociologically as being embedded both in social time and in social space at various societal levels, but particularly at the urban level. That is, they need to be understood, respectively, in the socio-historical terms of long-term urban change and also in the more spatial and material terms of the nature and impacts of events' constructions, sites and locations in the host's urban environment and cityscape.

In the course of this discussion we noted that, in many cities, the spectacular and iconic physical constructions which enhanced the experience of their mega-events at event-time continued to have an afterlife in post-event times. In many cases they have survived over many generations and continue to be of significance in the contemporary period both internally within cities in terms of the identities and heritages of cities, and also externally in terms of the interest and attractiveness of cities for international tourists. For mega-events and associated constructions created in the primary phase of Western modernisation these effects are likely to have been a matter of chance and good fortune. However for events and constructions created in the secondary phase these effects are more likely (and indeed they are increasingly likely) to be products of calculation and policy by event organisers and urban leaders. In addition, rather than, as in the primary phase, these effects being generated by an isolated event-originated construction, in the contemporary period it is more likely that post-event policy will be concerned with a set of co-located event constructions and related urban spaces.

The implications of the discussions in each of the preceding sections are that mega-events need to be understood as more than event-time spectacles. Their materially spectacular aspects can be an important concern in mega-event research and analysis. However, beyond this, events also need to be understood sociologically in a long-term perspective and in particular in terms of their potential urban impacts and role. This idea, or versions of it, has come to be increasingly recognised in mega-event policy and urban-policy circles over the last two decades. In these contexts it is referred to as understanding mega-events in terms of their legacies, that is in terms of the variety of things which events can be said to leave behind or bequeath to people in post-event times. Of course we need to be aware that the interest in event legacy tends to give a priority to intended rather than unintended event impacts, and also to positive or beneficial impacts rather than negative impacts (Mangan and Dyreson 2012). Bearing this in mind the following chapters will explore in more detail the physical and spatial legacies that mega-events such as Olympic Games (Chapter 5) and Expos (Chapter 6) can leave for their host cities. To help set the scene for this we now need to take a closer look at two topics. Firstly, we need to take account of the role of international 'owners' and controllers of the main mega-event genres, and their changing understandings of the urban impacts of their events, particularly their understandings of them as involving positive legacies for host cities. We will look into the concrete history of particular Olympic and Expo legacies overall and in key cases in the following chapters. So, secondly, to prepare for this we need to take a step away from the ideals and aspirations of mega-event organisations about such legacies, and to outline some relevant and realistic concepts of types of long-term event impact which will help in the analysis in Chapters 5 and 6.

Mega-event movements and event legacies

As we have seen so far, the two main mega-event genres of Expos and Olympic Games have long histories of having made long-term positive impacts on their host cities. In recent times each of their formats has come to be relatively standardised, and to include the expectation that they will plan for and bequeath such positive urban legacies. We will look a little further into this contemporary situation in a moment. However first it is necessary to provide some brief historical and organisational background. In their early decades in the late nineteenth and early twentieth centuries, if mega-events left positive long-term urban impacts these were likely to be ad hoc and not understood as legacies. They were patchy in that they might involve anything from an isolated construction to a co-ordinated set of facilities. They were not always particularly well thought through, and nor were they often understood as explicit and formal contributions to long-term urban development plans.

In the 'primary phase' of Western modernisation the earlier of the two genres, Expos, had notable, although often overlooked, long-term impacts and legacies in terms of the linkages to the creation of major urban parks in their host cities. And in some cases these were connected with broader urban development initiatives. We will look in more detail at this particular park-related legacy phenomenon later, in the case study of London and its mega-events in Chapter 8. However in this period Expos were less predictable in terms of whether or not they might leave isolated or multiple constructions to their host cities, and also in terms of whether or not they were designed with that in mind. Early Olympic Games events were even less engaged with processes of urban legacy-creation in this early period before the First World War. We look into the urban legacies of Olympic Games events in more detail in Chapter 5, but here it is sufficient to note that early Olympic events had few long-term impacts on their host cities. Olympic events and to a lesser extent Expos in this period could be characterised as often being ephemeral phenomena, transient socio-cultural processes leaving relatively light and/or unpredictable tracks in their host cities.

This situation began to change later in the primary phase, in the interwar period (1918–39) and the early postwar period (1945–70), when mega-events began to leave more substantial long-term urban impacts, and to do so more regularly and predictably. No doubt a number of factors contributed to this situation, but significant among them was the increasing institutionalisation, recognition and influence of the organisations which 'owned' and controlled the key Olympic and Expo genres of mega-events in this phase. These were, in particular, the International Olympic Committee (IOC) and the Bureau of International Expositions (BIE) – organisations which have continued to own and control these leading mega-events in the contemporary phase of secondary modernisation.[22]

From their beginning in 1896 Olympic Games events and programmes, together with their location and periodicity, were organised and owned by a committee, the IOC. Although unquestionably international in character the IOC was (and arguably remains) a self-recruiting and relatively secretive non-governmental organisation which has always exercised considerable control over the local operational event organisation created by host nations and cities. In the early stages of the modern Olympic Games the events took some time to become recognised and popular and did not compare with Expos in terms of scale and prestige. So this novel kind of 'international civil society'-based approach to event organisation had the chance to grow roots and be capable of sustaining itself long-term.

The situation with the Expo genre was rather different. From its origins in the London event of 1851 through to the interwar period Expo events were conceptualised and organised in ad hoc ways by the host nations and cities which were willing and able to host them. There was no overarching international controlling agency in this field comparable with the IOC in the sport field. That said, the need for a more organised approach to the location, periodicity and programme content of Expos had been recognised since the 1860s. But given the rise of competitive industrialising and empire-building European nations towards the end of the nineteenth century this recognition had little practical consequence at the time. However, after experiencing the unprecedented destructiveness and horror of the modern form of international conflict in the First World War, nations were eventually more disposed to co-operate, at least in cultural and sporting spheres (and albeit only for a limited period before the destructive passions and ideologies of competitive nationalism overwhelmed them again in the Second World War). In the interwar period, then, the leading genres of international events and the movements and networks associated with them grew organisationally stronger and became more institutionalised (Roche 2000, ch. 4).

Leading Western nations created the BIE in 1928 as a treaty-based inter-governmental agency to organise Expo events. The BIE organisation has decided on and licensed most, although not all, Expo events since that time. Thus most Expo events since the early twentieth century have been influenced by the BIE's categorisation of types or models of Expo events and of event–city relations. The BIE formalised previous Expo practice by controlling the calendar and venues of Expo events in relation to two main categories of event which were differenti-ated by the scope and scale of their themes and contents. Thus under the BIE system the biggest and most aspirational types of event have been registered as being 'Universal' and differentiated from more 'Specialised' types of events. These two main categories have been influential on host nations and cities through to the present, even if their labels and characteristics have evolved somewhat over the years.[23] The Universal type of event (now referred to as 'Registered') has broad themes 'of universal concern to all humanity', lasts for six months and enables participating nations to create temporary national pavil-ions within the central urban space provided by the host city. The Specialised type of event (now called 'Recognised') has a theme which while being of global concern is of a more specific kind, is shorter (lasting for three months) and nations do not have pavilions, instead exhibiting within common premises provided by the host city. In the primary modernisation and urbanisation period, both before and after the advent of the BIE and its system, the Special-ised types of Expo events tended to leave one or more large exhibition facilities as their urban legacies. In this period the bigger Universal type of Expo has left intangible legacies in the collective memories of host nations and cities. But there has been no official requirement for them to leave anything more tangible in their host city. That said, historically they have tended to leave at least the space of a new or renewed urban park, and sometimes also some other Expo-related iconic constructions (see Chapter 6 and Table 6.2). However, in a devel-opment in the period of secondary modernisation and urbanisation which has a parallel in a comparable development in the Olympic movement, the leaving of some positive legacies, particularly for the host city, has become a more explicit topic and expectation in BIE policy discourse, and this is particularly so since the 1990s (for instance see Loscertales 2008).

International event organisations and urban event legacies

The IOC and Olympic Game legacies

The IOC and Olympic movement began to get interested in the various possible legacies of Olympic Games events, including tangible legacies for the host city, in the 1990s. Important drivers for this development included a problem and a potential solution. The problem was the IOC's need to rescue and relegitimise itself and its showcase event after a period of serious self-inflicted damage due to organisational corruption in the late 1990s (Roche 2000, ch. 7). The potential solution emerged from the success of the Games events of Seoul 1988, of Barcelona 1992 and particularly of Sydney 2000.[24] Each of these events had been associated with wider urban renewal and development strategies which were generally viewed positively in the host cities. The IOC needed to relegitimise itself and its mission, and it was able to do this partly through a new incoming President (Jacques Rogge in 2001), partly through connecting with emerging social values (particularly relating to the environment) and partly (building on recent experience) by the parallel development of an urban impact and legacy policy agenda among cities bidding to host the Games event.

The latter was developed initially through the IOC's institutionalisation of research into and empirical assessment of the various urban impacts of staging an Olympic Games. This has been done through its OGGI (Olympic Games Global Impact) programme which was created in 2001, the year that Beijing won the right to stage the 2008 Games.[25] OGGI requires host city Olympic Games organising committees (OCOGs) to provide regularly updated data on a large number of indicators of impact over an 11-year period running from nine years prior to a Games event through to two years post-event. In 2002 the IOC held a major international conference on the idea of legacy and included OGGI in the programme. This provided some of the basis for the IOC's current recognition of the complexity of legacy and for its recognition of the main categories of legacy as being sporting, social, environmental, urban and economic, and also as being both intangible and tangible (IOC 2012d and 2012f). The IOC's publication of the proceedings of the 2002 conference (Moragas et al.

2003) contributed to the dissemination of its new policy of emphasising event impacts and legacies more widely in the Olympic movement, to potential bidding cities and beyond.[26] The Olympic Charter, effectively the constitution of the IOC and the Olympic movement, was modified to include an article on legacy. This now takes the form of a statement that part of the IOC's mission and role is 'to promote a positive legacy from the Olympic Games to the host cities and host countries' (IOC 2013b, ch. 1 para. 2.14). From this period, also, linked to the OGGI programme, the IOC's guide to bidding cities began to require information on the 'vision and legacy' relating to the Games they planned to stage.

The BIE and Expo event legacies

In the primary phase of modernisation Expos, as we have seen, went from being ad hoc events to being regularised through the organisational activities of the BIE from 1928 onward (Roche 2000, ch. 4). Both before and after the creation of the BIE Expos could sometimes leave significant marks on their host cities. But whether they did or did not do so was a largely arbitrary and unpredictable matter. This situation has changed in the secondary phase of modernisation, in parallel with the changes in the IOC's policy we have noted above, and particularly so since the 1990s.

BIE's policy relating to cities bidding for the right to stage Expos has been more flexible than that of the IOC in relation to cities bidding for the Olympic Games. However there is currently a clear expectation that cities bidding for registration or recognition must include a 'post-Expo plan'.[27] For BIE Secretary General Vincente Loscertales 'Expositions ... have always had a place in city planning as strategic instruments for urban, economic and cultural renewal. Despite only having a lifespan of three to six months Expositions belong to the realm of long-term projects for the transformation of the city ... The BIE places extremely high importance on the integration of the Expo site into the city and on the need to plan for its reutilisation' (Loscertales 2009, p. xi). This expectation has been an explicit feature of BIE policy since 1994 when the BIE General Assembly agreed the following Resolution: 'In order to ensure the contribution which exhibitions should make to the development and the improvement of the quality of life, the organisers should accord a primordial importance to: – the environmental conditions of the insertion of the site and the infrastructures of access; to the reduction of the risks of pollution, to the preservation and constitution of green spaces and to the quality of real estate development ... [and, in addition, to] … the re-utilisation of the site and its infrastructures after the exhibition' (quoted in Loscertales 2009).

For Loscertales Expositions can have 'transformational power' which can best be seen in a long-term perspective, and 'the BIE framework' aims to promote this power (Loscertales 2009, p. xii). BIE policy discourse elaborates on this understanding of the 'transformational power' of Expos: 'The real success of any EXPO lies in its ability to maintain its transformational power after the event. This is true of the meaning of sustainability: the capacity of an Expo to deliver its promise to maintain a positive impact both on the city and on the behaviour of citizens' (BIE 2014b, p. 10). Expos have educational and innovation objectives. So BIE 'places great emphasis on two aspects that are key for meeting' them, and these are 'the preparation phase and its legacy' (BIE 2014b, p. 11). Loscertales suggests that 'Expositions can be thought of as a rite de passage chosen by a city to enact a vision for its future layout, for the mobility within its walls and for the social, economic and cultural activities it will support. The actions that will accompany urban renewal fuelled by Expositions will involve, amongst others, the regeneration of certain areas, the overall (or partial) branding or rebranding, and the reconfiguration of the city's operational systems (transport, telecommunications, networks, and so on)' (BIE 2014b, p. xii). In addition he comments that 'the BIE … view [expositions] as opportunities to launch best practices for implementing sustainable urban solutions. Through a broad field of action that includes architecture, energy and resource usage, operations, communications and civil participation. The Expositions of the twenty first century will be real-life laboratories for innovation' (BIE 2014b, p. xii).

Mega-events and social dimensions of urbanism: conceptualising the long-term urban impacts and legacies of mega-events

We can now turn to look at the long-term urban impacts of mega-events a little more closely. As I have argued in the discussions so far, it is necessary to get beyond the limited discourse of spectacle, and rather to consider how any event-related spectacle is embedded in urban social time and space. Thinking within the discourse of the spectacle suggests that event, with its event-time performative and material spectacle aspects, can leave behind in the post-event period some particular piece of starchitecture or material spectacle which serves as an enduring memento of the event. However this is far too limited a perspective if the urban embedding of mega-events is to be understood and if the potential range and significance of mega-event legacies are to be seriously engaged with.

Mega-events can affect both the political-economic and socio-cultural aspects of host cities. In political-economic terms they have the potential to exert various influences both positive and negative. They can enhance or diminish either the quality of democracy or the scale of financial resources of cities, or both. However since the discourse of legacy is more concerned with the potentially positive impacts of their range of possible socio-cultural aspects I will focus on the latter here.[28] Mega-events are special cultural (sporting or exhibitonary) performances which require the provision and use of specialised cultural facilities (stadia and/or halls etc.) during event-time and which often leave some key elements of these facilities post-event as long-term urban legacies. Since these facilities are often located together in or around a single urban zone we can refer to these as 'functional facilities complexes'.

In effect, in the post-event period, functional facilities complexes, if they are adequately managed, invested in and developed, can create new, identifiable and permanent urban 'event places'. Thus mega-events can be urban place-makers. Such facilities complexes can be places which regularly stage small- and medium-scale events capable of attracting and mobilising publics composed not only of cross-city residents but also of national and international city-visitors. 'Functional complexes' can contain event-generated material spectacles, but they are not reducible to this, and as a whole they do not mainly relate to the public by means of the experience of spectacle. Rather, in the post-event period, they are more characterised by the degrees to which, and the ways in which, they come to be perceived to be dependably useful by publics. In this post-spectacle context publics can be conceived of as being more than merely reactive and awe-struck by spectacle as they might have been in some respects at event-time. Rather they can be characterised as recurrently using the post-event complex in their own active searches for meaning and satisfaction in their lives.

In large part post-event urban-space projects which take the form of functional complexes operate to create theatres and stages at a lower level than mega-events, for more frequent and diverse types of activities and performances. They can be referred to as 'event space' projects and processes in the sense that their assemblages of material spaces and places are the physical correlates of the social and cultural spaces that they open up for publics, and thus physical correlates also of the public place-making processes which they enable. If mega-event spectacle can be said to persist or recur over time then it is most likely to do so in such places, both in their recurrent performances and also in some of their most striking buildings. However, that said, many aspects of these 'facilities complexes' as constructions are inevitably oriented to functionality rather than material spectacle in the post-event period as they were during event-time. Any such event-legacy complex as a whole provides a non-spectacular physical context in which spectacular buildings may be spatially and organisationally embedded.

Evidently, however, as we have recognised in the preceding discussions, mega-events can also be used as leading and catalysing agents in wider and longer-term urban development projects. They are increasingly conceptualised and used in this way by urban leaderships in the contemporary period, and indeed mega-event organisations have increasingly required that they be seen and used this way. In this case we need to recognise that mega-event impacts often include at least three further types of urban place and space in addition to functional facility complexes. With one exception, these are not best charac- terised as involving the maintenance or reuse of material spectacle elements of the original mega-event. Rather they involve aspects of mega-event projects and their meanings and uses which are oriented to other, albeit usually non- spectacular, dimensions of urban social experience and urban social process, namely those of open spaces, infrastructures and communities.

The open-space type of physical corollary of mega-events is particularly important, in my view, if we are concerned to understand the general impacts and legacies of mega-events for people in host cities in the contemporary period. Mainstream discussions of the urban impacts and legacies of mega-events, including assessments of their costs and benefits, successes and failures, tend to focus either on individual and iconic constructions or on functional complexes. This kind of academic and policy discourse has tended to underplay, and even overlook, the fact that the staging of such events has often also been associated with processes and projects related to the restoration of polluted and dangerous urban land to human use and also to the construction or qualitative enhance- ment of major urban parks. This echoes the more general overlooking of what we can refer to as the park movement in areas such as the social history of modern cities and of the welfare state, and so we will look further into this topic later (see Chapter 6).

Finally, we can briefly note, in addition, the two further general categories of urban social processes and urban development projects which have increasingly been connected with mega-events in the contemporary period, namely the development of new urban infrastructures and new urban communities. 'Urban infrastructures' can be used to refer to the material and organisational systems which enable city residents and visitors to be mobile and communicate both within and without any given city. Thus the term refers to such things as new investments in transport services (including international airports, railway and metro systems, bridges and road systems), in telecommunications systems (optic fibre/broadband cabling, wifi systems, telecoms towers etc.) and accommodation and hospitality facilities (new hotels etc.). Mega-events can also be used to promote the development of new urban communities particularly in terms of the potential of any Olympics in particular to bequeath a post-event legacy of the athletes' village which is often created for the event. In addition such new residential centres typically require (at least in principle if not always in practice) associated public services (education and health), employment opportunities (local businesses) and private-sector/consumer-market services (in retail, entertainment and so on).[29]

While some elements of mega-events' infrastructure impacts may be capable of symbolic display in the form of event-related material spectacles (for instance impressive bridges and telecommunications towers), these are essentially embedded in the mundane non-spectacular public uses and flows of the urban transport and communication systems of which they are objectively only a minor part. And generally the other urban social processes contextualising the long-term impacts of mega-events, namely open spaces and new communities, have even less connection with event-spectacle and its post-event echoes.

Conclusion

In this chapter we have begun to focus on the urban places and spaces left by mega-events. They can be regarded as long-term physical legacies and are increasingly regarded by urban policy-makers as being matters of strategic significance in the development of host cities. We will explore these themes further in the following chapters. Of course we also recognise that such event legacies become social realities only in their human animation. That is they become socially realised and endure only in the varied uses to which they are actually put by people and in the varied meanings and memories that they acquire and accumulate in these processes. Unlike the event-time performance spectacle and its starchitecture aspects, these post-event uses and meanings are likely to take various non-spectacular rather than spectacular forms. That is, they are likely to extend into domains of people's experience which range from the active and instrumental pursuit of interests or passions to the unfocused enjoyment of reverie or memory, none of which have an intrinsic connection with experiences typically associated with spectacle.

We have suggested that the collective experiences and memories of a mega-event's performative spectacle(s), together with the continuity of those of its material spectacles which have been retained, need to be understood as being socially embedded in such wider event-time and post-event processes. Post-event urban space and place planning projects and public uses provide the main social contexts and processes in which mega-events can be analysed as being embedded. These processes are physically embodied in the form of people's presence in and usage of physical locations, and this is the aspect we are exploring in this and the following chapters. The understanding of mega-events from this socially and physically embedded-spectacle perspective challenges the understandings associated with more familiar spectacle-centred analyses and their related critiques of mega-events.[30]

In Chapter 4 we have suggested that there are two main types of physical urban legacy relating to mega-events. The main type is that of place-filling and place-making buildings and facilities which may be examples of starchitect architecture or functional architecture or both. The more secondary type is that of the space-making creation or renewal of major green parks and open public areas. We will be looking into each of these types of mega-event-related urban legacy in the following chapters. Of course we should be wary of overly concretising concepts. The main mega-event genres can each leave both of the main types of urban physical legacy, namely both functional complexes and open spaces. That is these types of physical legacy, when viewed as urban realities rather than as abstract concepts, can be found to co-exist with each other, and even overlap and hybridise with each other, in the diverse contexts of real cities and in the civic life and flow of real publics' interests, uses and politics. However, that being said, Olympic mega-events have traditionally tended to leave more of the functional complex type of urban space, and Expos have tended to leave more of the open space, recreational green park type.

Expo mega-events since at least the late nineteenth century, have tended to have a much stronger, if less well recognised, track record of leaving an urban legacy which has often included the recreational green-park type of urban space. In addition they have also, although more intermittently, sometimes left important venues and functional complexes which are used for cultural exhibitions and/or performance. We look into each of these aspects of Expos, but particularly the urban green-park-making and space-making aspects later (in Chapter 6). By contrast Olympic mega-events, Summer Olympics, over the last half a century or more have tended to leave behind functional complexes for spectact-ing and participating in sport. These usually include the main Olympic stadium and/or other main event facilities such as those for swimming and cycling. Sometimes these physical legacies can also include more culturally oriented venues for exhibitions and/or performances. In the next chapter we explore further this variation snd range of Olympic urban legacy-making.

Notes

1 The anthropologist and Olympic studies scholar John MacAloon was the first to note and analyse these multiple-performance aspects of Olympic Games events (MacAloon 1984, also see his 1992 and 2006). These aspects are reviewed in Roche 2000, ch. 6, pp. 165–7. The spectacle aspect is discussed in Tomlinson 2002 and Tom-linson and Young 2006, and it is used and developed in a number of contributions in Horne and Manzenreiter 2006 and in Gruneau and Horne 2016b. One of the main theoretical resources used to support the preoccupation with the spectacle aspects of events is Guy Debord's philosophical critique of the alleged spectacle nature of con-temporary culture (see Debord 1990 and 1995). Critical discussions of Debord's views are given in Kellner 2003a and 2010, and particularly in Tomlinson 2002 and Roche 2016a, the latter of which also proposes the 'embedded spectacle' perspective on events which is further developed in this book. The distinct festival aspect of mega-events is discussed in Roche 2011a and 2016b. On urban festival events also see Giorgi et al. 2011, Sassatelli 2011, Picard and Robinson 2006 and Olsen 2013; also see Gold and Gold 2004. For spirited arguments about the nature of people's experiences and inter-ests in cultural events and festivals see, for instance, Ehrenreich 2007 and Rojek 2013.
2 On starchitecture see Sklair and Gherardi 2012, and also McNeill 2008, also Jones 2011. For the architectural debate see for instance Russell 2014 and Buchanan 2015.
3 On risk-oriented and risk-management approaches to the study of mega-events see work by Will Jennings and his colleagues, for instance Jennings 2012. For an analysis of mega-events largely as risky and questionable 'gambles' see Zimbalist 2015.
4 See Essex and Chalkley 1998, 1999 and 2004, and to a lesser extent Gold and Gold 2011b, also see Cashman 2008.
5 On Speer's career and biography see Sereny 1995, Speer 1970.
6 On Paxton's career and biography see Colquhoun 2004.
7 On the project to build a new version of the Crystal Palace building see Copping 2013 and Dezeen 2015.
8 For information on these and other constructions built for Expos see the main histories and sources for this event genre. These include Allwood 1977, Findling and Pelle 2008, Greenhalgh 1988 and 2011, Jackson 2008, Monclus 2009 and Rydell 1984 and 1993. See also Table 4.1 sources.
9 For information on these Expos see note 12 below and on relevant architects see McNeill 2008 and note 10.
10 See note 2.
11 The Pritker Prize is funded by the Hyatt Foundation of Chicago, see McNeill 2008, p. 74; also see its website www.pritkerprize.com/.

12 Frei Otto created designs for a number of mega-events. These included the West German national pavilion for the 1967 Montreal Expo and the 'green' Japanese pavilion (with Shigeru Ban) for the 2000 Hanover Expo. He was awarded the Pritker Prize specifically for his creation of the main stadium and site for the 1972 Munich Olympics. However the timing of the award left something to be desired. It was given to Otto in 2015; this was not only 43 years late, but also just before his death. See the Prizker Prize site, www.pritkerprize.com/, and Stott 2015.

13 In relation to the design of the Beijing Olympic stadium it is also worth noting the involvement of the Chinese artist and political activist Ai Weiwei along with Herzog and de Meuron. While not exactly a starchitect, Ai Weiwei, who has cultural celebrity status both in China and internationally, no doubt helped to lend this mega-event-related project some further creative cachet at the time, although this is something he came to regret (Ai 2008, BBC 2012c).

14 On the Millennium Dome, now known as the O2 Arena, see Chapter 8 below on London's mega-events.

15 On the topic of mega-event 'legacies' which can be unintended as well as intended, see Chapter 6 below, also Mangan and Dyreson 2012, Viehoff and Poynter 2015 and Zimbalist 2015.

16 Two relevant cases of Olympic Games which initially appeared to be problematic but which in a longer perspective appear more positive are those of Montreal 1976 and Athens 2004. These cases are considered in Chapter 5.

17 Contributions to the recent growth in mega-event security studies include Bennett and Haggerty 2012, Boyle and Haggerty 2009. Eisenhauer et al. 2014, Giulianotti and Klauser 2010, Houlihan and Giulianotti 2012, Samatas 2011, Farred 2016 and Spaaij 2016.

18 See for instance Phil Scraton's authoritative case study of the Hillsborough tragedy, Scraton 2009.

19 On neoliberalism in general see Davies 2014 and in relation to cities and developing countries see Brenner et al. 2010, and Parnell and Robinson 2012. On the connection between neoliberalism and mega-events see for instance contributions to Gruneau and Horne 2016b including Darnell and Millington 2016, also Rojek 2013.

20 For an analysis of mega-events as transient theme parks see Roche 2000, ch. 5. The relevant context here is the ever-increasing importance of tourism in modern societies as both a cultural form (see for instance Picard and Robinson 2006) and a cultural industry (on the latter see for instance ITB 2014 and UNWTO 2014). Mega-events, if effectively planned, can play a part in stimulating tourism in host cities both at event-time and also as a legacy effect in longer post-event periods. In relation to the latter see Roche 1994 and 2009a, also see the discussion of the relevance of London's history of staging mega-events for its tourism economy in Chapter 8 later. On the general socio-cultural and policy significance of the touristic theme park idea for cities and societies see respectively Zukin 1995 and Bryman 2004, also Ritzer 1999.

21 On the idea of the public sphere see Habermas 1991 (original 1962). Habermas's early-career analysis of the public sphere analysis contains a thesis about the historical decline of the public sphere over the course of modernity. For a set of theoretical and historical critiques of this see Calhoun 1992. The latter also contains some of Habermas's late-career responses to his critics in which he displays a less declinist and more positive perspective. On the cultural aspect of the public sphere see Sassatelli 2011, McGuigan 1996, and Giorgi et al. 2011 passim. My reading of the

cultural aspects of concepts like the public sphere is in terms of the concepts of (1) 'public culture' (see Roche 2000, part 1 passim) and of (2) the structural and life-world aspects of mega-events (see Roche 2000, ch. 8). In the discussions in the present chapter, and in Part II more generally, I aim to emphasise the idea that people's public cultural and public sphere experiences and activities need to be understood in embodied and spatial terms as requiring material conditions, notably, in cities, in public spaces including parks. Mega-event projects have been and are connected with the construction and/or reanimation of such material conditions in a range of significant cities both in the West and beyond.

22 On the origins of these mega-event organisations see Roche 2000, ch. 4.

23 See the BIE website, www.bie-paris.org.

24 The Barcelona 1992 and Sydney 2000 cases are discussed, in Chapter 5 and also see Roche 2000, ch. 5; also see the comments on Seoul 1988 in Chapter 1 above.

25 On the 'Olympic Games Impact Study' (OGGI) see IOC 2007, also the discussions of Olympic impacts and legacies in Chapter 6 below.

26 For a critical discussion of the discourse of legacy in IOC-related contexts see MacAloon 2012.

27 BIE's advice to bidding cities on 'how to organise an Expo' refers to a city's 'Post-Expo' plan (that is, effectively, the city's plans for the event to leave legacies (i.e. 'the host city develops its post-expo plan' (BIE 2014a, para. 7)).

28 See Gratton and Preuss 2012 for an alternative model of event legacies.

29 On the urban legacies of mega-events see for instance, Essex and Chalkley 1998, 1999 and 2004; Gold and Gold 2011b; Kassens-Noor 2012; Monclus 2009; Gratton and Preuss 2012; Preuss 2015 and the discussions in Chapters 5 and 6.

30 For an account and critique of Guy Debord's thinking on 'the spectacle' and related spectacle-centred approaches to the understanding of mega-events see Roche 2016a, also note 1.

5

Mega-events and urban development: Olympics and legacies

Over the history of the modern Olympics the long-term urban impacts and legacies of these events have developed from leaving minimal and practically invisible traces in the earliest editions to leading major and highly visible urban development projects in contemporary editions. Along the way they initially tended to focus on leaving sport facilities and little more. Research into the urban impacts of Olympic events, as of mega-events more generally, has long been of variable quality. However over the last decade or more, stimulated on the one hand by growing academic interest in Olympic studies and also by growing stakeholder engagement, it has deepened and improved in analytical and methodological quality.[1]

Some early seminal work in this area was undertaken by Stephen Essex and Brian Chalkley (see Essex and Chalkley, 1998 and 1999; also 2004). Their work reviews the urban impacts of the modern Olympics mainly in the twentieth century through to the 1990s, and we refer to this as a guide in this chapter. Since they distinguish four main stages in the development of these impacts, namely (1) 1896–1904, (2) 1908–32, (3) 1936–56 and (4) 1960–96, I should indicate how these stages map on to my analysis and its alternative periodisation. As I indicated in Chapters 1 and 4, my analytic perspective on mega-event urban impacts and legacies involves a general periodisation of primary (1850–70) and secondary (1970 to present) phases of modernisation and related urbanisation. This is a key organising theme throughout Part II of this book and thus for the tables and discussions not only in the previous chapter but also in this chapter and in the following chapter, where the schema is explained in more detail. In these terms most of Essex and Chalkley's stages (1, 2 and 3) can be seen as details of what I refer to as the primary phase; and their stage 4 (1960–96) is split between my primary and secondary phases, with most of the events covered being in what I refer to as the secondary phase. This periodisation provides a framework for the discussion in this chapter. In the first section we begin by looking at the focus from early Olympic Games onwards on the construction of sport facilities. Recognising the historical evolution of the Games in the twentieth century we then look at the way other types of urban development which are not particularly relevant to sport, including urban infrastructures and community-building projects, were increasingly commonly associated with the Olympic events. Ultimately by the end of the twentieth century these wider urban impacts of Olympic events came to be understood as Olympic legacies.

While the dominant meaning of legacy in this context is normatively positive, implying benefits for host cities, evidently, as we have noted in the previous chapter, staging mega-events such as Olympics is an inherently risky business. At times they can fail and create normatively negative legacies such as under-used facilities ('white elephants') and long-term public debt. In the second section of this chapter we look into some important cases of these different types of wider impacts and legacies, on the one hand the arguably negative Olympic legacy cases of the Montreal 1976 and Athens 2004 Games events, and on the other hand the widely recognised positive Olympic legacy case of the Barcelona games of 1992.

Finally, in the third section of the chapter we look into the unavoidable structural complexity of mega-event projects and the equally unavoidable struggles they involve and the determination they require from their planners and organisers to promote positive event legacies in host cities and avoid the risks of negative legacies. We do this through the lens of one strategically very important mega-event case, namely that of the Sydney Olympics in 2000 which we look at in some detail. On the surface this is a case of an especially successful Games event which left unequivocally positive legacies in both urban space-making terms (e.g. new parklands) and urban place-making terms (e.g. new facilities complexes and communities).

The IOC regarded the Sydney Olympics at games time as 'the best ever' (ESPN/AP 2000). In addition arguably this perception of the event contributed substantially to the permanent strategic shift in the IOC's thinking and policy in the 2001–2 period relating to the intercity bidding process for hosting Olympic Games. As we have seen in the previous chapter this shift involved a new emphasis within the bidding process on the long-term urban and other impacts or legacies of staging Olympic Games events. In addition, and as a consequence, the Sydney case came to be seen as a model for bidding cities of how to plan and deliver Olympic Games with a positive legacy. In this respect it has had considerable influence within the world of Olympic bidding cities over the last decade or more. This is not least in relation to the case of London and its Olympics in 2012 which we look into in more detail later in the book. However, appearances can be deceptive and it can be wrongly assumed that the contemporary post-event success of the Sydney Olympic site was easily rolled out from the success of the event at games time. As we will see in our case study of the Sydney Olympic project, the reality was rather different. Our discussion will indicate that the Sydney organisers faced considerable challenges in the post-event period in avoiding negative legacies and in promoting positive legacies. We will also see that these problems in turn were the result of a failure (rather than any exemplary achievement) in their approach to the planning of Olympic legacies.

Olympic mega-events and cities: sport complexes and wider urban contexts

Olympics, stadia and sport facilities complexes

Summer Olympic Games events have often left behind them a complex of facilities and spaces concerned with promoting the culture of sport in either or both of that culture's main aspects, namely mass spectatorship of professional sport events, and mass participation in sport. These complexes have usually been situated around the main Olympic stadium which is used as the centrepiece of the event. Such stadium complexes were often newly built, or significantly refurbished for the Games event. (For a summary of some relevant Olympic constructions see Tables 4.1 and 4.2). During event time they constituted the core of what we can refer to as the Olympic theme park (Roche 2000, ch. 5). In the post-event period these complexes were often left as the core of the urban legacy of the event. However, as we noted earlier, the construction and maintenance of such complexes can be risky projects. This is not only in terms of cost but also, importantly in the context of Olympic Games, in terms of post-event facility usage.

Olympic event projects frequently aspire to leaving a sport legacy in their host society by stimulating a lasting increase in public sport participation. In principle this might be achieved in part by means of the sport experts and celebrities typically involved in Games events, their attractiveness for mass audiences and the demonstration and modelling effects of their high-quality and often spectacular performances. Again, in principle, it might also in part be achieved, particularly in the host city, by means of the potential attractiveness of the sport facilities complex the event often leaves behind. Olympic events and their facilities complex can leave a positive legacy in a variety of ways, notably in social, economic, touristic and other ways. However, whether for good or for ill, the fact remains that they are rarely successful in leaving very much of a sport legacy involving increased public sport participation. The recent London 2012 Olympics is an interesting illustration of this issue. It was judged to have been successful on a number of fronts, and to have left positive legacies. But whether it has left the UK very much in terms of the sport legacy it promised is very much open to question, and we will return to this issue in more detail later.

In principle the modern Summer Olympic Games events have always required the provision of a main stadium for the opening and closing ceremonies including the parade of national teams, and for the track and field events. In practice, however, in the early history of the modern Olympics (phase 1), the Games did not always get this kind of stage. With the exception of the reconstruction of the Pan-Hellenic Games stadium in Athens for the 1896 event, which remains a heritage tourist attraction in our times, Games in phase 1 had little or no impact on the host cities. The lack of a main stadium as a focal point in the 1900 Paris and 1904 St Louis Olympics meant that these Games events were very poorly organised and also poorly remembered by host publics. Olympic programme elements were scattered around among Expo sites and programmes at these two events. Thus they had little identity and public recognition as being distinctively 'Olympic' events. However these Games were clearly not a sustainable model for the Olympics and had things continued in this way the Olympic event genre would probably not have survived as an institution in modern international culture.

There was evidently a need for a coherent performance programme situated in dedicated facilities on a centralised or coherently organised space. This developed in what Essex and Chalkley refer to as phase 2, 1908–32. The Olympics made its first main bid to be recognised as an independent international cultural event genre in the run-up to and immediate aftermath from the First World War (i.e. from 1908 to 1928). In these cases (that is, at London 1908, Stockholm 1912, Antwerp 1920, Paris 1924 and Amsterdam 1928) the host nations and cities made efforts at least to provide a dedicated stadium venue. However these tended to be fairly small-scale. With the possible exception of the White City Stadium built for London's 1908 Olympics these stadia made a fairly minor urban impact during event-time and for later generations they left a fairly minor urban legacy from the experience of hosting the Olympic event. However, the potential for the Olympics to attract the attention of mass publics in the host nation and internationally, and thus to appear to justify the provision of a higher-profile urban stage, first began to be understood in the 1930s in the Games of Los Angeles 1932 and Berlin 1936.

Large-scale stadia had begun to be built in Europe to house the commercial operations of professional association football clubs and their league competitions since the late nineteenth century and the turn of the century.[2] Similar developments had occurred in the US in the same period for the housing of big league baseball and American football. In the 1932 Los Angeles Olympic Games the Olympic movement, as the leading and still amateur section of the modern international sport movement, first began its fateful encounter with American mass consumer culture in the form of informal links with US corporate marketing and film industry celebrity. The stage for the event was the LA Coliseum stadium which was located in a central city park. Basing the 1932 Olympics at this venue provided a stimulus to significantly increase its pre-existing capacity to over a hundred thousand seats. The stadium was temporarily 'borrowed' from the growing world of American professional sport, and was returned to it immediately afterwards. The physical legacy of the 1932 event, in addition to the stadium's extra capacity, included a specially built swimming centre which was built for the Games nearby on the park site. The resulting sport complex was extended after the Second World War with the addition of a large indoor arena. From this period onwards the uses of this complex of venues evolved to include entertainment alongside of sport, and in 1984 the stadium was again the focal point of an Olympic Games event.[3]

Essex and Chalkley's periodisation phase 3, 1936–56, was one involving some purpose-built sports facilities which in most cases had some recognisable impact on the infrastructure of host cities. It was inaugurated by the 1936 Berlin Olympics. In this event the scale and spectacle of the American way of staging the Olympics Games at the 1932 event was matched by a more overtly political and ideological way of staging the event. Here the mass political culture of Nazi Germany rather than American-style mass consumer culture created an exceptional propaganda opportunity for Adolf Hitler's regime. The event was seen to require the creation of an impressive hundred-thousand-seat stadium at the heart of a large complex for sports (including athletics and swimming) and state ceremonies in the Grunewald area of the city. The stadium was redesigned, enlarged and enhanced from a pre-existing structure by Hitler's favourite architect and event designer, Albert Speer, who the following year was to direct the construction of the German pavilion at the 1937 Paris Expo. An impressive athletes' village was constructed in a distant suburb and the central city area was used for Games-related public activities and festivities.[4]

The Berlin Olympic Games event no doubt had considerable propaganda value at the time within the Third Reich. However it was much less effective internationally. This was due in part to the highly visible dominance of black American athletes – such as the sprinter Jesse Owens – who were regarded in the Nazis' racial mythology as 'inferior' types of human being over German and other white athletes. However the Olympic stadium and its environment made a mark within the Olympic movement and it also left a lasting urban legacy. Today, in post-fascist and post-communist times, this continues to have some distinctive functional sporting and heritage values for Berliners and for city visitors.

The Games of the immediate postwar period, by contrast, namely London 1948, Helsinki 1952 and Melbourne 1956, were on a smaller scale than those of Berlin and had less of an impact on their host cities. London's 'Austerity Games' had little urban impact or legacy. They used pre-existing facilities such as Wembley stadium and large exhibition halls which were the legacy of the Expo of 1924–25. Helsinki involved the building of a new stadium and also an athletes' village which was converted for urban housing purposes post-event. Melbourne involved the expansion of the Melbourne Cricket Ground (the MCG) to its contemporary capacity of a hundred thousand, and also the creation of a sport complex in a park setting for swimming and cycling venues. While the MCG remained popular post-event as it had been pre-event, some of the other sports venues declined in popularity and usage. Again an athletes' village was constructed which was used for urban housing post-event.[5]

The wider urban impacts and contexts of Summer Olympic Games

The main impacts of the modern Olympic Games on various types of urban places and spaces in host cities are summarised in Table 5.1 (with the exception of their role in the creation or reanimation of major urban parks and open spaces, which we will discuss separately later, see the third section below). Overall there is a clear difference in the pattern of impacts between earlier Games in the primary phase of modernisation (nineteenth century to 1970) and more recent Games in the secondary phase of modernisation (1970–2020). The urban impacts and legacies of the Games of the earlier period (with some exceptions, namely Rome 1960 and Tokyo 1964) tended to be limited and to be focused on the provision of a main stadium and associated sports facilities. By

Table 5.1 Summer Olympic Games' impacts on host cities

Primary modernisation phase: nineteenth century to 1970			Secondary modernisation phase: 1970 to present	
			Urban development catalyst: sport facilities complexes; transport and communication infrastructures;new communities	
No impact / low impact	Sport facilities impacts	Urban development catalyst	*Olympic Games*	*Comments*
1900 Paris	1896 Athens	1960 Rome	1972 Munich	–
1904 St Louis	1908 London	1964 Tokyo	1976 Montreal	Cost problem
1948 London	1912 Stockholm		1980 Moscow	–
	1920 Antwerp		1984 Los Angeles	–
1968 Mexico City	1924 Paris		1988 Seoul	Transformative
	1928 Amsterdam		1992 Barcelona	Transformative
	1936 Berlin		1996 Atlanta	–
			2000 Sydney	Transformative
	1952 Helsinki		2004 Athens	Cost/use problem
			2008 Beijing	Cost/use problem
			2012 London	Transformative
			2016 Rio de Janeiro	Partially transformative
			2020 Tokyo	Partially transformative

Sources: Adapted from Essex and Chalkley 1998, with additional information from Gold and Gold 2011b, IOC 2012b, 2012f

contrast (and allowing for a couple of exceptions, namely Los Angeles 1984 and Atlanta 1996) the urban impacts and legacies of the Games of the more recent period tended to be much wider. The latter events have typically been far more associated than those in the preceding period with major urban development projects involving significant improvements in transport, communication and hotel infrastructures together with the development of new urban communities and their housing, employment and other needs.

As we noted in the previous chapter, the main factors influencing this differ-ence are changes both in social structures and in mega-event policy. The macro-structural social changes include post-industrialisation (requiring cities to reimagine, renew their economies and rebrand themselves), globalisation (increasing intercity competitiveness in relation to the attraction of global capital investment and tourism) and mediatisation (involving technological transformations in media and communications requiring the upgrading of urban infrastructures). The mega-event policy changes, as we have noted in Chapter 4, have been the increasing requirements from international mega-event organisations that the cities they select to host their events should receive some long-term benefits or legacies from this process.

Essex and Chalkley's phase 4, 1960–96, coincides with the television age (see the discussions in Part I). This was the period in which the advent of the new communications technology of mass television began to alter and expand popular interest in the Olympics, not only within host nations but also internationally. This strengthening of the public's interest in sport culture made it credible for urban planners to be more ambitious in attempting to use the Olympic event as a catalyst in urban renewal projects. With some notable exceptions this began to become clear from the time of the 1960 Olympics in Rome and the 1964 Olym-pics in Tokyo. The connection of this broader urban development agenda with the staging of Olympics started to emerge in what I refer to as the primary phase of modernisation, albeit at the very end of this phase, due in part to the factor of the media developments noted above and also to the historically specific factor of the need to counter the negative effects of the Second World War. They were both located in nation-states which had been on the losing side in the war and which thus urgently needed to symbolise and mark the restoration of their politi-cal reputations and status in the international community. More practically, both host cities were in need of physical reconstruction after the destructive effects of the Second World War and the staging of the Games events gave them the opportunity and confidence to tackle some of these problems.[6]

Macro-structural social changes such as de-industrialisation and post-industrialisation began to grow in the 1970s, marking what I refer to as the 'secondary phase' of Western modernisation. This was associated with new challenges and developments in urban policy involving attempting to re-imagine and re-image cities and regenerate de-industrialised urban areas. This in turn increased urban leaderships' and planners' interests in mega-event projects which had some capability to act as markers and catalysts of wider urban changes beyond the specialised fields of sport culture and exhibitionary culture.

In this context a long-term multi-thematic urban development-based Olympic model began to emerge which involved building a new sports complex, usually centred on a new Olympic stadium and situated in a central urban park environment. This model often also involved new transport infrastructures (such as major extensions to subways, roads and airports), new telecommunications infrastructures (to provide for increasingly intensive (locally comprehensive) and extensive (global) television coverage) and often also new urban housing and community developments. It was particularly in evidence in the Olympic Games events of the 1970s, namely Munich 1972 and Montreal 1976. As we noted in Chapter 4, in the 2001–3 period the IOC began to formally recognise the need for host cities to use their Games events to provide long-term urban legacy benefits. However it is clear that, as in the cases of Munich and Montreal, and also in subsequent editions of the Games in the 1980s and 1990s, the practice of using Games events to help address wider urban contexts and challenges predated the IOC's formal legacy expectations and requirements. However this practice was not without its problems, as we consider next.

Olympics and host cities: positive and negative legacies

Olympics and negative legacies: Montreal 1976 and Athens 2004

The emergence of the 'sport plus urban development' model of Olympic Games events was (and remains) associated with high levels of costs and risks. When considering the economic costs of this model of event we need to bear in mind distinctions between, on the one hand, the costs of event organisation per se (which is often the minor part of the overall event budget) and ,on the other hand, the costs of such elements as the construction of (1) sport- and other event-related facilities (i.e. sports stadia, athlete villages, media complexes etc.) and (2) wider urban infrastructures (i.e. transport, communications and energy systems) (often by far the major parts of overall event budgets). Given these distinctions there is a degree of ambiguity about judgements of the economic and financial success or failure of an Olympic mega-event. For instance it is always possible that the budget for event organisation (the event per se) can end in balance or even record a surplus, while, simultaneously, the budget for construction and infrastructures can be in deficit, generating losses and long-term debts for the overall event budget. Another source of ambiguity about judgements of success or failure in terms of the economics of events is the fact that the wider urban infrastructures often associated with them, and even some sport facilities, might well have been constructed anyway as part of the long-term urban economic and social development strategy of a city which happens to a host an Olympics. That is, the fact of staging the event may only have accelerated such constructions. In this kind of case it may not be appropriate to take the overall event budget at face value, since it contains expenditures which would have been undertaken even if the event had never occurred.

Mega-events and their associated costs naturally reflect the long-term inflationary movement of prices in modern economies. So they have always had a tendency to increase from case to case over time. More troublingly, however, in the course of preparing each event, costs always have the potential to escalate in unplanned and uncontrolled ways. Such vulnerability reflects various factors such as, among other things, the essential uniqueness of each mega-event project and thus the lack of comparisons against which to reliably assess and measure them; the changing requirements of the international mega-event 'owners'; the status aspirations of urban leaderships; the opportunistic demands of event-construction workers; and the financial incompetence and/or corruption of local event organisers. Such high and/or escalated costs carried increased risks that they might not be fully covered or compensated for by measurable benefits not only over short-term timeframes but even over long-term timeframes. In such negative scenarios financial losses might be made and long-term debt-repayments ('negative legacies') might be incurred, along with short- and long-term reputational damage to city images.

A rational observer might suggest that all participants in mega-event processes – particularly event organisers, but also national and city 'boosters', and hopeful or anxious publics – are well advised, in the pre-event preparation phase, to be guided by such familiar virtues as foresight, coolness, criticalness, clarity and realism. Such virtues are needed in relation to such things as estimation of the probable scale and strength of the various possible sources of event income (e.g. central and local state, mega-event owners, spectator ticketing at event-time and in post-event periods, sale of media rights, corporate sponsorship etc.) and the nature of the relationships between them (particularly the probable balances between public and private sector funding before, during and after the event). However the inevitable stresses and the public and media exposure of mega-event processes mean that these virtues can often be in short supply when they are most needed. We can summarise these negative impacts and legacies associated with mega-events as follows. From a socio-economic perspective mega-event projects in the contemporary period are essentially risky ventures and can be afflicted by various cost and post-event-use problems. In addition, from a socio-psychological perspective, mega-events are also essentially stressful processes for all stakeholders involved in them. Thus they are vulnerable to being influenced by poor-quality and even non-rational judgements, decision-making and management practices.

To some degree or another no doubt aspects of these socio-economic risks and socio-psychological vulnerabilities feature in the stories of every mega-event in the contemporary period, even those which have been acclaimed as successes. The latter category includes the Olympic Games events of Sydney 2000 and London 2012. In spite of their positive achievements which we look at later, in each case the dominant theme of public acclaim for them has been accompanied by a minor counterpoint of criticism for the alleged escalation and/or high level of their costs, and also for their creation of arguably underused ('white elephant') main stadia and sports facilities. However these and other related sorts of criticisms have been made much more loudly and justifiably about other urban development-oriented Olympic Games events, most notably those of Montreal 1972 and Athens 2004. While each of these Olympics operated well as short-term performances, their post-event impacts and legacies for their host cities have proved to be much more controversial

The Montreal Olympic stadium was a spectacular multi-use facility which was originally planned to cost (Canadian) \$134 million (US\$104.89 million) and to open ahead of the Olympics in 1972. Owing to various factors – including the difficulties posed by construction-worker strikes and also by the innovative design (particularly of the flexible and retractable roof and the massive sloping tower rising over the stadium which was intended to contain it) – the opening was delayed until 1976. The roof was completed as planned only in 1987, over a decade after the event; it never functioned well, was mothballed in the 1990s and has been kept closed for over twenty years. Currently it needs to be completely replaced at considerable public expense, something which is unlikely to happen while policy-makers are unable to envisage viable uses and a future role for the stadium.[7] The cost of the drawn-out construction of the stadium escalated in an uncontrolled way both before and after the event. The debt and interest charges it incurred took thirty years to repay, and by that time they amounted to US\$1.61 billion (Canadian \$1.48 billion), over ten times the original budget (Newton, 2012; Wiki 2015a). Generally there seems to have been little detailed planning for the post-event uses and finances of each of the elements of the main Olympic facilities complex.

However the situation of the Olympic event legacy in Montreal is not completely bleak. Overall, from a legacy perspective, Montreal's Olympic project
could be said to have benefited from having used a centralised site next to an
established central urban park (the Montreal Botanical Garden) and from not
being burdened with very much of a need for expenditures on infrastructures.
Post-event the great inclined tower of the Olympic Stadium was made publicly
accessible by a funicular rail system in 1987 and has been operated as a unique
kind of viewing tower since that time. In 1992 the cycling Velodrome building
nearby was successfully converted to a completely different use as a Biosphere
recreating and exhibiting a number of world eco-systems. Each of these contin-
uee to function for the city as a tourist attraction through to the present time.
The remaining sport facilities, including the Olympic pool, continue to service
the physical activity needs of city residents. Also the iconic pyramidal structure
of the athletes' village building was successfully converted into an apartment
complex and thus an urban community, albeit a 'gentrified' one largely restricted
to people with middle-class incomes (Latouche 2011; Economist 2013).

Nearly thirty years later this negative kind of Olympic legacy story, even if it
is one of more mixed fortunes than might appear to be the case at first sight,
was echoed in the Athens Olympics of 2004 (Kissoudi 2012; also Zimbalist 2015,
pp. 65–7). In recent years the Greek economy has been in crisis, having been
badly served by a succession of governments willing to finance public expenditures by running up unsustainable debts in international bond markets, and also
having been badly affected by the Western economic recession post 2008–9.
From the perspective of this present negative situation it is hard to view the
troubled 2004 Athens Olympic project as other than a sign of (and even a causal
factor in) what was to come. As in the Montreal case, construction programmes
were subject to delays and to significant and unplanned cost escalations. In
particular, as in Montreal, the challenging design of the spectacular main
stadium was a particular source of problems. However the Athens project differed from the Montreal project in a number of significant respects. Although,
as with Montreal, it used a centralised site for many of the sport facilities including the main stadium (OAKA Athens Olympic Sport Complex), unlike Montreal this was combined with a decentralised and dispersed approach to a
significant number of the sport facilities and the Olympic village. Venues were
located from the hilly north-east suburbs (e.g. mountain biking and the Olympic
village in the Parnitha area) and the south-eastern periphery (e.g. equestrianism
and shooting at Markopoulo) to coastal areas in the southern suburbs (e.g.
hockey, baseball and softball at Helleniko and beach volleyball, handball and

taekwondo at Faliro) and various sites scattered in between (e.g. the badminton and pentathlon at Goudi, the gymnastics at Galatsi, the boxing at Peristeri, the weightlifting at Nikaia).

The construction difficulties and delays, the degree of venue dispersal and the lack of realistic planning for post-event uses of venues led to mismanagement of the event's finances and its potential legacies. The event's direct and related costs were initially understood to be $5.7 billion, around half of which was to be covered by event revenues from such sources as ticketing and television rights sales. However, as early as 2005 it was officially estimated that event-related costs had more than doubled to $13 billion, and even that they might end up at $16 billion, triple the initial budget (Washington Post 2005). A decade after the event the exact nature and scale of this financial overrun is still not properly understood and is currently the subject of an official investigation. However the estimates of the costs remain of a similar order to those given earlier, namely $11.4 billion, with the possibility that the overall sum might ultimately be as high as $17 billion (MacKay 2014).

In addition to the fact that the 2004 Olympics became associated with financial failure there is also the fact that it has been visibly associated with waste and mismanagement in terms of its sport and sport-related legacies.[8] While a number of the facilities have eventually been turned to a positive use, many of them have remained uselessly and expensively closed for years awaiting new investment or demolition. Athens's sad group of Olympic 'white elephants' currently includes, among others, the canoeing and softball venues at Helleniko, the volleyball arena at Faliro, the weightlifting centre at Nikaia and the outdoor swimming and diving pools at OAKA. The Olympic village at Parnitha, which was originally designed to be a new post-Olympic community of ten thousand people, is only partially occupied, lacks most basic community services and suffers from vandalism and neglect. In addition many venues have existed for a decade in a 'twilight zone' of partial and/or under-capacity use. These include the Velodrome and the Olympic stadium at OAKA and the large indoor arena at Helleniko. However there are some post-event developments which have generally been socially positive: these include the conversion of the International Broadcast Centre into a popular shopping mall at the OAKA site and the conversion of the Goudi badminton venue into a theatre,

The aspirations of the Greek and Athenian leaderships to make long-term use of the opportunity presented by the Olympic 2004 event were distinctively ambitious. They intended to try to use the Games for major city-wide urban regeneration and development purposes, and in spite of the problems of cost and venue use they had some success in this. The Olympics provided the opportunity and stimulus for a major upgrade of the city's transport infrastructures, notably including a new international airport, an extension to the subway system, a new light tram system and a new ring road. These developments were long overdue and have generally been welcomed. So too has the pedestrianisation of some areas in the historical parts of central Athens which improves access to heritage sites. The transport and site-access improvements connected with the staging of the Olympics have been important for the health of the city's vital tourism economic sector. In spite of the country's recent economic crisis this has managed to double in the post-Olympic decade. In the recent view of Spyros Kapralos, President of the Hellenic Olympic Committee, in spite of the cost escalation and other problems the staging of the 2004 Olympics helped to change the face of the city of Athens for the better and 'the positives outweigh the negatives, but unfortunately we weren't able to communicate that' (quoted in MacKay 2014).

In spite of going through successive difficulties with its Olympic project over many years in the full glare of the international media, Athens's experience has not appeared to dampen the enthusiasm of major cities around the world for bidding to host the Games. In this respect the contemporary situation is different from that of the 1970s when Olympic Games went through a period of appearing to promise only bad publicity for host cities. The organisational risks of mega-events to the negative publicity and security costs associated with terrorist spectacles were graphically illustrated in the case of the Munich Olympics in 1972. And their financial risks were equally graphically illustrated in the case of Montreal Olympics in 1976. These cases undoubtedly scared many Western cities away from bidding for the Olympics throughout the 1970s. However this situation changed after the success of the Los Angeles Olympics of 1984 and the Seoul Olympics of 1988. In the 1980s cities' confidence and interest in the Olympics returned. Six cities entered the bidding process for the 1992 Games ultimately won by Barcelona. And, in spite of the Athens case along the way, the intercity bidding competitions have remained popular among world cities from that time through to the present, with around half a dozen cities bidding for each Games since Barcelona.

Olympics and positive legacies: Barcelona 1992

The multi-thematic model of mega-events and their impacts brings into view the broader urban contexts we need in order to appreciate the continuing significance of Games-derived constructional icons and material spectacles such as Roger Taillebert's Olympic stadium in Montreal and Frei Otto's Olympic stadium in Munich (Table 4.2). The reputation of this multi-thematic urban-development-based model of long-term Olympic impacts was further enhanced by its association with three well-regarded Olympic Games events in the late 1980s and 1990s, namely those of Seoul in 1988, Barcelona in 1992 and Sydney in 2000. We looked at the case of the Seoul Games in Chapter 1, so here we can focus here on the influential cases of the Games events of Barcelona and Sydney.

Barcelona's Olympic event was used by the city as a catalyst in a very long-term urban development strategy to modernise the city and to promote its international recognition and role in European and global markets and peer-groups of comparable cities.[9] The Olympics event was used to stimulate, focus and accelerate urban projects which had long been recognised as being necessary, and which have continued to be rolled out long after the occurrence of the Games. Barcelona had a tradition of using mega-events for major urban development purposes, having used the two Expos of 1885 and 1929 in this way in previous generations. This in turn meant that earlier Expo-legacy developments were available for temporary reuse by the 1992 Olympic event, and thus resources could be more focused on contemporary urban needs and developments. For instance the Olympic media operation, which needed to provide large-scale office and studio facilities for over twelve thousand television and print journalists, could be housed in the 1929 Expo-originated exhibition halls at Montjuïc. Resources could thus be focused on radical improvements to the city's telecommunications infrastructures needed both by the Games event and also by the city's post-event development plans and aspirations. These included key elements of a new city-wide broadband cable network, together with Santiago Calatrava's telecoms tower on Montjuïc hill and Norman Foster's telecoms tower in Barcelona's Collserola hills, both of which also happened to be touristically attractive and useful pieces of starchitecture. The city's broader urban-policy goals included fully integrating a previously marginal area (Vall d'Hebron, where a significant set of sport facilities were located) and creating a new central city post-industrial mixed-use area out of a previously declining industrial zone (the Parc de Mar, involving a new beach and port, and new housing, retail and business facilities).

The city's broader urban-policy goals also included promoting the new image and enhanced attractiveness of the city internationally to attract both mobile capital investment and also international tourists. The post-event impact of the Olympic event on international tourism into Barcelona has generally been assessed to be very positive. For instance over the 1990–2001 decade both hotel capacity and tourist numbers using them, and overnight stays, roughly doubled, with international visitors overtaking national visitors as a proportion of Barcelona's tourism market (Gratton et al. 2006). Although the event organisers used a multi-site approach rather than the more traditional concentrated 'main site' approach to the Olympic theme park, Barcelona was successful on each of the urban development policy fronts indicated above (among others). The 1992 Barcelona Olympics exemplifies the urban-development-led model of organising the Olympic mega-event and managing its aftermath. It undoubtedly created Olympic-related material spectacles (Calatrava's Montjuïc tower, Foster's Collserola tower and Gehry's Parc de Mar sculpture). However these cannot be understood in isolation, nor purely through the discourse of spectacle. As we have argued in general throughout the preceding and current chapters, to be adequately understood these pieces of starchitecture need to be contextualised in relation to the wider urban development process within which they were conceived, and within which they remain embedded.

The Sydney 2000 Olympics: performance, planning and legacy in a key mega-event case

Background

The Sydney Olympics, at least at games time in 2000, was widely perceived as a success – as a theatre of memorable sporting performance, as an entertainment spectacle, as an impressive building project and as a source of pride by the sports-literate public of the host nation. Indeed the President of the IOC at the time, Juan Samaranch, went so far as to give Sydney the accolade of being 'the best Olympic Games ever'.[10] Indirectly this can also be interpreted as an accolade to the IOC itself, and particularly to its chief co-ordinator with Sydney, Jacques Rogge, a rising star within the IOC who was soon to take over as President in 2001. No doubt Sydney's success created an optimistic afterglow for a period both in Australia and in the Olympic movement and its leadership in the immediate post-event period. As we have seen in Chapter 4, it was in this 'afterglow' that the IOC, under the influence of its new President, developed its new thinking, expectations and policies about Olympic legacy. So the Sydney experience and case could reasonably be assumed to have been influential in this regard. However in this section we need to take a closer and more critical look at this assumption, particularly in relation to the urban dimension of Olympic legacy.

Sydney was the first contemporary-era Olympic project to explicitly commit itself to leaving a positive legacy. From the launch in 1992 of their campaign to win the 2000 Olympics the Sydney organisers gave a high profile to their intention to make their event a 'Green Games'. Thus what they meant by legacy was mainly a model of urban development which would embody values of sustainability and ecological conservation. In this the project was significantly successful in the preparation period, providing a model which, by games-time, was judged capable of contributing to the green character of succeeding Olympics (Taylor 2000; Greenpeace 2000; Furrer 2002). In the post-Games period these 'green legacy' credentials and achievements have been further enhanced.[11] However, apart from these important environmental aspects, over a decade after the Sydney Games the event remains something of a puzzle to interpret and assess in terms of its Olympic legacy.

The positive afterglow of the games-time success of the event did not last long in the host city. Inevitably the special emotional buzz associated with a successful mega-event, the public sociability and collective vitality in the host city, fades with time, mutating into nostalgia and passing into memory.[12] There were organisational delays and uncertainties about the post-event reconfiguration and uses of the key elements of the main Olympic sport facilities complex, together with public and media concerns about their possible costs and status as wasteful 'white elephants'. This involved what one notable Olympic analyst has referred to as a 'bitter-sweet awakening' by the host public after the Olympic 'party' (Cashman 2006). Apart from the largely positive environmental dimension, significant aspects of Sydney's overall event legacy are less than positive and present a picture which is more mixed than is often recognised. Some other key aspects include the nature of the planning process and the adequacy of transport infrastructures.

We can now look into these aspects, beginning with the dimension of the event and its legacy which is probably most uncontroversially positive in the Sydney case, namely that of the project's green or environmentalist character and aspirations. In this part of the discussion note needs to be taken of the suburban location of the main Olympic site. It will be suggested that, while this was a strength as far as the environmental aspect of the event went, it contributed to transport and access problems in the post-event period. We can then look into the Olympic site and its key component venues in more detail, noting the centralised spatial model involved in the Sydney Olympics as compared with the decentralised spatial model used in the Barcelona 1992 Olympics (and again more recently in the Athens 2004 Olympics). Given these contexts we then turn to the issue of the quality of the legacy-planning process relating to the Games. There are clearly divergent perspectives on this issue, from the view that Sydney is an exemplary model for subsequent Olympic cities to the view that its legacy planning was flawed and that the lessons other cities can learn from Sydney include avoiding its mistakes. Finally we summarise some of the main post-event positive impacts and legacies which have derived from Sydney's project to stage the 2000 Olympics and we indicate how it is planned to develop these legacies further in future years up until 2030.

Mega-event space-making: the 'Green Games' and a sub-urban legacy

The city of Sydney's long-term urban development strategy is significantly influenced and operated by the regional or state-level government of New South Wales (NSW).[13] NSW is a major public land-owner in and around the city, and thus has levers to pull to enable its plans to make progress. Its strategy has long aimed, among other things, at coping with the rising tide of the city's population growth by means of an expansion of urban development. Given the long-established settlement of Sydney's east central and ocean-facing suburbs, this new wave of expansion needed to be into and beyond the city's inland-facing inner western suburbs. These inner western suburbs are deeply penetrated by the tidal Paramatta river and its tributaries which ultimately run eastwards into Sydney harbour and the Pacific. One significant location in these suburbs was Homebush Bay, 17 kilometres upriver from central Sydney.

Historically Homebush Bay had been a largely industrial area. However by the 1990s it had become largely disused and derelict, with polluted land and waterways. The land in this area needed, at the very least, to be 'remediated' or brought back to being usable by people. In addition its riverside and suburban location also suggested that the area and its immediate environs had significant 'green' potential. That is, they could be upgraded into parklands, wetlands and wildlife conservation zones which would offer recreational and quality-of-life benefits to residents of the growing western suburbs. As we have seen already (and as we will see further in relation to parks and open spaces in the following chapter), mega-events have traditionally provided prime opportunities and powerful motivations to enable such urban transformations to occur.

NSW recognised this in the early 1990s and thus gave strong support for a campaign to win the right for Sydney to stage to 2000 Olympics, an event which would be based at Homebush Bay. A mega-event project of such national significance promised to unlock public resources of a scale capable both of addressing the environmental problems of this area and its environs, and also of transforming and 'greening' them. NSW's evolving plans for the Olympic complex at Homebush Bay and its environs envisaged the creation of a complex of sport facilities which would be bounded by and linked to the east and north by over 430 hectares of open and/or green spaces of various kinds (i.e. Centennial Park, the Brickpit quarry and industrial heritage space, Wentworth Common, Badu Mangrove forest, Silver Water Nature Reserve, Millennium Parklands and Blaxland Riverside park). To the north-west it would be bounded by and linked to the athletes' village and subsequent residential housing developments at Newington, and to the east it would be bounded by Haslam's Creek, a tidal tributary of the Paramatta river. However, arguably the planning vision for the environs around the Olympic complex at Homebush Bay was clearer, and more purposefully pursued and delivered, than the vision for the complex itself, as we consider in a moment.

This strategy for green and open spaces in the environs around the Homebush Bay site set the scene for the Olympic project's pre-event commitment to a 'Green Games' and also for its success in delivering green impacts and legacies both at games-time and in the post-event period. However, arguably, the challenges of achieving the project's green aspects and legacies may have distracted organisers somewhat from making equal progress on other urban-legacy fronts connected with the project. One key issue here was transport. Homebush Bay's significant distance from downtown Sydney meant that public access for city-wide residents and tourists to the Olympic complex needed to be given a consistently high priority. This refers to the management of mass crowds not only during games-time but also in the post-event period as the sports complex established itself as a permanent major sport and cultural events destination. Road access by car or bus has always been adequate, but access by train has not. Homebush Bay was only minimally linked to Sydney's overground suburban train system by a specially built spur line. While special direct train services were run from central Sydney during the few weeks of the Olympic event, public access in post-Olympic years has typically been indirect, requiring a change of trains. In spite of plans for a city metro system which have developed in recent years, easy mass public access to the area remains a problem, and we return to it later (see the comments on legacies below).

As we have seen in Chapter 4, many cities have used the staging of mega-events as a catalyst to significantly improve urban transport infrastructures. This cannot be said to have occurred in the case of Sydney. Given that transport infrastructure developments can be extremely costly it is reasonable to suppose that Sydney's minimal investment in them was part of a defensible effort on the organisers' part to live within their budget. In post-industrialising cities like Sydney, people's needs for connectivity, mobility and accessibility in order to be able to be included and participate in the urban economy and social world are critical issues which need to be given a priority in urban policy-making. On this assumption it is reasonable to speculate that the relative lack of attention to this aspect of the Sydney Olympics and its legacy acted as a drag factor on the socio-economic development of Sydney's Olympic Park complex and its neighbouring areas in the post-event period.

Mega-event place-making: the Olympic complex in a centralised spatial model

There are evidently various different ways of designing and organising a successful Olympics which is both successful at games-time and also carries some potential to generate positive legacies in the post-event period. For instance Barcelona, as we have noted above, opted for what has been referred to as a decentralised spatial model, with multi-sites, some situated accessibly in the downtown area and others at more distant locations (such as Vall d'Hebron, about five kilometres away). The accessible downtown sites included the main stadium and the athletes' village. The Olympic stadium was a renewal and reuse of a pre-existing stadium. It was located on Montjuïc hill, some distance (about four kilometres) away across the central city from the athletes' village, which was a new construction on the coast near Barceloneta. By contrast Sydney's spatial model (with the exception of the media facilities which were sited at Darling Harbour in downtown Sydney) was simultaneously much more detached from the downtown city but also much more centralised.

As we have seen, Sydney's Olympic project differed from Barcelona's in that most of the main venues and facilities it required were newly created in a single integrated sport complex at the Homebush Bay site. They included the very large main stadium and also the nearby Olympic Village at Newington. The difference between these two facilities post-event highlights some further ambiguities relating to Sydney's Olympics and its urban legacies. The athletes' village was long planned to be the core of a new Sydney suburb and was designed to a high environmental standard. This involved the recycling of building-waste during the construction phase, and, for post-event housing, the building-in of solar-energy-powered water heating together with the use of recycled water for toilets and garden irrigation. The housing was sold to the public post-event, thus contributing to event costs, and the suburb has subsequently developed into a functioning community with health, educational and retail infrastructures and services.

The Sydney Olympic Park site consists of a complex of specially created sport, exhibitionary, cultural and multi-purpose event facilities. The sports-related facilities include the main Olympic (now ANZ) stadium (seating 110,000 during the Olympic Games, but scaled down to 83,000 post-event in 2003); a large indoor arena (the 'Sydney Super Dome', now the 'Allphones Arena', seating 21,000); and an aquatics centre (the Sydney Olympic Park Aquatic Centre, SOPA, seating ten thousand), together with a series of venues for athletics, tennis, hockey, archery and BMX mountain biking. Other significant sports-related and also exhibitionary facilities are provided by the Sydney Showground organisation, and these include the Sydney Showground Stadium (now the 'Spotless Stadium', seating 25,000), and the Dome and Exhibition Complex (seating ten thousand). While these large-scale facilities were fully utilised during the Games event, the immediate post-event period which brought an afterglow for some brought fears of 'white elephants' and waste for others.

Evidently the full complex could not have survived on the basis of local public interest and demand from the city's inner western suburbs. Their appeal and usage had to be effectively developed at cross-city and national levels, even (in some cases relevant to international tourists) at international levels rather than merely at local levels. Initially it was not clear that the facilities complex could be continuously programmed with events of a scale and public attractiveness to be fully used at these levels and to cover their costs. These fears have been largely overcome in most of the venues by the build-up mainly of spectator sport programmes and also by public take-up of the sport and fitness participation programmes that are available. In terms of the former the Allphones indoor arena is now one of the top three or four most successful such venues in the world (SOPA 2012). However concerns remain about the underuse of facilities which, in the pre-event period, were seen as costly and sometimes controversial commitments of public expenditure. The great centrepiece of the Olympic Park complex, the main Olympic Stadium, perhaps most exemplifies these concerns.

Sydney's Olympic Stadium had to be closed for two years post-event in order for its capacity to be reduced and to enable its seating to be made flexible and capable of being reconfigured to serve a variety of sports. Since then it has staged many significant sports events, sometimes to near capacity crowds, particularly in rugby league, but also in rugby union, association football, Australian rules football and cricket, at all levels from international to club level. However, difficulties remain and these include the following. The stadium's large size makes it costly to run and difficult to regularly fill; its periodic needs to be reconfigured reduce the time it can be available for normal uses; the quality of the experience of spectators at its major client sports (rugby league, rugby union and soccer), who are denied the proximity to the pitch they would normally expect because of the stadium's need to be capable of catering for the large pitch lay-outs required by its minor client sports (cricket and Australian rules football), is less than ideal. Finally, as we have already noted, there is the issue of the stadium's distance from downtown Sydney and its unimpressive public transport access for fans and tourists. It would not at all be accurate to describe this stadium as a 'white elephant'; but none the less, in these and other respects, it remains a problematic venue.

Legacy planning problems

The case of the Sydney Olympic mega-event enables us to recognise the multi-dimensional complexity both of the events themselves and also of their impacts and legacies. It also, thereby, illuminates what is involved in the idea that to understand event spectacle it is necessary to appreciate that and how they are embedded in social processes which have 'reach' in terms of social space and time, particularly those of urban development both at games-time and also in the post-event period. We have touched on a number of types of urban legacy, namely those relating to ecology, transport, sport and leisure, and community. In the case of Sydney's Olympics and its aftermath the picture these various legacies present is mixed but, ultimately, largely positive, and we will summarise that in a moment. First however it is worth reflecting on what the Sydney case shows about the process of planning mega-event legacies.

We have seen that, from the beginning of Sydney's campaign in 1992 to host the 2000 Games through to the delivery of the event, the idea of legacy was not an IOC requirement. Rather the Sydney Olympic Games organisers and their NSW backers generated and promoted the idea themselves for their own reasons concerned with the long-term urban (or more appropriately suburban) development of the proposed event site. Their version of the character and legacy of the Olympic event was particularly oriented towards green ecological values of environmental remediation, sustainability, habitat conservation and recreational green space, with special reference to the spatial frame around the site of the Olympic complex. The successful implementation of Sydney's green legacy plan, together with the performative success of the Games event itself in sporting and popular entertainment terms, together also with the leading participation in this project of an incoming IOC President, fuelled a new and lasting interest in event legacy on the part of the IOC.

In this respect Sydney's Olympic project represents something of a turning point in the development of the Olympic movement, and there are good grounds for claiming that it has a special status in the history of the movement in the contemporary period. However, with the passing of time, and with the occurrence of a lot of post-event positive urban development in the area, it is possible to imagine that the Sydney organisers always had a strong plan for Olympic legacies and succeeded in delivering that plan. A good illustration of this perception is the recent view of Alan Marsh, the current Chief Executive Officer of the Sydney Olympic Park Authority (SOPA): 'The Sydney 2000 Olympic Games were the first Games to explicitly incorporate legacy planning into the Olympic bid, outlining a future for the Games infrastructure that extended beyond the hosting period [...] The legacy with respect to sport, the environment and venues were very well thought out in advance of the Games, particularly at Sydney Olympic Park' (quoted in IOC 2012g). Marsh is correct in principle that mega-event projects like Olympic Games ought to involve pre-event plans for a variety of legacies which are 'well thought out in advance'. However he is not correct to claim that the Sydney Olympic planning processes exemplified such an approach and that it represents 'the exemplar of Olympic legacy planning' (SOPA 2012, p. 15).

Other 'insiders' and close observers effectively dispute Marsh's view and imply that it misrepresents Sydney's actual planning process. According to them in the pre-event period (and apart perhaps from the green legacy aspirations mainly directed at the spatial frame surrounding the Olympic complex, including the athletes' village, which we have discussed above) the Sydney organisers did not have any serious legacy plans for the post-event use and development of the sport and facilities complex. A key insider was Professor Sue Holliday who, at the time, was Director-General of the New South Wales state planning department, with a leading responsibility for the planning of the Sydney Olympic project. Contrary to Marsh's claim, Holliday is clear that 'We didn't really have a policy for what would happen to the Olympic site after the Games' (quoted in Usborne 2008). Also she has stated that 'Planning for the legacy on the site only began *after* the actual event' (quoted in IOC 2012g, my emphasis). This situation has been confirmed by various independent observers and event planning researchers. For instance Searle's study of the Sydney planning process found that 'planning for the Olympics did not incorporate further development at Sydney Park after 2000' (Searle 2008; also Cashman 2008). Smith's study of the process observes that 'not enough thought had gone into planning the legacy of the event' (Smith 2012, p. 236). And Cashman and Horne's recent analysis of Olympic legacy planning observes that even in Sydney's immediate Post-Games Report 'There was no mention of any specific plans to enhance positive legacy outcomes and to minimise negative outcomes' (Cashman and Horne 2013, p. 53).

In the immediate post-Games period it is clear that there was a significant hiatus concerning the event's legacy lasting a number of years, and to some extent justifying, at least for a time, public concerns and criticisms of waste and 'white elephants'. Venues were closed for long periods in order to be reconfigured for post-event use, and the main stadium was not reopened until 2003. Both this core facility and also the indoor arena remained very large venues which were both costly to operate and difficult to fill on a regular basis. The indoor arena was particularly financially troubled and went into receivership in 2004.

In this early post-event hiatus the NSW authorities recognised that a critical situation was developing and that a new plan needed to be developed. Given its relative spatial disconnection and its problematic access from downtown Sydney, the Olympic site needed to be rescued and re-energised by the constant presence of people working and living in and around it. And this, in turn, needed the commitment of new focused planning agency together with a new and detailed long-term plan for the development of the Homebush Bay site not only in sport events terms but also in terms of cultural and exhibitionary events. More broadly it was necessary to attract new businesses and sources of employment, and also to create new on-site residential communities (beyond the nearby former athletes' village at Newington). After a process of public consultation in 2001, NSW created the necessary agency (Sydney Olympic Park Authority, SOPA) in 2002. In turn, in the same year SOPA created the first detailed 'Master Plan' for the post-Games development of the Olympic site. The plan was to be periodically reviewed and updated as its delivery was being was rolled out, and the most recent version ('Master Plan 2030' created in 2008–9) contains guidelines for development and projections through to 2030 (SOPA 2009).

Although this plan was created and implemented after and not before the Games event it has, none the less, been relatively successful (for instance Searle 2008). We have noted elements of this success earlier in the discussion, and to conclude this case study they will be briefly summarised next. However at this point it is worth noting that, setting idealised misrepresentations of it to one side, Sydney's *actual* approach to much of its event-related legacy planning was risky. The immediate post-event legacy hiatus might have led to loss of planning commitment and creativity in the project of event-related development of the site, a loss of public legitimacy for it and a significant rethink and alteration of planning vision for the site. Sydney's eventual post-event site-development practice has much to recommend it as a model for cities bidding to stage the Olympic Games (Cashman 2008). However any such 'Sydney model', to have integrity and utility for future event policy-makers and planners, needs to recognise weaknesses in the Sydney case and to learn lessons from them. On the basis of our discussion these weaknesses can be said to include Sydney's lack of pre-event legacy planning and also the hiatus in its immediate post-event legacy planning.

Legacy achievements

Olympic-related post-event legacy developments in and around the Olympic complex site can be summarised as ultimately being, with some exceptions, significantly positive. We can note both current developments and future plans in three main areas, namely sport and leisure/entertainment, community (housing and employment) and transport and ecology. The performance of the Sydney Olympic Park as a sport and leisure/entertainment events complex, after a weak and uncertain start, has stabilised, gathered momentum and made progress. Now, over a decade after the reconfiguration and reopening of its main stadium, it can be said to be doing well in terms of sport and leisure legacies, and also in terms of community legacies. Regarding sport and leisure legacies the Park has become one of the most popular and important destinations for events not only in the state of New South Wales (SOPA 2012) but also in Australia more generally (SOPA 2009).

In 2011–12 it staged six thousand events, and twelve million people made a visit to the site to watch sport or to participate in sport, exhibitions or recreation (SOPA 2012). Given the ultimate achievement of success in this sport and leisure/entertainment dimension of the Olympic legacy it is understandable that the planners at NSW and SOPA aim to maintain and build on such capacity for staging events in the future (Searle 2008; SOPA 2009).

'Community' legacies can be said to relate particularly to employment and housing. From a housing legacy perspective we earlier noted the achievement of a functioning and expanding new community at the former athletes' village at Newington near to the Olympic complex site. More recently plans have been made to add more new housing developments within the site itself. Thus in addition to the former Olympic Village development six thousand new homes for fourteen thousand new residents are planned to be added in and around the Olympic complex site by 2030 (SOPA 2015). In general successive post-event Master Plans have scaled up the Olympic Park site in its residential and community-building aspects to the status of being a new township (Searle 2008).

From an employment legacy perspective in the post-event period there have been some positive socio-economic developments in the Sydney Park complex as a whole. The original complex was supported on-site at games-time by the construction of a small group of hotels and a railway station. In the post-event period it has also come to be flanked by the development of commercial office space for over two hundred organisations (including, among others, core divisions of a major national bank, the Commonwealth Bank of Australia, from 2006), together with some additional hotel development from 2008 and various retail and related services. Currently fourteen thousand people are permanently employed across the range of activities now undertaken in the Park (SOPA 2014). The complex has already grown to being something of a busy economic hub in the inner western suburbs of the city, and the planners' vision for the future is to build on this and grow this 'busy economic hub' aspect and its associated employment significantly. The Master Plan 2030 document envisaged 24,000 workers on the site by 2030 (SOPA 2009) and more recently this target has been increased to 31,000 (SOPA 2015). More generally the aim is, by 2030, to achieve a permanently large daily presence of around fifty thousand people on the site, working on it or actively using it in other ways. Besides employees this figure also includes five thousand higher-education students and a daily average of fifteen thousand visitors (Searle 2008) and of course the planned growth of residents noted above can be added to this.

Finally there are the contrasting fortunes of transport and ecology in the Sydney legacy development. Earlier we noted the planning authorities' unimpressive approach to the public-transport challenge posed by the location of the Olympic Park. This weakness has persisted over a decade after the event in spite of tangible evidence of the Park's long-term economic growth potential. Sydney has long had problems and weaknesses in its city-wide transport system, for instance as a major city which still lacks an underground rapid-transit metro system. In 2008 as part of a response to this situation the NSW government created a new agency to begin to plan such a system. Their initial plans included the possibility of creating a line which would directly link downtown Sydney with the inner western suburban hub of Paramatta township. This would have passed through both the Olympic complex site at Homebush Bay and the former Olympic village at Newington, and would have required the building of new metro stations in both locations. However owing to the global financial and economic recession from 2008 onwards and local political changes, plans relating to the metro were officially shelved in 2010 (SMH 2010 and AAP 2010). The new Sydney metro system which is currently being constructed and which will open in the 2020s does not include a link to Homebush Bay and Paramatta (NSW 2014). Access to the Olympic Park may have benefited from other ongoing improvements to the city's overland suburban rail system. In spite of this, in the absence of a direct metro link, the general problem of the connectivity of the Olympic site and of ensuring permanent mass public access to it which we noted earlier looks set to continue into the third decade of the post-Olympic-event period.

The situation is very different and much more positive, as we noted earlier, in relation to the ecological legacy of the Sydney Olympics, the first self-proclaimed 'Green Games'. The approach of the NSW government and SOPA to developing a green frame of various kinds of parklands and open spaces surrounding the Olympic complex to the east, north and north-west has been strategic, sustained and successful. In 2011–12 the parklands attracted 2.7 million visitors (SOPA 2012). In addition part of the planning vision for the new residential community developments envisaged in the coming years, which we have noted above, involves proximity and access for new residents to these publicly valued parklands (Searle 2008, p. 99).

Conclusion

In this chapter we have begun to engage in more detail with the phenomenon of the embedding of mega-event spectacles in various social contexts. We have looked in particular at the Summer Olympic Games and the evolution of their character as potentially transformative projects with long-term impacts and legacies in relation to their host cities. The discussion has recognised the intrinsic structural complexity and multi-dimensionality of mega-events like the Olympics. It has also recognised their inherently risky character – on the one hand typically aiming to promote positive legacies and benefits for host nations and cites, but on the other hand being readily capable of being mismanaged and generating negative legacies instead. In the cases of the Olympics of Montreal

1976 and Athens 2004 we saw that the attempt to manage the balance between risks and benefits arguably resulted in a relatively negative outcome and legacy for each of these host cities. As against this in the cases of Barcelona 1992 and Sydney 2000 we saw that this balance was generally much better managed and resulted in relatively positive outcomes and legacies for these host cities.

Our focus in this chapter has been particularly on Olympic mega-events as urban 'place-makers'. That is they often involve new constructions, on the one hand of sports- and related event-facilities complexes, and on the other hand of community-related developments in housing and employment. And, of course, since the turn of the millennium they are now effectively required by the IOC bidding system to make provision for such tangible urban legacies. We explored these types of event legacy aspects in some detail in the case of the Sydney 2000 Olympic project together with ita ambiguous claims to represent a model for subsequent Olympic cities, However what the Sydney case also pointed to was how mega-events can also be urban space-makers as well as place-makers. That is they have often been associated with the strategically important values of environmentalism and the work of humanising modern urbanisation through the provision of open and green spaces in the heart of cities. As we saw, Sydney's Olympic project gave a powerful stimulus and opportunity to the creation not only of a new urban place (namely a new suburban township constructed in and around the Olympic complex) but also a new urban 'space' (namely the series of parklands surrounding much of the township). However, arguably Expo mega-events have a longer and stronger track-record of such urban space-making than Olympics do, and we will explore this theme in the following chapter.

Notes

1 See for instance Preuss 2004, Gratton and Preuss 2012, Jennings 2012, Kassens-Noor 2012, Chalip 2014 and Preuss 2014. For a recent critical contribution to the debate about the economic nature, costs and benefits of sport mega-events see Zimbalist 2015. For edited collections of mega-event and Olympic studies see for instance Horne and Manzenreiter 2006, Girginov 2010, Gold and Gold 2011b, Mangan and Dyreson 2012, Frawley and Adair 2013, Girginov 2014, Grix 2014, Viehoff and Poynter 2015. Also see OECD 2010, KAS 2011, UNDESA 2012, Economist 2013 and Gotham 2016.

2 For information on the history and significance of major sport stadia see Spampinato 2015 and also Inglis 1996.

3 On the Los Angeles Olympics 1932 see Dyreson and Llewellyn 2012, also Masters 2012, Rosenberg 2015 and Zimmerman 1976.

4 On the 1936 Berlin Olympics see Roche 2000, ch. 4, pp. 112–19, also Meyer 2011.
5 On the urban aspects of the 1948 'austerity Olympics' in London see Essex and Chalkley 1999, p. 379; also Gold and Gold 2011b, pp. 34–5. On the event in general see Hampton 2012 and Polley 2011, ch. 9. On the urban development aspects of the Melbourne and Helsinki Olympics see Essex and Chalkley 1999, p. 379, and also their 1998, pp. 193–4; also Gold and Gold 2011a, pp. 356. On Melbourne's Olympic stadium see MCG 2015, and generally on the Olympics of Helsinki 1952 and Melbourne 1956 see the archives at IOC's website (IOC 1952 and IOC 1956).
6 On urban development aspects of the Rome and Tokyo Olympics see Essex and Chalkley 1999, pp. 379–80, also their 1998, p. 195; also Gold and Gold 2011a, pp. 36–8.
7 See CBC 2013, Latouche 2011, Newton 2012, Wiki 2015a.
8 See for instance Govan 2011 (relating to the post-event outcome for the athletes' village) and Paphitis and Tongas 2014 (generally).
9 On Barcelona see Roche 2000, ch. 5, and for more recent reflections see Monclus 2012 and also Zimbalist 2015, ch. 5.
10 See ESPN/AP 2000. For a more negative assessment of Sydney's event, in both economic and ecological terms see Zimbalist 2015 (e.g. ch. 3).
11 For instance see Cashman 2011, IOC 2012g, also COHRE 2007a, p. 21.
12 On the buzz at Sydney see Waitt 2003, also more generally MacAloon 1992 and Hiller 2012.
13 On NSW and Sydney planning see Marrs 2006, Searle 2008, and SOPA 2009.

6

Mega-events, urban space and social change: Expos, parks and cities

In this chapter we take further the exploration of the relationship between mega-events and cities in the context of long-term social change and with particular reference to the important theme of the significance of social space for modern cities. This develops some of the issues which were considered in relation to cities and Olympics in the previous chapter, this time with special reference to the other main mega-event genre of Expos. As we have seen, discussions at the interface between urban studies and mega-event studies often focus on the built urban environment and on mega-events. They tend to show that mega-events can be what I refer to as place-makers through the spectacular or functional architectural legacies they often leave. Such place-making is, of course, as much a characteristic of Expos as it is of Olympic Games. However, while recognising this characteristic, this chapter aims to give more of an emphasis to what we can refer to as mega-events' role in urban space-making. As we have seen, the cases of the Sydney Olympics and some of its successors appear to embody a substantial interest on the part of contemporary Olympic mega-events in environmental or green themes and legacies. In this chapter we investigate the idea that this is also true of Expos.

The history of Expos, which we look into in this chapter, shows that the greening of this genre of mega-events has been going on for a long time. A focus for an interest in both the greening of mega-events and also their roles in urban space-making is their connection with the conservation or creation of tangibly green spaces in modern cities, in the form of major central city parks. These themes in the analysis of Expos have tended to be overlooked in mega-event studies. So this chapter is intended to contribute to raising their profile in this field and to initiating a better appreciation and understanding of them. To provide historical and empirical foci for and illustrations of more general issues the chapter is organised in four sections and makes use of tabular summaries of relevant information together with detailed case studies

In Chapter 1 we noted the relationship between on the one hand Western modernisation and its associated urbanisation and on the other hand its Faustian pact with the environment (or 'nature' as we might ordinarily refer to it). In the growing global ecological crisis we are currently living through, particularly in our cities, modernity is beginning to 'reap the whirlwind' of its long and determined use and abuse of Nature. In the context of contemporary cities this has led to a growing awareness of, and public discourse and political debate about, the need for concrete and effective actions to promote environmental sustainability at all levels, from that of urban policy leaders to that of ordinary citizens. In some cases, arguably too few and too late, this in turn has led to relevant green actions. Mega-events have become implicated in such actions, and have increasingly been subject to a greening process, particularly in the secondary phase of modernisation. In this context mega-events are imagined and promoted as urban policies which can be (or at least which can be credibly presented to national and international publics as aspiring to being) carriers of green environmentalist and sustainability messages, and can also be potentially influential models for green urban policies in other areas, beside also leaving green legacies for urban citizens.

The chapter is organised in four sections. The 'greening of mega-events' theme whether understood as a committed and substantial policy or more critically as an ideological legitimation, or as a pragmatic combination of both, is the focus of the third and fourth sections. To introduce this theme the first two sections look at the changing versions of 'green city' awareness during and since the first phase of modernisation, with particular reference to the history of the creation and changing public uses of urban parks in the course of the modern development of Western cities. There are strong, if often overlooked, parallels and indeed tangible inter-connections, between what we can refer to as the urban park movement on the one hand and the urban Expo movement on the other. These sections outline the park side of this relationship in order to prepare the way for the consideration of the Expo side of this relationship in the following section.

In the third section, then, the discussion is more focused on Expos and a general exploration of their history of operating as urban park-creating projects, and thus as both space-creating and green projects. It covers both of the two main phases of modernisation and urbanisation, namely the primary phase from the mid-nineteenth to the late twentieth century and the secondary phase from the late twentieth to the early twenty-first century. The discussion in the final section moves to the contemporary period and focuses on a set of case studies of Expos as urban policy projects, particularly in terms of their space-creating, park-creating and green aspects. The cases are those of the European set of contemporary-era Expos, namely Seville 1992 and particularly Lisbon 1998 and Zaragoza 2008.[1]

Cities, culture and nature

An early form of what we might now refer to as green urban culture was that of botanical gardens[2] which originated in the Europe in the early modern period during the Italian Renaissance (for instance in the 1540s in Pisa, Padua and Florence). They were associated with the cultivation of medicinal herbs and the development of university faculties concerned with medical science and technology. Botanical gardens and orangeries developed substantively during the Northern European Renaissance and Enlightenment in the seventeenth and eighteenth centuries in parallel with Europeans' increasing access to and exploitation of other societies and civilisations, particularly in Africa and Asia. This was led at the time by colonisers, traders, explorers and botanical scientists in particular from England and the Netherlands. A notable example of an urban botanical garden from the early part of this period is Amsterdam's Hortus Botanicus founded in 1638, and an influential example from the late eighteenth and early nineteenth centuries is Kew Gardens in London founded in 1840. Another early form of nature culture incorporated into modern urbanism was that of 'zoological gardens'.[3] These developed in Europe from the mid-nineteenth century onwards, as Europeans' abilities to trap and transport exotic animals improved, particularly with the advent of the new technology of steam- powered engines and thus steam ships and railways. Paradigmatic early examples are the zoos established in London (at Regent's Park) in 1828 and Berlin (at the Tiergarten) in 1844. These urban cultural forms and institutions in general, including the particular examples noted here, originated in the primary phase of modernisation. However it is interesting to observe that, in spite of the passage of time and social changes involved in the shift from primary to secondary modernisation, none the less they continue to persist as highly valued and economically valuable elements in the repertoire of contemporary secondary-phase urbanism. However they are now reinterpreted in environmentalist rather than nature-mastery terms, as urban 'heritage' sites and as urban touristic attractions.

One of the foci of our discussion in this book in general and this chapter in particular, namely the Expo genre of mega-events, can be seen as having some of its origins in, and family connections with, a strategic set of modern urban cultural institutions like botanical gardens and zoos. This set also includes museums and art galleries which, in the early and mid-nineteenth century began to migrate socially from being socially exclusive to becoming inclusive, from being private elite preserves to being more open to middle-class and later working-class publics.[4] Exhibitions in these focal urban institutions could be said to contain a mastery of nature theme related to that contained in zoos and botanical gardens, in the capacity of modern 'realist' painting and sculpture to capture (through imagination and creative re-presentation) such things as landscapes, animals and human bodies. However publicly accessible museums and art galleries also contained additional aspects of modernity's civilisational worldview of progress and mastery. Museum collections and exhibitions could be said to display the West's cognitive and political mastery of non-European (colonised) cultures and even of time itself (through the new science and findings of archaeology about classical-era Greece and Rome). Meanwhile art galleries could be said to display Western modernity's mastery of human nature itself (through mimetic technique and experimentalism, and aesthetic creativity) in the fine arts.

The Expo genre of large-scale but transient exhibitions which were staged in the central areas of major Western cities from the mid-nineteenth century onwards drew on and adapted the experience of such permanent urban cultural institutions as museums and art galleries in particular, but also botanical garden and zoos, and in turn they recurrently stimulated public interest in such institutions. A particularly notable and controversial adaptation of one of these institutions into the Expo genre was the development from the late nineteenth to the early twentieth century of 'human zoo' displays. This involved the inclusion of groups of tribal people in Expo programmes, often presented less as alternative non-modern cultures and more as 'primitives' and 'savages' in a discursive frame built on pseudo-scientific ideas of social evolution and 'race'.[5]

In the course of these developments, Expos, along with the urban cultural institutions which influenced them, can be seen to have reflected primary-phase modernity's 'civilisational worldview'. Indeed Expos were often explicitly designed as festivals of progress including the mastery of nature theme that this involved, and they succeeded in communicating this to mass publics throughout the course of the primary phase of Western modernisation.[6] If Expos provided special times for national communities and the international community to celebrate modernity's progress and nature-mastery then the other cultural institutions we have considered here (i.e. botanical garden, zoos, museums and art galleries), which influenced Expos, can be said to have provided special places in cities in which to do so on a less spectacular but more permanent basis. However one additional urban cultural form which was crucial for the existence of both the set of institutions we have discussed here and also for Expos is that of the special space of the urban park.

Cities, parks and the environment

Parks typically provided the open-air spaces within which botanical gardens and zoos were set, and within which museums and art galleries also were often set. In the primary phase of Western modernisation and urbanisation parks played an important if ambiguous role. On the one hand urban parks represented yet another example of modernity's capacity to control nature, in this case to recreate versions of it in the heart of the 'un-natural' and artificial city. On the other hand, even if they were artificially achieved, urban parks offered a tangible alternative to the city's otherwise all-encompassing 'concrete jungle' environment. Such urban spaces were green alternatives, at least in aesthetic terms, and perhaps also in embryonic environmentalist terms. And in addition they were potentially psychologically 'recreative' for people given the pervasive alienation and stress of life in the modern city. We need to consider the topic of urban parks in general, together with their relation to mega-events such as Expos in particular, in more detail and we do this later (in the third section of this chapter).

Contemporary European cities no doubt retain much from premodern historical periods and particularly from the primary phase of Western modernisation. These inheritances include major institutional, architectural and spatial legacies of the kinds of urban cultural forms we have considered here, and which are now often regarded as key elements of urban heritage.[7] However, as we saw in Chapter 1, contemporary cities, together with both the societies in which they are located and also the cultural institutions and events located and staged within them, have all changed considerably in the course of the shift to the secondary phase of modernisation and urbanisation. The main dimensions of this shift were summarily indicated earlier in Tables 1.1 and 1.3. A key element here is the underlying shift in the 'civilisational worldview' away from a nature-mastery version of progress to a new nature-conservation version. We can usefully differentiate and label this new civilisational worldview as being a neo-progress view concerned with the management of late modernity's volatile dialectics between its potential on the one hand for industrially based and now digitally based cornucopia, and on the other hand for ecological apocalypse.

Some causes and reasons for this change no doubt relate to the growing scientific, public and media awareness, in the period from the 1970s to the 1990s and beyond, of the serious and existential nature of the medium- and long-term threats to human livelihoods and life itself around the planet of various inter-related ecological crises. A major driver of these problems has been and remains the excessive use of non-renewable carbon-based energy resources and the air pollution associated with this. The resulting crises take the form of global warming, climate volatility, regional desertification, the melting of polar ice, rising sea levels, oceanic pollution and species extinctions. These crises are now widely recognised to be human-made. That is, they have resulted from unanticipated and/or ignored consequences of the model of economic growth which was created, developed and globally diffused in the primary phase of modernisation, together with the realisation of the profound limitations of its nature mastery worldview and version of its progress.

Modernity's potential global ecological crisis initially developed slowly in the primary phase, but has become manifest and transformational in the secondary phase. Public and policy awareness of this has led to what we can refer to as a green paradigm shift, at least at the level of ideas and ideals, in the contemporary period, and particularly so since the turn of the millennium. This is towards more of a conservationist approach to nature and an approach to economic growth which emphasises sustainability.[8] The latter involves the recognition that the release of carbon into the atmosphere and other negative environmental impacts from the production of commodities, buildings and energy need to be systematically anticipated and minimised, while the technological development and widespread adoption and use of renewable energy sources needs to be maximised. The capacity for societies to achieve some (neo-)progress in these directions has been aided (if largely fortuitously) by the simultaneous occurrence of the digital revolution and associated science-based technologies and their generally potentially positive environmental implications for most forms of production and consumption.[9]

The greening of mega-events and cities

As we have seen, first-phase modernisation and the urbanisation which embodied it involved a self-deluding mastery of nature, which not only resulted in profound damage to nature but also stimulated it to threaten the habitats and lives of its putative masters. In the twenty-first century we are discovering just how profoundly difficult and daunting is the challenge of practically achieving a very different pro-nature green society and economy. None the less a greening of public understandings and policy ideals and aspirations (as distinct from practices) can increasingly be seen, particularly in the West, at all levels, from the international to the national and to the urban. To explore, characterise and assess the forms of greening under way at each of these levels would be a complex task. However it is not necessary to undertake such a task here, as the focus of our discussion remains on mega-events and aspects of urban development connected with them. In Chapter 5 we noted the tendency towards a 'greening of mega-events' tendency in the case of the Olympics, particularly in the influential case of the Sydney 2000 Olympics.[10] In succeeding sections of this chapter we look into the history and contemporary analysis of Expos and also into their contemporary character, particularly in some contemporary European examples of Expos (the 1998 Lisbon and 2008 Zaragoza Expos). In the course of this discussion we will look particularly into the relationship of Expos with the green and open spaces of major urban parks in both the primary and secondary phases of Western modernisation and urbanisation. In order to understand this relationship we need a conceptual and analytical framework, and the following discussion addresses this.

Earlier we noted that the list of urban cultural forms and institutions which have both influenced and been expressed in Expos is a substantial one, including botanical gardens, zoos, museums and art galleries and importantly also in terms of our focus here including urban parks. Indeed the urban cultural institution of the park has largely made the other cultural forms possible in that it has provided the space and material location for most of them as well as for all Expos. In the first phase of modern urbanisation these park-based cultural forms could be said to have an ambiguous meaning. On the one hand they were harbingers of the green worldview which was to become influential in the second phase of modernisation. In this latter aspect they cultivated the growth of a conservationist approach to nature and history. And, particularly in the case of parks, they offered urban publics new opportunities and facilities for recreation, and spaces in which to withdraw from modern urbanism and to encounter nature, albeit in a planned and 'cultivated' form. However, on the other hand, in the primary phase such green aspects are best seen as being embryonic characteristics which came to be more fully developed only in the secondary phase. In their construction and to a lesser extent in their operation each of the urban cultural forms we have discussed, including parks and Expos, incurred environmental costs. In addition each of them contributed to creating a cultural crown for its city, the material reality of which was itself the apotheosis of nature-mastery and of the unnatural. Also, as we saw earlier, each symbolised in its own spheres and in its own ways the subordination of the environment which was involved in the progress worldview.

Nevertheless these observations suggest that in attempting to understand the green aspects of Expos and the parks they are related to, particularly in the secondary phase, we need to give special attention to a number of elements. These are firstly the theme or message that Expos seek to communicate to the mass publics which visit them, secondly the model they provide for other urban projects in terms of their construction and operation, and thirdly the experience of recreational space they offer visitors. Expos and parks in the primary phase tended, in various different ways, to communicate progress messages and to provide an ambiguous combination of nature-mastery and nature-conservation when seen both as model urban projects and also as experiences of lived space.

We can apply these terms of reference when considering the idea that, in the course of the secondary phase of urbanisation, there has been something of a greening of mega-events and also of their varied interactions with host cities. So in the contemporary period mega-events can be said to function as potential 'green messages' in that they can be designed and labelled as carriers of ecological themes. These themes are primarily intended to be communicated widely to the international audience for the event, but also, secondarily, they are intended to be communicated as legitimations within the host city, as legitimations to its residents in the pre-event period and as attractions to its tourists in the post-event period. Mega-events can also be seen as potential green models in their form as demonstrations (to organisations, agencies and policy-makers within the host city) of practical and realisable forms of sustainable venue construction, site operation and event production.

Finally mega-events can be seen as potentially green to the extent that they manage to provide new or renewed urban spaces in which people's lived experience can be described as recreational and recreative. In this recreational space aspect arguably the main type of nature which is being conserved and sustained, or greened, is human nature rather than the eco-system.[11] In tangible terms this aspect refers to the experience not only of mega-event-related parks but also of event-related plazas and other such open and accessible public spaces, in the otherwise built-up and filled-in environment of host cities. Metaphorically put, to the extent that mega-events create or renew such recreational public spaces they can be said to be creating oases in the city's 'concrete jungle' and 'concrete deserts', and thus greening the city by cultivating the humanity of its citizens.

The idea that we are witnessing a greening of mega-events in the contemporary period refers to the idea that they increasingly aim to involve one or more of these three potentially green characteristics relating to message, model and lived space. Later in this chapter this scheme for understanding the greening of mega-events is applied in an exploration of the history and contemporary cases of Expos (see the fourth section below). There we need to address the relationship between Expos and the ostensibly quintessentially green phenomenon of urban parks. The latter are both a vital spatial precondition for Expos and also typically one of their main, if often overlooked, urban legacies. So, to prepare the way for this discussion, we next take a step back to encounter and assess the development and role of urban parks, the main original form of the greening of cities, in relation to the development of Western urbanisation.

Parks, urban space and the public sphere

Urban parks are one of the main physical legacies which some mega-events have left to their host cities and, as we detail later in the following section, this was particularly true of Expos. However first it is necessary to introduce the phenomenon of urban parks and their development more directly and generally, and this requires a reference to the process of industrialisation and the urbanisation associated with it. The processes of industrialisation, the development of capitalist market economies and modernisation in Europe and North America from the nineteenth into the twentieth century were expressed and reflected in the socio-spatial processes of what we can refer to as waves of primary urbanisation.[12] This involved mass internal rural-to-urban migration, mass international migration and, as a result of these migrations, the growth and building of cities. As is well known, primary urbanisation created, as well as expressing, many social problems for the new city-dwelling working classes. These included congested, polluted and insanitary living conditions as well as spatially located poverty and illiteracy. Social policy and ultimately welfare states developed in Europe from the late nineteenth through to the mid-twentieth century in order to counter these problems and literally re-form society. Given the social reality of urbanisation it is comprehensible why this growth of social policy, in fields such as health, education and housing, initially developed in large part at city level and in the form of practical and political interventions in and reconstructions of urban (rather than rural) physical environments.[13]

However, what is less well known is that a key part of this urban social policy prelude to the later development of formal welfare states in Europe involved urban social movements actively promoting the creation of green spaces and parks in Europe's cities.[14] This trend was also followed in the North American cities in this period. That is, parks were often developed precisely as proto-social policy projects through new combinations of city-level governments and urban civil society. Urban social-reform movements promoted the building of parks by landscape architects and associated professions for reasons of public welfare, public education and collective therapy. This was particularly evident in Britain, the leading society in the West's industrial revolution, and we look in a little more detail at this in the following section on Expos and parks, and also again in Chapter 8 on mega-events in London.

The great central city parks we are familiar with in Western cities were largely a product of the nineteenth-century park movement. This occurred within the primary urbanisation process which was such a core feature of early Western industrialisation and modernisation. They continue to be popular and well used both by resident communities and visiting publics in the contemporary period and are increasingly recognised as part of cities' and national societies' civic and national 'heritage'.[15] The public and policy meanings and experiences associated with urban parks in Western societies have evolved over the course of the modernisation process. The original rationales were those of welfare and education, literally people's 're-creation', related to needs and rights of public access to such things as daylight, relatively clean air, natural grasslands, woodlands and lakes, varieties of trees and flowers including from foreign countries, and 'official' national and local state monuments and memorials of various kinds. However over time other rationales have come to be attached to parks. Increasingly in the twentieth century in the West, and thus into the phase of secondary urbanisation (deindustrial and post-industrial etc.) parks came to be seen as sites of public leisure and entertainment. Later, into the early twenty-first they also came to be seen as sites of public awareness and appreciation of ecological values, as well as potential hubs of economic development. The development of these and other related rationales for and models of parks in Western societies is summarised in Table 6.1.

Table 6.1 maps out five main types of park which have been distinctive expressions and achievements of five main periods in the development of urban policy and social policy, namely the 'pleasure ground' (1830–1900), the 'social reform park' (1900–30), the 'recreation facility' (1930–70), the 'open space urban system' (1970–90) and the ecologically oriented 'green park' (1990 to present). This analysis was originally created by the American sociologist and

Table 6.1 The development of park types in city-building in modernity: an American typology

	The Pleasure Ground 1830–1900	The Social Reform Park 1900–30	The Recreation Facility 1930–70	The Open Space Urban System 1970–90	The Green Park 1990 to present
Site size and shape	Large, e.g. 1,000+ acres	Small, city blocks	Small to medium	Varied; irregular sites	Varied; 'wetland' parks; use of linear 'corridor' parks to link sites
Social policy aims	Public health, Sport and fitness, and social reform	Social reform; children's play; class and ethnic assimilation	Recreation service; response to public demand	Participation; revitalise city	Human health; ecological values
Main promoters	Idealists; health reformers; land speculators	Social reformers; recreation professionals	Politicians; bureaucrats; planners	Politicians; ecologists; artists; designers	Ecologists; localists; volunteers
Main intended users	All urban citizens (in reality = middle class)	Children, working class, immigrants	Suburban families	Diverse: from poor urban youth to middle class	All urban citizens; wildlife
Relation to the city	Compare and contrast (Nature against city life)	Accept migrants and adapt all people to city life	Help incorporate suburbs into city	Reflect 'city as work of art'	Links with city as nature plus art; part of urban life-quality system

Source: Adapted from Cranz and Boland 2004

urban policy researcher Galen Cranz (Cranz 1989).[16] It is presented in conceptual and heuristic terms and not as a set of empirical descriptions. So in the complex realities of any particular city it may be possible to see the co-existence of a number of these types as features of the organisation and public usage of particular major parks. The types are fairly self-explanatory, and further information about key aspects of each of them is contained in Table 6.1. These aspects include the various distinctive shapes and sizes of park site, the changing social policy aims they embody, what social interest groups supported their development, which social categories and groups were their main intended users and what their general relation was to cities and urban life.

It is noticeable that the health-oriented pleasure ground type was the first and probably most important type.[17] This type's sites involved the largest commitments of urban land, and also it was dominant for the longest period, throughout the mid- and late nineteenth century. The fortunes of this type of park have waxed and waned over the generations and on into the current phase of secondary urbanisation in Western societies. But it still remains influential and is basic for understanding the subsequent additions and modifications in the concept of public open spaces in cities which have occurred since. The most recent of these is the emergence of a type we can refer to as the 'green park model.[18] This type of park can involve such projects as the restoration of land damaged by the modern city and its industries, the restoration of pre-existing waterways both in their courses and water quality, the re-creation of wetland and wildlife habitats, and a commitment to the recycling of park waste and to sustainability in park constructions, infrastructures and technologies. It responds to public awareness of and concern about the contemporary global ecological crisis which has grown markedly on all continents and in all societies and cities in recent times. Major city parks can have the effect of making ecological values and meanings into tangible experiences for the denizens of our contemporary crowded metropolises. As we see in the following section, mega-events, and particularly Expos, have tended to promote the major pleasure ground type of park in the past, and its aspects remain important in the kind of urban parks which mega-events continue to promote in the present. In addition, as we saw earlier in the case of the 2000 Sydney Olympics, and as we will see later in the case of the 2010 Shanghai Expo, mega-events in the contemporary period typically aim to make a contribution to the ecological policy agenda by leaving green parks, often including wetlands, as key elements in their urban legacies.

The original typology of parks which underlies Table 6.1 is based on Cranz's study of the history and nature of parks in cities in the US. Arguably it is also a useful guide to some of the main stages and characteristics of the development of urban parks in their relation to wider social changes in the long process of Western modernisation. However it needs to be interpreted and enhanced when considering its application also to the history of urban parks in Europe. Firstly, the political, economic and cultural history of European countries and their cities is evidently much longer and deeper than that of the USA. In particular, unlike those in the US, European political systems, even in the period of early modernity, were monarchical until the seventeeth century (Britain) and eighteenth (France), and were composed of conflicting and changing combinations of monarchism and democratic parliamentarianism throughout the main stage of modernisation in the nineteenth and early twentieth centuries. Monarchical power and authority manifested themselves materially in European cities in the form of the building of great palaces and great parks. The former advertised monarchs' and aristocrats' status to the urban public, the latter advertised their culture and quality of life (including their commitment to hunting, horseriding and associated elite leisure pursuits).

Parks endured in the primary phase of European modernisation and its associated urbanisation for various reasons deriving from other aspects of pre-modern tradition beyond the rootedness of many urban open spaces in monarchical authority and aristocratic class interest. In addition there was the rootedness of areas of common land in traditions of public access and usage (for instance for food gathering and animal grazing). These open spaces (in Britain identifiable in cities through such place names as 'commons' and 'fields') may have originally been part of rural life, but became incorporated into urban life as cities expanded, often carrying their traditional rights and uses with them. The open spaces of parks and common lands within cities also served the important political purpose of providing sites of assembly and training for citizen militias and armies, and the important economic and cultural purposes of providing sites for periodic markets and trade fairs.

Given all of this it is clear that, as useful as it is, the American-angled picture of the development of urban parks in Table 6.1 needs to be modified and interpreted in relation to Europe's history in a number of respects. The pleasure ground type and its appearance and development in the period 1830–1900 may be the place to begin the story of the creation and sustaining of parks and open spaces in prominent locations in towns and cities in the US. However this does not work in the same way for European towns and cities. Other factors, including class-based and political dynamics involving democratisation helped to shape the origins of European cities and their parks. Apart from periodic and usually short-lived revolutions, the mainstream history of democratisation in Europe is what the British cultural sociologist Raymond Williams usefully conceptualised as a political and cultural 'long revolution'.[19] In relation to parks this meant that movements of people from the new middle and working classes mobilised themselves for a number of goals. Undoubtedly, as in America, the creation of new major public parks had a high priority for such movements. But in Europe, unlike America, there were also parallel movements and projects aimed at opening up access for all citizens to pre-existing and long-established urban parks which had traditionally been claimed as an exclusive and exclusionary preserve of the upper classes. These traditional parks needed not only to be initially accessed by and for the public but also, in the longer term, to be defended by the public against predatory land development and capitalistic development. In the contemporary period such parks are often regarded as important heritage sites with significance both for the collective memories and identities of national and urban citizens, and also for national and international visitors' interests in cities and thus for urban tourism economies. These factors and dynamics inevitably make both the prehistory and also the recent history of nineteenth-century public pleasure grounds more complex in the European case than in the American case.

In other respects the European experience with the development of urban parks is arguably less complex than the American experience. Firstly, the economic background was very different in the two continents. American economic growth in the twentieth century was faster and stronger than that of Europe for many reasons, for instance the self-destructiveness of Europe's world wars and the decline of its ability to exploit overseas empires. Thus America became more ostentatiously engaged with consumer-based capitalism and consumer culture, and associated urban dynamics such as car-ownership and suburbanisation, earlier than Europe. Parks as 'recreation facilities' incorporating suburbs into cities (see Table 6.1) may have developed as early as the interwar period in America, but this was a much later postwar experience for much of Europe.

Secondly, there is the social role of parks as common spaces promoting co-existence in ethnically diverse societies. This was a further development of the social role they had developed prior to this of providing a common space, or a tangible spatial and cultural public sphere (see note 4) for co-existence between social classes in Britain as well as the US. As a society founded on successive waves of immigration America has always had to engage one way or another, and particularly in its cities, with the challenge of culturally integrating a rapidly changing society composed of a variety of ethnicities. Parks, particularly the social reform park model, evidently played an important role in this process for the US and its cities as early as the early decades of the twentieth century. As a continent of emigration rather than of immigration Europe was not in this kind of position in this period. However in the twenty-first European societies have begun to face mounting waves of immigration from Africa and the Middle East, as well as accelerated migratory flows within the EU stimulated by the EU's continent-wide labour market. They have begun to become as culturally complex and effectively multicultural as American society always has been. Europe's early twentieth-century experience of parks as having some potential for promoting cultural integration mainly related to the common space they offered to different social classes. However, a century later Europe's experience of the integrationist potential of parks has belatedly followed the American path. It now includes policy and public understandings of the role of parks in relation to the challenges of ethnic diversity and multiculturalism in modern European societies as well as those related to persistence within them of class differences and inequalities.[20] In contemporary European cities parks can be interpreted as providing sociologically significant spaces and opportunities for both special and mundane displays of multicultural co-existence and tolerance by immigrants and natives.

Overall in Western societies, particularly the phase of secondary urbanisation, parks provide significant points of reference in the urban landscape for the promotion of various (and sometimes conflicting) types of values and policies, from traditional recreation to consumer culture, from heritage and collective memory to contemporary arts and performances, from economic growth to ecology. But in addition contemporary urban parks can be interpreted as representing material incarnations of the otherwise abstractly political notion and value of the public sphere. As such in my view they remain an underrecognised, but objectively important, element in the cultural and social life of cities in our times.[21] Since mega-events have often contributed to the history of major urban parks in many cities around the world, past and present, we now need to explore this relationship further.

Mega-events, urban space and green challenges: Expos and parks

Expos and legacy spaces in cities

Our discussion of the history of Expos so far has indicated that Expos have left urban legacies of various kinds in their host cities since the mid-nineteenth century. These include notable material spectacles such as the Eiffel Tower in Paris and the Space Needle in Seattle. In addition they have left functional cultural complexes such as London's 'Albertopolis' museum zone (which we look at further in Chapter 8). However in this section I want to draw attention to something which is often underplayed or even overlooked about Expos' urban impacts and legacies. This is that they have often left notable urban physical legacies which are spatial rather than physical, and which are the product of landscape architecture rather than conventional constructive architecture. That is, Expos have often left important urban parks as one of their main urban legacies.

In the previous section we suggested that the urban park-making movement needs to be understood in the context of long-term social changes involved in the modernisation process, including from primary to secondary stages of urbanisation. In addition urban park-making processes have sometimes been assisted by the staging of mega-events in general, and Expos in particular. Some highlights from the history of the staging of Expos and their relevance for urban park creation (and/or park development) are noted in Table 6.2. We consider

Table 6.2 Expos and legacy urban spaces: urban parks and cultural complexes 1850–2010

Primary phase: 1850–1970		Secondary phase: 1970–2010	
Year and city	'Legacy' urban spaces	Year and city	'Legacy' urban spaces
1854 London	Crystal Palace Park[1]	1975 Okinawa	Ocean Expo Park entertainments complex
1862 etc. London	'Albertopolis' complex[1]		
1867 Paris	Champ de Mars[2]	1985 Tsukuba	New town
1873 Vienna	Prater Park[2]	1986 Vancouver	False Creek waterside, cultural and community spaces
1875 Philadelphia	Fairmont Park[2]	1988 Brisbane	Cultural and exhibition area, Brisbane riverside
1888 Glasgow	Kelvingrove Park[2]		
1888 Barcelona	Ciutadella Park		
1893 Chicago	Jackson Park	1992 Seville	Alamillo Park, Quadalquivir riverside
1904 St Louis	Forest Park[2]		

Table 6.2 Expos and legacy urban spaces: urban parks and cultural complexes 1850–2010 (Continued)

Primary phase: 1850–1970		Secondary phase: 1970–2010	
Year and city	'Legacy' urban spaces	Year and city	'Legacy' urban spaces
1929 Barcelona	Plaza d'España, Montjuïc complex	1993 Taejon	Expo Park, entertainments complex
1929 Seville	Maria Luisa Park, Guadalquivir riverside	1998 Lisbon	(See Table 6.3 and discussion in the fourth section below)
1935 Brussels	Heysel complex	2000 Hanover	(See Table 6.3)
1937 Paris	Trocadero gardens, Seine riverside	2005 Aichi	(See Table 6.3)
1939–40 New York	Flushing Meadow park	2008 Zaragoza	(See Table 6.3 and discussion in the fourth section below)
1951 etc. London	Southbank complex, Thames riverside		
1962 Seattle	Seattle Center Park	2010 Shanghai	(See discussion in Chapter 7)
1967 Montreal	Jean Drapeau Park, St Lawrence river		
1970 Osaka	Suita new town		

Sources: Monclus 2009, Findling and Pelle 2008, and the BIE website (www.bie-paris.org/)
Notes
1 See the discussion of 'Albertopolis' and the impacts of mega-events on London in Chapter 8.
2 These Expo sites were pre-existing urban parks which, none the less, were significantly conserved and/or developed as a result of staging Expo events.

them here in relation to the two main phases of Western urbanisation discussed earlier. For the purposes of this discussion these phases are those which are roughly indicated in Table 1.3 as the periods 1850–1970 (in the primary phase) and 1970 to present (the secondary phase) and in the information summarised in the table in the left-hand and right-hand set of columns respectively. We will take them each in turn.

Expos and urban parks (1): primary urbanisation phase (1850–1970)

The process of primary urbanisation associated with Western modernisation was experienced earliest in Britain owing to the country's leadership in the industrial revolution of the late eighteenth and early nineteenth centuries. In northern Britain in particular industrialisation was strongly accompanied by waves of urbanisation. These created numerous new dynamic hubs of population and production growth in ports and areas of coal-mining, steel and textile production such as Manchester, Liverpool, Newcastle and Sheffield, which rapidly evolved to become major cities. In Britain these processes in turn fuelled the push to social and political modernisation which characterises the country's history throughout the nineteenth century. They came to be matched by comparable primary urbanisation processes in other countries in the West, particularly in industrial and port regions in western European countries and in east and central US, and also around Western capital cities.

Primary urbanisation processes, as part of more general modernisation processes and together with the social conflicts they involved, were, of course, expressed in the extension and intensification of new building in cities (Table 1.3, first and second columns). These city-building processes necessarily consumed and filled urban space. However as we saw in the previous section simultaneously efforts were also made by some, particularly reformist, urban policy-makers both to create and to protect space in cities, in particular through the urban park movement. The staging of Expo events in the mid- and late nineteenth century gave an undoubted stimulus to the creation of central city parks, particularly in the US and Europe, and we consider this further below. However, as we noted in the previous section, primary urbanisation in Europe could also involve the conservation of pre-existing parks as well as the creation of new ones, and Expos can be argued to have made a contribution on this front also.

European cities had often inherited traditional parks from the eighteenth century and earlier, and a number of notable European Expos were simply able to make use of them as temporary stages and environmental frames for their events. The pre-eminent case of a city which periodically devoted a pre-existing central city park to the cause of staging Expos was Paris. Most of its great Expo events, namely those of 1867, 1878, 1889 and 1937, were staged in the Champ de Mars.[22] Other notable cases included the London 1851 Expo staged in Hyde Park, the Vienna 1873 Expo staged in Prater Park, and various

Glasgow Expos and national exhibition events (1888, 1901 and 1911) which were staged in Kelvingrove Park. In the London 1851 case the British Parliament required that the Expo should conserve and not remove some of Hyde Park's tall trees. This in turn required the architect of the Crystal Palace building housing the event, Joseph Paxton, to make an unanticipated modification to his original design. The need to make room inside the large structure for some of the park's trees led him to add a transept structure with a curved glass roof, which has since been seen as architecturally innovative and iconic.[23] In these and other such cases Expos' park-promoting influences can be said to have expressed cities' high collective valuation of their pre-existing traditional urban parks and demonstrated their public utility. In these ways these events can be said to have defended the conservation of some key urban public spaces against predatory commercially or politically driven development pressures and claims in the turbulent construction processes involved in primary urbanisation.

The case of Britain is relevant in this respect. Britain's capital city, London, and also its major ports and northern industrial cities tend to be marked by centrally located urban public parks. These are a mixture of traditional sites and modern creations. It is worth noting, at this point, that Joseph Paxton, the designer of 1851 London Expo's Crystal Palace, was an equally innovative designer in the park movement. He created a major park at Sydenham in south London as the recreational frame for the relocation and reuse of his Crystal Palace building in 1854. Earlier, in 1847 he had designed Britain's first ever public urban park in Birkenhead near Liverpool, and in 1852 he created a comparable central urban park for the city of Glasgow at Kelvingrove which, as we have seen, was subsequently used by a number of Expo-type events.[24]

Paxton's work helped to stimulate the park movement not only in Britain but also in the USA, particularly through his influence on the legendary nineteenth-century American park-builder and landscape architect Frederick Olmsted. During a long and pioneering career Olmsted was responsible for the design and construction of major pleasure-ground-type urban parks in many American cities. Cranz and Boland even refer to this park type as 'Olmsted parks'.[25] In particular he was ultimately responsible for the design of one of the most important and influential parks ever to be created in Western society's primary phase of urbanisation, namely Central Park on Manhattan in New York city (on Olmsted's Central Park masterpiece see Heckscher 2008). Olmsted had been originally inspired in his vocation by Paxton's work and example after a visit to Birkenhead Park in 1850. Also, as with Paxton, Olmstead contributed to Expos as well as parks. His most notable contribution in this respect is his responsibility for the design and construction of Jackson Park in Chicago. This was originally created for the 1893 Chicago Expo, but it remains an Expo legacy and part of the city's physical and historical heritage. Both Paxton in Britain and his followers in Britain, and also Olmsted and his followers in America, embody the early links between the park movement on the one hand and the Expo-staging movement on the other. The links continued through the twentieth century and, as we see next, they have, if anything, been revived in the early twenty-first.

Expos and urban parks (2): secondary urbanisation phase (1970 to present)

The rise of both the Olympic and the Expo forms of mega-event was associated with, as we have seen so far, and socially embedded in, the primary phase of modernisation which in turn was mainly characterised in the West by the process of industrialisation. The urbanisation connected with this primary phase was most visibly manifested in the rise of industrial cities and also of the port and trade cities associated with them whose operations enabled intercity economic networks to develop at national and international level. Mega-events in more recent decades, at least in the West, are associated with and embedded in a secondary phase of modernisation and in the secondary forms of urbanisation associated with this (see Table 1.3, third and fourth columns). Some of the main continuities and differences between these two phases can now be briefly indicated.

A continuity between these phases is the persistence of the dominant political economic ideology of pro-market liberalism. This has been reanimated in the contemporary era particularly since the oil crisis of the 1970s in what has come to be referred to as neoliberalism.[26] Apart from this the main differences between the phases, for the purposes of our discussion, can be simplified by referring to the post-industrial (and particularly digital) character of economy and society in the secondary phase. In addition, as we have already considered, this phase has been characterised, particularly since the 1990s, by the rise of globalisation in economic and other spheres. Finally it has also been characterised by the rise of 'environmentalism' as the industrial era's long exploitation of nature's finite and non-renewable resources has generated global warming and other such crises leading to the urgent need to move to a more sustainable economic system worldwide.

These secondary-phase structural tendencies have influenced the development of both national societies and also the international community of national societies in the West from the 1970s onwards. They have been felt and manifested at all levels in national societies, and most notably at the level of cities. Both individually and in their various complex and sometimes conflictual combinations these factors and vectors have been manifested generally in major Western cities, in their material cityscapes as well as in the quality and style of life of their communities. They have particularly been manifested in the recurrent spatio-temporal urban-policy focus among such cities which is provided by competing to stage mega-events and using such events as markers and catalysts of significant long-term urban changes and legacies.

As we have seen, mega-events can leave physical markers and legacies ranging from spectacular pieces of 'starchitecture' to unspectacular functional complexes for sport and/or cultural activities. Both the spectacle of the event as a short-term performance and these long-lasting event-originated constructions are manifestations of a combination of the factors and vectors we have discussed. No doubt the detailed nature of their combination varies from event to event, and from one host city context to another. However in our discussion of such event-originated material legacies and their impacts on host-city social life and cityscapes we have attempted to provide a more contextualised and balanced picture of them than is usually achieved. That is we have attempted to recognise on the one hand the new and persisting presence of substantive buildings which are often bequeathed to urban publics by mega-events and also, on the other hand, the new and persisting presence of urban spaces they can also often leave. The former is the product of forms of architecture (whether familiar or unfamiliar) and thus of projects of filling urban space: however the latter is very different. By comparison with event-originated conventional architecture the latter is the product of landscape architecture and thus of projects of renewing, creating or opening urban space. I suggest that when analysing the strategic urban spaces often temporarily occupied and then left behind as legacies by mega-events we need to recognise more than we have in the past this duality between space-filling projects (starchitecture and/or functional complexes) on the one hand and space-opening projects (park renewal or creation) on the other.

In Chapter 5 we saw that Olympic events in both primary and secondary phases of modernisation and urbanisation have often left host cities with space-filling constructions involving great stadia and associated sport complexes. In the secondary phase, since roughly the 1970s, some of these have been framed within elements of an urban park context which they have, none the less, tended to dominate and overshadow. In more recent times, particularly since the Sydney 2000 Olympics, they have been associated with the construction of major new urban parks. As is indicated in Table 6.3, in this period Expos have sometimes also bequeathed space-filling cultural and/or entertainment-oriented constructions and complexes to their host cities, as in the cases of Okinawa 1975, Brisbane 1988, Taejon 1993, Lisbon 1998, London 2000 and Shanghai 2010. Also they have increasingly been associated with urban development projects of various kinds, including new housing and communities, as in the cases of Tsukuba 1985 and Vancouver 1986. However these urban developments have often included, as they had done in the primary phase, major urban space-opening projects involved in creating or reanimating parks, whether of a conventional kind or of a more unconventional linear (e.g. waterside or riverside) kind. Examples here include Vancouver 1986, Brisbane 1988, Seville 1992, Lisbon 1998, Aichi 2005, Zaragoza 2008 and Shanghai 2010.

In the secondary phase parks in general and event-generated parks in particular are coming to have a new significance for urban publics and leaderships as attractive and open spatial hubs serving a number of post-industrial purposes. The most basic of these is often that of the rescue (or remediation) of strategically located zones of urban land which industrial-era activities had polluted, rendered dangerous for human uses, and thus effectively made useless. Mega-event projects require the restoration of such urban land in a form which is demonstrably benign and available for ordinary human uses. The creation of post-industrial-era parks in previously industrial areas is a notable way of doing this. It can provide a particularly clear and meaningful exemplification and symbol of the potential for event-legacies to contribute to positive urban transformation for contemporary publics. However, in addition contemporary event-generated parks can also revive and renew, in ways adapted to post-industrial times, the original primary-phase or industrial-era purposes of parks as social-policy and cultural-integration projects, namely as urban pleasure grounds and recreation facilities. In the industrial era this kind of park-building was mainly for urban citizens; in the post-industrial era, in addition, it usually aims to add to a city's attraction for national and international tourists.

The other main post-industrial-era purpose served by event-generated parks relates to ecology. Recent Expos, notably those in Europe at Zaragoza in 2008 and in China at Shanghai in 2010, have each involved the creation of significant new green parks as permanent urban legacies on parts of the event-site. Each of these event-legacy parks has been designed to exemplify environmental values as well as providing opportunities for recreation. These are some of the more explicit examples of what can be referred to as the greening of mega-events in the early twenty-first century. We look into the case of Zaragoza in the following section, and the case of Shanghai in the following chapter.

The greening of contemporary mega-events: European Expos, environmentalism and urban space
Background

Since their origins in the mid- to late nineteenth century, mega-events genres have often been designed and delivered in ways which could be wasteful of materials and energy, not to mention also of financial resources. However, as we have noted earlier, the contemporary period has witnessed the growth of the global ecological crisis and also of public awareness of this. Mega-event organisers and interested publics now increasingly expect that both Expo and Olympic events will be designed and operated in ways which can be seen to respect environmentalist values. For instance it is expected that the carbon footprint of such events' building materials and energy needs should be minimised. In addition, where possible, it is expected that mega-events should leave a legacy of urban spaces which, among other things, are likely to have a green and recreational park character. So, as was suggested earlier, we can say that a development has occurred in the contemporary (or secondary-phase) period which can be referred to as the greening of mega-events.[27]

Cases of mega-events which particularly exemplify this greening process in the contemporary period include the Lisbon 1998 Expo, the Sydney 2000 Olympics, Zaragoza Expo 2008, the Shanghai 2010 Expo and the London 2012 Olympics. Many of the main contemporary cases are listed in Table 6.3 together with their urban spatial legacies, which have often been new urban parks. We discuss this summary in a moment, and then look into two of the Expo cases listed which exemplify the greening of mega-events in more detail, namely the European Expo events of Lisbon 1998 and Zaragoza 2008. In addition we explore the Shanghai 2010 and London 2000 cases later (in Chapters 7 and 8 respectively). However, to help analyse this greening phenomenon in these cases, it is first useful to rehearse some of the relevant framework ideas which were introduced earlier.

In the first section of this chapter it was suggested that a useful conceptual framework for analysing the greening of mega-events and their impacts and legacies in the contemporary period needed to be one which recognised and addressed three aspects of mega-events and their legacies. These aspects are their messages, their status as policy models and their provision of recreational space. To apply this framework in concrete cases, however, it needs to be allowed that that 'green' aspects of mega-event messages and models can sometimes be taken at face value, rather than, as in some cases, as deliberately misleading 'greenwash' (as, for instance, in the 2014 Sochi Winter Olympic project).[28] It also needs to be recognised that such messages and models can co-exist with other aspects which are not necessarily environmentally relevant. So mega-event messages to international audiences are often mixed, and alongside any green message they can also include messages relating to the renewal of host-city images aimed at attracting tourists. Similarly mega-events can be influential as policy project models in various ways in addition to being green models. For instance as policy models they can be influential in terms of their general effectiveness in delivering various legacies, particularly that of the urban regeneration associated with socio-economic development.

Finally, to apply the framework in concrete cases, the idea of urban recreational space, and indeed of the urban quality of life and public sphere more generally, needs to be enriched by being interpreted as including people's freedoms and capacities for mobility and access to such places and spaces. Thus this aspect and version of the greening of mega-events and their legacies suggests that a wider view should be taken of them which includes the degree to which they provide new public transport infrastructures. As with so many other aspects of life in the contemporary period, mega-event projects are increasingly recognised by environmentalist organisations as important fields of policy and are assessed by them in a technical manner in terms of their environmental impacts.[29] The approach I am taking here to the characterisations of mega-events as potentially 'green' projects is less formal, more qualitative and also more sociologically oriented. We return to these topics when considering the two contemporary European Expo cases later. To prepare the way for that we can first briefly review a relevant aspect of the greening of contemporary mega-events in Table 6.3.

Table 6.3 The greening of urban events: mega-events and legacy parks, 1998–2012

Expos		Summer Olympic games
Universal	Specialised	
Hanover 2000 (Only an Exhibition facilities complex)	*Lisbon 1998* Jardim do Passeio dos Herois do Mar Waterfront access	*Sydney 2000* Sydney Olympic Park Wetlands Waterfront access
	(London 2000) (Only an Exhibition facilities complex)	
	Aichi 2005 Expo Memorial (Morocoro) Park	*Athens 2004* (Only a Sports facilities complex)
Shanghai 2010 Houtan wetland park Waterfront access	*Zaragoza 2008* Water Park Waterfront access	*Beijing 2008* Olympic Forest Park
		London 2012 Queen Elizabeth II Olympic Park Waterfront access

Sources: Monclus 2009, Findling and Pelle 2008. On Olympics see the IOC website (www.olympic.org/). On Shanghai and Beijing see chapter 7; on Lisbon and Zaragoza see this chapter; on Sydney and Athens see chapter 5; and on London see chapter 8

Part II of this book has suggested that contemporary mega-event projects need to be seen as consisting of both their preparations for and their staging of an event, and also of the post-event urban legacies these processes leave and/or present for further development. In addition, as we have seen, these projects commonly claim, as one of their main dimensions, to have a nature-conserving environmentalist or green character, not only in theory (e.g. as an Expo theme or message) but also in practice. The practical and tangible aspect often takes the form of the renewal or creation of a major urban green park, which in the post-event period becomes a permanent space within the hosts' cityscapes. In my view this is an important but too little noticed and commented on fact about contemporary mega-events and their legacies. It connects with the increasing importance which is being more generally given to the provision of recreational space in contemporary cities. In this respect arguably mega-event urban-park legacies have the potential to act not only as practical contributions but also as more widely influential models for both the greening and the humanisation of urbanisation processes in the contemporary period.

Table 6.3 summarises the linkage between the main mega-events and urban-legacy parks and spaces in this period. New green parks were created as urban legacies of the Expos staged in Lisbon 1998, Aichi 2005, Zaragoza 2008 and Shanghai 2010 and also by the Olympic Games of Sydney 2000 and London 2012. There were, of course, some 'exceptions which prove the existence of the rule'. Thus in the Expo at Hanover in 2000 and the Olympic Games at Athens in 2004, and in their site legacies, there was an emphasis on the provision of built-up facilities and an absence of strong environmental or green aspects. The same can be said for the large-scale Expo-type but nationally oriented event, the Millennium Exhibition, staged in London in 2000. In Table 6.3 mega-events' recreational space legacies are mainly indicated by green parks. But, as the Table also notes, they can be said to also include waterfront access. This public access can involve linear parks and walks giving people the opportunity to experience new open spaces and vistas over water. In the mega-event cases of new water-front access listed in the Table 6.3, namely those of Lisbon, Sydney, Zaragoza, Shanghai and London, the new urban recreational spaces this offers are those of riverscapes. However in principle and in the future they could also include seascapes, as they have occasionally done in the past (for instance the Port Olimpic and Port Vell seafront developments which were among the legacies of the Barcelona 1992 Olympics).

Before we move on it is worth noting some interesting absences from the set of mega-events covered in Table 6.3, namely Winter Olympic events. Although somewhat smaller-scale than their Summer Olympic relatives, Winter Olympics remain usually large-scale and costly events with the capacity to create long-term socio-economic development and environmental legacies. However, they are not included in Table 6.3 because our focus here is on host cities rather than host regions, as would be needed to incorporate Winter Olympics. For obvious reasons Winter Olympics need to be set in high mountainous regions which are dominated by agricultural industries and where it is rare to find major cities. These regions may have the status of being (national) parkland, even if they might also be relatively near to a city and thus be relatively accessible to the public. However their relationship with the environment and environmentalism can be ambiguous. Their mountainous settings guarantee that, at least in their media coverage, they can appear as celebrations of a picturesque version of nature and of the natural environment as a context and challenge for winter sport. In addition the transport infrastructures they require to access the sports sites and settings can open up what are effectively rural areas and populations to new publics and to social and economic development associated with sport- and entertainment-based tourism. Thus they can increase the recreational space available to nearby urban populations as much as or more than might be achieved by the creation of a major new park within the host city of a Summer Games.

Winter Olympics in the contemporary period, particularly after the IOC's post-Sydney formalisation of its interest in Olympic legacies including 'green legacies, have tended to be assessed as having fairly positive green characteristics. The Games events of Salt Lake City 2002, Turin 2006 and Vancouver 2010 fall into this category, although Sochi 2014 does not.[30] Unlike urban events' frequently demonstrated capacities to remediate polluted 'brownfield' land, Winter Olympics inevitably run risks of inflicting significant damage on relatively pristine natural environments by opening up and building winter sports facilities and townships in these areas. The world was reminded of these risks in the case of the 2014 Sochi Winter Olympics in Russia and its negative environmental impacts and legacies in an area which is both a national park and also a UNESCO World Heritage site.[31]

European Expos, environmentalism and urban space

To recognise the trend towards the greening of mega-events in the contemporary period and to grasp it more concretely we can now take a look at some Expos in more detail. To do so we focus on the cases of the Lisbon Expo in 1998 and the Zaragoza Expo in 2008, prefaced with some observations about the Seville Expo in 1992.[32] Earlier we noted the BIE's category differences, together with the associated organisational differences, between 'Universal' and 'Special' types of Expo.[33] So it is worth mentioning at this point that the Seville Expo was categorised as an example of the bigger and longer universal type, and the Lisbon and Zaragoza events were categorised as being examples of the somewhat smaller and shorter type. It is also worth observing that these three events taken together represent an interesting development in the history of Expos in the twentieth and early twenty-first centuries. That is they represent a re-entry of medium-sized European cities into the world of staging Expos in what we have been referring to as the secondary phase of modernisation. In much of the preceding postwar period, for over a generation since the Brussels Expo of 1958, all European cities – whether, on the one hand of first-tier world city status, or on the other hand of second-tier medium-sized city status – had withdrawn from engagement with this particular genre of mega-event. This was unlike the situation in North America and Asia in this period where cities' interests in staging Expos had been continuous. Thus the three cities under consideration here represent a new European re-engagement with the potential contemporary usefulness and relevance of this mega-event genre.

The Lisbon and Zaragoza events have been generally regarded as reasonably successful examples of environmentally conscious Expos. And in my view this assessment can be supported when considering the green character of the messages, models and recreational spaces they provided in their events and event-legacies. In these respects they differed somewhat from the Seville event's environmental weaknesses. Indeed it has been observed that the planning processes for the Lisbon and Zaragoza events were each influenced by an awareness of the preceding Seville event and its weaknesses, and thus by the aim to improve on this record in terms of both the regeneration and the greening of cities which host Expos (Monclus 2009, p. 88). However while they can be reasonably assessed as having some success in terms of the greening agenda, outcomes have been more mixed in terms of regeneration.

A flawed model: the 1992 Seville Expo

Seville's Expo site was located on an island-type area across the river Guadalquivir from the centre of the city. The thematic message of this Expo was an updated version of the long-familiar idea of progress through science and technology. It was well attended at event-time, attracting over forty million visits. Its main urban legacies were a science, technology and business park, a theme park ('Isla Magica') and improved river crossings (particularly via the spectacular Alamillo bridge designed by the 'starchitect' Santiago Calatrava). Over the course of the post-event period, and after a problematic beginning in an uninspiring setting, the technology park has become reasonably successful and now provides around ten thousand jobs (Monclus 2009, p. 93). Also over the course of this period there have been some green developments. On the one hand public access to and use of the banks of the river have been improved by means of linear parks. And on the other hand what had been, at event-time, a limited nearby nature reserve has subsequently been developed into a substantial public wetland and green park (the Alamillo Park).

However the development of this general area of the city has not been as successful as it might have been. In the year of 1992 Seville's event was overshadowed both within Spain and internationally by the perceived success of the simultaneous Olympic mega-event which was staged in Barcelona. Perhaps with that in mind, construction of a large multi-purpose sport stadium, optimistically labelled the Olympic Stadium of Seville, near Alamillo Park was begun in the mid-1990s and completed in 1999. This project was part of the next steps in the city's mega-event aspirations and strategy, namely its bids in the 1997–2001 period to stage the 2004 and 2008 Olympics. The bids failed and the city now possesses a major but underused sport and cultural performance facility. In addition, the pre-event planning of the Expo's post-event legacies and its potential contribution to the city's urban development was not impressive. It involved a conceptual disconnection between the two main elements, namely the technology park and the entertainment-based theme park, which was embodied in a spatial disconnection between their sites and an experiential disconnection in their public uses and meanings. Arguably also, in spite of its objective proximity to the centre of Seville and the creation of new river crossings, the technology park in particular does not present itself as being very well connected with the central city.

The Seville planners' conceptualisation of their new post-Expo high-technology and business park at the time was apparently influenced by currently fashionable American thinking and experience with university-related spin-off facilities complexes such as those in California's 'Silicon Valley'. These are rather spatially disconnected and self-contained constructions in outer-urban and sub-urban campus-type settings. So instead of making a virtue out of the site's proximity to the city centre the planners seem to have been rather indifferent to this aspect.[34] Subsequent American urban-planning thinking about the spatial conditions needed to stimulate technology-based start-up businesses in the creative industries has revised the Silicon Valley model. It now tends to emphasise the benefits of proximity and accessibility achievable by organisational clustering in multi-use central city locations.[35] In principle Seville's Expo site location and its post-Expo development, particularly in relation to the technology park, would have been better served by adopting this latter kind of planning approach rather than the former type, which was the one which actually seems to have been taken. This may have helped avoid the underuse of the technology park site which was exacerbated but not caused by the economic recession of 1993, and which was a problem for some years after the Expo.[36]

Consistently with this approach to the technology park, little role or priority seemed to have been given at the time to factors which might have provided more public interest in and integrated uses of the Expo site in the post-event period. For instance the development of new communities in the area does not seem to have been much envisaged or promoted. In particular, in relation to our theme of the greening of mega-events, surprisingly little recognition seems to have been given to the potential post-event importance of cultivating the natural environment both in and around the site and in relation to the river nearby. The subsequent green developments in the post-event period noted above (namely riverside walks and the Alamillo Park) appear rather as after-thoughts, and as not having been fully anticipated and integrated into the Expo's planning process.

We have suggested that in 1992 Seville's Expo event suffered by comparison with Barcelona's Olympics in the same year. However, in retrospect arguably it also could be said to suffer by comparison with Seville's own prior experi-ence of staging an Expo. The 1929 Ibero-Hispanic Expo could be claimed to have made much more than the 1992 Expo of a lasting, visible and valued contribution to the city's material, cultural and socio-economic development. This is particularly arguable in relation to the green and recreational space legacies of the 1929 Expo which include the currently valued and touristi-cally important sites of the Plaza de España and the Marie Luisa Park (and see Table 6.2 above).

The 1998 Lisbon Expo

The city of Lisbon is located mainly on the north side of the wide mouth of the river Tagus where it flows out to the west to join the North Atlantic ocean. This location gave the city its traditional capacity to be the great port, and ultimately the capital, of the Portuguese nation. As such it played a unique and strategic role in the history of the economic and cultural development of Europe in the early modern period. It was one of the key bases for Europe's era of oceanic explorations from the late fifteenth onwards. In addition it was one of the key gateways for the entry into Europe of Asian spices and commodities, African produce and slaves, South American bullion and generally information and knowledge about the rest of the non-European world particularly the 'East'. This role helped to set Europe, which was now beginning to understand itself as 'the West', on the road to primary-phase modernisation and global domination. This historic role is connected with the original motives of urban leaders to envisage and pursue their 1998 Expo project. The Expo originated as a project of national as well as civic interest and significance.[37] It was intended to commemorate and celebrate the five-hundredth anniversary of the historic arrival of the Portuguese explorer Vasco da Gama in southern India in 1498, the first demonstration of the oceanic accessibility of Asia from Europe. In the course of the city's bid for official recognition from the BIE which succeeded in 1992 the theme or message of the event as a 'special' Expo was altered from commemoration to a more contemporary green concern for the nature of the oceans and their role in human life, under the slogan of 'The Oceans, a Heritage for the Future'.

The historic role of Lisbon as a port involved access to the river from the waterfronts in the central and west-central areas of the city. The waterfronts on the east-central side of the city were not accessed in this way, and during the development of the city in the primary phase of modernisation the urban land adjacent to them was given over to industrial, commercial and transport uses which effectively ignored them and cut them off from public access and use. Thus, apart from its green message the Expo could also lay a claim to being a green project in the other relevant ways. That is it was part of a longer-term strategy aiming at the transformation of the east-central area of the city. This transformation would involve the remediation and urban regeneration of disused and damaged ex-industrial urban land together with the creation of new public access to the east-central waterfront.

In these and other ways the project had the potential to be seen as significantly green both as a model and also as a provider of new public recreational space. In addition the Lisbon organisers were aware of the need to avoid the kind of planning weaknesses manifested in the Seville Expo. These included not only a clearer vision of the role of the event's environmental and socio-spatial legacies but also a more financially beneficial and organisationally effective approach to ensuring take-up and use of Expo-related land and facilities in the immediate post-event period. Thus all of the event's main buildings were pre-sold or otherwise pre-committed before the event in order to ensure their immediate use after the event. In addition land was sold for residential development and new community-building post-event. In these respects also Lisbon created a mega-event legacy-aware planning model which was not only influential on subsequent Expos, including that of Zaragoza, but which, in addition, anticipated later developments in the field of Olympic Games events, including, as we see in Chapter 8, that of London 2012.

The Expo involved the building of some physically spectacular constructions on and around its site, which in the post-Expo period is now referred to as the Parque das Nações (Park of Nations). The Expo's green message relating to the oceans was symbolised and embodied in the construction of a large aquarium, or oceanarium. This is the largest aquarium in Europe (MNN 2015), and it was designed to enable animal species from the world's major oceanic environments to be exhibited. The Expo's standing as a positive urban-planning model could be said to be symbolised by the building of two new large-scale pieces of urban transport infrastructure bordering the Expo site and integrated with its construction process. These were the Vasco da Gama bridge and the Oriente station. The bridge, to the north and east of the Expo site, was at the time the longest road bridge in Europe (BBC News 1998) and frames an impressive vista of the river Tagus when seen from the site. The station on the western edge of the site was the major gateway into the Expo at event-time. It is a major new transport hub for the city as a whole, giving access to the city's metro system, to national and international bus services, and to all levels of overground train systems, from high speed to local; in addition it contains a shopping centre. Construction of the station was a key element in beginning the extension of the metro system into east Lisbon, a process which would later enable central Lisbon to be linked by metro to the city's nearby international airport.

Other impressive constructions which the Expo project has also left as urban legacies include a viewing tower and a large indoor arena. The Vasco da Gama viewing tower, on the waterfront at the northern end of the site, offers unique perspectives on the nearby bridge and the river. The arena, now renamed the MEO Arena, is another legacy of the Expo and can seat up to twenty thousand people. It is a facility of relevant scale for attracting internationally significant sport and pop and rock performances, and also for benefiting the urban tourism and entertainments economy by attracting attendance for its performances from national visitors as well as local people. Finally Lisbon's 'special' Expo BIE status required the host city to provide large-scale exhibition halls for the participating nations to use for their displays. These more functionally designed halls were part of the event's economic legacy and provide a focus for commercial and other exhibitions on the Expo site in the post-event period.

The Expo's aim to include physical spectacle in relation to its event-time attraction and post-event legacy was emphasised in its commissioning of work by a number of high-profile architects and designers, including the starchitects Santiago Calatrava (Oriente station) and Peter Chermayoff (the Oceanarium). This aspect, together with the new recreational space of the park's waterfront location, undoubtedly contributed to its success in attracting over ten million visits during its four months' duration as well as the post-event popularity of the site and its venues. The Expo event is widely assessed as being a success and as having contributed substantially to positive social and economic change across the whole city of Lisbon. The 'Park of Nations', as a multi-use complex, adds substantially to Lisbon's visitor and tourism attractions. The Oceanarium alone typically attracts one million visitors annually in the post-event period.

In tourism and business terms it is noteworthy that in the year of its Expo, 1998, Lisbon also became the biggest Atlantic cruise ship terminal in Europe, a position it has succeeded in retaining since that time. The Expo-led development of the 'Park of Nations' riverside complex in east Lisbon has been followed in west Lisbon by other riverside cultural and touristic developments. As a result of these and other such developments the city's tourism sector has grown and plays a significant role in its economy, accounting for approximately ten per cent of the city's employment and gross domestic product (WTTC 2007). Besides stimulating the city's capacity to provide entertainment for visitors, the Expo's urban heritage also includes more tangibly green dimensions which also have some relevance for them. Two new urban parks were constructed for the Expo and its aftermath. These were an urban riverside park in the north end of the Expo site (Jardim do Passeio dos Herois do Mar) and a waterfront park in the central part of the site (Jardim Garcia de Orta). As parts of the new 'Park of Nations' area and its neighbourhood they provide new recreational spaces both for residents and for visitors.

The 2008 Zaragoza Expo

After a decade and a half had passed from the time of the troubled Seville Expo, another Spanish city decided to take the risk and stage one, albeit of the smaller 'special' type like that of Lisbon's Expo, rather than the larger 'universal' type undertaken by Seville.[38] Zaragoza's Expo project was influenced by the general success of the Lisbon project a decade earlier and shared some similarities with it. Both cities (as also with Seville) are historic European second-tier cities with populations around six to seven hundred thousand. Both Lisbon and Zaragoza were in need of urban regeneration and each used its Expo projects as leading and catalytic components of wider long-term urban development strategies. Both cities are situated on rivers and, in the course of their Expo and wider urban strategies, both aimed to make use of this fact in the locating and theming of their Expo projects. In all of this Zaragoza, like Lisbon, was aware of the planning and green environmental weaknesses of Seville and aimed to avoid these. And, like Lisbon, it can be said to have contributed to the picture of contemporary mega-events having a distinctively green character, for instance in terms of their public messages, as planning models and as providers of recreational space in modern cities.

Before we look into these green aspects of Zaragoza's Expo a little further it is necessary to make a general critical observation about the event. Arguably the ghost of Seville's problematic Expo haunted Zaragoza. The event and its immediate aftermath had the misfortune to coincide with the international and national economic recession and European financial crises of 2008–10. Due to this the event made a financial loss of roughly €500 million and the city found it difficult to gain much lasting economic benefit from its plans for post-Expo uses of the event site. Also in terms of the city's image and its tourism industry, while the Expo boosted the city's appeal to the domestic market of Spanish travellers, it had minimal impact in the international tourism market and left practically no legacy in this regard.[39]

The event aimed to communicate a green message about the importance of the role and management of water in human development to an international public. However, given what we have noted about Zaragoza's weaknesses in communicating messages about its own city image to international tourists, it would be unconvincing to assume that it was able to achieve much more than this with its environmentalist message. Having said that, the Expo project did succeed in providing some international recognition of and respect for the city's special interest in and connection with this important green theme. Thus the city became one of the hubs of global thinking about water-related technologies and polices in the years following the Expo. In particular the United Nations environmental organisation gave the city a leading role in hosting international seminars and conferences of experts and decision-makers in this field for the period 2009–15. In this particular respect hosting the Expo could be said to have helped the city to promote an important green message internationally.

The two leading new green developments which were left as urban legacies by the Expo are a major park and a major aquarium. The Water Park is a large area of parkland (120 hectares) which takes up the bulk of the Ramillas Meander area, and it includes extensive wetlands, riverside woods and a botanical garden. In addition, as with most such parks, it contains opportunities and facilities for a range of leisure activities aimed not only at urban residents but also at tourists (including such things as open-air swimming pools, a river beach, a spa, golf, and river and canal trips). The River Aquarium focuses on exhibitions and conservation in relation to freshwater fish species and wildlife habitats from many of the world's greatest rivers. It is the largest such facility in Europe, and as such, besides its green significance, it is also an important contribution to the city's cultural distinctiveness and its otherwise heavily traditional and heritage-oriented tourist attractions.

Earlier we suggested that green can be interpreted to refer to the humanising aspects of both recreational space and also mobility space. On this interpretation also the Expo can be argued to have contributed various long-term urban legacies. In addition to the Water Park, the Expo site left the city an extensive series of interlinked landscaped open-air public spaces covering 25 hectares interwoven with the various buildings left behind on the site. Also the two new bridges and the nearby (albeit irregularly used) cross-river cable car all contribute new mobility spaces. They offer walkers the possibility of gaining special perspectives on the river. Beyond this they promote cross-river connectivity between the two new post-2008 development hubs (the post-Expo site and the AVE-Delicias station zone) in the city's central-north-western area. In this respect part of the Expo's green urban legacy can be argued to lie in its transport improvements and the new space-making and place-making perceptions and practices which they offer the public in Zaragoza.

Conclusion

In Part II we have explored the general relationship between cities on the one hand and mega-events together with their urban impacts and legacies on the other, in the context of the long-term social changes involved in modernisation. The discussions have aimed to combine historical with contemporary perspectives, and in terms of the latter they have been illustrated with reference to mega-events which have been staged within the last two decades. Each of the chapters has focused on a special field or phenomenon in which key aspects of the general relationship between cities and mega-events can be engaged with. In Chapter 4 the focus was on the phenomenon of the embodiment of mega-events in legacy architecture, and on various key characteristics of this phenomenon, particularly those of its spectacle, place-making and spatio-temporal embedding. In Chapter 5 the focus was on the phenomenon that is the Olympic mega-event genre and various aspects of it such as its potential to create negative as well as positive urban legacies. A discussion of the influential case of the Sydney 2000 Olympics and its legacies allowed each of these aspects to be illustrated in a single concrete example. This case also allowed a light to be shone on the increasing importance in the contemporary mega-event world of events' potential role as urban space-makers, particularly park-makers, as well as 'place'-makers, and also on their related potential role as green urban policy projects. Chapter 6 has focused on these latter 'space'-making and 'green' phenomena, and has attempted to give them some of the recognition and analytic attention they both deserve and require.

The discussion in this chapter has covered a number of topics relating to these phenomena. The topics have ranged from the very general to the very particular. A key general topic has been the problematic relationship throughout the modernisation process, between on the one hand urbanisation and its artificial environments and on the other hand the natural environment. The emergence of a global ecological crisis in the contemporary period has influenced cities, particularly in the West, to attempt to promote more ecologically aware, green, urban development policies. We saw that a precedent for such policies was the growth of urban parks in cities in the early phase of modernisation, and that the Expo genre of mega-events played a distinctive and leading role in this green space-making movement.

The contemporary greening of urban policy concerned with sustainability and conservation is, of course, potentially much more transformative of the conditions of urban life than anything undertaken in the earlier period, and it covers many more fields of urban experience than the creation of parks. Nevertheless the role of parks as tangible and everyday forms of 'green urbanism' for publics in contemporary cities – helping to promote conservationist and recreational ideas, values and practices – remains as significant in our times as it has been in earlier times. So too does the fact that mega-events can be used to promote such green urbanism in host cities, through their longstanding connection with the renewal or creation of urban parks. In this chapter we have seen how these links between mega-events, parks and green policies have operated in relation to the Expo genre of mega-events both in general and in historical terms, and also in some particularity and detail in the case studies of the Lisbon 1998 Expo and Zaragoza 2008 Expo with which the chapter concluded.

The chapter has opened up a number of general issues in the analysis of mega-events and host cities. For instance there is the issue of the policy balance in terms of the public experience of urbanism terms between mega-events' roles either as urban place-makers or as urban space-makers. Also there is the issue of policy balance between their roles as catalysts either of socio-economic or of environmentalist change. These and other issues can be explored further in other relevant contemporary mega-event cases in their contexts, and we turn to some notable examples of these in the final part of the book.

Notes

1 The 2015 Milan Expo occurred too late to be covered in this book.
2 On botanical gardens see Monem 2007 and Brockway 2002, also note 4.
3 On zoos see Baratay 2002 and Rothfels 2008, also note 4.
4 On the origins and history of art galleries in the modernisation process see Prior 2002, and on the origins and history of museums from early modernity see Bennett 1995 (also Impey and McGregor 1985, Horne 1984 and MacKenzie 2010). In my view these urban cultural institutions, together with others, such as libraries, parks etc., contributed importantly to the development of a lived public sphere in European societies in the primary modernisation period. The idea of the 'public sphere' was notably recognised and analysed by the critical social theorist Jürgen Habermas. It developed in connection with the European Enlightenment and it included a cultural as well as a political dimension (see Habermas 1991 and contributions to Calhoun 1992). However Habermas saw it in mono-cultural terms and as declining in the twentieth century, and he tended to underplay its cultural dimension. As against this the contemporary sociology of culture sees the public sphere in our times in multicultural or cosmopolitan terms and as growing, and it seeks to address its cultural dimension. See for instance the recent work of Monica Sassatelli and her colleagues on modern European festivals in their collection *Festivals and the cultural public sphere* (Giorgi et al. 2011, also Sassatelli 2011). My conception of the urban social space and time created by major urban events in Part II of this book, and particularly in this chapter, shares in the spirit of this work (also see Roche 2010a, ch. 8).
5 For a study of the application of the 'zoo' concept to non-Western humans who were deemed to be 'savage' and 'exotic' in the period of colonialism and imperialism, an application which also, unfortunately, found a place in the programmes of late nineteenth-century Expos, see Blanchard 2008. Also on the Expo aspect of this topic see Greenhalgh 1988, ch. 4, and Roche 2000, ch. 3.
6 Expos were most strongly connected with the ideology of progress in the US. For instance the Expo or World's Fair which was staged to celebrate the centenary of the founding of the city of Chicago was given the title and theme of 'A Century of Progress'. On this Expo and more generally on American Expos and the theme of Progress see Rydell 1993 (also see Benedict 1983a and Rydell 1984).
7 On 'urban heritage' particularly in Europe see for instance Ashworth and Tunbridge 1990; Richards 2001; and Bandarin 2012. Urban heritage, particularly in Western countries, is typically recognised, conserved and developed by national-level laws, policies and agencies. However it is also worth noting (as another instance of both cultural 'globalisation' and 'glocalisation') that urban heritage can sometimes be recognised, conserved and developed within the trans-national framework of UNESCO's 'world heritage' concept and system (see UNESCO 2015). On early urban parks as urban heritage see note 15.
8 For a current United Nations-level statement of the nature and implications of sustainable development see UN-SF 2015. On the need for ecological conservation see WWF 2014. On the ecological crisis see Chapter 1.
9 For a recent brief but suggestive discussion of the potentially positive implications of the spread of digital technologies in the contemporary world for the concept of sustainable development which was pioneered by E. F. Schumacher (among others), see Lent 2014. On the digital age see Chapter 3.

10 On the greening of mega-events see Hayes and Karamichas 2012, chs 6–9; also Mangan and Dyreson 2012, ch. 1. For a critique of both the 'sustainability' event planning discourse and, particularly, its implications for the case of the Rio Olympics of 2016 see Gaffney 2013.

11 On leisure and recreation as 'human rights' see the discourse of the international legal system surrounding the United Nation's various relevant treaties and conventions, particularly the Universal Declaration of Human Rights (1948, article 24) and the International Covenant on Economic, Social and Cultural Rights (1976, article 7) (and see UN 1948 and UN 1976 respectively which relate to rights to rest from work and paid holidays away from work). The discourse has been further elaborated more recently in the Convention of the Rights of Persons with Disabilities (2006, article 30) which carries the implication that rights which are assumed to be appropriate to and enjoyed by people without disabilities also need to be guaranteed for people with disabilities. With that in mind it is relevant to note that article 30 concerns human rights to 'Participation in cultural life, recreation, leisure and sport' (UN 2006).

12 On primary urbanisation (i.e. urbanisation in the primary-phase modernisation) see discussions in Chapter 1 and also Chapter 7.

13 Social policy grew in the West, and particularly in Europe, first at the urban level in fields such as health, education and housing, and in the form of practical and political interventions in and reconstructions of urban physical environments. In the late nineteenth century in British cities this occurred initially in the building of state schools for primary- and (later) secondary-age children, and then public washhouses. Later, into the early twentieth century city councils would build swimming baths, public libraries, and publicly funded ('council') housing. See for instance Fraser 2009, Bailey 1978 and Cunningham 1980.

14 For histories of the development of parks in Britain see Williamson 1998 and Downing 2009. On the history of Central Park in New York city, the iconic modern urban park, see Heckscher 2008. For the history of parks in general see Jones and Will 2005, and on the development of urban parks in the USA see Cranz 1989. On the study of social aspects of contemporary park see Chiesura 2004, Cranz and Boland 2004, Walls 2009. On the background social history of leisure in Britain, that is, relating to the facts and forms of free time in which people could make use of parks, see Bailey 1978, Cunningham 1980, and Malcolmson 1973.

15 On early parks as currently valued aspects of urban heritage see for instance the UK. In Britain many urban parks are officially registered as 'national heritage' by the English Heritage organisation in order to help protect their funding and operation (see Layton-Jones 2014), and they are recognised as 'an enduring legacy of the industrial revolution' by the Heritage Lottery Fund organisation which has some responsibilities for supporting them (HLF 2014, p. 2). However, even given this cultural and political understanding it remains the case that, in the current recession-induced governmental climate of 'austerity' and cuts in national and local public expenditure, urban parks are beginning to be put at risk (HLF 2014 passim).

16 This work was subsequently developed further in Cranz and Boland 2004.

17 It is worth noting in terms of the historical analysis of urban parks and public spaces that Cranz's category of 'pleasure ground' has a different meaning in the American context from the category of 'pleasure garden'. The latter referred in Britain to a type of central urban private and profit-making entertainment-oriented place, usually but

not always outdoors, and set in a spatial frame of gardens and promenades. They were popular among the middle and upper classes in London and other British cities from the mid-eighteenth century and to the mid-nineteenth century (see Downing 2009).

18 Cranz and Boland refer to it as the 'sustainable park' model

19 On the idea and history of the 'long revolution' see the seminal work of Raymond Williams (Williams 1961).

20 On the relevance of parks in European cities for contemporary multi- and inter-cultural relations see general discussions in Edwards and Tsouros, 2006 Beumer 2010 and case studies in Green 2013 (on Copenhagen) and InfoRegio 2012 (on Antwerp).

21 Rising inequality and social polarisation, as well as immigration, in contemporary Western societies tends to produce urban spatial segregation. Public spaces and places like parks are currently important in sociological and in policy terms because they provide some resources which can be used by both policy-makers and ordinary people to defend against this trend. On the sociology, anthropology and social psychology of urban parks and spaces see work on 'Rethinking urban parks: public space and cultural diversity' by Low et al. 2005, also Tonnelat 2010.

22 For initial background information about the Paris Expos of 1867, 1878, 1889 and 1937 see appropriate chapters in Findling and Pelle 2008.

23 On the 1851 Crystal Palace Expo in London see Roche 2000, ch. 2, also Allwood 1977 and Greenhalgh 1988.

24 See Colquhoun's biography of Paxton (Colquhoun 2004).

25 See Cranz and Boland 2004, and also Twombly's collection of Olmsted's writings (Twombly 2010).

26 On neoliberalism see references in Chapter 1, note 20.

27 For instance the United Nations Environmental Programme (UNEP) has made formal assessments of mega-events such as the Turin Winter Olympics 2006 and the Shanghai Expo 2010 (UNEP 2006, 2010; also on Vancouver as a 'green Games' see Lew 2010). It rated Turin very positively and took a more mixed view of the achievements and problems in Shanghai. It treated the Shanghai assessment as an opportunity to provide advice to major cities in developing countries about the environmental challenges of hosting mega-events. It rated the London Olympic Games positively (UNEP 2012). But it has been criticised for its consultancy involvement in the Sochi Winter Olympics (G. Russell 2014) which has been widely judged to be an environmental failure (Time 2014). Greenpeace was formally involved in the environmental monitoring of the Sydney Olympics 2000, generally endorsing the organisers' claims to have staged a green Games (although its involvement and assessments have been criticised). Greenpeace used the experience to develop guidelines for cities planning to stage major events sustainably (Greenpeace 2000). On this basis it publicly criticised the organisers of the Athens 2004 Olympics for their failure to deliver on their green aspirations for the event (Greenpeace 2004).

28 On the environmental problems of the 2014 Sochi Winter Olympic event see Muller 2015b and also Boykoff 2016.

29 See sources in note 27.

30 On Turin 2006 and Vancouver 2010 see sources in note 27.

31 On Sochi 2014 see Muller 2015b and Boykoff 2016.

32 For initial overviews of each of these three Expos see the appropriate chapters in Findling and Pelle 2008.

33 See the discussion of BIE's categories of Expos in Chapter 4.
34 See Monclus's observations on the roles of the international expert academic consult-
    ants who were involved in the Seville Expo project, namely the sociologist Manuel
    Castells and the geographer Peter Hall (Monclus 2009, pp. 91–2).
35 A leading US advocate of this approach to urban economic development analysis
    and planning in the US in the current period has been Bruce Katz. The approach
    stresses the new economic importance in the digital age of 'creative clusters', net-
    works and proximity in cities. See Bradley and Katz 2014, also Katz 2010. Beyond
    the US elements of this approach are evident in the UK in national and urban gov-
    ernments' interests in promoting 'Tech City' zones within and between British cities.
    On the leading zone of this kind, namely Tech City in London, and its relevance for
    post-2012 Olympic economic developments around the new Queen Elizabeth II
    Olympic Park see Chapter 8.
36 See Findling 1994b, Marteau 2008, also Smith 2012, p. 73.
37 On the Lisbon Expo see the official account of its origins, contents and visitor reac-
    tions on ParqueExpo 2014 and an overview in Huntoon 2008. Some insightful and
    generally positive studies of the Expo as an urban project are given in Carrière and
    Demazière 2002, Edwards et al. 2004, Monclus 2009, pp. 93–7; note also observations
    in Smith 2012 pp. 58–9 and passim. A useful recent informal observation of the
    wider urban and touristic context in Lisbon into which the post-Expo park fits is
    given in Milheiro 2012, and information about the city's wider tourist economic
    context is given in WTTC 2007.
38 On the 2008 Zaragoza Expo the most substantial and authoritative study is that of
    Javier Monclus (see chs 4 to 6, plus the epilogue in Monclus 2009) and also insightful
    are Rollin 2008 and Molina 2013. Other useful points on the event are contained in
    Kambli 2011 and also the notes in Ramo 2005. Pradas and Arnal 2007 and Episa
    2014 contain information from groups involved in the Expo project and Schwartz
    2008 indicates the negative nature of the wider economic context of the event. A
    more detailed version of the account of the Expo and its legacies provided in this
    section is given in Roche 2016c.
39 On the scale of recession in the Spanish economy in the years preceding and follow-
    ing the Zaragoza Expo see trend tables for Spanish GDP in EU 2015d and for
    unemployment in EU 2015a and EU 2015b. On Zaragoza's tourism see Wall 2014.

III

Mega-events and global change in East and West

7

Mega-events, globalisation and urban legacy: events in China in the early twenty-first century

The sociological perspective taken in this book is that to understand mega-events and their legacies it is necessary to understand their social contexts, together with the ways in which they reflect, mark and influence these contexts. So far we have investigated the relevance for mega-events of two major vectors of twenty-first-century structural change, namely change in the media environment relating to the rise of the digital age (Part I) and change in the urban environment relating to 'secondary-phase modernisation and post-industrial urban regeneration (Part II). In Part III, in this chapter, and also in the following one, we are particularly concerned about a third vector of secondary-phase social change, namely globalisation, particularly in its complex and differentiating aspects.[1] On the one hand, in geopolitical and political-economic terms globalisation is currently operating as a process of differentiation in that it appears to involve the emergence of greater 'world regionalism' and a 'multipolar world order'.[2] On the other hand at the urban level globalisation is also reconfiguring social systems in 'glocal' ways. In this glocal form globalisation appears simultaneously both to strengthen the role of global agencies and forces at the local urban level and also (and thereby) to produce greater distinctiveness at that level. Mega-events have always been international as well as urban phenomena, and are now readily viewable as simultaneously global and urban phenomena. As such they are likely to exemplify, embody and propagate these complex forms of globalisation which are influencing societies in our period.

The world-regionality dynamic is particularly visible in such processes as the development of the European Union as a multi- and supranational governance system in the European world region, in the rise of China in the East Asia and also in the new power and potential of some developing societies across the world's continents. To explore globalisation's world-regionality dynamic and its implications for mega-events in this chapter we look East. We discuss the role of mega-events such as the Beijing 2008 Olympic Games and the Shanghai 2010 Expo and their legacies in China's contemporary development, both at the national level and also particularly at the urban level. By contrast in Chapter 8 later we look West and explore the implications of the glocalisation dynamic for mega-events in the case of the city of London. We discuss the influence of mega-events on the development of London as a world city, and we look in particular at the London 2012 Olympic Games and its urban legacies. In addition in each of these chapters we also look again at the issues raised in Chapter 6, concerning the urban policy balances which are struck in staging mega-events between place-making and space-making, and also between socio-economic and environmental development. We will see how these urban-policy balances are struck in two very different world regional and 'glocal' contexts. This chapter is then organised in three main sections: it firstly outlines some of the stage-setting background of social change in China; secondly it addresses China's early twenty-first-century major sport events; and finally the discussion focuses on China's Expo in Shanghai in 2010.

China, mega-events and social change: background themes and issues

A key element and dynamic force within the global shift in the world economy over the last two decades has been the rapid and large-scale emergence of China. China will be the biggest economy in the world, overtaking the US certainly well before 2050 and possibly as early as 2025.[3] In his later writing the economic analyst Jim O'Neill recognises the limitations of his BRIC analysis (see Chapter 1) and that China is a special case and not just an exemplar of the BRIC group. Indeed, along with many commentators, he is willing to see the twenty-first century as a whole as 'The Chinese Century' (O'Neill 2013, ch. 3), in recognition not only of the great economic significance but also the wider political and cultural significance of China's re-emergence to a dominant position both for the East Asian world region and also for the global society as a whole. These processes involved in the rise of China underlie the fact that in the decade or more since the turn of the millennium the People's Republic of China (PRC) has also currently begun to bid for and to stage mega-events along with other types of large-scale and international events. In this the PRC has been joined by the set of mainly small polities which are located near the Chinese mainland in which the peoples have mainly Han ethnicity and mainland origins, and which are influenced by the PRC but which retain various degrees of autonomy from it. This set consists of Hong Kong, Macau, Taiwan and Singapore. Together with the PRC they can be seen as a cultural (although *not* a political) complex which I will informally refer to here as Chinese regions.[4] Table 7.1 indicates some of the major events and mega-events which have been staged in Chinese region societies in the early years of the twenty-first, and in the following discussion we focus in particular on the PRC.

East Asia, including the developed countries of Japan and South Korea but also including its newly emerging (or, given history, its re-emerging) global superpower China, has become a leading world region over the last two generations or more (Dolles and Soderman 2008, Shin 2012, also Guthrie 2006). Mega-events have long been important in this region. Japan marked its emergence in the postwar period by staging the 1964 Tokyo Olympics, and South Korea did the same kind of thing a generation later either by staging the 1988 Seoul Olympics. China has followed this pattern and has even elaborated on it over the last decade or more. From the turn of the new millennium leaders in the central Chinese state and also in some of its major and rapidly growing cities

Table 7.1 Major events in the Chinese regions in the twenty-first century

Country	Year and city	Event
People's Republic of China (PRC)	2008 Beijing	Summer Olympics
	2010 Shanghai	World Expo
	2011 Shenzen	World Student Games
	2013 Tianjin	East Asian Games
	2014 Nanjing	Youth Olympic Games
	(2022 Beijing)	*(Winter Olympics)*
Hong Kong and Macau	2005 Macau	East Asian Games
	2009 Hong Kong	East Asian Games
Taiwan	2010 Kaohsiung	World Games
	(2017 Taipei)	*(World Student Games)*
Singapore	2011	Youth Olympic Games
	(2015)	*(South East Asian Games)*

Sources: See the websites of the following event organisations: the IOC (www.olympics.org/); the BIE (www.bie-paris.org/); FIFA (www.fifa.com); IWGA (for World Games) (www.theworldgames.org/); YOG (for Youth Olympics) (www.olympics.org/youth-olympic-games); OCASIA (for East Asian Games) (www.ocasia.org/); FEI (for South East Asian Games) (www.fei.org/); FISU (FOR Universiade) (www.fisu.net/en/Summer-Universiades-3490.html).
Note: Italics indicate future events.

collaborated to embark on processes of bidding for and staging a number of mega-events (see also Wasserstrom 2010a, pp. 86–93). These include the Summer Olympics in Beijing in 2008, the Asian Games in Guangzhou in 2010 and the World Expo in Shanghai in 2010. The general aims of what we can refer to as this national multi mega-event strategy could be said to have been to use the events to communicate about China both externally to the rest of the world and also internally to the Chinese public. Externally the events have been generally used to showcase the fact of China's (re-)entry into full membership of the international order. They have been used to symbolise its progress, achievements and future potential in terms of economic, cultural and urban modernization, and to exercise 'soft (cultural/symbolic) power' in global international relations. Internally they have been used to communicate with the Chinese public about the need to imagine and to achieve a new urban and socio-economic model in a context of urbanisation dynamics which are operating at a historically unprecedented scale and pace.

China has achieved spectacular economic growth since the 1980 reforms initiated by the 'paramount leader' Deng Xiaoping in the post-Mao Zedong era. This growth, according to some estimates, is likely to propel the country's GDP to a position of parity with the USA by 2020 (Chow 2010, ch. 7) and to a position of global domination by 2050, when it is likely to double the size of the USA's GDP.[5] China's economic growth has been achieved largely through the mobilisation and use of massive resources of low-cost labour drawn from China's huge 1.3 billion population by means of rapid and linked processes of industrialisation and urbanisation. The Deng-era national economic strategy has been largely export-led, devoted to supplying Western consumer markets. However this strategy and the underlying social and economic processes which have delivered it so successfully have been shown to carry heavy costs in terms of environmental pollution, social dislocation, social inequality and polarisation, the urban quality of life and underlying international economic (inter-) dependency.[6]

In the post-Deng era, 1979 to 2009, China's urban population is estimated to have grown by between 440 million and 622 million. Much of that has been due to rural-to-urban migration.[7] And the process is predicted to continue, with another 243 million flowing into China's cities by 2025 (Wiki 2013b). China's urbanisation challenges are exacerbated by the fact that the state monopolises the ownership of all land in the country. Thus the Communist Party, as the sole governing authority, has total control through its urban and provincial representatives of this crucial social asset and factor of production. Importantly state agencies control all of the land in the undeveloped rural countryside surrounding cities and into which these cities have been rapidly expanding in recent times. In this situation, and in the absence of a political and legal system committed to public accountability, the potential for corruption is a pervasive problem in relations between urban leaders, party officials and bureaucrats on the one side and on the other side private capitalists, property developers, industrialists and others interested in land development.[8]

What is also clear is the potential for coerciveness in the relationships between urban leaders and officials and both rural villagers using land in the environs of the cities and also urban migrants within the cities. Economic migrants from rural homelands make up large proportions of the population of China's major cities, and in some cases, as in Shenzhen, they make up the majority. China's long-established 'hukou' system of official registration of individuals (and thus of providing social rights to access state resources and support for such things as housing, education and employment) identifies people in terms of the location of their original household (Wang 2007). It differentiates strongly between rural and urban household locations and in practice denies rural migrants living in cities the full recognition and rights which are accorded to the urban residents who happened to originate from those cities (Wang 2008, Whyte 2010).

The system was introduced in the 1950s in order to enable the state to control economic migration from the countryside to the cities, but in the post-Deng era it has had little impact on stemming this flow. However the operation of the system creates large social categories and spatial zones in China's cities of people who are effectively defined and treated as official second-class citizens. Their communities and residential areas are even more vulnerable to the power of city leaderships and their urban planning projects (including mega-events) than those of urban residents already are. That said, the recent economic growth which has stimulated migration into China's cities has also simultaneously created a new very large-scale and growing urban middle class. This class is creating a social pressure for versions of urban Western consumer culture, for gentrification and for the quality-of-life agenda.[9] Between corruptible power elites at the top of the system, a large and growing middle class and precariously located second-class citizens at the bottom, China's cities are becoming as socially unequal and polarised as Western cities are (Ramstetter et al. 2009, and Chow 2010, ch. 28).

In relatively recent years China's leadership has become increasingly aware of the range of deep social structural and urban environmental problems associated with economic growth (Jacka et al. 2013), and of the pressing need to address them by shifting towards a new socio-economic model (NPC 2011). Since the problems it faces are multi-faceted, any such new model must inevitably be multi-dimensional. One aspect of it needs to involve attempting to reorientate the economy and economic growth towards a significantly greater role for domestic consumption. Simultaneously there is also a need to promote environmental sustainability in industrial and urban areas. In addition any such model also needs to involve attempts to manage the tension between the governmental coerciveness which is often involved in China's rapid urban development (including the disruption often involved in the organisation of its urban mega-events) with the development of forms of urbanism which support rather than threaten the quality of citizens' lives. This awareness and search for a new socio-economic model was confirmed in the accession of Xi Jinping, who is a leading advocate of it, to the country's Presidency in 2012–13.

In this new millennium context China's recent and current multi-mega-event strategy can be seen as an effort to use these particularly powerful cultural-policy instruments in order to communicate not only with an international audience but also with China's own massive population, and to do the latter in relation to themes of consumerism, environmentalism, social inclusiveness and urban quality of life. These multi-themes, together with the conflicts they imply and the policy challenges they present, are clearly visible in both the 2008 Beijing Olympics and the Shanghai Expo 2010, which we consider in more detail in a moment.

China and major sport events

Second-order mega-events in Guangzhou and Shenzhen

China's rapid economic growth and urbanisation in the post-Deng period generated an unprecedented interest among Chinese urban leaderships in strategies of bidding for and staging mega-events. From the perspective of the Chinese state as a whole, as we noted earlier, this can be referred to as a multi-mega event strategy. This has been particularly noticeable over the last five years as event preparation processes which had been begun in the first decade of the new century have come to fruition in a number of China's leading cities, particularly Beijing, Shanghai, Guangzhou, Shenzhen, Tianjin and Nanjing. Beijing and Shanghai are world cities, respectively the political and economic capitals of China as a newly emerging global superpower. They have also become extremely large-scale urban concentrations of population, respectively approximately 20 million and 23 million people. The southern cities of Guangzhou and Shenzhen, the east central city of Nanjing and the northern city of Tianjin are somewhat smaller. However they have also grown to become what in Western terms would still count as very large-scale cities (with populations respectively of approximately 11–14 million, 10 million, 8 million and 12 million). All of these cities are major international ports. Together with the port city of Shanghai they act as economic hubs linking the production and consumption of south, central and north-east China, on the one hand, with, on the other hand, economies in the East Asia region, in the West and in the rest of the world. Their growth has led, facilitated and reflected the rapid growth of the Chinese national economy over the last two decades.

Urban leaderships in these cities, authorised and funded by the national government, have been interested in investing in, bidding for, preparing and staging mega-events for various familiar sorts of reasons. These include, internally, using mega-events to catalyse and symbolise urban infrastructural transformations. Externally, they include using mega-events to create international recognition, particularly among the global peer group of comparable cities, and to put host cities on the international map for inward investment and tourism. The most prominent cases involve the staging of two first-order mega-events of 'universal' (generalist, non-special) character and of global interest and significance, namely the Beijing 2008 Olympics and the Shanghai 2010 Expo, and we look at these cases in more detail in a moment. In addition China has staged a number of second-order mega-events. While these events are still of a large scale and of an international character, they are typically smaller than first-order mega-events. They are typically of a more specialist character, or mainly of interest to a particular world-regional interest, or both. These include the Asian Games in Guangzhou in 2010, the World Student Games (or 'Universiade') in Shenzhen in 2011, the East Asian Games in Tianjin in 2013 and the Youth Olympic Games in Nanjing in 2014.

In spite of their second-order mega-event status a number of these events had very high budgets allocated to them. In the cases of Guangzhou and Shenzhen these were respectively $18 billion in Guangzhou and in Shenzen roughly between $30 billion (Yuan 180 billion) and $50 billion (Yuan 300 billion) (if major new urban transport systems costs are included).[10] These expenditures were considerably more than the cost of the Olympic Games events staged in the cities of Sydney ($6.29 billion), Athens ($10 billion) and London ($15.41 billion) (IOC 2012a and Gold 2011). Major cities in emerging countries, as noted earlier, face a dual challenge in their development. On the one hand there is the basic need to accommodate and manage massive inflows of economic migrants, and on the other hand, simultaneously, there is the imperative to catch up and to better Western urban models. This possibly helps in understanding the high expenditures for mega-events and related developments in Chinese cities. Large elements of the event-related costs were for the completely new transport infrastructures connected with new housing projects which their rapid physical growth required, as well as for new and potentially long-term leisure and sport-related legacy facilities.

Guangzhou, historically known in the West as Canton, lies on the Pearl river and is the hub of the southern coastal region, which also contains Shenzhen. This region has been one of the main drivers of China's economic growth over the past two decades. Guangzhou's 2010 Asian Games event was only slightly smaller than an Olympic games in terms of the number of athletes participating, and the requirements for the building of an athletes' village and a media centre. And, as we have noted above, it was considerably more expensive than many Olympic Games events. Although a range of new sport facilities was constructed, this did not need to involve a new main stadium or other large stadia, since the city already possessed these. In particular in 2001 it had already constructed an eighty-thousand-seat stadium and hotel complex to provide support for the Beijing Olympic bid. (The latter's event involved a certain amount of long-distance distribution of venues, as for instance in the location of the sailing competitions at Qindao, the equestrian competitions in Hong Kong, and some of the football events in Shanghai and Tianjin.) Newly constructed facilities included a major gymnasium, an indoor arena (the 18,000 seat Guangzhou International Sports Arena, GISA) and also an outdoor performance stadium (the 35,000 seat Haixinsha Stadium). Each of these is multi-functional and is likely to have viable long-term uses for the city.

The Games in general aimed to have regenerative impacts across the city, so its events were distributed among venues at many sites in and around the city. However there were three main clusters of venues, each involving significant new constructions. One was in the city centre at Haixinsha (a new stadium for the Games opening and closing ceremonies), a second was in an eastern suburb, Luogang (where GISA was sited), and a third was in a southern suburb, Panyu (the site for the athletes' and officials' villages, the media centre and the new gymnasium). Each of these three areas involved some additional development of new green space or parkland (and/or the making of new connections with existing urban parklands, as in Panyu and particularly Luogang). The post-event legacy conceptualisation of the Panyu site was that it would be developed effectively as a new urban village oriented to housing and employment, while the vision for Luogang was that it would be a new hub of sport and entertainment for Guangzhou residents and tourists. The Games as a whole was intended to be an environmentally conscious low-carbon event in terms of its energy uses.

The city-centre games site of Haixinsha was in Zhujiang New Town. Zhujiang is centrally located in Guangzhou city, on the banks of the Pearl river. It is a newly developed centre for the city of Guangzhou and contains the city's commercial and business district. In the year of 2010 a number of major developments were completed in Zhujiang. These included a major architectural and functional feature of the central business district, the Guangzhou West Tower, the first of what is now an iconic set of twin towers, each over a hundred storeys. Other developments completed in 2010 in this district included major new cultural facilities (e.g. the Guangdong museum and the Guangzhou Opera House), new communications facilities (e.g. the iconic Canton Tower telecoms tower) and new transport infrastructures (e.g. the Zhujiang automated people mover, a driverless metro-type system). These developments at Zhujiang are the centrepieces of an urban masterplan for Guangzhou which aims to improve the quality of life for its residents and also to attract international business visitors and tourists. Thus the staging of the Asian Games in 2010, which was communicated to both national and also world-regional publics, helped to provide both a catalyst in the planning of these new central urban developments and a launch celebration for them. In this respect and in others it is possible to argue that, in spite of its high costs, the event and its associated developments have the potential to be seen eventually as having made a positive contribution to urban legacy in Guangzhou. In addition it is worth noting that the IOC President Jacques Rogge, who observed the Asian Games, took the view that the event had demonstrated that Guangzhou had the capacity to bid for and to successfully stage an Olympic Games (Messakh 2010).

Compared with Guangzhou's Asian Games experience, Shenzen's 2011 Universiade event involved a similar or greater level of infrastructural construction (e.g. a number of new metro lines) and sports facilities construction (e.g. including a new sixty-thousand-seat main stadium and sport complex) (for instance Wiki 2011). Some of these may well be ultimately assessable as providing a positive legacy for the city. However the staging of this second-order mega-event proved controversial within China for a number of reasons. Firstly, as we noted earlier, there was the very high level of event-related expenditures, which some estimates put at nearly $30 billion or more (see above), which was double the level of London's spending on the significantly bigger 2012 Olympics event.

Secondly various officials have been sacked for corruption related to the Universiade event. These include Liang Daoxing, one of the leaders of the Shenzhen Universiade organisation and a previous vice-mayor of the city, and some of his associates including Xu Zongheng, previously a mayor of the city (Tam 2012b, WantChina Times 2012, China Sports Review 2013). Thirdly, in a city which is largely composed of economic migrants there was the high number of allegedly 'high-risk' migrants (eighty thousand) who were summarily evicted from the city by a police force assembled for the event and said to number 284,000 (Xinhua 2011, Chan 2011).

The second-order multi-sport mega-events of Guangzhou's relatively positive Asian Games in 2010 and Shenzhen's controversial Universiade in 2011 had followed in sequence from the first-order multi-sport mega-event of the Beijing's Olympics in 2008 which we look at in a moment. It is hard to see too much of the green legacy Sydney model (see Chapter 5) in either of the two post-Beijing events. In Guangzhou's case, although there was a green environmentalist aspiration, arguably this concept was somewhat dissipated by the distribution of Asian Games venues around the city. In Shenzen's case whatever improvements the Universiade might have helped to catalyse in the quality of urban life for city residents is counterbalanced by the corruption and coerciveness of the event organisers and city authorities and the damage they have done to the city's image both externally and internally. The Sydney model was arguably more influential on the previous Beijing Games which preceded these two events. However all of these Chinese sport mega-events – including more recent and smaller-scale international sport events like Tianjin's 2013 East Asian Games and Nanjing's 2014 Youth Olympics – have been criticised in respect of one of their themes and (hoped-for) legacies.

The criticism is that these events are costly promotions of an elite form of sport culture and of national glory through the achievements of Chinese champions in the world of international sport. However, whatever other urban legacies the events may or may not leave, they have had very little, if any, impact on ordinary Chinese people's health, whether in the cities or elsewhere in the country. Critical voices have been raised within the Chinese Communist Party itself not only about the potential lack of a public-health legacy from sport mega-events but even about the very purpose of developing a sport policy at all, whether through these or other means. For instance Jiang Xiaoyu, the vice-chair of the Party's main relevant advisory body, the Education, Science, Culture and Public health Committee, is reported as criticising the fact of the measurable decline in the overall health (including agility and strength) of China's young people in the contemporary period, in spite of the country's high levels of spending on sport mega-events (Zhen 2010). We will return to this criticism in the conclusion, but before that we can take a look at the first and biggest of the recent series of Chinese sport mega-events, Beijing's 2008 Olympic project

The Beijing 2008 Olympic mega-event and its legacies

The Beijing 2008 Olympics, unlike the Athens 2004 Olympics, was in a position to learn from the Sydney 2000 model since it won the right to stage the Games in 2001. It could be interpreted as applying some of the Sydney features, although with variable degrees of success.[11] However whereas the Sydney Olympics, like the London Olympics later, were designed to have a minimal impact in terms of the compulsory relocation of urban residents, the Beijing Olympics, like the Shanghai Expo, involved the pressured relocation of very significant numbers of people. Large-scale relocations, whether pressured or not, are common in contemporary China. This is because of the great pace and scale of the country's urbanisation together with the authoritarian and democratically unaccountable character of its political systems at state and urban levels. Between 2000 and 2008 it is estimated that over one million people were relocated and rehoused in Beijing due to the various processes of urban reconstruction and infrastructure modernisation that the city was undergoing in this period. However, how much of this was with or without the acquiescence of the residents is unclear and a matter of debate, and so too is how much of it was specifically due to the Olympic project (see COHRE 2008 as against Ferguson 2008).

The pre-event period was dogged by negative international media coverage and comment about China's human rights record, its censorship of news and the internet, its oppressive political record in Tibet, the human cost of its clearances and conversions of central areas of the city of Beijing, and the state of air pollution in the city. But the opening ceremony celebrating some of China's contributions to the history of human civilisation, staged in the iconic 'Bird's Nest' Olympic stadium, was widely regarded as one of the most impressive which had ever been seen. Overall the Games was effectively organised and the event acted as a catalyst for a significant amount of long-term urban development and modernisation in Beijing.

As with previous Olympic cities a considerable amount of transport infrastructural and related developments was undertaken. These included a number of new road systems encircling the city, extensions to the metro system and improvements to the international airport. The city's stock of hotels was increased and so too was its ability to attract and manage growing flows of international visitors. The main Olympic sports facilities were positioned on a linear site in a developing north-central area of the city and grouped around the Olympic stadium in the 'Olympic Green' area. Echoing the Sydney model, Beijing's Olympic site included, besides this complex of new sports facilities, also a major new urban green space, namely the Olympic Forest Park.

Beijing's level of spending on the Olympic event was at an unprecedented level for Olympic Games, $43 billion (Wiki 2013a) and the city had good intentions to create a 'green Games' with sustainable legacies. However the interim assessment of this effort must be a mixed one. On the negative side the main sports facilities, particularly the Olympic stadium, but also including to some extent the aquatic centre (the 'Water Cube'), have not been well used in the post-event period and could be said to be blighted by the 'white elephant' syndrome. As we saw in Part II, this negative legacy syndrome is a common occurrence in the history of mega-events, and it is a predictable outcome of a lack of adequate planning for post-event uses for event-based facilities.[12] However the development in China of public interest in the Western culture of sport (and thus the use of sport facilities whether as spectators or participants) was always likely to be a slow and complex process, one which was unlikely to be much accelerated by the staging of a single sport mega-event. The common Western critical assessment of Beijing's post-Olympic 'white elephant' problem (or, more excessively, its 'ruin porn' problem, as McDonald refers to it (McDonald 2012)) may appear to be justified in relation to the experience of the few years which have elapsed since the event. But it can also be judged to be premature, unbalanced and misleading. On the one hand a longer timeframe was always going to be needed for a fuller assessment of the post-event use of the sport facilities, one which takes into account the long-term development of sport culture in China (Brownell 1995, 2008). On the other hand Western commentary on the Beijing Olympics usually seems blind to its green legacy aspects, perhaps discounting them in the face of the massive scale of the city's recognised pollution and ecological problems and challenges. None the less it is worth noting that in particular the Olympic Forest Park tends to be largely overlooked as a positive event legacy. While it is a recreational centre rather than a sporting one, its material and symbolic contribution to the social and natural environment of north central Beijing is considerable.

As with many other of China's great cities Beijing is expanding rapidly and thus the pressures on urban land usage, on the quality of human habitat and on the natural environment in the city are also increasing rapidly. In principle new urbanisation requires new human and community facilities such as green spaces. The new Olympic Forest Park, which is twice the size of New York's iconic Central Park, has been created from scratch from prior industrial and housing land. It consists of a number of artifical elements, including a lake, a hill, a stream system, wetlands, wooded areas and a meadow in an area close to part of the river system running through Beijing. The park was carefully planned to achieve a number of aims, including the following. Firstly it aimed to show deep traditional Chinese (imperial-era) cultural understandings of nature and of how they can be represented through constructed parkland, located in the modern city and opened up to ordinary (i.e. post-imperial) people. Secondly it aimed to provide the city with a technologically sophisticated working model of urban parkland which includes such features as animal and plant habitat conservation, naturally based water purification processes, uses of solar energy and communication to the public about these and other aspects of the natural environment (Hu 2008, Grove 2012). Finally it aimed to be attractive and popular, to be a well-used recreational facility in the middle of the dense housing developments and commercial life of north central Beijing. In these aims, unlike the post-event problems with its sports facilities, Beijing's Olympic Forest Park has arguably been something of an Olympic legacy success story, and in terms of popularity it attracts over five million visits annually (Grove 2012).

China's Expo: the Shanghai Expo 2010 mega-event and its legacies

If Beijing is China's political capital then Shanghai, the country's second city and now a mega-city with a population of around 23 million, can be seen as its economic capital. The idea that Shanghai might stage an Expo and the connection of this with China's need to modernise has a long history, dating back to the pre-Communist period of the late Qing Empire in the late nineteenth and early twentieth centuries (Hur 2012). However it was only after a turbulent century of war, revolution and economic development that Shanghai was finally in a position in 2010 to stage an Expo. Having waited to stage an Expo for so long it was perhaps appropriate that the event it finally staged was on an unprecedented scale.

Shanghai's 2010 World Expo event was held in the centre of the city, in its Pudong district and on an ex-industrial site in the southern sector of this district. The site was on Shanghai's river, the Huangpu, next to the Lupu bridge which had been completed recently in 2009. The Expo was based mainly on the east bank, but also included an area across the river on the west bank. The Expo's theme was 'Better City, Better Life' and it aimed to explore challenges and possibilities for the future of urban life across the world in the twenty-first century (Busa 2012). However this display of idealistic urbanism was achieved at what was a significant social cost to people living in the area, if, as it has been alleged, eighteen thousand Shanghai residents were pressured to relocate to homes elsewhere in order to enable the Expo site to be created (UN Watch 2010a and 2010b).

Over two hundred nations, corporations and cities participated, creating pavilions and exhibitions of future-oriented visions and technologies around the Expo theme. The target audience for the Expo was mainly a domestic one and particularly the relatively wealthy East Chinese regions around and accessible to Shanghai (Expo 2010). The Expo attracted a world record attendance of 73 million visits, most of which were by Chinese citizens (68.75 million) with foreign tourists making up the rest (4.25 million) (Barboza 2010). A great army of local volunteers (170,000) was mobilised to help organise and service the flows of visitors (Waldmeir 2010). In spite of its relative lack of profile in the international media and for international tourists the Expo was generally deemed to have been successful, not least in China among the national leadership and within the city of Shanghai (Xinhua 2010, NPC 2011).

Beijing may be China's political capital, but since the nineteenth century (and excluding consideration of the special case of Hong Kong) Shanghai has been its financial capital as well as one of the country's major ports (see for instance Wasserstrom 2009). The modern city now sits across the Huangpu River which feeds into the Yangtse River, traditionally the greatest of the historic arteries of trade which reach deep into central China. The Pudong district within which the Expo was located is on the east side of the river, and looks across the river at the older and more populated west side. In particular it looks across at the area called the Bund, a prime location in Shanghai, which originally held European and American banks and trading houses from the late nineteenth century through to the interwar period. The Bund's distinctive period architecture contributes to its contemporary status as mainly a heritage and tourism area. It faces back across the river at Pudong's distinctive and towering skyline as Shanghai's new-era financial and commercial district. Pudong New Area on the east side of the river has been developed since the 1990s as an important new urban zone and is itself of strategic importance nationally for contemporary China both internally and externally. In 2013 the Chinese government gave Pudong the unique official status of being a 'Free Trade Zone' (BBC 2013a, Lewis 2013) to encourage the kind of cultural presence and economic participation among Western companies which they have long experienced in the administratively separate city-state of Hong Kong. Among other Western-style liberties to be allowed in this zone, Western-based social media, internet and press would not be monitored, censored or blocked as they are in every other part of China.

Shanghai aspires to be, and arguably already is, a 'world city' (see for instance Wasserstrom 2009). In the twenty-first century there is an evident link, for instance in the Gulf Arab states and across East Asia, between on the one hand rapid national economic and cultural modernisation and aspiration for future development, and on the other hand the need to symbolise these things by world-class cultural developments such as the construction of iconic (or mega-) urban architecture together with the staging of mega-events. For instance in 2009, as part of its rapid urban expansion, the city of Dubai, in the United Arab Emirates, constructed the tallest tower in the world, the Burj Dubai. This is designed for mixed uses from office, hotel and residential to entertainment and tourism. Consistent with this high-profile approach to urban development the city will be staging a World Expo in 2020.[13] Shanghai's Pudong area is also a leading example of these global/urban trends, specifically the spectacular tower cluster which has been planned and developed over the last twenty years. This cluster consists particularly of the Oriental Pearl TV Tower (opened in 1994), the Jinmao Tower (1999) and the Shanghai World Finance Centre (2008), together with the recently constructed Shanghai Tower, the second tallest structure in the world. Besides its various financial and media functions in and for Shanghai and East China, Pudong's tower cluster also operates as one of the city's main tourist attractions and tourism marketing images both nationally and internationally. However the 2010 Shanghai Expo mega-event was intended to convey a different version of world-class urbanism from that of the tower clusters of central Pudong and we consider this further in a moment.

Shanghai's Expo-related expenditures totalled $45 billion which is slightly more than the cost of the Beijing Olympics ($43 billion) (Knowledge Wharton 2010). The event is estimated to have made an operating profit of $157 million (Eastday 2011) which was reinvested in Expo-related cultural legacy buildings (see later). The Expo is assessed as having had a beneficial short-term economic impact on overseas tourist visits to Shanghai which increased from 6.29 million in 2009 to 8.5 million in 2010 (Eastday 2011), and on associated hotel and residential property sectors of the city (Knowledge Wharton 2010). The event provided a significant catalyst for important long-term improvements in transport infrastructures, including a new road bridge (the Lupu Bridge, 2009), a new road link to the city's international airport (Shanghai Pudong), a major addition to the capacity of its domestic airport (Shanghai Hongqiao), a new terminal to take the largest cruise ships (north Shanghai), a number of new lines on the metro system and a new road tunnel under the Huangpu river linking Pudong with west central Shanghai.

By 2016 the post-Expo development of the Expo site was planned to include a hotel cluster containing two five-star hotels, representing an overall investment into this area of $490 million (CNNGo 2011). It is also worth mentioning another post-Expo urban development in Shanghai, which even though it is elsewhere in Pudong none the less has a 'family relationship' to the Expo. There is a link in American cultural history between the staging of Expos and the creation of theme parks, specifically through the activities of Walt Disney and his corporation (Roche 2000, ch. 5). Arguably this experience is being replayed with contemporary modifications in Shanghai. The city's planners and authorities not only created a successful Expo in Pudong in 2010 but as a follow-on from this they committed the city in 2009 to a joint venture with the Disney corporation to create the Shanghai Disney Resort elsewhere in Pudong at a cost of $5.5 billion. This will eventually contain a large-scale Disneyland theme park, two themed hotels and an entertainment and retailing complex, together with additional smaller theme parks. The first stage opened in 2016 and the resort aims to become one of the most visited tourist attractions in the world, with around fifty million visitors annually (see Barboza and Barnes 2011, also Phillips 2016).

The design of the 2010 Shanghai Expo reflected a number of the macro factors and structural themes relating to contemporary China and to mega-events generally in the twenty-first century which we noted earlier, as well as more local and urban issues relating to Shanghai city. In terms of macro factors and themes, three sets of them are relevant. Firstly, there are the structural and economic changes in China relating to the country's external international image and the promotion of a consumer culture among the country's population. In the Expo this theme was addressed in a creative but essentially familiar way through the quantity and quality of national and other pavilions, from over two hundred nations and other organisations. Secondly, there is the rise of the environmental (greening) theme in twenty-first-century mega-events. In the Expo project this theme was addressed through the clearance of industrial uses and land pollution from the riverside site, in the design of the main buildings and particularly in the construction of a riverside green wetland park (the Houtan park) incorporating a water purification process to decontaminate and use water from the otherwise contaminated river Huangpu nearby. Thirdly, there is the general and rapid urbanisation process which has been experienced in many developing countries, but particularly during China's industrialisation and economic rise since the 1980s. In the Expo this theme was expressed and addressed generally by the official theme of the Expo, namely 'Better City, Better Life' which we noted earlier, and also by the more local and urban aspects of the Expo relating to Shanghai city to which we can now turn.

We have already indicated some of the Expo's main short- and long-term local urban impacts. However it is also worth considering that in various ways the Expo was also attempting to make a longer-term statement about central Shanghai's future development against the background of some of the recent and current developments we have noted. In particular the Expo can be seen as offering imaginative and human-scale alternatives to the kind of high-profile internationally oriented urbanism Shanghai had already been pursuing nearby in central Pudong. This latter kind of urbanism, with its tower cluster which is both spectacular and functional, could be seen as creating places for people either to merely work in or, as tourists, to gaze at, to stay in overnight and then to leave behind. That is, central Pudong does not particularly present itself as offering an urban space in which to live long-term. By contrast, both through its theme and associated exhibitions and also through its legacy the Expo aimed to indicate and to model what an alternative Shanghai urban environment might look like.[14] This is one which was equally as future-oriented as central Pudong, but which might also be qualitatively more sociable and ecological, a zone in which to live and have leisure.

Various of the Expo's legacies, together with its planners' concepts for the post-Expo plans for the future development of the Expo site, are relevant to this vision of a more liveable central urban area and a more leisure and consumption-oriented lifestyle for central urban residents. The housing which is planned for the site will be relatively low-rise and stepped back from the river in order to provide for river views and for access to the riverside wetland park.[15] In addition the Expo is leaving a number of significant and iconic buildings and cultural institutions as its legacy (Xinhua 2012). These include the China Art Museum (or Art Palace) which is housed in the monumental building which served as the China national pavilion during the Expo. One of the Expo's star attractions from that pavilion was the massive digitally animated projection of an eleventh-century Song-dynasty panoramic painting of a medieval Chinese village. This was Zhang Zeduan's work 'Along the River During the Qingming Festival', and this technologically renewed masterpiece also features in the new China Art

Museum. The Expo's legacies also include a second art museum devoted to modern art, the Power Station of Art, together with a large indoor arena (eighteen thousand seats) and entertainment complex (the Mercedes-Benz Arena).

Shanghai already hosts high-quality museums, most notably the Shanghai Museum with its nationally and internationally important collection of Chinese heritage bronzes and porcelain. However the major new art galleries in the (post-) Expo district are intended to add to this and to enable Shanghai to rival the museum clusters of London, New York and Paris, confirming the city's entry into this peer group of world cities (Xinhua 2012, CNNGo 2012). In terms of the history of Expos the Shanghai Expo will be remembered not only for its record-breaking crowds but also because one of its legacies is the world's only World Expo Museum, which opened in 2015. The museum features collections from around the world from the sites of previous Expos together with documentary archives and research facilities. This project has been authorised by the Bureau of International Expositions in Paris and its Secretary General, Vincente Loscertales. The BIE clearly envisages the possibility that another Chinese city could undertake the staging of an Expo in the not-too-distant future (CNNGo 2011). Indeed Guangzhou has already expressed an interest in doing this (Hamlin and Dingmin 2010). The Shanghai experience and its future Expo museum is likely to provide an invaluable resource for any such venture.

Conclusion

Mega-events typically both reflect and symbolise aspects of the social context and social dynamics of the period in which they are staged. The contemporary period is one in which countries, cities and mega-events are all affected and marked by complexities imposed by globalisation and also by discordances involved in the pursuit of renewed forms of modernisation in these conditions. This is particularly the case for countries and cities in non-Western world regions. In these contexts countries and cities face the dual challenge of simultaneously achieving on the one hand such things as primary-phase industrialisation and urbanisation as well as, on the other hand, such things as secondary-phase post-industrialisation, ecological sustainability and life-enhancing forms of urbanism. In this chapter a wide-ranging sociological perspective was used to understand some aspects of the nature and role of mega-events in these globalization-related processes in the contemporary period (Roche 2006b, 2010) particularly in the context of rapid urban development (Roche 1994, 2009a). I suggested that contemporary mega-events organized by cities in non-Western world regions are likely to reflect and symbolise these sorts of discordances. This analysis has been explored and illustrated in this chapter in relation to the non-Western world region of East Asia and its emerging great power China.

The chapter has attempted to convey something of the pace and scale of China's economic emergence and also of how the urbanisation associated with this is being reflected in the country's development of a multiple mega-events strategy. In recent years this has involved the serial staging of multiple mega-events in China's leading cities, particularly Beijing, Shanghai and Guangzhou. China is, undoubtedly, from historical and social scientific perspectives something of an exceptional case in many respects (in the same way, as we saw earlier in Chapter 1, that this has also been long argued in relation to the understanding of the US).[16] As such it is possible to argue that its experiences of staging mega-events may carry few implications for other countries, even those it is categorised with as large-scale and 'emerging' economies (such as the so-called BRICS group of nations).

No doubt China is distinctive and arguably exceptional because of many factors. These include its sheer size and rate of change; the 'civilisation-state' character of its history and culture (Jacques 2012, ch. 7); its one-party state-based political system and relatively undeveloped non-state civil society (and thus the consequent major inequalities in power between state officials and party members on the one hand and ordinary citizens on the other); the state's control of land (and thus the presence of structural incentives for corrupt and collusive relations between state officials and private property developers); and the large migrant component in the make-up of many of its new urban populations (together with the structural denial of the full rights of urban residence and citizenship to them which is involved in the 'hukou' system of local residential registration). As a result of the distinctive level of relatively unaccountable power by party and state officials over migrants, residents and land in China's cities, the clearing and relocation of large numbers of people to create sites for mega-events and their urban legacies is possible to a degree that it is not in the West, or more generally in many other countries and world regions. In these respects, and no doubt in others, we should be aware that the possibility of deriving generalisations which might be relevant to other countries and world regions from China's experiences with mega-events (and indeed its experiences with urban development in general) may well be very limited.

However, while fully acknowledging China's potential exceptionalism, it can also be argued that its recent mega-events have shared some distinctive commonalities with contemporary mega-event projects in other world regions.

Throughout much of the late twentieth century, mega-events were conceived of as essentially short-term projects which needed to be organised as transient cultural or sporting theme parks (Roche 2000, ch. 5). This was the case even if the events did actually happen to have long-term impacts in their host urban environments. However since at least the time of the Sydney 2000 Olympics event organisers around the world, generally including China (with exceptions, such as in the case of Shenzhen) have become much more aware than ever before that their events are intrinsically complex in their characteristics and contexts, and that they are thus risky projects which need careful, well-informed and committed planning. In addition they have become more aware than before that the variety of impacts mega-events can have on cities can potentially be of long-term significance, and thus that they need to be planned for on this legacy basis.

Beyond event organisers and the national and urban political leadership circles they are part of, this kind of awareness of the potentially multi-thematic complexity of contemporary mega-events, together with the longevity of their legacy influences, is also present to a greater or lesser degree among affected urban publics and the urban media they use to interpret public issues. This is particularly visible in the case of mega-events in Western world regions and cities with developed traditions of civil society organisation and media independence (for instance see Hayes and Karamichas 2012b). Not only have mega-event projects been much debated and criticised in Western host cities but also projects to create them have sometimes been rejected by urban citizens (e.g. the Munich public's vote in 2013 against bidding for the 2022 Winter Olympics (Mackay 2013)). Such debate and criticism have not been completely absent in China. This is illustrated in the controversial character of coercive relocation of urban residents to create the space for mega-events which we have considered throughout this chapter, and the visibility of these issues in elements of China's contemporary media systems, including both official media and also internet-based social media.

While recognising the importance of world-regional and national differences for mega-events in all periods, none the less in this chapter and throughout Part III I have suggested that in the contemporary period there is some evidence for the emergence of a new general model of mega-events. This has occurred particularly in response to the nature and success of the Sydney 2000 Olympics (Toohey 2008, Cashman 2011, IOC 2012d). Around the world, and almost irrespective of which world region they are staged in, mega-events in our times are better understood, whether by organisers, by publics or indeed by researchers, by means of the model of open and socially inclusive multi-theme legacy parks rather than by means of the preceding late twentieth-century model of closed and exclusive theme parks (Roche 2000, ch. 5). The former concept means that in the contemporary period mega-events are now commonly expected, on the one hand, to achieve long-term policy goals (or legacies) and on the other hand to do so across a range of varied urban development and other such policies.[17] The urban policies often involve material goals (like the creation of new buildings and infrastructures related to urban parks) together with immaterial goals (like the use of these facilities to drive new economic activity, including in the tourism economy and cultural industries, and the organisation of new urban communities).

In addition, in the preceding late twentieth-century period the environmental or green character of mega-events and their legacies was of little perceived importance (Mol and Zhang 2012). However, as we have seen in Chapter 6, in the contemporary period this aspect has come to be seen as of major significance in various ways wherever mega-events are organised. So not only is the concept of mega-events as involving the creation of multi-theme legacy parks increasingly characteristic of contemporary mega-event production and reception in cities around the world, in addition there is also a greater emphasis within that concept on a realistic and more traditional green and recreational meaning of the concept of the urban park or green space.

This chapter has begun to explore this new concept of contemporary mega-events as being multi-theme legacy parks. The new concept seems particularly well adapted to a period of global shifts at all levels, a period in which mega-event locations are being redistributed away from the West and increasingly include non-Western world regions. We have illustrated both the new concept of mega-events, and also their new contexts, by reviewing mega-events in contemporary China, particularly the cases of the Beijing 2008 Olympics, the Guangzhou 2010 Asian Games and the Shanghai 2010 Expo 2010. The Sydney 2000 Olympic model was only partially and fitfully followed in China's mega-events, and this is no doubt because of the influence of the distinctive features of Chinese society we noted earlier. However at least one concrete commonality from the Sydney model to the Chinese mega-events we have looked at is that they have tended to feature the construction of a major new urban green space. These urban park-building and park-renewing projects have typically aimed to embody, on a permanent basis, environmental and recreational (rather than sporting) values. They can thus be argued to have attempted to make a tangible and practical commitment to a similar understanding of what the urban quality of life now requires in the heart of some of the world's biggest and most dynamic cities. In addition these mega-event projects all aimed, in comparable ways (even if to greater or lesser extents), to use these new urban parks as hubs and catalysts from which some of the other mega-event legacy themes might be addressed.

The early years of the twenty-first century's global shift processes of social change both at the political-economic organisation level and in cultural spheres such as mega-events represent a period of disruptions. This is not least for the West and the international institutions it originated. These include the mega-event owner organisations of the IOC and the BIE which continue to understand and project their Olympic and Expo events as bearers of Western-originated ideas, values and ideologies relating to universal human progress, educability and rights. Mega-event organisations have long needed to manage both their dependence on finance from commercial sources and also the corruption this can engender. These problems and their management have periodically clouded mega-event movements' ideas and values without, however, completely undermining their legitimacy, credibility and popularity in the West. However the global shift in mega-event locations to more regularly shared patterns with non-Western countries, many of which might be authoritarian or otherwise uncommitted to values such as human rights, is more existentially threatening to mega-event movements and their controlling organisations. How far might they go to retain the new global reach and access to finance they are offered by regularly locating in authoritarian or rights-abusing states? Do they have the desire and capacity to be harbingers of progressive political change in host nations as well as catalysts of urban development in host cities?

The global shift means that it is becoming imperative that mega-event organisations and movements face up to these and other related issues. Whether they can discern and commit to credible and sustainable strategies in terms of host-city selection and event location remains currently unclear and an open question.[18] Time will tell.

Notes

1 On globalisation see the discussion and related notes in Chapter 1 above, also Roche 2010a, chs 1 and 7.
2 On world regionalism see Roche 2010a, ch. 2.
3 In relation to 2040 see O'Neill 2001, in relation to 2025 see e.g. CEBR 2014. Indeed some argue that if the comparison of economies is undertaken in terms of 'purchasing power parities' (PPPs) then China had already achieved this dominant position in 2014.

4 Although this is a cumbersome expression to use it is descriptive of a *cultural* category of political communities, and thus it is hopefully much less politically misleading than is its main alternative, namely 'Greater China'.

5 See Jacques 2012, p. 5, also more on recent trends for instance see Ward 2011 and CEBR 2014.

6 For instance see Chow 2010, Jacka et al. 2013, Yang 2007.

7 See ILO 2013, Wang 2008, Whyte 2010.

8 For instance the Shenzen case below, and Chow 2010, ch. 29

9 For instance Smith 2012. One indicator of the existence of a middle class, that is a social category with some assets and disposable income, particularly in a developing country context, is use of the internet (being a 'netizen'). Being a netizen carries implications for people's literacy and education level, for their disposable time as well as income, for their valuation of individuality and privacy, and for their location in the infrastructure-rich environments of cities. At the time of the Beijing Olympics in 2008 China already had over 150 million netizens (see Chapter 4). Only a few years later this figure has ballooned to 650 million (including over 550 mobile internet users (via tablet PCs and 3G mobile phones), many of whom are young people, indicating the emergence of massive middle-class and upper-working-class social categories (see Millward 2015). The vast bulk of these people live in China's expanding cities, since the national policy to roll out broadband and wifi to rural China has not yet been enacted (Yanan 2015).

10 On event costs in Guangzhou see Hamlin and Dingmin 2010, and in Shenzen see Wiki 2011 and Tam 2012a (the latter source includes urban transport costs).

11 For instance Ong 2004, Close et al. 2006, Brownell 2008, Price and Dayan 2008, Cook and Miles 2011, Shin and Bingqin 2013.

12 For instance Roche 1994, Branigan 2012, Bond 2012.

13 The official website for Dubai's planned 2020 Expo is http://expo2020dubai.ae/en/.

14 Information from urban planning academic Prof. Jiang Jun, Tongji University, Shanghai, who was part of the planning group for the Shanghai Expo (interview conducted 7 December 2012, Tongji University).

15 See note 14.

16 On Chinese exceptionalism see for instance Callahan 2012 and Tatlow 2014 and on American 'exceptionalism' see for instance Lipset 1996.

17 On mega-events' urban impacts see Preuss 2004, Gratton et al. 2006, Essex and Chalkley 1998, 1999, Gold and Gold 2011a; on mega-event legacies see Moragas et al. 2003, Kassens-Noor 2012, IOC 2012b, 2012c, 2013b.

18 The IOC's recent Olympic Agenda 2020 was determined after an extensive Olympic Movement-wide consultation process. It includes improvements to the host-city selection process and the further integration of human rights into the process, and the IOC has committed to implementing these aspects (IOC 2014a).

8

Mega-events, glocalisation and urban legacy: London as an event city and the 2012 Olympics

The city of London has a long experience of staging great events, including mega-event genres, though to the contemporary period. This chapter looks into the enduring influences on the city of its experiences of being, in significant respects, an event city.[1] In terms of the past, the chapter considers the long-term and contemporary impacts and legacies of London's Expo events, from both the distant and the recent past. In terms of the present and future it also considers the potentially transformative and legacy-leaving characteristics of the city's most recent mega-event, the 2012 London Olympics. The history of London as an event city and also the recent case of London's 2012 Olympic event illustrates a number of the book's themes. These include firstly the changing balance between Western and non-Western locations of mega-events, secondly the way spectacular mega-events can generally be seen as embedded in socially trans-formative urban legacy projects, and thirdly, within such urban embedding, the potential and emerging relationship between mega-events and urban cultural policy.

London was for a number of centuries the capital and political economic hub of the British worldwide trade and colonial system, a system which gave itself the formal status of being an empire in the late nineteenth century. Thus throughout much of the primary phase of modernisation London was the capital of a worldwide empire through to Britain's decolonisation process in the 1945–60s period. As such it was, de facto, a world city as well as a national city.[2] In the postcolonial period London has retained this world city status largely because of its special strategic role in the global economy as a hub of the global finance industry, and more recently as a target for global property investment and speculation. In these and other respects for London to stage a mega-event is as much a representation of 'the West' as it is of Britain as a host nation. Thus the broader significance of the 2012 Olympics can be interpreted (in relation to the global shift theme) as being that of a 'return to the West' for the Olympics after the 2008 Olympics in China. However, notably, this return to the West in London is in reality something of a brief interlude, since the Games of 2016 and 2020 see the Olympics once again being located outside of the West, in Brazil and Japan respectively. The history of London's mega-events surveyed in this chapter offers a series of cases which bear witness to our theme of the imperative to understand how event-related performative and material spectacle is embedded in changing urban contexts. Finally there is the theme of the potential and emerging relationship between mega-events and urban cultural policy. And the case of the London 2012 Olympics illustrates this very well. Contemporary mega-events and their associated legacy projects like that of London 2012 can involve the promotion of cultural industries and cultural institutions including recreation and tourism as well as sport. Such exercises of 'cultural policy', as we see in this chapter, can be understood as being primary and leading elements, rather than as secondary elements, in the socio-economic and environmental transformations which contemporary mega-event projects can aspire to offer their host cities. As a key element in this discussion we reflect on the fact that the London Olympics attempted to give a strategic centrality to green themes in its post-event legacy-development activities, specifically the creation and uses of a major new urban park, the Queen Elizabeth II Olympic Park.

As we saw in Chapter 6 major events can be used to legitimate the creation of open green space in crowded modern cities. And in the contemporary period this, in turn, can help to serve a number of direct and indirect social goals in urban development policy, particularly in the West in cities undergoing secondary-phase (e.g. post-industrial) regeneration. Events' space-creating capacities can contribute directly to urban society and social policy in three ways. Firstly, the construction of parks can contribute to the general greening of cities which has become an urban policy imperative everywhere given the global ecological crisis. Secondly, parks can contribute directly to the recreational opportunities and thus the life-quality of cities' citizens, denizens and visitors. Finally parks can be used as a spatial hub around which (or near which) new housing and communities can be located. In addition parks can contribute to the urban social-policy agenda more indirectly. From this perspective the focus is on their economic potential to provide spatial hubs for the location of new enterprises in the cultural and creative industries. In this aspect they have the potential to contribute to employment, and thus to urban social-policy goals indirectly by enabling the generation of incomes for employees and also by promoting the social welfare and cultural inclusion associated with both work and work-based consumption. The discussion in this chapter emphasises how the promotion of positive post-event impacts and legacies requires consistent and sustained commitment to social and economic development in and around the event site and its spaces, as well as the capacity to recognise changing circumstances and opportunities and to adapt policies pragmatically to take advantage of them. London's experience with major events, particularly with the 2012 Olympics, provides good illustrations of these issues.

The chapter proceeds in four stages. In the first stage we look briefly at some of the history of London's major events in the modern era. This enables two points to be made. On the one hand the passage of time from the initial events can be considerable in the case of London, and this enables us to recognise the reality of long-term impacts and legacies and their continuing contemporary relevance. On the other hand the continued relevance of event legacies into the present is particularly evident in the field of London's contemporary urban cultural tourism. London's experience contains some interesting examples of both of these points: they are discussed in the first section. The three stages of the discussion which follow in this chapter all focus on the particular case of the London 2012 Olympics and its impacts and legacies. Thus the second stage of the discussion introduces the general policy and planning context and aims of the Olympic project, particularly in relation to its long-term social and sport policy goals and aspirations. The third stage looks in more detail at the project's directly social aspects and legacies, in terms of such things as the construction of housing and of the Olympic Park. Finally the fourth stage of the discussion looks into the Olympic project's indirectly social character in terms of its economic and employment impacts and legacies, particularly in terms of the cultural and creative industries. It also notes the role of the Olympic Park, in addition to its primary socio-environmental role, in relation to this economic context.

London, major events and modernity: event legacies and contemporary tourism

Like any major capital city London has always had a history of being an event city.[3] That is it has always been a focal point for mass public gatherings with some explicitly national political dimension, whether conservative (e.g. royal weddings, public executions or state funerals) or radical (e.g. anti-war demonstrations, political rallies etc.). And this has particularly been so in stages of modernisation from the nineteenth century through to contemporary times. In addition it has been an event city in that it helped to create and develop mass public-event genres of international interest and significance, which, even if they implicitly had a political character, were explicitly promoted as being mainly cultural or sporting events and thus as aspiring to be apolitical. As we have noted in earlier discussions London took a lead in relation to the Expo mega-event genre. It staged the first international Expo, the legendary Crystal Palace event in Hyde Park in 1851.[4] And it contributed to the development of the genre by staging a subsequent series of international and 'imperial' expos in the South Kensington area neighbouring the former Crystal Palace site in central London in 1862, 1871–74 and 1886. The 1851 Expo and some of London's other major nineteenth-century and contemporary cultural and sport events are summarised in Table 8.1. The selection aims to emphasise those cultural or sporting events which have left some notable architectural legacies and cultural economy legacies to the city, particularly those which continue to have significance into the present in the field of popular and cultural tourism.

Table 8.1 presents an overview of some of the major international events staged in London from the 1851 Crystal Palace Expo event through to the present. This covers the two periods of the modernisation process we have been concerned with in this book, namely the primary phase (early nineteenth to late twentieth century) and the secondary phase (late twentieth century to present). In the primary phase Expos or Expo-type events dominated over Olympics and sport events in London's experience of major events which have left long-term urban legacies. Even though London hosted two Olympics in this general period, in 1908 and 1948, neither of them was primarily responsible for leaving an urban legacy.

The 1908 London Olympics was staged in the context of, and in the stadium built for, the Franco-British Expo. The Expo's other main temporary neo-classical buildings were clad in white marble, attracting the name White City, a name which had been previously used in Expo-related media and popular discourse (and for the same reason) to characterise the main buildings of the Expo in Chicago in 1893.[5] The White City Stadium was thus an Expo legacy rather than an Olympic legacy. From 1908 onwards it was a notable and popular element in London's twentieth-century national and international sport infrastructure for over two generations through to its closure in 1970. The 1948 London Olympics was held during the early post-Second World War period of austerity, in a city which was still being physically reconstructed after suffering extensive damage during the War.[6] Since there were many other priorities at the time for public expenditure and private philanthropy, the funding available for the event was minimal. So it was fortunate that an existing football stadium, the

Table 8.1 London's major international events and urban legacies, 1851–2012

Period of modernisation	Event	Location in the city	Nature of zone	Key places and spaces
PRIMARY PHASE (nineteenth to late twentieth century)	1851 Expo	Central London (South Kensington)	Cultural complex	*Albertopolis* V&A Museum Natural History Museum (and later Albert Hall, Science Museum, Royal College of Art, Imperial College etc.)
	(1862 Expo) (1871–74 Exhibitions) (1886 Expo)	Central London (South Kensington) for all these		
	1908 Expo and Olympics	West Central London	Sport complex	*White City* Sport Stadium (1908–70)
	1924–25 Expo	North West London	Sport and exhibition complex	*Wembley Stadium*
	1948 Olympics	North West London	Sports complex	*Wembley Stadium (and pool, halls etc.)*
	1951 Expo	Riverside, Central London	Cultural complex	*Southbank* Festival Hall, (and later National Theatre, Globe Theatre, Tate Modern etc.)
	1966 FIFA World Cup	North West London	Sport stadium	*Wembley Stadium*
SECONDARY PHASE (Late twentieth century to present)	2000 Expo	South East London	Entertainment complex	*O2 Arena* (originally Millennium Dome)
	2012 Olympics	East London	Sport and entertainment complex; Cultural economy complexes; Park	Olympic Stadium, Olympic Park, 'Olympicopolis'

Sources: On Expos the information is drawn from Expo histories by Allwood 1977, Greenhalgh 1988, Findling and Pelle 2008, Monclus 2009, and the BIE website (www.bie-paris.org/). On other events the information is drawn from Inglis 1996 and World Stadiums (www.worldstadiums.com)

Notes: Column 5, 'Wembley Stadium' etc. italicised to indicate the location of the 1948 Olympics and 1966 World Cup Final in the legacy building of the 1923–24 Expo. The two events themselves did not leave any significant legacy legendary home of English football at Wembley, could be used together with its complex of facilities. These included a swimming pool and large exhibition halls which could be used for the gymnastics competition and other elements of the sport programme. Wembley's stadium and halls were actually urban legacies from the 1924–25 British Empire Exhibition, one of a series of imperial Expos staged by Britain and also by France in the early twentieth century.[7] The 1948 Olympics used these legacies but did not add any of its own. The same can be said of the FIFA World Cup mega-event which England hosted in 1966, the Final match of which was staged in the Wembley stadium. By contrast in the secondary phase of modernisation the dominant event in London, both as a performance and in its aspirations to create urban legacy, has been an Olympic Games event, namely the 2012 Olympics, and we will look into this case in much more detail in the following sections.

The dominant role of Expos in the primary phase of modernisation in London, both as performances and also as urban legacy-creators, was established by the very first such event in 1851. The Crystal Place event, which was staged in Hyde Park, attracted six million visits and made a financial surplus. This enabled the organisers to purchase an area of land in South Kensington adjacent to the Park. Their purpose was to develop a permanent cultural legacy on this new site to commemorate both the Crystal Palace Expo and also the leading role in the Expo project of Queen Victoria's husband, Prince Albert. Over the course of the remaining decades of the nineteenth century the original and accumulated surplus would be invested in various facilities on the site to enable the work of collection, curation and public exhibition of science, technology, arts and crafts which had been begun at the Expo to be maintained and built up (Roche 2000, ch. 2). Understandably this urban enclave and its facilities both at the time and later came to be popularly known as 'Albertopolis'.[8]

Expos were held on this parkside neighbourhood in 1862 and 1886, and smaller-scale exhibitions were staged there in the years 1871–74. Over time a cluster of museums of international significance was developed there, including the Victoria and Albert Museum (V&A, a design and craft museum), the Natural History Museum (commemorating Charles Darwin's achievements in biology) and the Science Museum. Other relevant facilities in the area which were developed as part of this cluster of cultural institutions included the advanced teaching and research institutions of the Royal College of Art and Imperial College (now a world-leading science and technology university), and also the Albert Hall, a major six-thousand-seat venue for musical performances of national and international significance.[9] Albertopolis is a physical and organisational embodiment of the potential for mega-events to contribute long-term urban legacies to their host cities. It remains important for contemporary London as a leading element in the city's current repertoire of cultural tourism attractions, and we return to this topic in a moment.

In 1951, a century after the original 1851 Expo which left the Albertopolis legacy, another Expo-type exhibition event, the Festival of Britain, was held in London, and its urban legacy has turned out to be nearly as significant as that of the Great Exhibition.[10] The 1951 event's programme was staged on a number of sites on the south bank of the Thames, but the main site was in the very centre of London, slightly downstream and across the river from Britain's Parliament and seat of government. The event celebrated Britain's contributions to modern twentieth-century life, from science and technology through to art, design and architecture. Although this was a nationally rather than internationally orientated event, it was on the large scale of an Expo, and it attracted ten million visits. It had some of the same kind of programme elements as an Expo, including spectacular temporary architecture. Also, as a symbol of Britain's cultural and material postwar reconstruction, it left the city with some important physical and cultural legacies. The key architectural legacy was the Royal Festival Hall, a 2,500-seat concert hall built in what was then the relatively avant-garde international modernist style. Later, in 1967, this was accompanied by the Queen Elizabeth Hall incorporating the Purcell Roon, smaller music and performance venues in a more extreme, 'brutalist' version ot the modernist architectural style style. Public access to these halls with their various facilities also involved giving the public access to the south central area of London's Thames riverside. This spatial group provided the kernel of what, echoing the slow development of the Albertopolis cultural quarter, has over time become the 'Southbank' cultural cluster and quarter.

The Southbank quarter[11] is a linear riverside cluster of cultural institutions, and a centrally important group within this cluster is the Southbank Centre. This includes the two halls (above) together with an art gallery (the Hayward) which was developed in the late 1960s. Other cultural venues in the same riverside area which were developed in the same general period or later were the British Film Institute (BFI) and the National Theatre. The BFI opened its main set of screens next to the Southbank Centre in 1957 in what is now 'BFI Southbank'. Next to the BFI the National Theatre, which was opened in 1976–77, represented a further major development of the core area of the Southbank cultural quarter. A riverside pedestrian walkway (opened in 1977) links these central sites to three further notable nearby riverside tourist and cultural attractions. On the eastern side of the Southbank Centre the walkway links to 'Shakespeare's Globe' (a 1997 reconstruction of a sixteenth-century theatre in the style of, and near the original site of, William Shakespeare's Globe theatre) and the internationally recognised Tate Modern art gallery (opened in 2000). And on the western side of the Southbank Centre the walkway links to the nearby 'London Eye' (a modern version which opened in 2000 of a Ferris Wheel-type of rotating public-viewing system).

Before we conclude this section it is worth briefly noting the urban legacy of the most recent Expo-type event staged in London, namely the 'Millennium Experience' exhibition held in 2000.[12] In terms of content this was a poor-quality event compared to the 1851 and 1951 Expos. However it enabled an industrially polluted riverside site on the Greenwich peninsula, next to the historic Thames-side urban village of Greenwich in south-east London, to be reclaimed, connected to the London metro system and developed for leisure and housing purposes. In particular it left a spectacular piece of architecture, namely Richard Rogers's 'Millennium Dome', a large-scale tent-like structure which had originally contained the entire Expo. Post-event in 2007, after a long and controversial planning hiatus, a successful and sustainable use was finally developed for this building. It was restructured by the US entertainment company AEG into a large (twenty-thousand-seat) world-class indoor arena (renamed the 'O2 Arena' after the telecoms company sponsoring it) plus an indoor entertainment zone containing restaurants, shops and exhibition areas. The current popularity and success of this venue as an attraction for both London residents and tourists is indicated by the fact that for some years the arena has been recorded as the busiest in the world in terms of accumulated ticket sales, attracting an annual aggregate audience of over two million people (Pollstar 2013, 2014). The O2 Arena and its entertainment complex in Greenwich is undoubtedly a substantial Expo-derived urban legacy for London which contributes to the city's popular cultural and tourism economy. However it is not on the same scale as the two Expo-originated cultural quarters of Albertopolis and Southbank with which we have been mainly concerned here.

The whole linear riverside area of the Southbank cultural quarter can be said to derive ultimately from and build around the original Expo-based legacy of the Southbank Centre and its various buildings and facilities. Like the Expo-derived Albertopolis cultural quarter, the Southbank area is now an extremely important element in London's cultural tourism economy and annually attracts millions of visitors. This is indicated in Table 8.2 which lists the ten most popular and most visited London tourism attractions in 2014. Half of them (column 3) are

Table 8.2 London tourism and event legacies: leading cultural tourism attractions, 2014

Rank order (top ten)	Cultural tourism attractions		Visitor numbers (millions)
	Leading tourism attractions	*Event legacy-related attractions*	
1	British Museum		6.69
2	The National Gallery		6.41
3		Southbank Centre	6.25
4		Tate Modern	5.78
5		Natural History Museum	5.38
6		Science Museum	3.35
7		V&A Museum	3.18
8	Tower of London		3.07
9	Somerset House		2.46
10	National Portrait Gallery		2.06

Source: Drawn from Association of Leading Visitor Attractions, (ALVA) information. See ALVA's website, www.alva.org.uk

located in London's two main Expo-originated cultural quarters. That is, the Southbank Centre and Tate Modern are parts of the Southbank quarter, and the Natural History Museum, the Science Museum and the V&A Museum are parts of the Albertopolis quarter.

In this section we have seen how London can be analysed as an event city and something of the long-term urban legacy implications of major events like Expos. Given this context we can now turn to consider the most recent London mega-event, the 2012 Olympic Games, and its legacy implications for the city.

The London 2012 Olympics: policy contexts and sport legacies

As a short-term event the London 2012 Olympics was widely regarded internationally to have been a success across a range of fronts.[13] In a longer-term perspective in my view it also promises to be eventually assessable as having had largely positive impacts and consequences in most legacy areas particularly those relating to the host city. The IOC President Jacques Rogge commented that London had 'created a legacy blueprint for future Games hosts'.[14] As we have discussed in earlier chapters, mega-events like Olympic Games are increasingly prospectively planned and retrospectively analysed as being multi-thematic projects with multiple functions. In this and the following sections we outline some of the distinct types of legacy plans and aspirations which were embodied in the London 2012 project, from the thematic fields of sport culture and sport policy to the non-sport thematic fields of urban social policy and urban economic-development policy. We do not yet have the benefit of the passage of time to consider the long-term working out of the legacies of this event, as we did in relation to London's earlier mega-events. However we will also attempt to make some provisional assessments of the progress which has been made in each of the main thematic areas of legacy in the early post-event years which have elapsed so far.

The political and urban background

Locating the 2012 Olympic Games in East London was a high-level policy project to introduce a powerful catalyst into the long-overdue effort to generate social and economic development in this disadvantaged area of the UK's capital city. This effort had got under way particularly with the advent of the New Labour government under the leadership of Prime Minister Tony Blair from 1997, the creation in 2000 of both the Greater London Authority (GLA) and with an influential new office of London Mayor to lead the GLA. In the same year a leading Labour Party politician, Ken Livingstone, was elected as the first Mayor in this new system. Blair and the UK government were interested in mega-events but their experience with them was not good. They had supported both the English Football Association's failed bid in 2000 to stage the 2006 FIFA football World Cup and also the staging, in 2000 of the Millennium Experience Expo-type event. The latter, as we noted earlier, was poorly conceived, poorly programmed and had no clear and immediate plan for post-event use and legacy.[15] Lessons were learned from the problems both with the FIFA event bid and with the Millennium Expo event when the possibility of bidding for the Olympics arose in 2004.

From the beginning London's Olympic project was seen in the wider planning context of the masterplan to bring economic and social development to the region of the 'Thames Gateway', situated roughly between the East End of London and the English Channel.[16] The notion of London having a distinctive 'East End' implicitly refers to the difference of this area from the affluent and fashionable central zone of London traditionally referred to as the 'West End'.[17] The East End, at least until very recently, has by contrast been commonly perceived as poor, unfashionable and disconnected. Core areas of the old East End close to the river Thames had been a zone of very large-scale dock and housing construction in the late nineteenth century when London was the main port and trading centre of the worldwide British Empire.

In the postwar and post-British Empire period the East End declined. The decline was particularly dramatic when container technology was introduced into the international merchant shipping and docking industries from the 1970s onwards. The East End suffered rapid and steep economic decline and physical dereliction. The dock industry moved away to deeper-water ports and to new purpose-built container terminals which were nearer the sea. These new port facilities were located outside of London, further down the Thames estuary at Tilbury and beyond. The East End of London suffered a major loss of employment and of sources of income together with a migration of significant elements of the traditional working class community to the new areas of dock-related employment. For two or three decades there was little to replace these losses.

From the 1980s through to the present the East End, as an area of low rents and low cost of living but also low standards of living, continued to attract immigrants looking for employment. It spiralled down to become one of the UK's worst urban areas in terms of social inequality and exclusion, multiple disadvantage and transience. Two years prior to the Olympics, in 2010, three of the four local authority areas (or 'boroughs', namely Hackney, Tower Hamlets and Newham) in which the Olympic Park and its Olympic sport venues were to be located were assessed as being in the twenty most socially deprived local authority areas in England.[18] The main Olympic borough, Newham, had particularly high levels of unemployment, household overcrowding, recent immigration and ethnic complexity.[19] Perhaps understandably, given the onset of both a global recession and a UK national economic recession from 2008, the poor social deprivation situation in the four boroughs had worsened over the 2007–10 period, the same period in which the Olympics site was being built (UK Gov 2011).

By the early 2000s the East End's social problems and needs were understood to be a priority in terms of public investment in urban socio-economic policy and urban regeneration.[20] And with the UK's surprise victory in 2005 in the international competition to become the host for the 2012 Olympics it became clear that the key policy instrument which would end up carrying responsibility for helping to address these problems and needs would be a sport-oriented mega-event. In spite of its national-level, international-level and sport-oriented characteristics, the Olympic project managed to conceive of itself, popularise itself with the public and legitimate itself as being an exercise in progressive urban socio-economic policy which was interested in and concerned about its location among particular communities in the city of London. Having said this, it none the less also remained the case that in the pre-event period the London Olympic project was always likely to be controversial, to be a topic of public debate among many and to provoke active opposition among some. This was possibly most visibly and vocally the case in 2007 when the UK government finally confirmed the project's budget. The figure of £2.37 billion ($3.12 billion) had been used for event costs as part of the original bid to the IOC in 2005 by the promoters of the project. However this had long been suspected to be a gross underestimate and the revised budget was £9.3 billion ($12.23 billion). The project ultimately kept to this figure, but understandably the quadrupling of the original budget attracted much public attention and national media criticism (for instance see Bond 2007 and Milland 2007).

A critical sociological research study undertaken in 2011–12 into 'critical and oppositional responses to the 2012 Olympics' (Giulianotti et al, 2015, hereafter referred to as Giulianotti et al., p. 105) elaborates on this national-level and media-based critical discourse which accompanied the Olympic project and which included the views both of local organisations (reported in the press) and also of the press themselves. Giulianotti et al's study noted that, beyond an undergrowth of small-scale and under-reported protest activities the only form of criticism of the Olympic project which achieved something of the substance of the national-level media criticism was local-level 'community complaint' in the four boroughs containing the Olympic Park (pp. 108–13). These included complaints about what they predicted to be a 'lack of local economic impact on jobs and business', the use of compulsory purchase orders to clear residents and businesses out of land allocated for Olympic site purposes, and the lengthy inconveniences and costs imposed on local residents and businesses by the construction of the Olympic Park and its venues. However, unlike the national-level criticism, the study indicates that local complainants were generally 'not opposed to hosting the Games' (p. 106).

Overall Giulianotti et al. clearly imply that the phenomenon of criticism of and opposition to the London 2012 Olympic project needs to be kept in perspective. On the one hand they acknowledge that in spite of it 'The Games were widely praised for succeeding in delivering secure venues, spectacular athletic performances and event ceremonies and sustained post-event support from the UK public' (p. 100). By comparison the overall picture they draw of the six types of criticism of and opposition to the Olympic project they identified (i.e. at national level and also at community level, plus the four small-scale types listed above) was that they were very fragmented, often on too small a scale, readily managed by the police and underreported. Thus it is not surprising that they are able to observe that generally such criticism and protest had 'relatively limited socio-political impact' (p. 100). We can now turn to look into the Olympic project in more detail, beginning with its sport-related aspects and, in this sport area, its legacy potential, and then moving on to consider its non-sport social and economic aspects and its legacy potentials in these areas.

Key elements of the London 2012 Olympic event

As noted earlier, London had originally budgeted only £2.37 billion ($3.12 billion) for the Games (IOC 2012a) but later this wholly unrealistic cost estimate was raised by the government to a more realistic £9.3 billion ($12.33 billion) in 2007. This latter figure was still less than half the budget the Chinese were at the time devoting to the 2008 Beijing Olympics, and this discrepancy was initially a source of concern about the potential for later uncontrollable cost escalation in a mega-project such as this. The onset of the Euro-American economic recession in 2008 and the rise of the politics of austerity in the UK (as elsewhere) from 2010 created the conditions for a continuing public debate about the costs of the Olympic project in the British media throughout the 2005 to 2012 period. These concerns deepened when, on the one hand, the post-event view of the Athens Olympics revealed the extent to which money could be wasted on 'white elephant' facilities and also when, on the other hand, the Beijing Olympics indicated just how high expenditure might need to be in order to stage a Games which would be recognised internationally as being impressive and successful. However the London 2012 project was well-organised financially and the event and its facilities were eventually delivered £528 million ($851.8 million) under budget (BBC 2013c).

To justify the large public investment in the Olympic project and to maximise its capacity to stimulate positive social and economic development in London, the main base of the project had to be located in London's most needy area, the East End. Of course this was not a completely exclusive policy choice. Many of the Olympic sites for particular sports could be distributed around other parts of the city, although these tended to be in more affluent and less needy areas than the East End. For instance the numerous existing international-quality sport venues in London which the Olympic programme used included Wembley

Stadium (for football) and the All England Lawn Tennis Club at Wimbledon (for tennis). In addition the touristic image of London could be promoted to 'the world' watching the Olympics on television by using picturesque heritage sites for Olympic events. These included Hampton Court (for the start of some of the road cycling), Horseguards Parade (for beach volleyball), Lord's cricket ground (for archery), Greenwich Park (for horseriding), Hyde Park (for triathlon), the O2 Arena (for gymnastics) and the Mall near Buckingham Palace (for the marathon). Also large public television screens were set up in various locations, for the masses of fans and the public who were not able to get tickets for events. The big-screen venues included Victoria Park for East End residents and Hyde Park for both Britons and international visitors to London.

Allowing for exceptions such as these, however, the bulk of the Olympics' core sport programme (for instance most of the athletics and swimming events) was focused in the Olympic Park. And it was agreed early on between the main stakeholders (the UK government, the Greater London Authority (GLA) and the British Olympic Association (BOA)) that the Park and its new sports and related facilities would be located in the heart of the old East End, at Stratford. The Stratford location was at the confluence of four socially disadvantaged boroughs (Newham, Hackney, Tower Hamlets and Waltham Forest) and thus contained the possibility that the influence and stimulus of the event might be capable of being experienced by each of them, particularly Newham. The Olympic Park site is a fairly irregular and linear one running on a north–south axis along the line of the Lea river. The Lea is one of the many tributaries of the river Thames which since the nineteenth century had been part buried in culverts and part canalised, and it had become significantly polluted. The area was largely an underused complex of railway land and areas used for low-level industrial, commercial uses and low-rent housing. Much of the land was contaminated from previous dock-related industrial uses and also from the results of Second World War bombing. This created barriers to land and property development since developers would not carry the costs of remediation, perhaps understandably seeing them as being matters of public interest requiring public expenditure and investment. In addition the area's education and crime problems created further barriers to inward investment and economic development. The Olympic project gave a once-in-a-generation opportunity to make a significant financial, organisational and cultural investment in the area which might help to address both its physical environmental problems and also its social problems.

London's Olympic project had learned from previous Olympics, particularly from Sydney 2000. Like Sydney, London attempted to use the Games event to

go beyond sport culture and to achieve positive socio-economic and environmental legacies for the host city. Also like Sydney and Beijing, London
approached the design of the main Olympic Park site and its urban legacies from
a green planning perspectives (for instance see Hartman 2012). As with previous
Games organisation the London Olympic project was functionally split between
an agency devoted to ensuring the construction of the facilities for the event
(the Olympic Delivery Authority, ODA) and one devoted to ensuring the performance of the event itself (the London Organising Committee of the Olympic
Games, LOCOG). However the London Olympic project was distinctive in that
its organisation also contained a third agency devoted to ensuring, in the pre-
event period, the planning and contracting of post-event land and facility uses
and legacies (the Olympic Legacy Delivery Company, OLDC, which was controlled by the London Mayor as part of the GLA as the London Legacy Delivery
Corporation, LLDC).[21]

The creation of the OLDC/LLDC was an important organisational innovation. London organisers attempted to avoid repeating the 'white elephant' facility problems which had beset both the Athens and Beijing Olympic projects,
and which caused unnecessary and demoralising delays in post-Olympic developments in both Sydney and Beijing. The main topographical and architectural
elements of the Olympic Park were essentially designed for long-term uses. But
the underlying park was given a temporary overlay (for instance special larger-
scale pedestrian routes, bridges and catering venues) to enable the unusual scale
of Olympic event crowds to be safely managed (London Assembly 2007, LLDC
2014, IOC 2013d). This Games-event overlay was removed in the immediate
post-event period and the underlying and post-event Park was revealed in two
stages in 2013 and 2014. The innovativeness and functionality involved in the
work of an agency such as this as part of the organisation of an Olympic Games
has been recognised by the IOC and recommended by them as good practice
to future bidding cities.[22]

Overall the post-event park (named the Queen Elizabeth II Olympic Park)
was planned to consist of a multi-thematic complex of places and spaces which
would enable a range of direct long-term urban legacies to be developed
(Hartman 2012). These included legacies in the thematic areas of sport and
related entertainment; employment and commercial development; social participation and cultural inclusion; housing and community-building; and recreation and environmental improvement. In addition there are a number of areas,
such as transport, tourism and technology in which legacy effects of the Olympic
event and its Park might be describable as being more indirect – a consequence

of rather unplanned synergies between the event and other factors in East London's social environment. We can now briefly look in particular at sport-related aspects of the event and their potential for creating a sport legacy.

Sport legacies of the 2012 Olympics

The sport facilities created for the 2012 Olympic Games event in the Olympic Park, both during and after the event, were intended to leave 'sport-related legacies'. That is, they aimed to promote sport as offering entertaining experiences to ordinary people whether through spectatorship or participation, and in the latter case also offering the promotion of public-health policy goals. Post-event the audiences addressed range from local East Enders to Londoners more generally, and they also include domestic and international visitors. The main sports to be supported and promoted post-event by facilities built for the Games include athletics, cycling, swimming, football, tennis and basketball. Some of the Games sport facilities were temporary (e.g. the Olympic basketball and the hockey venues) and these were removed post-event to make way for other uses of the spaces as parts of the construction of the post-event Park. Others were always intended to be permanent features in the Park, even if some temporary adaptations were made to them for the purposes of the event. These include the Aquatics centre (designed by the starchitect Zaha Hadid)[23] and the much-debated main Olympic Stadium.[24]

The event's sport facilities may well stimulate an increase in East Enders' involvement in sport culture as spectators of professional sport events. However the picture seems to be more mixed in relation to local people's participation in sport and physical activities. In the post-Olympic period trends in physical activities among the population in Hackney, which is one of the main boroughs neighbouring the Olympics Park, have been generally positive, and the percentage which is physically inactive is now lower than the national UK average. However trends in physical activity in other neighbouring boroughs, notably Newham (which encompasses the south side of the Olympic Park, including many of its sport venues) and also Tower Hamlets, have been negative. Newham in particular has now declined (by 2014) to being the local borough with the lowest percentage in England of the population engaging in physical activity (UKactive 2014a and 2014b).

More generally, in spite of the London organisers' pitch to the IOC in 2005 that staging the Olympics in London would 'inspire a generation' of Britons to increase their engagement with sport, they are unlikely to achieve this at the national UK level.[25] National sport and physical activity participation levels in the UK are low in international comparative terms (UKactive 2014b, p. 6, figure 1). What is more, they seem to be getting lower over time. Sebastian Coe, the London Olympic project leader and promoter of the idea of an Olympic sport legacy, seemed to recognise this in his contribution to a recent post-Olympic report on the problem of physical inactivity in Britain. Thus he observes that 'physical inactivity accounts for nearly one-fifth of premature deaths in the UK. [But] ... inactivity levels are due to increase by a further 15 per cent by 2030.' He recognises that the problem requires 'urgent action' and that 'turning the tide of inactivity would be hugely important for our legacy story'. However it is evident from what Coe says that the London 2012 Olympic sport mega-event. understood as a policy action, whatever else it may have achieved, has not been adequate to the task of 'turning the tide' in terms of Britons' participation in sport and physical activities. For instance national adult obesity rates, which are currently already historically high at 26 per cent among males, are set to treble in future to 74per cent by 2030 according to the World Health Organisation (WHO) (UKactive 2014a, also Meikle 2015 and HSCIC 2015).

From a sociologically informed policy perspective, physical activity levels in national populations need to be understood as a function of a complex range of structural, policy and cultural factors. These include such factors as the extent and quality of physical education in the national school system, the degree of sedentariness in the organisation of economic activity, the nature and power of national food and drink industries and the consumer culture surrounding them, as well as the enduring pattern of national social divisions and inequalities.[26] They also include cultural differences between societies in their degree of familiarity with and commitment to Western sport traditions, differences which would be manifest, for instance in any comparison between the Sydney and Beijing Olympics. These sorts of factors are the long-term responsibility of governmental social, sport and health policies and not of one-off mega-events. Sport mega-events can promote sport culture in the wider public in diffuse ways. But they should not be expected to have the capacity to transform public sport participation in any 'single shot' or 'quick fix' way.[27]

However, as we have seen earlier in the case of various past and recent Olympic Games events (e.g. Chapter 6), the situation in relation to multi-thematic *non*-sport legacies at the urban level of the host city can potentially be more positive. Here the staging mega-events, particularly where they are part of a long-term urban planning process, can potentially 'make a difference' and can act as both a signal and a catalyst for long-term social and economic change.

It can be argued that, over time, the London 2012 Olympics and its legacies could turn out to be good examples of this. So now we take a look into some of these non-sport areas and their potential for promoting event-related legacies.

Social impacts and legacies of the London 2012 Olympics
Social and cultural inclusion dimensions

The potential for the London 2012 Olympics to have positive long-term legacy influences on the entrenched social divisions of traditional and contemporary British society generally is no doubt limited. To the extent that such a potential exists, it is likely to be strongest within East London, with a lesser influence on the metropolis of London more generally. Given East London's generally socially disadvantaged situation, the various explicitly social-policy-oriented aspects of the post-event developments in and around the Olympic Park Games promise to have a relatively positive although limited influence (Vanderhoven 2012, Watt 2013). This is likely to be particularly so in legacy areas like employment and economic growth, and also in housing and community-building, each of which we discuss in more detail below. In addition, as we have indicated above, there is reason to be sceptical about the Olympics' influences on long-term sport participation in the UK. That said, it is reasonable to expect some medium-term increase in sport participation, particularly among the young, in the East End boroughs bordering on the Olympics Park as school and sports clubs become more familiar with accessing the Park's critical mass of high-quality sport venues and facilities.

We can speculate that the Games event might have some long-term legacies in terms of social participation and cultural inclusion beyond the practical aspects mentioned so far. If so this may have to do with the popularly perceived character and success of the event and the *memorability* of this. Unlike the 2000 Millennium Experience event, but more like the 1951 Festival of Britain event, the 2012 Olympics created, at the time, a distinctive national 'feel good' factor and an experience of positive national identity and pride. Arguably these experiences are likely to endure long in collective and personal memories in Britain. This is even more the case given the rarity value of the Olympic mega-event. For most people in most countries which stage an Olympic Games this will be a once-in-a-generation and maybe once-in-a-lifetime experience.

Various aspects of the Olympic event communicated a contemporary socially inclusive and culturally inclusive version and vision of British identity. Under the influence of factors such as post-colonialism, globalisation and EU-based Europeanisation, British society in the early twenty-first century has objectively become very multicultural in its composition to a historically unprecedented degree. While this has generated some reaction and division at the national-istic fringes of British society, the national public generally has been open to change and difference, and has become increasingly cosmopolitan in many of its mainstream attitudes and values. This is evident in the nation's leading cities like London and particularly so in city areas like the East End. Various aspects of the London 2012 Olympic event reflected this emergent British identity in which a large proportion of the population, at least superficially, has seemed comfortable with cultural plurality and social change. Arguably these aspects are likely to contribute to the long-term memorability of the event. This is even more the case given the British public's unexpected and marginal decision in a referendum in 2016 to exit the EU, which promises to usher in a future domi-nated by more nationalistic, monocultural and introspective versions of British identity. In this context the contrasting multiculturalism and internationalism of Britain's Olympic 2012 'moment' is likely to endure as an important and even contested 'national' memory, discordant for some but inspirational for others. Identity-relevant aspects of the London Olympics included many ele-ments such as the Olympic Torch relay and the Paralympic Games which space does not permit us to explore here. However they also include the elements of the Opening Ceremony, the 'Gamesmaker' volunteers and the achievements of British Olympic Champions, and we can now briefly look at each of these in turn.

The Opening Ceremony

The Opening Ceremony of the 2012 Olympic Games was designed by the renowned film-maker Danny Boyle and scripted by Frank Cottrell Boyce as a television show (also see observations on the mediation of this ceremony earlier in Chapter 3). In the course of the show a great national pageant was broadcast to the watching world representing Britain's contribution to the modern world in terms of both the industrial revolution and also social progress (IOC 2012c). The vision of the industrial revolution was that it was built on technologically innovative entrepreneurship. This was symbolised, among other things, by the well-known British actor Kenneth Branagh playing the figure of the leading and innovative nineteenth-century engineer Isambard Kingdom Brunel. In a dra-matic industrial staging it was implied that the Olympic project, symbolised by the 'forging' of the Olympic rings, had been created in Britain. The vision of social progress in general was that it was built on civil-society-based social and democratic movements such as the women's movement and the movement to create a welfare state. The former was symbolised through a depiction of early twentieth-century 'suffragette' demonstrations for the enfranchisement of women, and the latter was symbolised by reference to the National Health Service. With the involvement of various other internationally recognisable symbols and icons of traditional and contemporary British popular culture including the Queen, James Bond and British rock music, the Opening Ceremony was an imaginative, impressive and lively experience, and it was favourably received not only domestically but also internationally.[28] As noted earlier, for a variety of reasons aspects of these generally progressive and inclusive representations of British national identity are likely to remain memorable, thus constituting intangible cultural legacies, at both collective and inter-personal levels in British society.

The 'Gamesmaker' volunteers

Every mega-event, and particularly Summer Olympic Games, needs the help of a 'civil army' of unpaid volunteers to work on the complex range of operations and functions which enable such events to occur. The UK has a long and strong tradition of civil society activity and participation. This has been given a higher political profile and public status in recent years because of the recessionary rise in unemployment and also the ideological preferences of Conservative-influenced governments elected since 2010. So, in the case of the London 2012 Olympics, it is understandable that the UK public showed a lot of interest in participating in the volunteer army needed for the Games, and nearly 250,000 applied to join. From these 70,000 were recruited and trained to take on the role of what LOCOG decided to refer to as 'Gamesmaker', a title which stressed their vital importance to the delivery and success of Britain's Olympic project.

The civil army of Gamesmakers was praised practically universally by the public and the media for its enthusiasm, pride and effectiveness across the range of the varied tasks it was required to perform (DCMS 2013, ch. 9). This was particularly so for those tasks involving the public in and around the main venues, for instance informing and guiding members of the public and managing crowd flows. Olympic mega-events can be experienced as large-scale, formalised and overawing occasions. But the work of the Gamesmaker volunteers helped to give the London Olympics a human face, and to project that face through the domestic and international media coverage of the Games. They helped to give it the feeling of being an informal, hospitable and inclusive 'street-level' community celebration or festival. And in this way they can be said to have contributed to its memorability and thus to one aspect of its cultural legacy. In addition many Gamesmakers experienced their work as contributing to positive developments in their lives, whether through further volunteering or a movement into employment. Finally, the public visibility and example of the Gamesmakers had an immediate, if short-term, legacy. That is, it appeared to have stimulated an increase in public interest in and valuation of volunteering more generally in Britain in the 2012–13 period. However it is debatable whether this attitudinal effect actually generated more volunteering in practice, and also there is no evidence to indicate that this effect would not diminish as time passes and as distance from a uniquely motivating event increases (DCMS 2013, Jozwiak 2013, Legacy Trust 2013).

The achievements of British Olympic champions

The British team generally performed well, as the teams representing the national Olympic host typically tend to do. Among the British athletes who managed to succeed in the competition to become Olympic champions, the most publicly recognised and celebrated at the time were Mo Farah and Jessica Ennis (now Ennis-Hill). Farah won both the men's 5,000 and 10,000 metres and Ennis-Hill won the women's heptathlon. Farah was born in Somalia to a British father and Somalian mother, and Ennis-Hill was born in Britain to a Jamaican father and a British mother. Because of their outstanding achievements, but also because they reflect the multicultural dimension of contemporary British identity, they are likely to remain memorable and potentially inspirational to the nation's youth as sport role models in the longer term. As such, given their practical embodiment of the values and practices of cultural pluralism and inclusion, such aspects of the performances of Britain's Olympic and Paralympic teams can reasonably be assessed as being positive contributions in any assessment of the legacies of the London 2012 Olympics for British society.[29]

Housing and community-building dimensions

Housing aspects of Olympics and their legacies have two main aspects. On the one hand there is the issue of compulsory purchase of urban land in order to build the sport facilities and create the Olympic Park in the pre-event period.

On the other hand there is post-event use of the athletes' village and the use of Olympic land for house-building purposes. The latter can be affected by the dynamics and trends in the local urban housing market. To stage the London 2012 Olympics (unlike Beijing and Shanghai) the Olympic organisers' project did not require large-scale relocation of urban residents. The compulsory purchase of homes was kept to a minimum, ultimately only 425 people (Games-Monitor 2008).

On the positive side, relating to the reuse of the athletes' village and use of Olympic site land for new-build housing, the event's contribution in the East End of London is likely to be fairly substantial and generally positive. It is of a comparable order of magnitude with that of Sydney's Olympic project and is over a comparable medium-term time period (see Chapter 6). In East London six new neighbourhoods and communities are being developed around the borders of the Park, although their completion is being staggered over a decade or more (LLDC 2011, Robertson 2013). Ultimately they will create new Parkside communities on the east and west side of the northern sector of the Park (East Village, Chobham Manor and East Wick) and also on the west and south sides of the southern sector of the Park (Sweetwater, Marshgate and Pudding Mill). When they are fully developed by 2030 the Park's new neighbourhoods will ultimately provide around 10,800 new homes and contain around thirty thousand residents.

Most of the housing is intended to reflect a 'human-scale' vision of urbanism, being relatively low rise and with a majority having gardens. Given the gardens and also these new neighbourhoods' proximity to the open green spaces of the Park, this community-building process could be said to embody a contemporary version of the English interwar urban planning ideals which created the UK's garden cities and many of the green suburban expansion areas around its cities. Their construction will contribute to addressing some of the East End's enduring housing shortage problems. It is planned that around a third of the homes will be sold at 'affordable' sub-market prices to contribute to social mixing and accessibility in these communities (see BBC 2011 and LLDC 2011; also Robertson 2013).[30]

Overall the community-building and house-building impacts of the Olympic project can be generally assessed to be socially positive. They involve a degree of inclusion and mixing of social classes, provide some access for local people and avoid the extremes of intrusive and exclusive development associated with the previous experience of gentrification in London. However the project's wider economic context and the limitations that this implies should be borne in mind.

As a world city the demand for housing in London in recent years, whether as a capital investment or a status symbol, has become truly global. This has created high levels of house-price inflation since the end of the global recession in 2011. The glocal character of the top end of London's housing market has deformed the local functioning of the market. It has inflated prices throughout the whole market, creating major barriers at the bottom end of the market to initial entry for all young London adults, even those in well-paid and professional occupations. This, combined with the UK's persistent failure to increase the supply of urban housing over recent decades, means that the effects of the Olympics on either the supply or the price of housing in London are inevitably likely to be limited.

Park-related dimensions: green aspects, recreation and tourism

Britain's urbanisation from the mid-eighteenth century on through the nineteenth was accompanied by waves of conflicts over the control and uses of urban land and space. Along with other British cities London, particularly in its central, northern, southern and western areas, benefited from initially private-based and later public-based movements of park-building and green-space defending and renewing. The East End did not completely miss out on this process, and it benefited from the creation and protection of large green spaces like Victoria Park and Hackney Marshes. But these were limited developments by comparison with many of London's other areas, and they were in a region of the city which needed much more. As we noted earlier, the East End was a part of London that became rapidly and densely built up as the docks and related industry, transport and housing construction developed from the mid-nineteenth century. Urban park-creation slowed down considerably in the twentieth century in London and other British cities as cities expanded through suburbanisation and encroached into surrounding countryside. A major urban park had not been created in London for over a century prior to the 2012 Olympics, and certainly not in the East End. However the current creation of the post-Games Queen Elizabeth II Olympic Park in and for the East End of London is on a relatively large scale, roughly equivalent in size to the largest green space in central London, Hyde Park. Much of the Olympic Park's new green space consists of recreational parkland and the whole development is intended to embody environmentalist values and practices. In this respect, as we saw earlier, the London 2012 Olympic project can be seen as an attempt to take the greening of twenty-first-century mega-events to a new level, building on the Sydney and Beijing Olympic experiences in particular.

Throughout the consideration of post-event legacies of the Games in this chapter it is clear that the Park and its facilities is at the heart of the attempt to produce multi-thematic but inter-connected long-term regenerative social and environmental legacies and changes in this central area of the East End (see for instance UK Gov 2013, chs 3 to 5). The Park is an irregular and somewhat linear green space flanking both sides of a central section of the newly revived river Lea. For organisational, developmental and analytical purposes it can be very roughly and summarily divided into North Park and South Park sections. The North Park section is intended to contain most of the Park's green spaces, particularly those bordering the river Lea. As such it will cater more for the kind of casual recreational uses familiar elsewhere in London's urban parks, and can be expected to be an amenity which will be regularly used by individuals and families living in the neighbourhoods bordering the park. However, as with the South Park section, it is a space which has a variety of uses since the main housing projects and the 'Here East' business district border on to it. Also it contains the cycling facilities of the Velodrome and the BMX biking centre. Because of the nearby housing this section of the Park will be particularly carefully controlled in security terms, and although it will be fully open to the public during the day it is possible that key areas will close to all except residents at night.

The South Park section is intended to be a more actively used, entertainment-oriented and tourist-oriented space. It contains the main large-scale sport venues and tourist attractions, particularly the Olympic Stadium, the Aquatic centre, the Orbit Tower and a planned new plaza containing eating and drinking venues. The Copper Box indoor arena was reopened for the various post-event uses in 2013 and it can also be seen as belonging to this part of the park. Large-scale sporting and cultural events will be programmed particularly in the Olympic Stadium and also in the Copper Box. Given that the Olympic Stadium is now committed long-term to staging West Ham FC's English Premier League home games, these are likely to regularly attract crowds into the park in the range of thirty to forty thousand per event from autumn through to spring in a typical year. And the stadium is likely to also stage large events such as one-off sport events and/or pop music performances.

Two other visitor attractions relevant to the tourism and entertainment aspects (and economics) of the Park, particularly its South Park section, should also be noted here. These are, in the Park, the iconic ArcelorMittal Orbit Tower, and, next to a main entrance to the Park, the Westfield shopping mall. We post-pone discussion of the Westfield development to the following section on employment impacts, so here we focus on the Orbit Tower.

The Tower is the result of a decision by the New Labour Olympics Minister, Tessa Jowell, and the Conservative London Mayor, Boris Johnson, in 2008. During the construction of the Olympic Park they felt that a structure which they thought of as an 'Olympic Tower' was needed to give some added public interest and profile to the Park and its facilities. The steel magnate Lakshmi Mittal, Chairman of the ArcelorMittal steel company, was willing to supply the steel and cover the bulk of the cost of such a structure (£22.7 million, $29.85 million) in return for its naming rights. The structure which emerged from the design competition is located in the South Park near the Olympic Stadium.[31] It is essentially a large-scale 114-metre-high piece of public art (created by the internationally renowned artist Anish Kapoor) which is also designed to act as a public viewing tower. As a world city London has long compared unfavour-ably with other such cities in terms of its provision for visitors to take a bird's eye view of the city, of its quarters, major buildings and skyline, from high platforms. This is one of the reasons for the success of the iconic London Eye located on the Thames in central London. (It is worth noting here that the inspi-ration for the Eye, as a Ferris Wheel-type structure, is derived from the large urban viewing wheels created for the 1893 Chicago and Paris 1900 Expos among others, and of course the concept of an urban viewing tower was given its first incarnation at the 1889 Paris Expo in the form of the Eiffel Tower.) The Orbit's scarcity value, although at a lower level than the Eye, together with its unique look are likely to make it part of the circuit of London tourist attractions in its own right.

The Orbit Tower, opened in 2014, was expected to attract around 800,000 visitors annually (LLDC 2012), and it was hoped that its ticketing income would make a contribution to its operating costs. However initial demand turned out to be lower than anticipated, and the decision was taken in 2016 to add a giant slide to the tower, designed by the artist Carsten Holler (Wainwright 2016). In my view, whatever the artistic hybridisation involved in this development, it is likely to add to the reasons why domestic and also international visitors might be expected to visit the Olympic Park in the future. Seen in the broader context of the image of the Park the demonstrably non-sporting character of the Orbit Tower and its slide makes a clear statement to the public that the Park is not just a massive sport complex but that it is also about entertainment and recrea-tional (not to mention aesthetic) experiences. And, in a less spectacular way, the green space characteristics of both sections of the Park also communicate a version of this kind of non-sporting message.

Although most of the post-Games Olympic Park's green space is in the North Park, the South Park also contains some. The internationally known New York-based landscape designer James Corner was commissioned to create a tree-lined promenade in the vicinity of the Olympic Stadium and running north–south along the line of the river Lea. This is linked to a series of 'green rooms' (or small 'pocket parks') of various size which are able to accommodate a range of cultural activities and uses from informal picnics to music festivals. In the 2012–14 period the LLDC spent £300 million ($394.54 million) removing the Olympic event overlays and refitting the Park for post-event uses. The alterations included restructuring pedestrian paths, cycle ways and bridges in order to construct many new connections with the surrounding neighbourhoods (which, of course, had been physically excluded from the Park site during the Olympic event). The North Park was opened in summer 2013 and the South Park a year later. However further developments of the river system, parklands, facilities and park-edge housing will continue for years, certainly into the medium term.[32]

Economic impacts and legacies of the London 2012 Olympics: developing the cultural and creative economy

Background

London's Olympic project planners set themselves the ambitious socio-economic policy target to create around seventy thousand jobs related to the Games in the pre-event and event-time periods. The city's final official report after the event confirms that this target was in fact achieved (GLA 2013). In the post-event period the project's longer-term capacity to stimulate urban employment growth, both directly and indirectly, and both current and planned, is also considerable, and we discuss this further in a moment. At the macro-economic level of the UK economy an official government report after the event estimated that the boost it provided to the national economy (and thus to national employment) was £9.9 billion ($13.02 billion). It also suggested that in the longer post-event period through to 2020 the economic legacy of the event could be of the order of £40 billion ($52.61 billion) (BBC 2013b, DCMS 2013, p. 5).

At this point it is important to note that if positive medium- and long-term economic impacts are achieved then this will not just be a product of London's pre-event plans and aspirations for post-event economic legacy.[33] London's experience suggests that this is a necessary but not sufficient condition for success. In addition what is required is an approach to urban planning which is both consistent and committed as well as being both pragmatic and creative. Post-event development possibilities can emerge which were simply not envisaged in the pre-event period. The approach to the development of legacies and investment in them orchestrated by relevant governance agencies (in this case particularly by the LLDC) needs to be proactive, sustained and capable of adapting to this and turning it to the area's advantage. This was the general urban planning lesson taught by the initial problems and ultimate achievements of Sydney's experience with its Olympic mega-event project and its legacies, as we have seen earlier (Chapter 6). London's planners and policy-makers seem to have learned from this.

Economic growth and employment in and around the Olympic Park in the post-event medium and longer terms are likely to come from a number of distinct and related sources such as tourism, entertainment (including retailing) and also in digital technology and design-based industries including in cultural and media sectors. A significant proportion of this is likely to be related to what is developing in other economic zones in and around central London. These include a potential triangle of relationships involving links between the Olympic Park-based enterprises and, on the one hand, London's existing major international financial industry (importantly including its deep resources of venture capital, located partially in the East End at Canary Wharf) and, on the other hand, London's creative cultural and digital industries zone (also located partially in the East End in the 'Tech City' area of Shoreditch). In spite of the constraints of the recent economic recession Oxford Economics predicts a net annual growth of jobs in London due to the Olympic project and the Olympic Park of 4,500, and thus an overall growth in the post-event period through to 2020 which is likely to be over thirty thousand. The LLDC has recently extended the overall planning projection to 45,000 jobs within the longer timeframe of 2015–31.[34]

In what follows we focus on some distinctive and high-profile Olympic Park economic zones and projects which are capable of generating employment growth on a significant scale. However it should also be borne in mind that even prosaic functions like the operation of the Olympic Park infrastructures of sports venues and transport portals have had and will continue to have positive, even if low-level and unspecified, impacts on employment.[35] In 2015 there were five main projects in and around the Olympic Park. These are located in distinct spatial zones which have potential for economic and employment growth. They operate in three main economic sectors, they are outlined in Table 8.3 and are as follows. In the cultural and creative sector there are three main projects and zones, namely 'Olympicopolis', 'Here East' and 'UCL East'. In the popular and consumer culture sector there is the Westfield shopping mall and its associated elements. Finally in the services category there is the potentially considerable employment growth associated with 'The International Quarter' project. We can take a look at each of these in turn.

Services: The International Quarter

The International Quarter (TIQ)[36] is a zone on the south-eastern periphery of the Olympic Park, outside of the Olympicopolis and Aquatics Centre sites, in which new office buildings for national and international agencies and enterprises are being located. The quarter was due to begin to open in 2018 and organisations committed to moving to the site include the Financial Conduct Authority (FCA), which is the UK's independent regulatory body for the financial services sector, and its three thousand staff, and the headquarters of the Transport for London (TfL) organisation, which is the body within the GLA which operates all aspects of public transport in the city. Unlike the other new Park zones which are potentially more innovative, TIQ's contribution to the Olympic Park as an economic stimulus and legacy-leaver operates in the more familiar sector of general office services, as is indicated by the examples of the FCA and TfL. However TIQ could be the most substantial Park-based economic zone of them all. For instance planners are currently aiming in the medium term to generate 25,000 jobs in the zone together with investment valued at £2 billion.

Within London the Park's and TIQ's relatively low office costs and the higher quality of life which it offers employees are valuable assets for incoming and relocating businesses. But equally important are the factors of the Park's spatial proximity and transport connectivity to London's main business districts of Canary Wharf and the (old) 'City of London' to the UK government quarter at Westminster, and to London's consumer culture hub in the West End. Of course these are positive factors not just for services but also for the cultural and creative industries developments at the Park which we consider next. Overall these economically relevant issues of proximity and connectivity are much stronger in the case of London's Olympic Park than they were (and are) in the case of Sydney's less centrally located Olympic Park which we considered earlier (Chapter 6).

Table 8.3 Economic legacy developments related to the London 2012 Olympics

Economic sector	Zones	Elements	Cost/value	Employment
Cultural and creative	Olympicopolis	V&A Museum Sadler's Wells (music and dance) Arts University (Smithsonian Museum)	Olympicopolis overall: £400 million ($525.20 million) (UK government £140 million, $183.8 million)	(3,000–10,000)[1]
	Here East	BT Sport, Loughborough University, Infinity Data centre, etc.	Here East overall: £1 billion ($1.32 billion)	(5,300 onsite) (2,200 offsite)
	UCL East	UCL centres and departments (design, engineering, technology etc.)	£270 million ($355.09 million)	(6,500 students and staff)
Popular/consumer culture	Westfield	Major shopping mall, plus two hotels, casino, film complex	£1.6 billion ($2.10 billion)	10,000
Services	The International Quarter	National and International companies' offices	£2 billion ($2.63 billion)	(25,000 after 2017)

Sources: LLDC 2014, table 1, p. 22; London Gov 2013; also Johnson 2013, QEOP 2015a and b.

Notes: Column 3: Parentheses indicate provisional and subject to final agreement; Column 5: Parentheses indicate planning targets for jobs.

1 The target of 3,000 is given in QEOP 2015a; however earlier projections are higher; see Johnson 2013, and London Gov 2013 give 10,000. The latter seems to be a gross figure for the three elements in the Cultural and Creative sector.

Cultural and creative industries

'Here East'

The 2012 Olympic Games, as with previous Olympics, was a media event and as such required the creation of special non-sport media-related facilities. These included large-scale buildings and communications infrastructures for the army of media personnel required to broadcast the event to mass audiences in nations around the world. During the London Games this army totalled 28,000 media workers housed in the London Olympic Media Centre building containing the International Broadcast Centre and the Main Press Centre. Post-event it was envisaged that these large-scale facilities, which also now include a large (750-seat) auditorium, would be taken over by one or more commercial companies. These are preferably to be in new digital industries which would be capable of making best use of the state-of-the-art communications infrastructures and connectivity this Olympic Park site offers. It was hoped that such developments might provide a new long-term hub for growth in the area in new creative cultural and knowledge industries and a boost for local employment, income and investment.

The Media Centre is now one of the core areas of the Olympic Park as a business zone and it has been renamed 'Here East'.[37] It is controlled by the iCity company which is aiming to use it to generate redevelopment to a value of £100 million. In 2013 a substantial part of the main building was leased on a ten-year contract to the UK's main telecoms company British Telecom (BT).[38] Part of BT's current corporate strategy involves developing its subscription cable television service. A key programme content to attract a new base of consumers to a subscription television service is live sport, particularly live football, and particularly live EPL games. Rupert Murdoch's Sky TV company has demonstrated this reality in the UK since the early 1990s by practically monopolising the purchase and broadcasting of EPL football, as we have seen earlier in Chapter 4. However, a BT company, BT Vision, has acquired the broadcast rights to a package of EPL games in each of the last two EPL auctions of their rights (for the periods 2013–16 and 2016–19). In addition in 2013 BT out-bid Sky to acquire exclusive rights to the high-profile and internationally important series of European football matches in UEFA's two club competitions (the European Champions' League and the Europa Cup) for the years 2015–18. Thus BT is evidently using the Here East facility as a production base from which to mount a serious and strategic challenge to Sky's dominance in the live media-sport field in the UK. In addition the Here East space and location have also attracted

Infinity SDC, an expanding data-centre services company, together with units from some tertiary education organisations (Loughborough University and Newham College). Because of the proximity and connectivity of the Park to central London, and also the East End's relatively lower business property prices it is reasonable to suppose that in the medium term this zone will attract more investment and new businesses in the digital, media and cultural industries

National and local governments have been encouraging the growth of an East London technological and commercial hub in the nearby Shoreditch area for a number of years. This is referred to as the Tech City project and, to a certain extent, it is based on a British adaptation of such American 'growth cluster' models such as California's 'Silicon Valley'.[39] The Tech City hub district is now becoming a leading growth sector in the UK's economic recovery from recession. The district focuses on digital-technology-based businesses from small start-up companies (over fifteen thousand were created there in 2012) to the biggest multinational companies (such as Google, Microsoft and Amazon). The Olympic Park is located a relatively short distance to the east of the Tech City hub area. It is hoped that a medium-term economic and employment legacy of the Games will be that the Park will provide a natural corridor of expansion for the Tech City hub. Given the hub's current rate of expansion it is reasonable to expect that such a corridor from Tech City to Olympic Park and Here East is feasible. If achieved it will create a new scale and critical mass of digitally based industries in the UK. This in turn may well have the capacity to contribute a new source of economic dynamism into the London economy more generally and to underpin and drive economic development both within and beyond East London.

'Olympicopolis' and 'UCL East'

The 'Olympicopolis' project[40] aims to develop an area on the waterfront at the edge of the Queen Elizabeth II Olympic Park (QEOP). The aim is to develop the area into a cultural and educational quarter or campus, as a cultural hub and a showcase for some of the highest quality of London's cultural industries. It was named in recognition of Albertopolis, the nineteenth-century Expo-legacy cultural quarter development in central London which we discussed earlier. The project is likely to cost around £400 million ($525.20 million). In 2014 the UK government contributed over £140 million ($183.82 million) and the rest is being raised from commercial sponsorship, philanthropy and the sale or rent of shops and housing on the site. The project was launched by London

Mayor, Boris Johnson, in mid-2014 and, after a competition, a design team was appointed in early 2015. The plan for the Olympicopolis project aims to create between three and ten thousand jobs and to increase the economic value of the area by a figure variously calculated as being at least £1.8 billion ($2.37 billion) and possibly as much as £5.2 billion ($6.84 billion).[41] 'UCL East' is a project involving a major expansion of University College London (UCL) which is a UK-leading and world-leading university.[42] UCL is investing £270 million ($355.09 million) to develop its own new campus site at the southern end of the South Park near to Olympicopolis. The campus will contain accommodation for 6,500 postgraduate and undergraduate students and staff using new teaching and research facilities in fields such as Design, Engineering and Technology.

So far leading cultural and educational organisations have committed either to set up satellite operations and venues in the quarter (the Victoria and Albert Museum, the V&A East, and Sadler's Wells theatre) or to relocate there (the London College of Fashion and University of the Arts, London (UAL)) (Bevan 2016, Morrison 2016). In addition the US's Smithsonian Museums Institution based in Washington, DC, is currently exploring the possibility of staging joint exhibitions of American culture with V&A East.[43] Of course, whether as a matter of cultural policy or fortunate accident, the metropolis of London has always also created opportunities for juxtaposition and crossover between high culture and popular culture. So it is relevant to observe that the Olympic Park contains a number of popular cultural operations aimed both at city residents, national visitors and international tourists. These include the main professional sport venues such as the Olympic Stadium, the Copper Box Arena and also the Orbit viewing and sliding tower. The economic impacts and legacies of these, however, are unlikely to match that of the consumer-culture industry represented by the Westfield shopping mall, which we look at next.

Popular and consumer-cultural industries

The Westfield shopping mall

The Westfield Stratford City shopping mall[44] is one of the UK's and Europe's largest malls, and is located at the periphery of the south-eastern section of the Park. This means that it is strategically positioned in a number of respects. It lies next to TIQ services development zone, and also it is a linking area between the main Olympic Park entrance (and its access to the Olympic Stadium) and the Stratford transport hub (with its metro station and fast access to the West

End). It opened in 2011, a year ahead of the Olympics, with the then-director of the mall observing 'We're the first piece of the Olympic legacy' (Barrett and Kortekaas 2011).

It was developed, and is owned and operated, by Westfield Group, an Australian-originated multinational corporation which runs over a hundred large shopping malls in the US and Australia as well as the UK. In the UK its most recent investment had been the developing of a large-scale mall in West London which opened in 2008. Ironically this was located on the disused site of the 1908 Franco-British Expo, the White City area. The Group's original investment in land in Stratford in the heart of the East End, to develop both for the mall and also for housing, occurred in 2004, a year before London won the right to stage the Olympics. It had already independently identified East London as a potential investment area given the longstanding and growing UK government and city-planning recognition of the need for strategic interventions in the area. An attraction for Westfield was that the UK's public sector was committed, in any case, to remediating the polluted watercourses of East London's river Lea, a tributary of the Thames, together with the polluted and derelict land around it, and generally to (re)connecting the area with Central London in terms of transport and also socio-economically. The public sector was also, more controversially, committed to financing this in part through the sale of under-used and disused ex-industrial and ex-railway land in the area. However the catalytic effect of London winning the right in 2005 to stage the Games meant that from then on the regeneration work would have to be coherently co-ordinated and also accelerated to fit the absolute requirements of the Olympic mega-event's timetable. From 2005 onwards the Westfield Group was closely involved in the development plans for the Olympic Park and its peripheries with the Olympic Delivery Authority and other agencies. The Group's housing project in Stratford became the basis for the athletes' village. Also the orientation of the main indoor and outdoor shopping streets of its shopping mall was designed to link the Stratford transport hub to the main Park entrance. The mall thus became the main pedestrian route and approach to the Park for most visitors during the Games. As convenient as this was for people attending the Games, and as necessary as it was to help finance the Olympic Park as a regeneration project, arguably this took the integration of the Olympic Games with commercialism and consumer culture to a new and controversial level.

The Westfield mall cost £1.6 billion ($2.10 billion) and employs around ten thousand people, at least twenty per cent from the local area. As a retail hub the mall contains three hundred shops, including the outlets of numerous high-end retailers. As an entertainment hub it contains also the UK's largest casino, a seventeen-screen cinema complex, two large hotels and seventy restaurants. In these respects it is in principle a self-contained 'short-break' tourist destination for consumers in the national UK market. In practice, in both its retail and entertainment aspects, it has already become one of London's most popular visitor destinations, registering 47 million visits in 2012 and generating sales of nearly £1 billion ($1.32 billion). As such it is likely to operate in a synergistic way with the Olympic Park and its critical mass of visitor attractions. It is likely to provide a source, as well as a route, for flows of visitors into the Park in the post-Games period, as it did during the Games period. There is evidence of good potential for positive synergies between visits to Westfield and also to the Olympic Park and its attractions. For instance, during the short four-week period of the Olympics and Paralympics in 2012, with massive numbers of spectators flowing into the Olympic Park, many of them using the Westfield mall route, Westfield's own visitor numbers also peaked at 8.5 million (see Magnay 2013, Ainsworth-Wells 2013, Cabinet Office 2013, Visit Britain 2012). In these and other respects the Westfield mall contributes to the notion that the Olympic Park, with its zones and its environs, has been a complex but trans-formative project for East London. It is creating a new and important social, cultural and economic hub which generally has positive implications and legacy-potential for city residents both in East London and for the wider city.

Conclusion

This chapter has focused on the relationships between mega-events, their urban contexts and urban legacies through the lens of the particular case of London. The discussion began by looking at London as an 'event city' and as having been physically marked and culturally influenced by a number of mega-events since the mid-nineteenth century, particularly Expos and Expo-type events. The point was emphasised here that these events left long-term urban legacies, most notably in the cases of the Albertopolis and Southbank quarters, which were invested in, added to and developed over many years. They thereby have the capacity to play a leading role in the cultural tourism industry which is an important sector of the city's economy, and more generally in relation to the city's image, identity and quality of life. However the bulk of the chapter in the following three sections was concerned with using some of these introductory and historical themes to inform a detailed look into the case of the London 2012 Olympics and its various legacies.

The second section took a look into the socio-economic context and needs of East London – the policy context in which the Olympics as a multi-thematic (sport, social and economic) project was embedded and which it was used to address. Attention was then turned to consider the event's various impacts and potentials for creating lasting legacies. The event has left a cluster of high-quality sport facilities and in this sense has left a sport legacy at least for the spectating of professional sport which is likely to be valued particularly by the young and by succeeding generations. However it was assessed as being unlikely to be able to make much difference to the established patterns of ordinary people's participation, or lack of it, in sport and physical activity, which is a growing health policy concern both in the UK in general and also among local residents in East London.

In the final two sections of the chapter the focus was on the events' socio-economic legacies. The discussion of the Olympic project's social legacies in the third section indicated a largely positive potential for both event-related housing and community-building developments to contribute to improvements in people's living conditions in and around Stratford. It also indicated the potential for the Olympic Park, as a significant new open and green riverside space within a great metropolis, to make a special and lasting contribution to the quality of life of residents and also to the recreational opportunities of visitors. The discussion of the Olympic project's economic and employment legacies also indicated a largely positive potential in the various zones located around the Olympic Park which are being devoted to service industries, cultural and creative industries and popular cultural industries. The Park's proximity and connectivity to central London and the West End are important contributors to the Park's capacity to develop as a new hub within the city for economic and employment growth

Without doubt the story of London's events and their urban legacies, particularly that of the most recent example, the 2012 Olympics, is unique in some respects. However it also has sufficient commonalities with other major cities, at least in the West, to be able to illustrate more general aspects of contemporary mega-event policy and practice. These issues are generally better recognised today, both by academic analysts and also by policy practitioners, than they were in, say, the last quarter of the twentieth century. Then the focus of mega-event organisers tended to be relatively short-term. They organised their events in ways which we have suggested can best be seen as the creation of transient theme parks, and mega-event analysts followed them in focusing on the assessment of short-term impacts and short-term costs and benefits.

By contrast now there seem to be some distinctive commonalities among contemporary mega-event organisers. This is in spite of other important contextual differences, such as whether events are staged in developed or developing or emerging societies; or whether those societies are in the West or outside of it (notably for instance in the East); or whether the times are economically booming or afflicted by recession. The commonalities are that organisers tend to be much more aware than ever before that their events are intrinsically complex in their characteristics and contexts, and that they are thus risky projects in changing urban contexts which need careful and well-informed planning. In addition there are a variety of mega-event impacts and they can each potentially contribute to the long-term legacy significance of the event the host city. This kind of contemporary awareness among mega-event organisers, and the political leaderships and publics surrounding them, can be expressed in the concept that contemporary mega-events are better understood as multi-theme legacy parks rather than as theme parks. The development of such multi-thematic legacies requires a consistent and co-ordinated approach from park or site planners and policy-makers, one which involves a pragmatic willingness to explore and invest in development opportunities as they arise over time. This is well illustrated in the case of London and its various mega-events, past and present.

Before we close there is an additional general comparison in respect of the conceptualisation and planning of mega-events between the contemporary period and the last quarter of the twentieth century, and this also is well illustrated by London's experience with its events, particularly its 2012 Olympic event. In the last quarter of the twentieth century the environmental or green character of the events and their legacies was of little perceived policy importance. However in the contemporary period it has come to be seen as of major significance in various ways. So, in terms of meanings, there is now a greater emphasis on a realistic and more traditional green and recreational meaning of the concept of 'park' as a leading element in the idea that contemporary mega-events tend to involve multi-theme legacy parks. We explored theoretical and practical aspects of the link between mega-events and green parks in some detail earlier in Chapter 6, and also in the discussion of Sydney's Olympics in Chapter 5. In this chapter we explored these aspects again in relation to the London 2012 Olympics and the multi-uses and legacy-potential of its post-event Olympic Park urban development project.

We have suggested that the 'legacy blueprint' which the IOC judged that London's 2012 Olympic Games offered to future games hosts (see above) needs at least to be understood as having multi-thematic sport, social and economic dimensions. The economic dimension can be further understood as an economic complex involving the development of a range of different but related post-industrial sectors, such as service industries, popular consumer and tourism-related cultural industries and also cultural and creative industries. However the focal point and hub of such ambitious event-legacy developments in the case of London and also of Sydney and other mega-event host cities in recent times, has been that of the creation of the new urban green space of one or more parks. Event-generated park-building projects in the heart of some of the world's biggest and most dynamic cities can give material and permanent embodiment to both environmental and recreational values. In the earlier generations of the modern era, in the first phase of modernisation, mega-events tended to create iconic places (monuments, starchitecture and sometimes 'white elephants') as their urban legacies and testimonials to versions of the ideal of progress. In the contemporary period, the second phase of modernization, they are just as likely to aim to interpret the meaning of progress as relating to urban residents' quality of life together with the quality of their environmental conditions. Throughout the final two parts of this book we have observed that, in order to give tangible and practical expression to these emerging life- and environment-related values and aspirations, mega-events will increasingly attempt to leave host cities with, among other things, progressive urban legacies such as parks, riverside walks and seashore spaces, that is with green and recreational urban spaces.

The future facing mega-events as the twenty-first century unfolds evidently involves risks and challenges, not least those connected with the major social changes we have considered in this book. Their relevance and credibility, and even their very existence, will depend on their ability to adapt successfully to these changes. As we saw in Part I, in large part the emerging risks and challenges derive from the need for mega-events, particularly those operating in the field of sport culture, to adapt to the new global media environment. In Parts II and III the focus moved to the issue of mega-events' responsiveness to the changes involved in modern urbanisation, particularly in the contemporary period. We explored the historical, current and possible role of mega-event projects, as potentially influential exercises in urban policy, together with the emerging importance of a life- and environment-related vision of contemporary urbanism and policy goals in this context. An implication of these discussions is that the future of mega-events will also depend significantly on their ability to adapt to contemporary urbanism, and to dependably deliver relevant life- and environment-related developments and legacies to their host cities

Notes

1 Contemporary cities typically have developed busy and professionally managed event programmes for many of the same sort of reasons (e.g. identity, morale, marketing, tourism and regeneration) that they periodically bid to stage mega-events. Such programmes use cities' public places and spaces to stage festivals, exhibitions and performances of various kinds and of various scales, from the small and local to the large and international. In the field of events policy and research a relevant way to refer to this phenomenon is by characterising cities as 'eventful cities' (e.g. Richards and Palmer 2010). London is evidently also an 'eventful city' in this respect. However my focus in this chapter is on mega-events and their legacies, so it is more appropriate to use the term 'event city' to refer to this particular phenomenon.

2 For a relevant critical analysis of the associated notion of global cities in which London is included see Sassen 2012, pp. 34–8 and passim. Also see discussions of cities in relation to globalisation in the chapters in Part II and Chapter 8.

3 For some relevant social and cultural background the history of London in the modern era see for instance Rasmussen 1974 and Porter 1994.

4 For some relevant accounts of London's 1851 Crystal Palace Expo, titled as 'The Great Exhibition' (of the Works of Industry of all Nations), see Roche 2000, ch. 2, also Allwood 1977, Greenhalgh 1988, ch. 1 and Davis 2008.

5 Chicago's 1893 Expo (which was officially dedicated in 1892) was titled 'The World's Columbian Exposition' and designed as a celebration of the four-hundredth anniversary of Christopher Columbus's arrival in the New World. Its site informally came to be known as the White City. See Findling 1994a, Rydell 1984, ch. 2, also Badger 2008.

6 On London's 1948 Olympics, also known informally as 'the Austerity Games' see Hampton 2012 and Polley 2011, ch. 10.

7 On London's 1924–25 Expo event, titled as 'The British Empire Exhibition', see Roche 2000, ch. 4; also Geppert 2008 and Rydell 1993, ch. 3.

8 On the background to the emergence of Albertopolis see note 4.

9 On the Albert Hall see BHO 1975, also Morgan 2012.

10 On the Festival of Britain event see Atkinson 2008.

11 On the Southbank quarter in general see South Bank London 2015, and on the Southbank Centre see Southbank Centre 2015.

12 On the 2000 'Millennium Experience' exhibition event see McGuigan and Gilmore 2000, also NAO 2008 on the UK government's planning hiatus and ultimate decision to back AEG and its project to re-create the Millennium Dome as the O2 Arena.

13 For instance Telegraph 2012, Observer 2012, Brown 2012 and Lawton 2012; also AP 2012, BBC 2012a, IOC 2012c and Giulianotti et al. 2015, p. 100. For more negative views of both the short- and long-run impacts of the London Olympics see contributions in Viehoff and Poynter 2015 and also Zimbalist 2015, ch. 6.

14 Jacques Rogge's assessment is quoted in DCMS 2012b.

15 See note 12.

16 For basic information about the Thames Gateway plan, which was introduced in 2007, see BBC News 2007b and BBC 2007.

17 On the social history of the East End of London see for instance Brodie 2004, and on the West End see for instance Porter 1994.

18 In official British social statistics the social deprivation of localities is understood in multi-dimensional terms and is assessed by a 'multiple deprivation index' (MDI). This consists of combined measures of income, employment, health deprivation, education skills, barriers to housing, crime and living environment quality (see UK Gov 2011).

19 See Giulianotti et al. 2015, p. 103. They also note the association between the social deprivation of the areas of East London in and around the Olympic Park zone like Newham and, in those areas, the contemporary urban phenomenon of a high degree of transience and turnover (or 'churn') with its associations of a low sense of community and a lack of social cohesion.

20 The planning and development approach in the related and neighbouring Docklands regeneration project (which decades on from the 1990s still remains something of a 'work-in-progress') arguably achieved much both economically and architecturally. But it achieved much less socially since it was significantly insensitive to the views of local communities in relation both to the architectural interventions in the area and to the newcomers the economic growth brought with it. For a sociological investigation into the nature and problems of the urban social changes associated with the Docklands regeneration project see Foster 1999, also Collins 2009. On the gentrification theme and literature more generally see Brown-Saracino 2010 and Smith 2002, and on the related urban regeneration context also see Smith 2012.

21 Information about the LLDC, its development, current activities and future plans is now available on its website for the Queen Elizabeth II Olympic Park (referred to in this chapter and the references by means of the acronym QEOP). See http://queenelizabetholympicpark.co.uk/planning-authority.

22 See Jacques Rogge's 'blueprint' comment, quoted in DCMS 2012b.

23 On the relationship between 'starchitects' like Hadid and mega-events like Olympic Games see Chapter 4.

24 On a number of controversies and changes in the planned uses, design and costs of the Olympic Stadium see London Assembly 2011, Clark 2014 and Gibson 2015d.

25 London's original bid promised to use the Games to get more young people into sport, and this was refined later prior to the event into the official event slogan that the Games aimed to 'inspire a generation' (for instance see Magnay 2012).

26 The idea that there are a number of dimensions of social inequality, particularly between social classes, genders and ethnic and 'racial' groups (and in principle we could also add between age groups and abled and disabled groups) is a familiar one in sociology. So too is the idea that the 'intersectional' connections between them (for instance the links between sexism and racism which are addressed by black feminist theory and practice) need to be recognised and understood, including in their systematic or structural nature. The work of Patricia Hill Collins is seminal in this area, for instance see her early paper on the sociological significance of black feminist thought and her analysis of 'the interlocking nature of oppression' (Collins 1986). This recognition of the multi-dimensionality and inter-connectedness of social inequality is relevant in many areas of people's everyday lives including those relating to physical health and illness. However, even if it is recognised by policy-makers, the complex matrix nature of social disadvantage and of the ill-health-producing

behaviours it generates are very difficult to change, even in a long-term perspective. In this context mega-events, as short-duration interventions, probably have little to contribute as policy instruments.

27 For instance see the meta-review of research by Mahtani et al. in the *British Medical Journal* which concludes that 'The evidence to support the notion that hosting an Olympic games leads to an automatic increase in mass sporting or physical activity is poor' (Mahtani et al. 2013, p. 7).

28 On international reception of the televising of the Opening Ceremony see note 13, and also the discussion of the event's media character in Chapter 2.

29 For different perspective on these athletes and their celebrity status for the British public see Andrews and Rick 2014.

30 For information on Olympic Park-related housing developments see Prynn 2013, Robertson 2013, and Out-Law 2013b.

31 For Kapoor's original ideas and sketches for the tower see Kapoor 2015. For press review of the unveiling and opening of the Tower see for instance H. Williams 2012.

32 The Olympic Park-related planning for housing and for economic development typically involves projections to the mid-2020s or later, see for instance Robertson 2013 and Work Foundation 2010. And the wider context of the Olympic Park's development is the Thames Gateway strategy which takes an equally long view (see note 16). On the work of the landscape James Corner in the Olympic Park see Gibson 2012, Ijeh 2014, also QEOP 2014.

33 The Mayor of London who helped the bid for the Games to succeed, Ken Livingstone, saw the Olympic mega-event project as an instrument to stimulate social regeneration and economic growth and not as a sport project. He made this clear after the bid had been won (see Standard 2008). It is also a theme in other early planning documents, for instance see London Assembly 2007.

34 The Oxford Economic projection is contained in Work Foundation 2010, p. 47, and the more recent projection is in LLDC 2014, p. 22. In addition it is relevant to note here that, in relation to the pre-event period, the organiser's short-term job target of seventy thousand jobs has been assessed as having been met (see report by GLA 2013).

35 For instance it is expected that the normal operation of the Olympic Stadium will generate over seven hundred jobs (Gibson 2015d), and that the normal retail and business activities associated with a residential area such as Chobham Manor will generate over four hundred jobs (LLDC 2014, table 1, p. 22).

36 On The International Quarter (TIQ) see the websites of TIQ and the Olympic Park (QEOP), that is TIQ 2014 and QEOP 2015a.

37 On Here East see Shead 2014a and 2014b.

38 On BT Sport's move to Here East and its plans for its operations on this site see BBC 2012c. On BT's strategic challenge to Sky TV in the field of media sport see BT 2013 and BBC 2015a. On the wider context of contemporary media sport, particularly in the UK, see Chapter 4.

39 On Tech City see Cowan 2013, Forsyth and Bird 2013.

40 On the 'Olympicopolis' project see Johnson 2013, London Gov 2013, Crerar 2013, Ellis-Peterson 2014, Brown 2015, Pickford 2015 and QEOP 2015b. Also see Woodman 2015 for a critique.

41 The 'Olympicopolis' idea seems to have come from the London Mayor, Boris Johnson. For instance in a press article in 2013 he proposed that 'the Olympic park will be the "Albertopolis of the east"' (of London). He also predicted that by 2030 the project

would generate an extra £5.2 billion in gross value added and 10,800 jobs (Johnson 2013) in the Stratford area. The same order of jobs is also given in London Gov 2013. It is likely that this figure is an overall one which, in addition to the cultural hub involving the V&A, includes calculations for Here East and possibly also UCL East (and see the Table 8.3 note 3). The lower range of projections noted in the text for jobs and value added are from QEOP 2015b.

42 On UCL East see UCL 2014 and Temperton 2014.
43 On the interest of the Smithsonian in having a location in the Olympicopolis project see Rosenfield 2015 and RT 2015.
44 On the Westfield Stratford City shopping mall see Barrett and Kortekaas 2011 and Moore 2011.

References

AAP 2010 'Taxpayers will compensate axed Metro losers: Keneally', 21 February, *Sydney Morning Herald*, Sydney. Online at: www.msmh.com.au/nsw/taxpayers-will-compensate-axed-metro-losers-keneally-20100221-on6h.html

AFP 2015 'Architect Frei Otto named Pritker prize winner one day after his death', 11 March, Agence France-Presse (AFP), Paris. Online at: www.theguardian.com/artanddesign/2015/mar/11/architect-frei-otto-named-pritzker-prize-winner-one-day-after-his-death

Ainsworth-Wells, M. 2013 'London's Olympic legacy, the results are in', 27 June, *Daily Telegraph*, London. Online at: www.telegraph.co.uk/travel/10146348/London-Olympic-legacy-the-results-are-in.html

Ai, Weiwei 2008 'Why I'll stay away from the opening ceremony of the Olympics', 7 August, *Guardian*, London. Online at: www.theguardian,com/commentisfree/2008/aug/07/olympics2008.china

Allen, K. 2010 'EU urged to crack down on internet piracy', 10 January, *Guardian*, London Online at: http://guardian.co.uk/technology/2010/jan/eu-illegal-internet-piracy-filesharing

Allwood, J. 1977 *The great exhibitions*. Cassell and Collier, London.

Andrews, D. and Rick, O. 2014 'Celebrity and the London 2012 spectacle', ch. 14, pp. 195–212, in Girginov ed.

AP 2009a '4 years later, Turin basks in its Olympic legacy', Sport ESPN. Online at: http://sports.espn.go.com/espn/wire?section=oly&id=4782888

AP 2009b 'Olympics urged to open content rights to online', *Sydney Morning Herald*, Sydney. Online at: www.smh.com.au/technology/biz-tech/olympics-urged-to-open-content-rights-online-20091006-gkma.html

AP 2012 'London 2012 opening ceremony audience hit 900 million predicts IOC', Associated Press reported 7 August, *Independent*, London. Online at: www.independent.co.uk/sport/olympics/news/london-2012-opening-ceremony-audience-hit-900-million-predicts-ioc-8015361.html

Apuzzo, M., Schmidt, M., Rashbaum, W. and Borden, S. 2015 'FIFA officials arrested on corruption charges; Blatter isn't among them', 30 May, *New York Times*. New York. Online at: www.nytimes.com/2015/05/27/sports/soccer/fifa-officials-face-corruption-charges-in-us.html

Arexpo 2014 'The tender for the post Expo 2015, developing Milan in the future' (sic), Arexpo. Online at: http://urbanpromo.it/2014/wpcontent/uploads/sites/4/2014/11/Brochure_Arexpo.pdf

Arrighi, G. 1998 'Globalization and the rise of East Asia: lessons from the past, prospects for the future', March, vol. 13, 1, pp. 59–77, *International Sociology*.

Arup 2013 'Museums in the Digital Age', Arup, London. Online at: www.arup.com/news/2013_11_november/05_november_museums_in_a_digital_age

Ashworth, G. and Tunbridge, J. 1990 *The Tourist-Historic City*, Belhaven Press, London.

Asprogerakas, E. 2007 'City competition and urban marketing: the case of tourism industry in Athens', Vol. 2, 1, pp. 89–114, *Tourismos: An International Multidisciplinary Journal of Tourism*.

Atkinson, H. 2008 'London 1951', pp. 316–18, in Findling and Pelle eds.

Attaran, A. 2016 'Off the podium: why public health concerns for global spread of zika virus means that Rio de Janeiro's Olympic Games must not proceed', Special Commentary, Harvard Public Health Review, May. Online at: http://harvardpublichealthreview.org/off-the-podium-why-rios- 2016-olympic -games-must-not-proceed/

Badger, R. 2008 'Chicago 1893', pp. 116–25, in Findling and Pelle eds.

Bailey, P. 1978 *Leisure and class in Victorian England: rational recreation and the contest for control, 1830–1885*. Routledge, London.

Baker, L. and Adegoke, Y. 2012 'Olympics fans find ways to circumvent NBC's online control', 31 July Reuters. Online at: http://in.reuters.com/article/2012/07/31/us-olympics-techworkaround-idINBRE86U02R20120731

Balfour, A. 2012 'London 2012 Olympic and Paralympic Games-time digital report', 13 August, Slideshare. Online at: www.slideshare.net/balf/london-2012com-olympic-games-digital-round-up-13-august-2012

Bandarin, F. 2012 *The historic urban landscape: managing heritage in an urban century*. Wiley Blackwell, Chichester.

Bandarin, F. and van Oers, R. eds 2015 *Reconnecting the city: the historic urban landscape and the future of urban heritage*. Wiley Blackwell, Chichester.

Baratay, E. 2002 *Zoo: A history of zoological gardens in the West*. Reaktion, London.

Barboza, D. 2010, 'Shanghai Expo sets record with 73 million visitors', 2 November, *New York Times*, New York. Online at: www.nytimes.com/2010/11/03/wprld/asia/03shanghai.html?pagewanted=all&_r=0

Barboza, D. and Barnes, B. 2011 'Disney plans lavish park in Shanghai' 7 April, *New York Times*, New York. Online at: www.nytimes.com/2011/04/08/business/media/08disney.html

Barnett, E. 2010 'Entertainment industry calls for EU internet piracy crackdown', 11 January, *Daily Telegraph*. Online at www.telegraph.co.uk/journalists/emma-barnett/

Barrett, C. and Kortekaas, V. 2011 'Shopping takes a lead at the London Olympics', 20 August, *Financial Times*, London Online at: www.ft.com/cms/s/0/d64763c-cfdd-11e0-a144feabdc0.html#axzz3ZVK49

Bauder, D. 2014 'NBC says thousands of illegal video stopped', 27 February, *USA Today*. Online at: www.usatoday.com/story/sports/olympics/2014/02/27/nbc-sochi-olympics-/5865535/

BBC 2007 'Thames Gateway: explained', 5 June, BBC London. Online at: www.bbc.co.uk/kent/thamesgateway/maps_facts/thames_gateway_facts_whos_who_feature.shtml

BBC 2011 'London 2012 Olympic Park neighbourhood names revealed', BBC News, London. Online at: www.bbc.co.uk/news/uk-england-london-14364485

BBC 2012a 'London 2012: How the world saw the Olympic Games', 13 August, BBC News, London. Online at: www.bbc.co.uk/news/uk-politics-19238284?print=true

BBC 2012b 'Profile: Rupert Murdoch', BBC, London. Online at: www.bbc.co.uk/news/uk-14078128

BBC 2012c 'BT Sport set to move to Olympic broadcast centre', BBC, London. Online at: www.bbc.co.uk/news/uk-england-london-20544533

BBC 2013a 'Shanghai free-trade zone launched', 24 September, BBC News, London. Online at: www.bbc.co.uk/news/business-24322313

BBC 2013b 'London Olympics "have boosted UK economy by £9,9 billion"', 19 July, BBC News, London. Online at: www.bbc.c.uk/news/uk-23370270

BBC 2013c 'London 2012: Olympics and Paralympics £528m under budget', 18 July, BBC Sport, London. Online at: bbc.co.uk/sport/0/olympics/20041426

BBC 2014 'Brics nations to create $100 billion development bank', 15 July, BBC News, London. Online at: www.bbc.co.uk/news/business-28317555

BBC 2015a 'Premier League in record £5.14bn TV rights deal', 10 February, BBC, London. Online at: www.bbc.co.uk/news/business-31379128

BBC 2015b 'Sepp Blatter: Coca-Cola among sponsors saying Fifa boss must go', BBC, London. Online at: www.bbc.co.uk/sport/0/football/34430729

BBC News 1998 'Europe's longest bridge opened in Portugal', BBC News, BBC World Service, London. Online at http://news.bbc.co.uk/1/hi/world/europe/71214.stm

BBC News 2007a 'YouTube facing football lawsuit', 4 May. BBC, London. Online at: http://news.bbc.co.uk/go/pr/fr/-/hi/business/6627135.stm

BBC News 2007b 'Thames Gateway plans unveiled', 30 December, BBC, London. Online at: www.newsbbc.co.uk/1/hi/uk_politics/7119540.stm

BBC News 2009 'Internet piracy plans', 28 October, BBC, London. Online at: http://news.bbc.co.uk/1/hi/technology/8329710.stm

Beck, U. 2000 *What is globalization*. Polity Press, Cambridge.

Bellaby, M. 2000 'Internet police protect Olympic broadcasting rights', ABC News Network, 22 September. Online at: http://abcnews.go.com/Sports/story?id=100482

Benedict, B. 1983a 'The anthropology of world's fairs', ch. 1 in Benedict ed. 1983b.

Benedict, B. ed. 1983b *The anthropology of world's fairs*. Scolar Press, London.

Bennett, C. and Haggerty, K. eds 2012 *Security games: surveillance and control at mega-events*. Routledge, London.

Bennett, T. 1995 'The exhibitionary complex', ch. 2 in his *The birth of the museum: history, theory and politics*. Routledge, London.

Bercht, A. 2013 'Glurbanization of the Chinese megacity Guangzhou – image-building and city development through entrepreneurial governance'. Vol. 68, pp. 129–38, *Geographica Helvetica*. Online at: www.geogr_helv.net/68/129/2013/gh-68-129-2013.pdf

Beumer, C. 2010 'Social cohesion in a sustainable urban neighbourhood', SUN Action 2. Online at: www.icis.unimaas.info/wp-content/uploads/2010/07/Beumer-2010-Social-cohesion-theory.pdf

Bevan, R. 2016 ' Olympicopolis architects on their £1.3 billion vision for E20', 8 March, *Evening Standard*, London. Online at: www.standard.co.uk/lifestyle/london-life/olympicopolis-architects-om-their-13-billion-vision-for-e20-a319804.html

BHO 1975 'Royal Albert Hall', British History Online. Online at www.british-history.ac.uk/survey-london/vol38/pp177-195

Biao, A. 2008 'Pirating the Olympics, then and now', 13 August, Waxy.org. Online at: http://waxy.org/2008/08/pirating_the_olympics_then_and_now/

Bidwell, J. 2008 '2012 spectacle can transform the capital and unify the nation', 20 August, *Evening Standard*, London. Online at: www.standard.co.uk/olympics/2012-spectacle-can-transform-the-nation-6878562.html

BIE 2008 'Foreword', pp. 1–3, in Findling and Pelle eds.

BIE 2014a 'How to organize an Expo?' BIE, Paris. Online at: www.bie-paris.org/site/en/publications/

BIE 2014b 'Speech at the AIHP Spring Meeting' (speech on behalf of the BIE President V. Loscertales), BIE, Paris. Online at: www.bie-paris.org/site/em/publications/speeches

Billings, A. 2008 *Olympic media*. Routledge, London.

Blanchard, P. 2008 *Human zoos: science and spectacle in the age of colonial empire*. Liverpool University Press, Liverpool.

Bond, D. 2007 'Tessa Jowell "knew Olympic bill would soar"', 7 September, *Daily Telegraph*, London. Online at: www.telegraph.co.uk/news/uknews/1562437/Tessa-Jowell-knew-Olympic-bill-would-soar.html

Bond, D. 2012 'Beijing's monuments to a lost Olympic era', BBC, London. Online at: www.bbc.co.ukblogs/davidbond/2012/05beijings_monuments_to_a_lost_o.html

Bookman, S. 2014 'Judges' tally: NBC scores historic online video numbers at Sochi Olympics, but will it bank on OTT viewers', 26 February, FierceOnlineVideo. Online at: www.fierceonlinevideo.com/special-reports/judges-tally-nbc-scores-historic-online-video-numbers-sochi-olympics-will-i

Borowy, M. and Ying, D. 2016 'Mega-events of the future: the experience economy, the Korean connection, and the growth of eSport', ch. 12 in Gruneau and Horne eds 2016b.

Both, A. 2015 'Super Bowl has ways to go in captivating global audience', 24 January, Reuters. Online at: www.reuters.com/article/2015/01/24/us-nfl-international-idUSKBN0KX0KK20150124

Boukas, N., Ziakas, V. and Boustras, G. 2013 'Olympic legacy and cultural tourism: exploring the facets of Athens' Olympic heritage'. Vol. 19, 2, pp. 203–28, *International Journal of Heritage Studies*.

Bowdin, G., Allen, J., O'Toole, W., Harris, R. and McDonnell, I. 2010 *Events management*. Routledge, London.

Boykoff, J. 2016 'Sochi 2014: politics, activism and repression', ch. 8 in Gruneau and Horne eds 2016b.

Boyle, P. and Haggerty, K. 2009 'Spectacular security: mega-events and the security complex'. Vol. 3, pp. 25774, *International Political Sociology*.

Boyle, R. 2013 'No longer the crown jewels of sport? – television, sport and national events in the UK', ch. 6 in Scherer, J. and Rowe, D. eds *Sport, Public Broadcasting and Cultural Citizenship: Signal Lost?* Routledge, London.

Bradley, J. and Katz, B. 2014 *The metropolitan revolution: how cities and metros are fixing our broken politics and fragile economy*. Brookings Institution Press, Washington, DC.

Branigan, T. 2008 'China relaxes internet censorship for Olympics', 1 August, *Guardian*, London. Online at: www.theguardian.com/world/2008/aug/01/china.olympics

Branigan, T. 2012 'London 2012: Legacy of Beijing is that Bird's Nest will take 30 years to pay off', 26 July, *Guardian*, London. Online at: www.theguardian.com/sport/london-2012-olympics-blog/2012/jul/26/2008-olympics-birds-nest-beijing

Brannagan, P. and Giulianotti, R. 2015 'Soft power and soft disempowerment: Qatar, global sport and football's 2022 World Cup finals'. Vol. 34, 6, pp. 703–19, *Leisure Studies*.

Brenner, N. 2004 *New state spaces: urban governance and the rescaling of statehood*. Oxford University Press, Oxford.

Brenner, N., Peck, J. and Theodore, N. 2010 'After neoliberalization?'. Vol. 7, 3, pp. 327–45, *Globalizations*.

Bridges, B. 2012 'The Seoul Olympics: economic miracle meets the world', ch. 4 in Mangan and Dyreson eds.

Briggs, A. and Burke, P. 2009 *A social history of the media: from Gutenberg to the Internet* (3rd edition). Polity, Cambridge.

Brockway, L. 2002. *Science and colonial expansion: the role of the British Royal Botanic Gardens*. Yale University Press, New Haven.

Brodie, M. 2004 *The politics of the poor: the East End of London, 1885–1914*. Clarendon Press, Oxford.

Broudehoux, A.-M. 2007 'Spectacular Beijing: the conspicuous construction of an Olympic metropolis'. Vol. 29, 4, pp. 383–99, *Journal of Urban Affairs*.

Broudehoux, A.-M. 2016 'Mega-events, urban image constructions, and the politics of exclusion', ch. 7 in Gruneau and Horne eds 2016b.

Brown, M. 2012 'London 2012 Olympics: two weeks of unbelievable spectacle that surpassed our wildest dreams', 13 August, *Daily Telegraph*, London. Online at: www.telegraph.co.uk/olympics/news/9471473/London-2012-Olympics-Two-weeks-of-unbelievable-spectacle-that-surpassed-our-wildest-dreams.html

Brown, M. 2015 'Plans for Olympicopolis arts hub in east London attract £45 million of private cash', *Guardian*, London. Online at: www.theguardian.com/culture/2015/nov/05/olympicopolis-east-london-arts-hub-stratford-boris-johnson

Brownell, S. 1995 *Training the body for China: sports in the moral order of the People's Republic*. University of Chicago Press, Chicago.

Brownell, S. 2008 *Beijing's games: what the Olympics mean to China*. Rowman and Littlefield, Lanham, MD.

Brown-Saracino, J. ed. 2010 *The gentrification debates*. Routledge, New York.

Bryman, A. 2004 *The Disneyization of society*. Sage, London.

BT 2013 'BT Sport wins all live UK TV rights to Champions League and Europa League', 12 November, BT Sport, London. Online at: http://sport.bt.com/sport-football/football/bt-sport-wins-all-live-uk-tv-rights-to-champions-league-and-europa-leagueS11363847946944

Buchanan, P. 2015 'Empty gestures: starchitecture's swan song', 27 February, *The Architectural Review*. Online at: www.architectural-review.com/essays/empty-gestures-starchitectures-swan-song/8679010.fullarticle

Busa, F. 2012 'Mega-events as catalysts for urban transformation', ch. 10 in UNDESA.

Butler, N. 2016a 'IAAF hit-back at WADA claims of "systemic failures" within world governing body', 11 January, InsidetheGames. Online at: www.insidethegames.biz/articles/1033160/iaaf-hit-back-wada-claims-of-systemic-failures-within-world-governing-body

Butler, N. 2016b 'Rio State Governor admits Olympics could be "big failure" if transport and security concerns not addressed', 27 June, InsidetheGames. Online at: www.insidethegames.biz/articles/1038956/rio-state-governor-admits-olympics-could-be-big-failure-if-transporrt-and-security-concerns-not-addressed

Butler, P. 2000 'The Millennium Dome', 6 September, *Guardian*, London. Online at: www.theguardian.com/world/2000/sep/06/qanda

Cabinet Office 2013 'Inspired by 2012: the legacy from the London 2012 Olympic Games and Paralympic Games', A joint UK Government and Mayor of London report, Cabinet office, Whitehall, London. Online at: www.gov.uk/government/publications/the-olympic-and-paralympic-legacy-inspired-by-2012

Calhoun, C. ed. 1992 *Habermas and the public sphere*. MIT Press, London.

Callahan, W. 2012 'Sino-speak: Chinese exceptionalism and the politics of history'. Vol. 71, 1, pp. 33–55, *The Journal of Asian Studies*.

Caratti, P. and Ferraguto, L. 2012 'The Role of Environmental Issues in Mega-Events Planning and Management Processes: Which factors count?', ch. 6 in Hayes and Karamichas eds 2012b.

Carbone, C. 2008 'Seville 1929–1930', pp. 254–6, in Findling and Pelle eds.

Carrière, J.-P. and Demazière, C. 2002, 'Urban planning and flagship development projects: lessons from EXPO 98, Lisbon'. Vol. 17, 1, pp. 69–79, *Planning, Practice and Research*.

Carter, B. and Sandomir, R. 2008 'A surprise winner at the Olympic Games in Beijing: NBC', 17 August, *New York Times*, New York. Online at: www.nytimes.com/2008/08/18/sports/olympics/18nbc.html?pagewanted=all&_r=0

Cashman, R. 2006 *The bitter-sweet awakening: the legacy of the Sydney 2000 Olympic Games*. Walla Walla Press, Petersham, NSW.

Cashman, R. 2008 'The Sydney Olympic Park model: – Its evolution and realisation', pp. 21–44, in Cashman and Hay eds.

Cashman, R. 2011 *Sydney Olympic Park 2000 to 2010: history and legacy*. Walla Walla Press, Petersham, NSW.

Cashman, R. and Hay, A. eds 2008 *Mega event cities*, SOPA, Sydney Olympic Park Authority (for Metropolis Congress 2008), Sydney. Online at: www.metropolis.org/sites/default/files/publications/2008/megaevents-complete_0.pdf

Cashman, R. and Horne, J. 2013 'Managing legacy', ch. 4 in Frawley and Adair eds.

Castells, M. 2002 *The internet galaxy*. Oxford University Press, Oxford.

CBC 2013 'Olympic stadium's roof rapidly deteriorates', 3 December, Canadian Broadcasting Corporation (CBC). www.cbc.ca/news/canada/montreal/lympic-stadium-s-roof-rapidly-deteriorates-1.2448439

CEBR 2014 'World economic league table 2015', 26 December, Centre for Economics and Business Research (CEBR). Online at: www.cebr.com/reports/world-economic-league-table-2015/

Chalip, L. 2014 'From legacy to leverage', ch. 1 in Grix ed.

Chan, K. 2011 '80,000 "High risk" people leave Shenzhen' (writer, Wang Yuanyuan), Shenzen Party.com. Online at: www.shenzhenparty.com/blogs/kelley-chan/109219-80000-high-risk-people-leave-she

Chiesura, A. 2004 'The role of urban parks for the sustainable city'. Vol. 68, pp. 129–38. *Landscape and Urban Planning*.

China Sports Review. 2013 'Shenzen Universiade Graft Cases'. Online at: www.chinasportsreview.com/2013/04/05/shenzen-universiade-graft-cases/

Chow, G. 2010 *Interpreting China's economy*. World Scientific, Singapore.

Chozick, A. 2012 'NBC unpacks trove of data from Olympics', 25 September, *New York Times*, New York. Online at: www.nytimes.com/2012/09/6/business/media/nbc-upacks-trove-of-data-from-olympics.html

Clark, N. 2010 'Business models jostle for space in digital revolution', 2 April, *Independent*, London. Online at: www.independenrt.co.uk/news/business/news/business-models-jostle-for space-in-digital-revolution-19552.html

Clark, R. 2014 'You're paying £175 million to give West Ham a new stadium', 22 November, *The Spectator*. Online at: www.spectator.co.uk/features/9374702/londons-real-olympic-legacy-to-build-the-stadium-twice/

Close, P. 2011 'The Beijing Olympiad's achievement and legacy in global perspective', *Play the Game*. Online at: www.www.org/news/news-articles/2011/the-beijing-olympiads-achievement-and-legacy-in-global-perspective

Close, P., Askew, D. and Xu, X. 2006 *The Beijing Olympiad: the political economy of a sporting mega-event*. Routledge, London.

CNNGo 2011 'World Expo Museum planned for Shanghai', CNN. Online at: http://travel.cnn.com/shanghai/life/world-expo-museum-break-ground-shanghai-727698

CNNGo 2012 '"Asia's largest art museum" set to open in Shanghai', 28 September, CNN. Online at: http://travel.cnn.com/Shanghai /life/asias-largest-museum-set-open-shanghai-874686

COHRE 2007a 'The impacts of the Sydney Olympic Games on housing rights', Centre on Housing Rights and Evictions, Geneva. Online at: www.ruig-gian.org/ressources/Sydney_background_paper.pdf

COHRE 2007b 'The housing impact of the 2004 Olympic Games in Athens', Centre on Housing and Evictions, Geneva. Online at: www.ruig-gian.org/ressources/Athens_background_paper.pdf

COHRE 2008 'One world, whose dream?: housing rights violations and the Beijing Olympic Games', Centre on Housing Rights and Evictions (COHRE), Geneva. Online at: http://cohre.org/topics/mega-events

Collins, M. 2009 'Legacy of the docks', 5 August, *Guardian*, London. Online at: www.theguardian.com/society/2009/aug/05/london-docklands-legacy-development-regeneration

Collins, P. 1986 'Learning from the outsider within: the sociological significance of black feminist thought'. Vol. 33, 6, pp. S14–32, Special Theory Issue, *Social Problems*.

Collins, S. 2012a 'Olympics 2012: NBC finds vindication in opening ceremony record', 28 July, *LA Times*, Los Angeles. Online at: http://articles.latimes.com/2012/jul/28/entertainment/la-et-st-nbc-olympic-2012-opening-ceremony-ratings-nielsen-20120728

Collins, S. 2012b 'London Olympics: NBC coverage most-watched TV event in U.S. history', 13 August, *LA Times*, Los Angeles. Online at: http://articles.latimes.com/2012/aug/13/entertainment/la-et-stlondon-olympics-dubbed-most-watched-in-us-history-by-nbc-20120813

Colquhoun, K. 2004 *A thing in disguise: the visionary life of Joseph Paxton*. Harper Perennial, London.

Compton, J. 2016 'Mega-events, media and the integrated world of global spectacle', ch. 3 in Gruneau and Horne eds 2016b.

Cook, I. and Miles, S. 2011 'Beijing 2008', ch. 17 in Gold and Gold eds 2011b.

Copping, J. 2013 'Plans for new Crystal Palace unveiled', 3 October, *Daily Telegraph*, London. Online at: www.telegraph.co.uk/news/uknews/1035367/Plans-for-new-Crystal-Palace-unveiled.html

Couldry, N. 2014 'Mediatization: What is it?', pp. 33–9. in Kramp et al. eds.

Couldry, N., Hepp, A. and Krotz, F. eds 2010 *Media events in a global age*. Routledge, London.

Cowan, M. 2013 'London's moment: the tech cluster in the east of Britain's capital is on a roll', 5 April, *Wired*. Online at: www.wired.co.uk/magazine/archive/2013/04/features/londons-moment

Cranz, G. 1989 *The politics of park design: a history of urban parks in America*. The MIT Press, London.

Cranz, G. and Boland, M. 2004 'Defining the sustainable park: a fifth model for urban parks'. Vol. 23, pp. 2–4, *Landscape Journal*.

Crerar, P. 2013 '"Olympicopolis": Multi-million pound cultural hub planned for Olympic Park', 5 December, *Evening Standard*, London. Online at: www.standard. co.uk/news/london/olympicopolis-multimillion-pound-cultural-hub-planned-for-olympic-park-8982657.html

Cunningham, H. 1980 *Leisure in the Industrial Revolution, 1780–1880*. St Martin's Press, London.

Curran, J. and Seaton, J. 2010 *Power without responsibility: press, broadcasting and the internet in Britain* (7th edition). Routledge, London.

Curtis, S. 2014 'Illegal downloading: four strikes and then … nothing', 21 July, *Daily Telegraph*, London. Online at: www.telegraph.co.uk/technology/news/10979918/ Illegal-downloading-four-strikes-and-then…-nothing.html

C2ES 2015 'The Paris Agreement', Center for Climate and Energy Solutions (C2ES). Online at: www.e2es.org/international/paris-agreement

Darnell, S. and Millington, R. 2016 'Modernization, neoliberalism, and sports mega-events: evolving discourses in Latin America', ch. 4 in Gruneau and Horne eds 2016b.

Davies, W. 2014 *The limits of neoliberalism*. Sage, London.

Davis, J. 2008 'London 1851', pp. 9–15, in Findling and Pelle eds.

Davis, L. 2011 'International events and mass evictions: a longer view'. Vol. 35, 3, pp. 582–99, *International Journal of Urban and Regional Research*.

Dayan, D. and Katz, E. 1992 *Media events*. Harvard University Press, London.

DCMS 2012a 'Post legislative assessment of the London Olympic Games and Paralympic Games (Amendment) Act 2011', Memorandum to the Culture, Media and Sport Select Committee, Department of Culture, Media and Sport, CM 8503, December, UK Government, London. Online at: www.gov.uk/government/uploads/system/ uploads/attachment_data/file/235982/8503.pdf

DCMS 2012b 'International Olympic Committee hail London as "legacy blueprint"', DCMS, UK Government, London. Online at: www.gov.uk/government/news/ international-olympic-committee-hail-london-as-legacy-blueprint

DCMS 2013 *Meta-evaluation of the impacts and legacy of the London 2012 Olympics Games and Paralympic Games: post-games evaluation, summary report*, Grant Thornton/Ecosys/Loughborough University for the Department of Culture, Media and Sport (DCMS), UK Government, London. Online at: www.gov.uk/government/ publications/report-5-post-games-evaluation-meta-evaluation-of-the-impacts-and-legacy-of-the-london-2012-olympics-games-and-paralympic-games

Debord, G. 1990 *Comments on the society of the spectacle* (French original 1988). Verso, London.

Debord, G. 1995 *The society of the spectacle* (French original 1967). Zone Books, New York.

DEFRA 2011 'London 2012: a spectacular opportunity for sustainable behaviour change', Department of Environment, Food and Rural Affairs (DEFRA), UK Government, London. Online at http://sd.defra.gov.uk/2011/08/london-2012-a-spectacular-opportunity-for-sustainable-behaviour-change/

Delanty, G. 2009 *The Cosmopolitan Imagination: The Renewal of Critical Social Theory*. Cambridge University Press, Cambridge.

De Moraes, L. 2014 'NBC says Olympic ratings success proves primetime strategy still works in digital era', 12 February, Deadline.com. Online at: http://deadline.com/2014/02/sochi-olympics-ratings-nbc-strategy-success-682016/

Department of Justice 2009 'PRO-IP Act: first annual report 2008–2009'. Department of Justice, US Government, Washington, DC. Online at: www.gpo.gov/fdsys/pkg/PLAW-110publ403/pdf/PLAW-110publ403.pdf

Desai, A. 2016 'Between Madiba Magic and spectacular capitalism: the FIFA World Cup in South Africa', ch. 5 in Gruneau and Horne eds 2016b.

Dezeen 2015 'London council cans controversial Crystal Palace project', 27 February, Dezeen. Online at: www.dezeen.com/2015/02/27/london-bromley-council-scraps-controversial-crystal-palace-project/

Dick, T. 2006 'At last, an Olympic dream we can bank on', 13 July, *Sydney Morning Herald*, Sydney. Online at: www.smh.com.au/news/national/at-last-an-olympic-dream-we-can-bank-on/2006/07/12/1152637740404.html

Dicken, P. 2015 *Global shift: mapping the changing contours of the world economy* (7th edition). Sage, London.

Di Maggio, P. 2014a 'The internet and the cultural industries', *MIT Technology Review*. Online at: www.technologyreview.com/view/531341/the-internet-and-the-cultural-industries

Di Maggio, P. 2014b 'The internet's influence on the production and consumption of culture: Creative destruction and new opportunities', *Open Mind*, BBVA. Online at: www.bbvaopenmind.com/en/article/the-internets-influence-on-the-production-and-consumption-of-culture-creative-destruction-and-new-opportunities/

Dolata, U. 2011 'The music industry and the internet: a decade of disruptive and uncontrolled sectoral change', Institute of Social Sciences, University of Stuttgart. Online at: www.uni-stuttgart.de/soz/oi/publicationen/soi2_dolata_music_industry.pdf

Dolles, H. and Soderman, S. 2008 'Mega-sporting events in Asia – impacts on society, business and management'. Vol. 7, pp. 147–62, *Asian Business and Management*.

Donner, M. 2014 'Olympic television channel launch put LA in spotlight', 17 December, *The Hollywood Times*. Online at: http://thehollywoodtimes.net/2014/12/17/olympic-television-channel-launch-put-la-in-spotlight/

Downing, S. 2009 *The English pleasure garden 1660–1860*. Shire Publications Ltd, Botley, Oxford.

Dyreson, M. and Llewellyn, M. 2012 'Los Angeles is *the* Olympic city: legacies of the 1932 and 1984 Olympics games', ch. 7 in Mangan and Dyreson eds.

Eastday 2011 'City's record-breaking Expo turns in a profit', English.EastDay.Com (original source, 1 October, *Shanghai Daily*). Online at: http://eastday.com/e/11101/u1a6133087.html

Eastwood, N. 2015 'Global growth in smartphones will change our digital lives', 29 January, The Huffington Post. Online at: www.huffingtonpost.co.uk/nigel-eastwood/global-growth-in-smartpho_b_6563888html

EC 2015, 'Paris Agreement', European Commission. Online at: http://ec.europa.eu/clima/policies/international/regulations/future/index_en.htm

Economist 2013 'Hosting Mega-Events: Managing Innovation in Infrastructure', The Economic Intelligence Unit Ltd (authors/editors McFarlane, T. and Freudmann, A.), *Economist*, London. Online at: www.economistinsights.com/technology-innovations/analysis/hosting-mega-events

Economist 2015 'The future of work: There's an app for that', 3–9 January, *Economist*, London, pp. 5 and 13–16,. Online at: www.economist.com/news/briefing/21637355-freelance-workers-available-moments-notice-will-reshape-nature-companies-and

Economy, E. and Segal, A. 2008 'China's Olympic nightmare', July/August, *Foreign Affairs*. Online at: www.foreignaffairs.com/articles/64447/elizabeth-c-economy-and-adam-segal/chinas-olympic-nightmare

Edwards, J., Moital, M. and Vaughan, R. 2004 'The impacts of mega-events: the case of EXPO '98 – Lisbon', pp. 195–215 in Robinson, M. and Long, P. eds *Tourism and cultural festivals and events*. Business Education Publishers, Sunderland.

Edwards, P. and Tsouros, A. 2006 'Promoting physical activity and active living in urban environments: the role of local governments', World Health Organisation (WHO). Online at; www.euro.who.int/_data/assets/pdf_file/0009/98424/E89498.pdf

Ehrenreich, B. 2007 *Dancing in the streets: a history of collective joy*. Granta, London.

Eisenhauer, S., Adair, D. and Taylor, T. 2014 'Neoliberalism and mega-event security legacies: the 2010 FIFA World Cup, Cape Town, South Africa'. Vol. 8, 1, pp. 35–51, *International Journal of Event Management Research*.

EIU 2015 'Democracy Index 2014: democracy and its discontents', Economist Intelligence Unit. Online at: www.sudestadacom.uy/Content/Articles/421a313a-d58f-462e-9624-2504a37f6b56/Democracy-index-2014.pdf

Elgan, M. 2012 'The newspaper industry must change, or become yesterday's news', 24 March, *Computerworld*. Online at: www.computerworld.com/article/2503168/mobile-wireless/the-newspaper-industry-must-change-or-become-yesterday-s-news.html

Ellis-Peterson, H. 2014 'London Olympicopolis culture hub plan gets £141m funding', 7 December, *Guardian*, London. Online at: www.theguardian.com/uk-news/2014/dec/02/london-olympicopolis-culture-hub-stratford

Episa 2014 'EXPOs as catalysts for innovation and transformation of the urban landscape: the case of EXPO Zaragoza 2008'. Online at: www.astanaforum.org/2014/WP-content/themes/aef2014/docs/?id=27

ESPN/AP 2000 'Samaranch calls these Olympics "best ever"', 1 October, Associated Press, ESPN. Online at: http://assets.espn.go.com/oly/summer00/news/2000/1001/794339.html

Essex, S. and Chalkley, B. 1998 'Olympic Games: catalyst of urban change'. Vol. 17, 3, pp. 187–206, *Leisure Studies*.

Essex, S. and Chalkley, B. 1999 'Urban development through hosting international events: a history of the Olympic Games'. Vol. 14, pp. 369–94, *Planning Perspectives*.

Essex, S. and Chalkley, B. 2004 'The Olympic Games: catalyst of urban change', Plymouth University. Online at: www6.plymouth.ac.uk/files/extranet/docs/SSB/eurolympicgames.pdf

EU 2007 'A European agenda for culture' (A Resolution of the Council), 29 November, *Official Journal of the European Union*, C287/1, Brussels. Online at: http://eu-lex.europ.eu/legal-content/EN/TXT/?uri=CELEX:32007G1129(01)

EU 2013 'Intellectual property rights intensive industries: – contribution to economic performance and employment in the European Union', Industry-level Analysis Report by the Office for Harmonization of the Internal Market and the European Patents office, September. Online at: http://ec.europa.eu/internal_market/intellectual-property/docs/joint-report-epo-ohim-final-version_en.pdf

EU 2015a 'Spain – Standardised unemployment rate', Eurostat. Online at: http://sdw.ecb.europa.eu/quickview.do?SERIES_KEY=132.STS.M.ES.S.UNEH.RTT000.4.000

EU 2015b 'Unemployment statistics – 2014', Eurostat. Online at: http://ec.europa.eu/eurostat/tatistics-explained/index.php/Unemployment_statistics

EU 2015c 'Creative Europe', European Commission, Brussels. Online at: http://ec.europa.eu/programmes/creative-europe/opportunities/index_en.htm

EU 2015d 'GDP per capita in PPS: Spain', DataMarket, Eurostat. Online at: http://datamarket.com/data/set/1qxc/gdp-per-capita-in-pps#!ds=1qx!1qht=d&display=line

Euramet 2013 'Mega cities' Euramet, mega city paper – MgC-January'. Online at: www.emrponline.eu/call2013/docs/MegaCities.pdf

EU-URBACT 2012 'Zaragoza: a challenge, a city', URBACT. Online at: www.urbact.eu/filedmin/Projects/Citylogo/documents_media/Zaragoza_baseline_citylogo.pdf

Expo 2010 'World Expo 2010, Shanghai China, communication & promotion plan', Expo 2010, Shanghai. Online at: http://en.expo2010.cn/expo/expo_english/documents/dc/userobject1ai48897/60000000.pdf

EXPOCheck 2012 'EXPOcheck reports'. Online at: http://jdpecon.com/expo/expocheck.html

Expo Zaragoza Empresarial 2015 'Expo Zaragoza Empresarial', Expo Zaragoza Empresarial website. Online at: www.expozaragozaempresarial.com/

Fallah, M. 2015 'Post-Expo Milano 2015: prospective visions of future voids', 3NTA. Online at: www.3nta.com/post-expo-milano-2015-prospective-visions-of-future-voids/

Farred, G. 2016 'The World Cup, the security state, and the colonized Other: reflections on Brazil, Russia, South Africa and Qatar', ch. 9 in Gruneau and Horne eds 2016b.

Ferguson, D. 2008 'Beijing's "1.5 million" evictions: – the making of a Western media myth'. Online at: www.china.org.cn/china/2008-11/12/content_16752591.htm

Fielding, R. 2013 'The Olympic Legacy: after the circus', *Economia*. Online at http://economia.icaew.com/business/july-2013/after-the-circus

FierceWireless, 2010, '190 million people watched the Olympics on the networks of NBC Universal', 2 March, FierceWireless. Online at: www.fiercewireless.com/press-releases/190-million-watched-olympics-networks-nbc-universal

Findling, J. 1994a *Chicago's great world's fairs*. Manchester University Press, Manchester.

Findling, J. 1994b 'Fair legacies: Expo '92 and Cartuja '93', in Rydell and Gwinn eds.

Findling, J. 2008 'Barcelona 1929–1930', pp. 251–4, in Findling and Pelle eds.

Findling, J. and Pelle, K. eds 2008 *Encyclopedia of world's fairs and expositions* (2nd edition). McFarland and Co. Inc., London.

Fine, R. 2006 'Cosmopolitanism and violence: difficulties of judgement'. Vol. 57, 1, pp. 49–67, *British Journal of Sociology*.

Fine, R. 2007 *Cosmopolitanism*. Routledge, London.

FirstRow 2015 'FirstRowSports'. Online at: www.firstrows.eu

Flinn, J. and Frew, M. 2013 'Glastonbury: managing the mystification of festivity', *Leisure Studies*. Online at: http://dx.doi.org10.1080/02614367.2012.751121

Florida, R. 2002 *The rise of the creative class*. Basic Books, New York.

Foley, M., McGillivray, D. and McPherson, G. 2012 *Event policy: from theory to strategy*. Routledge, London.

Forsyth, J. and Bird, M. 2013 'UK start-ups flock to Silicon Roundabout', 15 July, CityAM. Online at: www.cityam.com/article/uk-start-ups-flock-to-silicon-roundabout

Foster, J. 1999 *Docklands: cultures in conflict, worlds in collision*. UCL Press, London.

Fraser, D. 2009 *The Evolution of the British Welfare State* (4th edition). Palgrave Macmillan, Basingstoke.

Frawley, S. and Adair, D. eds 2013 *Managing the Olympics*. Palgrave Macmillan, London.

Freeman, C. and Soete, L. 1997 *The economics of industrial innovation* (3rd edition). Pinter, London.

Furrer, P. 2002 'Sustainable Olympic Games: a dream or a reality?' Online at: www. omero.unito.it/web/Furrer(eng.).PDF

Futterman, M. and Schechner, S. 2008 'NBC's Olympic ratings get a web-based boost', 11 August, *The Wall Street Journal*. Online at: www.wsj.com/articles/ SB121841383938428459

Gaffney, C. 2013 'Between discourse and reality: the un-sustainability of mega-event planning'. Vol. 5, pp. 3926–40, *Sustainability*.

Gaffney, C. 2016 'The urban impacts of the 2014 World Cup in Brazil', ch. 10 in Gruneau and Horne eds 2016b.

Games Monitor 2008 'London Olympic evictions', *Games Monitor*. Online at: www. gamesmonitor.org.uk/node/558

Garcia, B. 2011 'Sydney 2000', ch. 15 in Gold and Gold eds 2011b.

Gartner 2014 'Gartner says worldwide traditional PC, tablet, ultramobile and mobile phone shipments on pace to grow 7.6 percent in 2014', 7 January, Gartner. Online at: www.gartner.com/newsroom/id/2645115

Gatopoulos, D. 2010 'Did 2004 Olympics spark Greek financial crisis?', 6 March, *USA Today*. Online at: http://usatoday30.usatoday.com/sports/olympics/2010-06-03-3222710772x.htm

Geppert, A. 2008 'Wembley 1924–1925', pp. 230–6, in Findling and Pelle eds.

German Government 2006 'It truly was a time to make friends' (Review by the Federal Government on the 2006 FIFA World Cup), German Government. Online at: www.bmi. bund.de/cae/servlet/contentblob/150624/publicationFile/15402/Abschlussbericht_ WM206_en.pdf

Getz, D. 2012 *Event studies* (2nd edition). Routledge, London

Gibson, O. 2009 'Premier League TV model at risk as websites threaten lucrative deals', 11 August, *Guardian*, London. Online at: www.theguardian.com/football/2009/aug/11/ premier-league-tv-rights-deals-websites

Gibson, O. 2012 'Designer behind New York's High Line reveals plans for Olympic Park', 14 October, *Guardian*, London. Online at: www.theguardian.com.uk/2012/oct/14/ designer-high-line-olympic-park

Gibson, O. 2013 'Premier League drops copyright infringement case against YouTube', 11 November, *Guardian*, London. Online at: www.theguardian.com/football/2013/ nov/11/premier-league-copyright-case-youtube

Gibson, O. 2015a 'Question of state aid still lingers over West Ham's luxurious new home', 20 April, *Guardian*, London. Online at: www.theguardian.com/football/2015/ apr/20/west-ham-olympic-stadium-state-aid-question

Gibson, O. 2015b 'Luis Figo pulls out of Fifa presidential race to leave two-horse race', 21 May, *Guardian*, London. Online at: www.theguardian.com/football/2015/may/21/ luis-figo-fifa-presidential-race-two-horse-race

Gibson, O. 2015c 'Sky and BT retain Premier League TV rights for record £5.14 billion', 10 February, *Guardian*, London. Online at: www.theguardian.com/football/201/ feb/10/premier-league-tv-rights-sky-bt

Gibson, O. 2015d 'The troubled history of Zaha Hadid's Tokyo Olympic stadium project', 17 July, *Guardian*, London. Online at: www.theguardian.com/artanddesign/20215/ jul/17/the-troubled-history-of-zaha-hadids-tokyo-olympic-stadium-project

Gibson, O. 2015e 'Japan scraps Zaha Hadid plan for Olympic stadium', 17 July, *Guardian*, London. Online at: www.theguardian.com/world/2015/jul/17/japan-scraps-zaha-hadids-tokyo-olympic-stadium-design

Gibson, O. 2015f 'FIFA and IAAF endure grim 2015 but corruption crises far from over', 31 December, *Guardian*, London. Online at: www.theguardian.com/football/2015dec/31/fifa-iaaf-corruption-crisis-2015

Gibson, O. 2016 'Russian athletics: IAAF upholds ban before Rio Olympics', 17 June, *Guardian*, London. Online at: www.theguardian.com/sport/2016/jun/17/russia-rio-olympics-ban-doping-iaaf-sebastian-coe

Giddens, A. 2002 *runaway world: how globalisation is reshaping our lives* (2nd edition). Profile Books, London.

Gilbert, D. 2012 'Was the London 2012 Olympics a social media success?', 13 August, *International Business Times*. Online at: www.ibtimes.co.uk/social-media-olympics-london-2012-twitter-facebook-373114

Gill, A. 2010 'Glittering ceremonies cannot disguise the problems of the music industry', 19 July, *Independent*. Online at: www.independent.co.uk/artsentertainment/music/features/andy-gill-glittering-ceremonies-cannot-disguise-theproblems-of-the-music-industry-2030310.html

Gillies, C. 2014 'The spectacle of spectacles', 31 January, *Globe and Mail*, Toronto. Online at: www.theglobeandmail.com/sports/olympics/behind-the-games/the-spectacle-of-all-spectacles/article16636704/

Giorgi, L., Sassatelli, M. and Delanty, G. eds 2011 *Festivals and the cultural public sphere*. Routledge, London.

Giovinazzi, O. and Moretti, M. 2010 'Port cities and urban waterfront: transformations and opportunities'. Vol. 3, March, pp. 57–64, TeMALab journal. Online at: www.tema.unina.it/index.php/tema/article/viewFile/urn%3Anbn%3Ait%3Aunina-3515/125

Girginov, V. ed. 2010 *The Olympics: a critical reader*. Routledge, London.

Girginov. V. ed. 2014 *Handbook of the London 2012 Olympic and Paralympic Games. Volume 2, celebrating the games*. Routledge, London.

Giulianotti, R., Armstrong, G., Hales, G. and Hobbs, D. 2015 'Sport mega-events and public opposition: a sociological study of the London 2012 Olympics'. Vol. 39, 2, pp. 99119, *Journal of Sport and Social Issues*.

Giulianotti, R. and Klauser, F. 2010 'Security governance and sport mega-events: toward an interdisciplinary research agenda'. Vol. 4, 1, pp. 49–61, *Journal of Sport and Social Issues*.

GLA 2013 'Olympic jobs evaluation; final report', SQW, Mayor of London. Online at: www.london.gov.uk/sites/default/files/GLAOlympicJobsFinalreport.pdf

Goggin, G. 2013 'Sport and the rise of mobile media', ch. 2 in Hutchins and Rowe eds.

Gold, M. 2011 'Athens 2004', ch. 16 in Gold and Gold eds 2011b.

Gold, J. and Gold, M. 2004 *Cities of culture: staging international festivals and the urban agenda, 1851–2000*. Ashgate, Aldershot.

Gold, J. and Gold, M. 2011a 'From A to B: the Summer Olympics, 1896–2008', ch. 2 in Gold and Gold eds 2011b.

Gold, J. and Gold, M. eds 2011b *Olympic cities: city agendas, planning and the world's games, 1896–2016* (2nd edition). Routledge, London.

Goldberg, D. and Larsson, L. 2014 'Pirate Bay co-founder Peter Sunde: "In prison you become brain-dead"', 5 November, *Guardian*, London. Online at: www.theguardian.com/technology/2014/nov/05/sp-pirate-bay-cofounder-peter-sunde-in-prison

Goldwyn, S. 1949 'Hollywood in the Television Age', Cobblestone Entertainment. Online at: www.cobbles.com/simpp_archive/goldwyn_television.htm

Golson, J. 2014 'Selling its 500 millionth iPhone, Apple has time to create next big thing', 27 March, *TechRepublic*. Online at: www.techrepublic.com/article/selling-its-500-millionth-iphone-apple-has-time-to-create-next-big-thing/

Goody, J. 1977 *The domestication of the savage mind*. Cambridge University Press, Cambridge.

Goody, J. and Watt, I. 1975 'The Consequences of Literacy', pp. 27–68 in Goody, J. ed. *Literacy in traditional societies*. Cambridge University Press, Cambridge.

Gotham, K. 2016 'Beyond bread and circuses: mega-events as forces of creative destruction', ch. 2 in Gruneau and Horne eds 2016b.

Govan, F. 2011 'Greece's Olympic dream has turned into a nightmare for Village residents', 23 June, *Daily Telegraph*, London. Online at: www.telegraph.co.uk/finance/financialcrisis/8595360/Greecesolympic-dream-has-turned-into-a-nightmare-for-village-residents.html

Gratton, C. and Preuss, H. 2012 'Maximizing Olympic impacts by building up legacies', ch. 3 in Mangan and Dyreson eds.

Gratton, C., Shibli, S. and Coleman, S. 2006 'The economic impact of major sports events: a review of ten events in the UK'. Vol. 54, 2, pp. 41–58, *Sociological Review*.

Green, J. 2013 'Superkilen: global mash-up of a park', The Dirt, Copenhagen. Online at: http://dirt.asla.org/2013/03/14/superkilen-global-mash-up-of-a-park/

Greenhalgh, P. 1988 *Ephemeral vistas: the expositions universelles, great exhibitions and world's fairs*. Manchester University Press, Manchester.

Greenhalgh, P. 2011 *Fair world: a history of world's fairs and expositions, from London to Shanghai, 1851–2010*. Papadakis, New Architecture Group, Winterbourne, Berkshire.

Greenpeace 2000 'Greenpeace Olympic environmental guidelines: a guide to sustainable events', September, Greenpeace. Online at: www.greenpeace.org/eastasiaPageFiles/301173guidelines.pdf

Greenpeace 2004 'Athens 2004 disqualified from Green Olympics', 29 July, Greenpeace. Online at: www.greenpeace.org/international/en/news/features/athens-disqualified-from-green/

Greyser, S. and Kogan, V. 2013 'NBC and the 2012 London Olympics: unexpected success', 15 September, Working Paper 14-02, Harvard Business School, Cambidge, MA. Online at: www.hbs.edu/faculty/PublicationFiles/14-028_99a0100c-7dcc-4fc4-bf29-6c0bd2f5561d.pdf

Grix, J. ed. 2014 *Leveraging legacies from sports mega-events*. Palgrave, London.

Grove, M. 2012 'Beijing 2008: the Olympic legacy', Sasaki Associates. Online at: www.archive.uli.org/fallmeeting2012/thur/Olympics-MichaelGrove.pdf

Gruneau, R. and Horne, J. 2016a 'Mega-events and globalization: a critical introduction', ch. 1 in Gruneau and Horne eds 2016b.

Gruneau, R. and Horne, J. eds 2016b *Mega-Events and Globalization: Capital and Spectacle in a Changing World Order*. Routledge, Abingdon.

Guthrie, D. 2006 *China and Globalization*. Routledge, London.

Habermas, J. 1991 *The structural transformation of the public sphere* (German original 1962). Polity, Cambridge.

Hague, W. 2011 'Foreign Secretary on London Olympics: "The greatest show on earth" ', UK Government, London. Online at: www.gov.uk/government/news/foreign-secretary-onlondon-olympics-the-greatest-show-on-earth

Hamlin, K. and Dingmin, Z. 2010 'China to close Asian Games after spending more money than London Olympics', Bloomberg. Online at: www.bloomberg.com/

news/print/2010-11-25/china-to-close-asian-games-with-budget-toppping-london-olympics.html

Hampton, J. 2012 *The Austerity Olympics: when the Games came to London in 1948*. Aurum, London.

Harriss, J. 1975 *The tallest tower: Eiffel and the Belle Epoque*. Houghton Mifflin Co., Boston.

Hartman. H. 2012 *London 2012 – sustainable design: delivering a games legacy*. John Wiley and Sons, Chichester.

Harvey, D. 1985 *The urbanization of capital*. Blackwell, Oxford.

Harvey, D. 2006 'The political economy of public space', ch. 2 in Low, S. and Smith, N. eds *The politics of public space*. Routledge, New York.

Harvey, P. 1996 *Hybrids of modernity: anthropology, the nation state and the universal exhibition*. Routledge, London.

Hastac 2012 'The future of museums', HASTAC, US. Online at: www.hastac.org/initiatives/hastac-scholars/scholars-forums/future-musuems

Hatherley, O. 2010 'Shanghai Expo: this is new Confucianism writ large', 31 October, *Guardian*, London. Online at: www.theguardian.com/commentisfree/2010/0ct/11/shanghai-expo-architecture-China-development

Hayes, G. and Karamichas, J. 2012a 'Introduction: sports mega-events, sustainable development and civil societies', ch. 1 in Hayes and Karamichas eds 2012b.

Hayes, G. and Karamichas, J. eds 2012b *Olympic Games, mega-events and civil societies: globalization, environment, resistance*. Palgrave, London.

Heathcote, E. 2010 'The Shanghai Expo is the biggest ever', 5 June, *Financial Times*, London. Online at: www.ft.com/cms/s/2/2ba39b9e-6f65-11df-9f43-00144feabdc0.html

Heckscher, M. 2008 *Creating Central Park*. The Metropolitan Museum of Art and Yale University Press, London.

Held, D., McGrew, A., Goldblatt, D. and Perraton, J. 2000 *Global transformations: politics, economics and culture*. Polity Press, Cambridge.

Hepp, A. 2013 *Cultures of mediatization*. Polity, Cambridge.

Hesmondhalgh, D. 2005 *Cultural industries* (2nd edition). Sage, London.

Higgins, C. 2012 'London 2012 opening ceremony promises spectacle and surprises', 12 June, *Guardian*, London. Online at: www.theguardian.com.sport/2012/jun12/london-2012-opening-ceremony-spectacle

Hiller, H. 2012 *Host cities and the Olympics*. Routledge, London.

Hiller, H. and Wanner, R. 2015 'The psycho-social impact of the Olympics as urban festival: a leisure perspective'. Vol. 4, 6, pp. 672–88, *Leisure Studies*.

HLF 2014 'State of UK public parks 2014: Renaissance to risk?', Heritage Lottery Fund (HLF). Online at: www.hlf.org.uk/state-uk-public-park#.VWDiYUYucf4

HM Treasury 2014, *Public Expenditure: Statistical Analyses 2014*, HM Treasury, London. Online at: www.gov.uk/government/uploads/system/uploads/attachment_data/file/330717/PESA_2014_-_print.pdf

Horne, D. 1984 *The great museum: the re-presentation of history*. Pluto, London.

Horne, J. 2011 'Architects, stadia and sport spectacles'. Vol. 46, 2, pp. 205–27, *International Review for the Sociology of Sport*.

Horne, J. and Manzenreiter, W. eds 2006 *Sport mega-events: social scientific analyses of a global phenomenon*. Blackwell, Oxford.

Horten, M. 2013 'France wants to relaunch the EU "fight against piracy"'. www.iptegrity.com. Online at: www.iptegrity.com/index.php/france/912-france-wants-to-relaunch-the-eu-fight-against-piracy

Houlihan, B. and Giulianotti, R. 2012 'Politics and the London 2012 Olympics: the (in) security Games'. Vol. 88, 4, pp. 708–17, *International Affairs*.

HSCIC 2015 'Statistics on obesity, physical activity and diet – England 2015', Health and Social Care Information Centre (HSCIC). Online at: www.hscic.gov.uk/catalogue/PUB16988

Hu, J. 2008 'Sustainable practice in China – the Olympic Forest Park, Beijing', October, ASLA Annual Meeting & Expo. Online at: www.asia.orguploadedFiles/CMS/Business_Quarterly/0810-BeijingOlympicForestPark-HuJie-2.pdf

Huntoon, L. 2008 'Lisbon 1998', pp. 389–93, in Findling and Pelle eds.

Hur, H. 2012 'Staging modern statehood: world exhibitions and the rhetoric of publishing in late Qing China, 1851–1910'. Online at: www.ideals.illinois.edu/bitstream/handle/2142/31036/Hur_Hyunggju.pdf

Hutchins, B. and Rowe, D. 2009 'From broadcast scarcity to digital plenitude: the changing dynamics of the media sport content economy'. Vol. 10, 4, pp. 354–70, *Television and the New Media*.

Hutchins, B. and Rowe, D. eds 2013 *Digital media sport: technology, power and culture in the network society*. Routledge, London.

ICE 2014 'Federal agencies seize more than $21.6 million in fake NFL merchandise during "Operation Team Player"', Immigration and Customs Enforcement (ICE), US Government, Washington, DC. Online at: www.ice.gov/news/releases/federal-agencies-seize-more-216-million-fake-nfl-merchandise-during-operation-team

Ijeh, I. 2014 'It's not just a breathing space, it's a social space', BDonline. Online at; www.bdonline.co.uk/'It's-not-just-a-breathing-space-it's-a-social-space'/5067715.article

Illoniemi, L. 2014 'The Pritzker Prize: making architects "starchitechts" since 1979 (but at what cost?)', 27 March, *ArchDaily*. Online at: www.archdaily.com/490708/the-pritzker-prize-making-architect-starchitects-since-1979-but-at-what-cost/

ILO 2013 'Labour migration', International Labour Organisation, Geneva. Online at: www.ilo.org/beijing/areas-of-work/labour-migration/lang–en/index.htm

IMLS 2008 'National study on the use of libraries, museums and the internet'. IMLS, US. Online at: http://interconnectionsreport.org/

Imperial War Museum 2011 *The Imperial War Museum. London, guidebook*. Belmont Press, London.

Impey, O. and McGregor, A. eds 1985 *The origins of museums: The cabinet of curiosities in sixteenth- and seventeenth-century Europe*. Clarendon, Oxford.

InfoRegio 2012 'Urban park revitalises deprived city neighbourhood', Regional Policy, EU. Online at: http://ec.europa.eu/regional_policy/index.cfm/en/projects/belgiumurban-park-revitalises-deprived-city-neighbourhood

Ingle, S. 2016 'IAAF in crisis: a complex trail of corruption that led to the very top', 7 January, *Guardian*, London. Online at: www.theguardian.com/sport/2016/jan/07/russia-doping-scandal-corruption-blackmail-athletics-iaaf

Inglis, S. 1996 *Football grounds of Britain* (3rd revised edition). Harper Collins, London.

IOC 1952 '1952 Helsinki Olympics', IOC, Lausanne. Online at: www.olympic.org/helsinki-1952-summer-olympics

IOC 1956 '1956 Melbourne Olympics', IOC, Lausanne. Online at: www.olympic.org/Melbourne-stockholm-1956-summer-olympics

IOC 2000 'The Sydney 2000 Olympic Games', IOC, Lausanne. Online at: www.olympic.org/documents/reports/en_report_249.pdf

IOC 2002 'Salt Lake 2002, Section 3', IOC, Lausanne. Online at: www.olympic.org/Documents/EN/en_report_560.pdf

IOC 2003 'Candidature acceptance procedure: games of the XXX Olympiad 2012', IOC, Lausanne. Online at: www.olympic.org/olympic-charter/documents-reports-studies-publications

IOC 2004 'Athens 2004 Olympic Games, global television report', IOC, Lausanne. Online at: www.olympic.org/Documents/Reports/EN/en_report_1086.pdf

IOC 2006 'Global television report', IOC, Lausanne. Online at: www.olympic.org/Documents/Reports/EN/en_report_1087.pdf

IOC 2007 'What is the Olympic Games global impact study?', IOC, Lausanne. Online at: www.olympic.org/Documents/Reports/EN/en_report_1077.pdf

IOC 2008 *Marketing report, Beijing 2008*, IOC, Lausanne. Online at: www.olympic.org/Documents/Reports/EN/en_report_1428.pdf

IOC 2009 'Games of the XXIX Olympiad, Beijing 2008: global television and online media report', IOC, Lausanne. Online at: www.olympic.org/Documents/IOC_Marketing/Broadcasting/Beijing_2008_Global_Broadcast_Overview.pdf

IOC 2010 'Vancouver 2010 Olympic Winter Games: global television and online media overview', IOC, Lausanne. Online at: www.olympic.org/Documenets/IOC/Marketing/Broadcasting/Vancouver2010OlympicWinterGames-BroadcastCoverageAudienceOverview.pdf

IOC 2011 '2020 Candidature acceptance procedure: games of the XXXII Olympiad', IOC, Lausanne. Online at: www.olympic.org/Documents/Host_City_elections/2020_CAP.pdf

IOC 2012a 'Factsheet: – London 2012 facts and figures, update – November 2012'. Online at: www.olympic.org/Documents/Reference_documents_Factsheets/London_2012_Facts_and_Figures-eng.pdf

IOC 2012b 'Factsheet – legacies of the Games, Update – July 2012'. Online at: www.olympic.org/Documents/Reference_documents_Factsheets/Legacy.pdf

IOC 2012c *IOC Marketing report – London 2012*, IOC, Lausanne. Online at: www.olympic.org/Documents/IOC_Marketing/London_2012?LP_IOC_MarketingReport_medium_res1.html

IOC 2012d 'Olympic legacy', IOC, Lausanne. Online at: www.olympic.org/Documents/Olympism_in_action/Legacy2013_Booklet_Legacy.pdf

IOC 2012e 'Sydney's Olympic legacies praised', IOC, Lausanne. Online at: http://www.olympic.org/news/sydney-s-olympic-legacies-praised/167971

IOC 2012f 'Olympic legacy', IOC, Lausanne. Online at: www.olympic.org/Documents/Olympism_in_action/Legacy/Olympic_Legacy.pdf.pdf

IOC 2012g 'Sydney's Olympic legacies praised', 13 July, Olympic.org. Online at: www.olympic.org/news/sydney-s-olympic-legacies-praised/167971

IOC 2013a 'London 2012 – benefits of hosting London 2012 will be ongoing', IOC, Lausanne. Online at www.olympic.org/news/benefits-of-hosting London-2012-will-be-ongoing/172370

IOC 2013b *Olympic Games: legacies and impacts – bibliography*, IOC, Lausanne. Online at: www.olympic.org/Assets/OSC Section/pdf/LRes_7E.pdf

IOC 2013c *Olympic charter – 2013*, IOC, Lausanne. Online at: www.olympic.org/documents/olympic_charter_en.pdf

IOC 2013d 'Olympic marketing fact file' (2014 edition), IOC, Lausanne. Online at: www.olympic.org/Documents/IOC_Marketing/OLYMPIC_MARKETING_FACT_FILE.2014.pdf

IOC 2014a 'Olympic agenda 2020: 20+20 recommendations', IOC, Lausanne. Online at: www.olympic.org/Documents/Olympic_Agenda_2020/Olympic_Agenda_2020-20-20_Recommendations-ENG.pdf

IOC 2014b 'Factsheet: IOC financial summary, update – July 2014' IOC, Lausanne. Online at: www.olympic.org/Documents/Reference_documents_Factsheets/IOC_ Financial_Summary.pdf

IOC 2015 'The Olympic movement: introduction', Olympic.org. Online at: www.olympic. org/content/the-ioc/governance/introductionold/

ITB 2014 'The world travel and trends report 2014/15', ITB Berlin. Online at: www.itb-berline.de/itb/itb_dl_de/itb_itb_berlin/itb_itb_academy/ITB_2015_WTTR_Report. A4_4.pff

IWGA 2008 'Beijing 2008: new media records'. International World Games Association (IGWA). Online at: www.theworldgames.org/news/news-of-the-world-games/ 419-beijing-2008–new-media-records

IWS 2014 'Internet usage statistics', Internet World Stats (IWS). Online at: www.inter-networldstats.com/stats.htm

Izundu, C. 2010 'Illegal online sports streaming of matches "'increases"', 22 October, BBC News, London. Online at: www.bbc.co.uk/newsbeat/11549979

Jacka, T., Kipnis, A. and Sargeson, S. 2013 *Contemporary China: society and social change*. Cambridge University Press, Cambridge.

Jackson, A. 2008 *Expo: international expositions 1851–2010*. V&A Publishing, London.

Jackson, M. 2013 'EU ruling could extend internet piracy website blocking to all ISPs', 27 November, *ISPreview*. Online at: www.ispreview.co.uk/index.hp/2013/11/eu-ruling-extend-internet-piracy-website-blocking-isps.html

Jacques, M. 2012 *When China rules the world*. Penguin, London.

James. M. 2012 'NBC's London Olympic ratings defy expectations', 11 August. *LA Times*, Los Angeles. Online at: http://articles.latimes.com/2012/aug/11/business/fi-ct-olympics-ratings-20120811

Jennings, W. 2012 'Mega-events and risk colonisation: risk management and the Olympics', CARR Discussion paper 71, LSE, London. Online at: www.lse.ac.uk/accounting/ CARR/pdf/DPs/Disspaper71.pdf

Jessop, B. and Sum, N. 2000 'An entrepreneurial city in action: Hong Kong's emerging strategies in and for (inter) urban competition'. Vol. 37, 12, pp. 2287–313, *Urban Studies*. Online at: www.lancaster.ac.uk/sociology/research/publications/papers/ jessop-sum-USE-2000a.pdf

Ji, S.W. and Waterman, D. 2013 'The impact of the internet on media industries: an economic perspective', Indiana University. Online at: www.indiana.edu/~telecom/ people/aculty/waterman/EDITEDOnline_OfflineChapter12-11-2013.pdf

Jinxia, D. and Mangan, J. 2012 'Beijing Olympics legacies: certain intentions and certain and uncertain outcomes', ch. 8 in Mangan and Dyreson eds.

Johnson, B. 2013 'Boris Johnson: the Olympic park will be the Albertopolis of the east', 5 December, *Evening Standard*, London. Online at: www.standard.co.uk/ comment/comment/boris-johnson-the-olympic-park-will-be-the-albertopolis-of-the-east-8982871.html

Jones, K. and Will, J. 2005 *The invention of the park: recreational landscapes from the Garden of Eden to Disney's Magic Kingdom*. Polity, Cambridge.

Jones, P. 2011 *The sociology of architecture: constructing identities*. Liverpool University Press, Liverpool.

Jozwiak, G. 2013 'Olympic Games spark a volunteering boom', 30 April, *Children and Young People Now*. Online at: www.ypnow.co.uk/print_article/cyp/news/107093/ olympic-games-spark-volunteering-boom

Justia 2010 'The Football Association Premier League Limited et al v. You Tube, Inc. et al', Justia, Supreme Court Center, US. Online at: http://news.justia.com/cases/featured/new-york/nysdce/I:2007cv03582/305574

Kafka, P. 2008 'Olympic Committee outraged about USA fans watching live online, sends takedown notices', *Business Insider*. Online at: www.businessinsider.com/2008/8/olympic-organizers-to-blog-please-don-t-show-anyone-our-opening-ceremonies?IR=T

Kahn, M. and Auchard, E. 2007 'Premier League soccer sues YouTube over copyright', Reuters. Online at: www.reuters.com/assets/print?aid=USN0445675320070505

Kambli, N. 2011 'The changing nature of place in the 21st century: a story of Zaragoza'. Online at: www.geography.ssc.uwo.ca/faculty/Gilliland/ISUF2011-FullPapers/04011010Kambli_paper.pdf

Kamen, M. 2015 'Pirate bay struggling to stay afloat since return', 25 February, *Wired*. Online at: www.wired.co.uk/news/archive/2015-02/25/pirate-bay-failed-rsurrection

Kantar 2014 'Sochi 2014, global broadcast and audience report', Kantar and IOC, Lausanne. Online at: www.olympic.org/Documents/IOC_Marketing/Sochi_2014/sochi-2014-global-coverage-audience-summary-vaug14.pdf

Kaplan, R. 2012 'Between mass society and revolutionary praxis: the contradictions of Guy Debord's Society of the Spectacle'. Vol. 14, 4, pp. 457–78, *European Journal of Cultural Studies*.

Kapoor, A. 2015 'Orbit'. Online at: http://anishkapoor.com/32/Orbit.html

Karamichas, J. 2012 'Olympic Games as an opportunity for the ecological modernization of the host nation: The cases of Sydney 2000 and Athens 2004', pp. 151–71, in Hayes and Karamichas eds 2012b.

KAS 2011 'Sustainable mega-events in developing countries: experiences and insights from host cities in South Africa, India and Brazil', Kondrad Adenauer Stiftung (KAS), Johannesburg. Online at: www.kas.de/wfdoc/kas_29583-1522-1-30.pdf?120124104507

Kassens-Noor, E. 2012 *Planning Olympic Legacies*. Routledge, London.

Kassens-Noor, E. et al. (Kassens-Noor, E., Wilson, M., Muller, S., Maharaj, B. and Huntoon, L.) 2015 'Towards a mega-event legacy framework'. Vol. 34, pp. 665–71. *Leisure Studies*.

Katz, B. 2010 'City centred: investing in metropolitan areas to build the next economy', 1 November, Brookings Institute, Washington, DC. Online at: www.brookings.edu/research/articles/2010/1021-metro-economy-katz

Katzenstein, P. 2005 *A world of regions: Asia and Europe in the American Imperium*. Cornell University Press, Ithaca.

Kellner, D. 2003a *Media spectacle*. Routledge, London

Kellner, D. 2003b 'Media culture and the triumph of the spectacle', ch. 1 in Kellner 2003a.

Kellner, D. 2003c 'The sports spectacle, Michael Jordan, and Nike', ch. 3 in Kellner 2003a.

Kellner, D. 2004 'Media culture and the triumph of the spectacle'. Online at: http://pages.gseis.ucla.edu/faculty/Kellner/essays/mediaculturetriumphspectacle.pdf

Kellner, D. 2010 'Media spectacle and media events: some critical reflections', ch. 6 in Couldry et al. eds.

Killanin, L. and Rodda, J. eds 1976 *The Olympic Games*. Macmillan, New York.

Kiss, J. 2009 'The Pirate Bay trial: guilty verdict', 17 April, *Guardian*, London. Online at: www.theguardian.com/technology/2009/apr/17/the-pirate-bay-trial-guilty-verdict

Kiss, J. 2011 'BitTorrent: Copyright lawyers' favourite target reaches 200,000 lawsuits', 9 August, *Guardian*, London. Online at: www.theguardian.com/technology/pda/2011/aug/09/bittorrent-piracy

Kissell, R. 2015 'Update Super Bowl on NBC draws record U.S. television audience', 2 February, *Variety*. Online at: http://variety.com/2015/tv/ratings/super-bowl-ratings-it-all-time-high-with-patriotswin-on-nbc1201421267/

Kissoudi, P. 2012 'The Athens Olympics: optimistic legacies – post-Olympic assets and the struggle for their realization', ch. 6 in Mangan and Dyreson eds.

Knowledge Wharton 2010 'Expo 2010's legacy: what did Shanghai gain?' Wharton School of Business, University of Pennsylvania, Philadelphia. Online at: knowledge.wharton.upenn.edu/article/expo-2010s-legacy-what-did-shanghai-gain/

Kohli, S. 2014 'How much of the world watches TV vs. Internet video' (TNS data), Quartz.com. Online at: http://qz.com/233451/chart-how-much-of-the-worldwatches-tv-vs-internet-video/

Kondolojy, A. 2012 'London Olympics on NBC is most-watched television event in U.S. history', 13 August, TV by the Numbers. Online at: http://tvbythenumbers.zap2it.com/2012/08/13/london-olympics-on-nbc-is-most-watchedtelevision-event-in-u-s-history144780/

Kondolojy, A. 2014a '151 million viewers – more than half of all America TV viewers – have watched ther Sochi Winter Olympics on the networks of NBCUniversal', 14 February, *TV by the Numbers*. Online at: http://tvbythenumbers.zap2it.com/2014/02/14/151-milion-viewers-have-watched-the-sochi-winter-olympics-on-the-networks-of-nbcuniversal/237264/

Kondolojy, A. 2014b '76% of U.S. TV homes tuned in to Sochi Games coverage on networks of NBCUniversal', 25 February, *TV by the Numbers*. Online at: http://tvbythenumbers.zap2it.com/2014/02/25/76-of-u-s-tv-homes-tuned-in-to-sochi-games-coverage-on-networks-of-nbcuniversal/240155/

Kramp, L. et al. eds (Kramp, L., Carpentier, N., Hepp, A., Trivundza, I., Nieminen, H., Kunelius, R., Olsson, T., Sundin, E., Kilborn, R.) 2014 *Media Practice and Everyday Agency in Europe*. Edition Lumière, Bremen.

Kretschmer, M. 2005 'Trends in global copyright'. Vol. 1, 2, pp. 231–7, *Global Media and Communication*.

Krotz, F. 2009 'Mediatization: a concept with which to grasp media and societal change', ch. 1 in Lundby ed.

Krotz, F. 2014 'From a social worlds perspective to the analysis of mediatized worlds', pp. 69–82, in Kramp et al. eds.

Kung, L., Picard, R. and Towse, R. 2008 *The internet and the mass media*. Sage, London.

Lamond, I. and Platt, L. eds 2016 *Critical event studies: approaches to research*. Palgrave Macmillan, London.

Larson, J. and Park, H.-S. 1993 *Global television and the politics of the Seoul Olympics*. Westview, Oxford.

Latouche, D. 2011 'Montreal 1976', ch. 13 in Gold and Gold eds 2011b.

Lawton, J. 2012 'London Olympics 2012: The greatest show on Earth (and it's only just begun)', 28 July, *Independent*, London. Online at: www.independent.co.uk/sport/olympics/news/london-olympics-2012-the-greatest-show-on-earth-and-its-only-just-begun

Layton-Jones, K. 2014 'National review of research priorities for urban parks, designed landscapes, and open spaces, final report', English Heritage. Online at: www.services.english-heritage.org.uk/ResearchReportsPdfs/004_2014WEB.pdf

Lechner, F. and Boli, J. 2005 *World culture: origins and consequences.* Blackwell, Oxford.

Legacy Trust 2013 'Have we inspired a generation? Research highlights', Legacy Trust UK. Online at: www.legacytrust.org/news/london-2012-have-we-inspired-a-generation/

Lenskyj, H. 2000 *Inside the Olympic industry.* SUNY Press, Albany.

Lent, A. 2014 'Why E. F. Schumacher would embrace the digital revolution', The Schumacher Institute, Bristol. Online at: http://schumacherinstitute.org.uk/efschumacher-digital-revolution

Levine, R. 2011 'How the internet has all but destroyed the market for films, music and newspapers', 14 August, *Guardian*, London. Online at: www.theguardian.com/media/2011/aug/14/robert-levine-digital-free-ride

Lew, J. 2010 'Vancouver 2010: the greenest Olympics?', 28 January, *Mother Nature News* (MNN). Online at: www.mnn.com/lifestyle/eco-tourism/stories/vancouver-2010.the-greenest-olympics

Lewis, L. 2013 'The bold opening of a free trade zone that won't be bold at all', 1 October, *The Times*, London. Online at: www.thetimes.co.uk/tto/business/economics/article3883210.ece

Lipset, S. 1996 *American exceptionalism: a double edged sword.* Norton, London.

LLDC 2011 'Neighbourhoods on the Olympic Park named', London Legacy Development Corporation. Online at: www.londonlegacy.co.uk/neighbourhoods-on-the-olympic-park/

LLDC 2012 'ArcelorMittal Orbit'. Online at: www.londonlegacy.co.uk/investment-and-venues/venues-and-infrastructure/arcelormittal-orbit/

LLDC 2014 'Local plan 2015–2031', London Legacy Development Committee (LLDC), London. Online at: www.queenelizabetholympicpark.co.uk/~/media/LLDC/Local-Plan/LocalPlanAug14/Local Plan.pdf

Lo, V. and Hiscock, M. eds 2014 *The rise of the BRICS in the global political economy: changing paradigms?* Edward Elgar, Cheltenham.

Lodderhose, D. 2014 'Movie piracy: threat to the future of films intensifies', 17 July, *Guardian*, London. Online at: www.theguardian.com/film/2014/jul/17/digital-piracy-film-onlinecounterfeit-dvds

London Assembly 2007 'A lasting legacy for London? Assessing the legacy of the Olympic Games and the Paralympic Games', London Research Institute (LERI), University of East London, for the London Assembly of the Greater London Authority. Online at: www.uel.ac.uk/londoneast/research/documents/lasting-legacy.pdf

London Assembly 2011 'Park life: the legacy of London's Olympic venues', Economy, Culture and Sport Committee of the London Assembly of the Greater London Authority. Online at: www.london.gov.uk/mayor-assembly/london-assembly/publications/park-life-legacy-londons-olympic-venues

London and Partners 2013 'Olympic year provides a boost to London tourism', 19 April. Online at: www.londonandpartners.com/media-centre/press-releases/2013/130419-olympic-year-providdes-a-visitor-boost-to-london-tourism

London Gov 2013 'Mayor and Chancellor announce commitment to the development of major new education and arts centres on Queen Elizabeth Olympic Park', 4 December, LondonGov.uk, London. Online at: www.london.gov.uk/media/mayor-press-releases/2013/12/mayor-chancellor-announce-commitment-to-the-development-of-major

Loscertales, V. 2008 'Foreword' (to *Encyclopedia of world's fairs and expositions*), pp. 1–3, in Findling and Pelle eds.

Loscertales, V. 2009 'Foreword' pp. xi–xiii in Monclus.

Loscertales, V. 2010 'A pillar of the success of EXPO 2010: the Theme (of) Development'. Online at: www.bie-paris.org/site/en/publications/speeches

Loscertales, V. 2013 'Symposium Dubai 2020', 22 October. Online at: www.bie-paris.org/site/en/publications/speeches

Low. S., Taplin, D. and Scheld, S. 2005 *Rethinking urban parks: public space and cultural diversity*. University of Texas Press, Austin.

Lundby, K. ed. 2009 *Mediatization: concept, changes, consequences*. Peter Lang, New York.

MacAloon, J. 1984 'Olympic Games and the theory of spectacle in modern societies', pp. 241–80, in MacAloon, J. ed. *Rite, drama, festival, spectacle*. The Institute of Human issues, Philadelphia.

MacAloon, J. 1992 'The ethnographic imperative in comparative Olympic research'. Vol. 9, pp. 104–30, *Sociology of Sport Journal*.

MacAloon, J. 2006 'The theory of spectacle: reviewing Olympic ethnography', ch. 2 in Tomlinson and Young eds 2006b.

MacAloon, J. 2012 '"Legacy" as Managerial/Magical Discourse in Contemporary Olympic Affairs', ch. 10, pp. 177–88, in Mangan and Dyreson eds.

McCormack, G., Rock, M., Toohey, A. and Hignell, D. 2010 'Characteristics of urban parks associated with park use and physical activity: A review of qualitative research'. Vol. 16, pp. 712–26, *Health and Place*.

McDonald, M. 2012 '"Ruin Porn" – the aftermath of the Beijing Olympics', 15 July, *International Herald Tribune*, Paris. Online at: http://rendezvous.blogs.nytimes.com/2012/07/15/ruin-porn-the-aftermath-of-the-beijing-olympics/?_r=0

McDonald, S. and Lemco, J. 2015 *State capitalism's uncertain future*. Praeger, Santa Barbara.

McGuigan, J. 1996 *Culture and the public sphere*. Routledge, London.

McGuigan, J. and Gilmore, A. 2000 'Figuring out the Dome'. Vol. 10, 30, pp. 39–83, *Cultural Trends*.

MacKay, D. 2013 'Munich citizens vote against bid for 2022 Winter Olympics and Paralympics', 10 November, Inside the Games. Online at: www.insidethegames.biz/olympics/winter-olympics/2022/1016892-munich-citizens-against-bid-for-2022-winter-olympics-and-paralympics

MacKay, D. 2014 'Angelopolous-Daskalaki commissions study into true cost of Athens 2004', 7 August, Inside the Games. Online at: www.insidethegames.biz/Olympics/1021753-angelopolous-dakalaki-commissions-study-into-true-cost-of-Athens-2004

MacKenzie, J. 2010 *Museums and empire: Natural history, human cultures and colonial identities*. Manchester University Press, Manchester.

McLuhan, M. and Powers, B. 1989 *The global village*. Oxford University Press, Oxford.

McNair, B. 2006 *Cultural chaos*. Routledge, London.

McNeill, D. 2008 *The global architect*. Routledge, London.

McRae, H. 2015 'Is the concept of the BRICS countries still valid, 15 years after its presentation?', 2 April, *Independent*, London. Online at: www.independent.co.uk/news/business/comment/hamish-mcrae/hamish-mcrae-is-the-concept-of-the-brics-countries-still-valid-15-years-after-its-presentation-10150607.html

Magnay, J. 2012 'London Olympics: "Inspire a Generation" unveiled as official slogan for Games', 18 April, *Daily Telegraph*, London. Online at: www.telegraph.co.uk/olympics/9210790/London-2012-Olympics-Inspire-a-Generation-unveiled-as-official-slogan-for-Games.html

Magnay, J. 2013 'One year on: the transformation of London's Olympic park', 25 June, *Daily Telegraph*, London. Online at: www.telegraph.co.uk/sport/olympics/10127550/One-year-on-the-transformation-of-Londons-Olympic park.html

Mahtani, K., Prothroe, J., Slight, S et al. 2013 'Can the London 2012 Olympics "inspire a generation" to do more physical or sporting activities? An overview of systematic reviews', *British Medical Journal*, BMJ Open. Online at: http://bmjopen.bmj.com/content/3/l/e002058.full

Malcolmson, R. 1973 *Popular recreations in English society, 1700–1850*. Cambridge University Press, Cambridge.

Mangan, J. 2012 'Prologue: guarantees of global goodwill: post-Olympic legacies – too many limping white elephants?', pp. xviii–xxxi, in Mangan and Dyreson eds.

Mangan, M. and Dyreson, J. eds 2012 *Olympic legacies: intended and unintended*. Routledge, London.

Manzenreiter, W. 2010 'The Beijing Games in the western imagination of China: the weak power of soft power'. Vol. 34, 1, pp. 29–48, *Journal of Sport and Social Issues*.

Marrs, C. 2006 'Olympic legacy guru', *Planning Resource*. Online at: www.planning resource.co.uk/article/574365/olympic-legacy-guru

Marshall, P.D., Walker, B. and Russo, N. 2010 'Mediating the Olympics'. Vol. 16, 3, pp. 263–78, *Convergence*.

Marteau, V. 2008 'Seville 1992', pp. 377–86 in Findling and Pelle eds.

Martinson, J. 2015 'Google admits mistakes with news outlets as it announces new partnership', 27 April, *Guardian*, London. Online at: www.thegurdian.com/technology/2015/apr/27/google-mistakes-news-outlets-announces-digital-partnership

Masters, N. 2012 'Documenting and preserving LA's Olympic History', KCET.org. Online at: www.kcet.org/updaily/socal_focus/history/la-as-subject/la-olympic_history.html

Mattelart, T. 2009 'Audio-visual piracy'. Vol. 5, 3, pp. 308–26, *Global Media and Communication*.

MCG 2015 'Olympic Games' (1956), Melbourne Cricket Ground (MCG). Online at: www.meg.org.au/History/Olympic Games 1956.aspx

Meikle, J. 2015 'WHO: report: 74% of men and 64% of women in UK to be overweight by 2030', 6 May, *Guardian*, London. Online at: www.theguardian.com/society/2015/may/05/obesity-crisis-projections-uk-2030-men-women

Mellander, C., Florida, R., Asheim, B. and Gertler, M. 2014 *The creative class goes global*. Routledge, London.

Merrick, J. 2009 'The Net closes in on internet piracy', 16 August, *Independent*, London. Online at: www.independent.co.uk/arts/music/news/the-net-closes-in-on-internet-piracy-177820.html

Messakh, M. 2010, 'Guangzhou praised for perfect preparation', 5 November, *Jakarta Post*. Online at: www.thejakartapost.com/news/2010/11/15/Guangzhou-praised-for-perfect-preparation.html

Meyer, M. 2011 'Berlin 1936', ch. 11 in Gold and Gold eds 2011b.

Miah, A. 2014 'Tweeting the Olympic Games', ch. 7 in Girginov ed.

Milheiro, A. 2012 'On the Waterfront', 27 February, *Architecture Today*. Online at: www.architecturetoday.co.uk/?p=21731

Milland, G. 2007 'Now Olympics bill could soar again … to £10 bn', 11 December, *Daily Express*, London Online at: www.express.co.uk/news/uk/27968/Now-Olympics-bill-could-soar-again-to-10bn

Millward, S. 2015 'China now has 557M mobile internet users, grand total of 649M netizens', 3 February, *TechInAsia*. Online at: www.techinasia.com/cnnic-china-577-million-mobile-web-users-and-649-internet-users-2014

Minton, A. 2012 *Ground control: fear and happiness in the twenty-first-century city*. Penguin, London.

MNN 2015 '10 of the world's most impressive aquariums', Mother Nature Network (MNN). Online at: www.mnn.com/family/family-activities/photos/10-of-the-worlds-most-impressive-aquariums/lisbon-oceanarium

Mol, A. and Zhang, L. 2012 'Sustainability as global norm: the greening of mega-events in China', ch. 7 in Hayes and Karamichas eds.

Molina, M. 2013 'The role of tourism events in urban development: the case of Zaragoza'. Vol. 11, 1, pp. 57–71, *Journal of Tourism and Cultural Heritage*.

Monclus, J. 2009 *International Exhibitions and Urbanism*. Ashgate, Farnham.

Monclus, J. 2012 'Barcelona 1992', ch. 14 in Mangan and Dyreson eds.

Monem, N. ed. 2007 *Botanic gardens: a living history*. Black Dog, London.

Moore, J. 2014 'Move over America: China overtakes US as world's biggest economy', 8 October, *Independent*, London. Online at: www.independent.co.uk/news/business/news/move-over-america-china-overtakes-us-as-worlds-biggest-economy-kind-of-9783050.html

Moore, R. 2011 'Westfield Stratford City – review', 11 September, *Guardian*, London. Online at: www.theguardian.com/artanddesign/2011/sep/11/westfield-stratford-city-london-2012-3437305

Moragas, M., Kennett, C. and Puig, N. eds 2003 *The legacy of the Olympic Games 1984–2000*. International Olympic Committee, Lausanne.

Moragas, M., Rivenburgh, N. and Larson, J. 1995 *Television in the Olympics*. John Libbey Media, Luton.

Morgan, E. 2012 'Why was the Hall built?' (Royal Albert Hall), Life at the Hall. Online at: http://life.royalalberthall.com/2012/03/12/why-was-the-royal-albert-hall-built/

Morrison, J. 2016 'Olympicopolis trips at first hurdle', 28 July, *The Times*, London. Online at: www.thetimes.co.uk/article/olympicopolis-trips-at-first-hurdle-jg65jlzx

MSNBC 2008 'Part of Olympic display altered in broadcast'. Online at; www.nbcnews.com/id/6139005/ns/technology_and_science-tech_and_gadgets/t/part-olymic-display-altered-broadcast/#.VWh-bEYucf4

Muller, M. 2015a 'What makes an event a mega-event? Definitions and sizes'. Vol. 34, 6, pp. 627–42, *Leisure Studies*.

Muller, M. 2015b '(Im-)Mobile policies: why sustainability went wrong in the 2014 Olympics in Sochi'. Vol. 22, 2, pp. 191–209, *European Urban and Regional Studies*.

Muller, M. 2015c 'The mega-event syndrome: why so much goes wrong in mega-event planning and what to do about it'. Vol. 81, 1, pp. 6–17, *Journal of the American Planning Association*.

Muller, M. and Pickles, J. 2015 'Global games, local rules: mega-events in the post-socialist world'. Vol. 22, 2, pp. 121–7, *European Urban and Regional Studies*.

Mumford, L. 1966 *The city in history*. Penguin, London.

NAO 2008 'The regeneration of the Greenwich peninsula: a progress report', National Audit Office (NAO), London. Online at: www.nao.org/wp-content/uploads/2008/07/n0708338.pdf

Naughton, J. 2010 'Will the world back Murdoch's big gamble?', 4 July, *Observer*, London.

Neal, R. 2013 'FirstRow Sports banned in UK: sport streaming website defeated by English Premier League', 17 July, *International Business Times*. Online at: www.ibtimes.

com/firstrow-sports-banned-uk-sports-streaming-website-defeated-by-english-premier-league-135061

Neate, R. 2015 'Apple soon to be worth more than $1tn, financial analysts predict', 23 March, *Guardian*, London. Online at: www.theguardian.com./technology/2015/mar/23/apple-company-worth-1tn-market-value

Nemo 2013 'Museums in the digital age', Network of European Museum Organisations, Germany. Online at: www.nemo.org/fileadmin/Dateien/publicstatements_and_news/NEMO_21st_Annual_Conference_Documentation.pdf

Newshome 2013 'The Shenzen Universiade into a hotbed of corruption', Newshome. Online at: www.newshome.us/news-4244518-The Shenzhen-Universiade-into-a-hotbed-of-corruption.html

Newton, P. 2012 'Olympics worth the price tag? The Montreal legacy', 20 July, CNN. Online at: http://edition.cnn.com/2012/07/19/world/canada-montreal-olympic-legacy/index.html

Nielsen 2008 'Beijing Olympics draw largest ever global TV audience', 5 September, Nielsen.com. Online at: www.nielsen.com/us/en/insights/news/2008/beijing-olympics-draw-largestever-global-tv-audience.html

Nisbet, R. 1980 *History of the idea of progress*. Heinemann, London.

Nixon, A. 2013 'Premier League wins battle against foreign piracy websites', 6 August, LawInSport. Online at: www.lawinsport.com/blog/sheridans/item/premier-league-wins-battle-against-foreign-piracy-websites

NPC 2011 'Report on China's economic and social development plan', National People's Congress and Xinhua, Beijing. Online at: www.chinadaily.com.cn/china/2011-03/18/content_12193653_11.htm

NSW 2014 'Transforming Sydney', New South Wales Authority. Online at: www.nsw.gov.au/sites/default/files/miscellaneous/sydney-rapid-transit_sis2014.pdf

Observer 2012 'London 2012 Olympics: the world's journalists give their verdict', 5 August, *Observer*, London. Online at: http://theguardian.com/media/2012/aug/05/london-2012-olympics-journalists-verdict

O'Connell, M. 2014 'TV Ratings: Super Bowl XLVIII is most watched in history with 112.2 million viewers', 3 February, *Hollywood Reporter*. Online at: www.hollywoodreporter.com/live-feed/tv-ratings-super-bowl-xlviii-676651

OECD 2010 'Local development benefits from staging global events: achieving the local development legacy from 2012', OECD. Online at: www.oecd.org/cfe/leed/46207013.pdf

Olsen, C. 2013 'Re-thinking festivals: a comparative study of the integration/marginalization of arts festivals in the urban regimes of Manchester, Copenhagen and Vienna'. Vol. 19, 4, pp. 481–500, *International Journal of Cultural Policy*.

O'Neill, J. 2001 'Building better global economic BRICS', Goldman Sachs. Online at: www.goldmansachs.com/our-thinking/archive/building-better.html

O'Neill, J. 2011 *The growth map: economic opportunity in the BRICs and beyond*. Portfolio Penguin, London.

O'Neill, J. 2013 *The BRIC road to growth*. London Publishing Partnership, London.

Ong, R. 2004 'New Beijing, great Olympics: Beijing and its unfolding Olympic legacy'. Vol. 4, 2, pp. 35–49, *Stanford Journal of East Asian Affairs*.

O'Riordan, C. 2012 'The story of the digital Olympics: Streams, browsers, most watched, four screens', 13 August, BBC. Online at: www.bbc.co.uk/blogs/bbcinternet/2012/08/digital_olympics_reach_stream_stats.html

Out-Law 2013a 'Premier League wins injunction against website facilitating illegal football streaming', Out-law.com. Online at: www.out-law.com/en/articles/2013/

july/premier-league-wins-injunction-against-website-facilitating-illegal-football-streaming

Out-Law 2013b 'Plans for two new Olympic Park neighbourhoods are accelerated', Out-Law. com. Online at: www.out-law.com/en/articles/2013/july/plans-for-two-new-olympic-park-neighbourhoods-are-acceleerated

Paganoni, M. 2012 'City branding and social inclusion in the glocal city'. Vol.7, 1, pp. 13–31, *Mobilities*.

Page, S. and Connell, J. eds 2012 *The Routledge handbook of events*. Routledge, London.

Panethiere, D. 2005 *The persistence of piracy*. UNESCO, Paris.

Paphitis, N. and Tongas, T. 2014 'Athens Olympic site in ruins 10 years on from 2004 Games', news.com.au. Online at: www.news.com.au/sport/more-sports/athens-olympic-site-in-ruins-10years-on-from-2004-games/story-fndukor0-1227024073167

Parnell, S. and Robinson, J. 2012 '(Re)theorizing cities from the global south: looking beyond neoliberalism'. Vol. 33, 4, pp. 593–617, *Urban Geography*.

Parqueexpo 2014 'World EXPO'98'. Online at: www.parqueexpo.pt/conteuodo.aspx? lang=ing&id_object=692&name=World-EXPO'98-

Pavitt, M. 2016 'Pollution concerns raised at Rio 2016 venues after studies find "super-bacteria" ', 11 June, InsidetheGames. Online at: www.insidethegames.biz/articles/1038349/pollution-concerns-raised-at-rio-2016-venues-after-studies-find-super-bacteria

Peña, E. 2009 'Olympic Summer Games and broadcast rights: evolution and challenges in the new media environment', *Revista Latina de Comunicacion* 64. Online at: www. revistalatinacs.org/09/art/876_Barcelona/77_144_FernandezEng.html

Phillips, T. 2016 'Mickey Mao: fanfare for China's first Disney park', 17 June, *Guardian*, London. Online at: www.pressreader.com/uk/the-guardian/20160617

Picard, D. and Robinson, M. eds 2006 *Festivals, tourism and social change*. Channel View Publications, Clevedon.

Pickford, J. 2015 'London mayor's vision for Olympicopolis gathers steam', 30 January, *Financial Times*, London. Online at: www.ft.com/cms/s/0/7b9bf08e-a885-11e4-bd17-00144feab7de.html#axzz3V7cccznPM

Pirenne, H. 1969 *Medieval cities*. Princeton University Press, Princeton.

Politics.co.uk 2013 'Millennium Dome', Politics.co.uk. Online at: www.politics.co.uk/reference/millennium-dome

Pollard, S. 1971 *The idea of progress: history and society*. Penguin, London.

Polley, M. 2011 *The British Olympics: Britain's Olympic heritage 1612–2012*. English Heritage, Swindon.

Pollstar 2013 'Worldwide ticket sales, top 200 arena venues, 2013 year end', Pollstar. Online at: sprint_center.s3.amazonaws.com/doc/2013YearEndWorldwideTicketSale sTop200ArenaVenues.pdf

Pollstar 2014 'Worldwide ticket sales, top 100 arena venues, 2013 year end', Pollstar. Online at: sprint_center.s3.amazonaws.com/doc/2014MidYearWorldwideTicketSale sTop100ArenaVenues.pdf

Porter, R. 1994 *London – a social history*. Hamish Hamilton, London.

Pradas, J. and Arnal, J.-C. 2007 'Mille digital'. Online at: www.rudi.net/books/20055

Preuss, H. 2004 *The economics of staging the Olympics: a comparison of the games 1972–2008*. Edward Elgar, Cheltenham.

Preuss, H. 2014 ' "Legacy" revisited', ch. 3 in Grix ed.

Preuss, H. 2015 'A framework for identifying the legacies of a mega-sport event'. Vol. 34, 6, 643–64, *Leisure Studies*.

Price, M. and Dayan, D. eds 2008 *Owning the Olympics: Narratives of the New China*. University of Michigan Press, Ann Arbor.

Prior N. 2002 *Museums and modernity: art galleries and the making of modern culture*. Berg, Oxford.

Prynn, J. 2013 'First of 30,000 Olympic Park residents move in next month', 26 July, *Evening Standard*, London. Online at: www.standard.co.uk/news/london/first-of-30000-olympic-park-residents-move-in-next-month-8733271.html

QEOP 2014 'Queen Elizabeth Olympic Park springs into action', 15 January, Queen Elizabeth Olympic Park (QEOP). Online at: http://queenelizabetholympicpark.co.uk/news/news-articles/2014/1/queen-elizabeth-olympic-park-springs-into-action

QEOP 2015a 'Shortlist announced for UCL East master planners on Queen Elizabeth Olympic Park', Queen Elizabeth Olympic Park (QEOP). Online at: http://queenelizabetholympicpark.co.uk/media/press-releases/shortlist-announced-for-ucl-east-master-planners-on-queen-elizabeth-olympicpark

QEOP 2015b 'Olympicopolis', Queen Elizabeth Olympic Park. Online at: http://queenelizabetholympicpark.co.uk/the-park/attractions/olympicopolis

Qing, L. and Richieri, G. eds 2012 *Encoding the Olympics: the Beijing Olympic Games and the communication impact worldwide*. Routledge, London.

Rabb, T. and Rotberg, R. eds 1981 *Industrialization and urbanization: studies in interdisciplinary history*. Princeton University Press, Princeton.

Ramo, B. 2005 'The re-creation of the European city: "urban shopping list" for secondary cities', Monu. Online at: www.monu.org/monu7/Zaragoza.pdf

Ramstetter, E., Dai, E. and Sakamoto, H. 2009 'Recent trends in China's distribution of income and consumption: a review of the evidence', ch. 6 in Islam, N. ed. *Resurgent China: issues for the future*. Palgrave, London.

Rasmussen, S. 1974 *London: the unique city* (original 1934). The MIT Press, Cambridge, MA.

Reidy, T. 2016 'No mud but all the music: fans flock to watch festivals online', 14 August, *Observer*, London. Online at: www.theguardian.comculture/2016/aug/13/live-streaming-festivals-notting-hill

Reuters 2006 'Prime-time Olympics coverage stumbles at Turin', 26 February, Reuters. Online at: www.tv.com/news/prime-time-olympics-coverage-at-turin-3452/

Richards, G. ed. 2001 *Cultural attractions and European tourism*. CABI, Wallingford, Oxford.

Richards, G. and Palmer, R. 2010 *Eventful cities: cultural management and urban revitalisation*. BH, Elsevier, Oxford.

Ritzer, G. 1999 *Enchanting u disenchanted world: revolutionising the means of consumption*. Sage, London.

Robertson, A. 2010 *Mediated cosmopolitanism: the world of television news*. Polity, Cambridge.

Robertson, L. 2013 'Completion of homes at Olympic Park to be brought forward by six years', 8 October, *Inside Housing*. Online at: www.insidehousing.co.uk/development/completion-of-homes-at-olympic-park-to-be-brought-forweard-by-six-years/6528939.article

Robertson, R. 1992 *Globalisation: social theory and global culture*. Sage, London.

Roche, M. 1992 *Rethinking citizenship: welfare, ideology and change in modern society*. Polity, Cambridge.

Roche, M. 1994 'Mega-events and urban policy'. Vol. 21, 1, pp. 1–19, *Annals of Tourism Research*.

Roche, M. 1998 'Mega-events, culture and modernity: Expos and the origins of public culture'. Vol. 5, 1, pp. 1–31, *International Journal of Cultural Policy*.

Roche, M. 2000 *Mega-events and modernity: Olympics and Expos in the growth of global culture*. Routledge, London.

Roche, M. 2002 'The Olympics and "global citizenship"'. Vol. 6, 2, pp. 165–81, *Citizenship Studies*.

Roche, M. 2003 'Mega-events, time and modernity'. Vol. 12, 1, pp. 99–126, *Time and Society*.

Roche, M. 2006a 'Nationalism, mega-events and international culture', ch. 22 in Delanty, G.and Kumar, K. eds *Handbook of nations and nationalism*. Sage, London.

Roche, M. 2006b 'Mega-events and modernity revisited: – globalisation and the case of the Olympics', ch. 2, pp. 27–40, in Horne and Manzenreiter eds.

Roche, M. 2007 'Cultural Europeanisation and the "Cosmopolitan Condition": EU regulation and European sport', ch. 8 in Rumford, C.ed. *Europe and cosmopolitanism*, Liverpool University Press, Liverpool.

Roche, M. 2009a 'Mega-events and micro-modernization: on the sociology of the new urban tourism', ch. 13 in Page,S. and Connell, J. eds *Event tourism*. Routledge, London.

Roche, M. 2009b 'Cosmopolitanism, festivalisation and European culture: on the social significance of mega-events', paper delivered at the 'Public culture and festivals' international workshop, Euro-Festival Consortium, ICCR, Vienna.

Roche, M. 2010a *Exploring the sociology of Europe: an analysis of the European social complex*. Sage, London.

Roche, M. 2010b 'The Olympics and "global citizenship"', ch. 7, pp. 108–20, in Girginov ed.

Roche, M. 2011a 'Festivalization, cosmopolitanism and European culture: on the sociocultural significance of mega-events', ch. 8 in Giorgi et al. eds.

Roche, M. 2011b 'Olympics, mega-events and modernity: Changing models of Olympic mediation', unpublished paper given at the 'Olympics and the Social Sciences' conference, The British Sociological Association, London, available from the author, m.roche@sheffield.ac.uk

Roche, M. 2014 *Phenomenology, language and the social sciences* (original 1973). Routledge, London.

Roche, M. 2016a 'Background papers 1: – Rethinking mega-events: the embedded spectacle', (unpublished paper, available from the author, m.roche@sheffield.ac.uk

Roche, M. 2016b 'Background papers 2: – Mega-event and festivalisation: – origins, developments and Expos', unpublished paper, available from the author, m.roche@sheffield.ac.uk

Roche, M. 2016c 'Background papers 3: – The 2008 Zaragoza Expo – an urban event and its legacies', unpublished paper, available from the author, m.roche@sheffield.ac.uk

RocSearch 2007 'Internet piracy most harmful to global film industry – Rocsearch report' (Press release), 7 October, PR.com. Online at: www.pr.com/press-releases/55090

Rodas, C. 2008 'IOC asks Sweden to block Pirate Bay', 19 August, *The Local* (Sweden's News in English). Online at: www.thelocal.se/13800/20080819/

Rodrigues, M. ed. 2002 *The new knowledge economy in Europe*. Edward Elgar, Cheltenham.

Rogers, E. 1986 *Communications technology: the new media in society*. Collier-Macmillan, London.

Rogers, E. 2003 *The diffusion of innovations* (5th edition). Free Press, New York.

Rojek, C. 2013 *Event power: how global events manage and manipulate.* Sage, London.

Rollin, H. 2008 'International exhibitions and urban renewal: Zaragoza's Expo 2008 on "Water and Sustainable Development"'. Vol. 21, 3, pp. 263–72, *International Journal of Iberian Studies.*

Rosenberg, J. 2015 'History of the Olympics, 1932 – Los Angeles, United States'. Online at: http://history1900s.about.com/od/fadsfashion/a/olympics1932.htm

Rosenfield, K. 2015 'London "Olympicopolis" aims to host Smithsonian's first international venture', *ArchDaily.* Online at: www.archdaily.com/592870/london-s-olympicopolis-aims-to-host-smithsonian-s-first-international-venue/

Rothfels, N. 2008 *Savages and beasts: the birth of the modern zoo.* Johns Hopkins University Press. Baltimore.

Rowe, D. 2004a *Sport, culture and the media: an unholy trinity* (2nd edition). Open University Press, Maidenhead.

Rowe, D. ed. 2004b *Critical readings: sport, culture and the media.* Open University Press, Maidenhead.

Roy, A. 2009 'The 21st-century metropolis: new geographies of theory'. Vol. 43, 6, pp. 819–30, *Regional Studies.*

Russia Today. 2015 'Olympicopolis': Smithsonian plans new London museum, *RT (Russia Today)* UK, 28 January. Online at: www.rt.com/uk/227099-smithsonian-london-olympic-park/

Russell, G. 2014 'Fouled out: Sochi Games a PR debacle for UN greenwashing strategy', 5 March, Fox News. Online at: www.foxnews.com/world/2014/03/05/fouled-out-sochi-games-pr-debacle-for-un-greenwashing-strategy/

Russell, J. 2014 'The stupid starchitect debate', 13 August, *Architizer.* Online at: http://architizer.com/blog/the-stupid-starchitect-debate/

Rydell, R. 1984 *All the world's a fair: visions of empire at American international expositions 1876–1916.* Chicago: Chicago University Press.

Rydell, R. 1993 *World of fairs: the century-of-progress expositions.* Chicago University Press, Chicago.

Rydell, R. and Gwinn, N. eds 1994 *Fair representations: world's fairs and the modern world.* VU University Press, Amsterdam.

Samatas, M. 2011 'Surveillance in Athens 2004 and Beijing 2008'. Vol. 48, 15, pp. 3347–66, *Urban Studies.*

Sassatelli, M. 2011 'Urban festivals and the cultural public sphere: Cosmopolitanism between ethics and aesthetics', ch. 1 in Giorgi et al. eds.

Sassen, S. 2012 *Cities in a world economy* (4th edition). Sage, London.

Schmidt, E. and Cohen, J. 2013 *The new digital age: reshaping the future of people, nations and business.* John Murray/Hodder and Stoughton, London.

Schneider, F. 2013 'Political communication at the Shanghai Expo', 17 June, *Politics East Asia.* Online at: www.politicseastasia.com/research/shanghai-expo-research/

Schoen, J. 2014 'Megacities' explosive growth poses epic challenges', 21 March, Yahoo Finance. Online at: http://finance.yahoo.com/news/megacities-explosive-growth-poses-epic-challenges-123451190.html

Scholte, J. 2005 *Globalisation: a critical introduction* (2nd edition). Palgrave, Basingstoke.

Schwartz, N. 2008 'Zaragoza, beneficiary of Spain's heady years, feels the undertow',4 November, *New York Times,* New York. Online at: www.nytimes.com/2008/11/04/businessworldbusiness/04euecon.html?

Scraton, P. 2009 *Hillsborough – the truth*. Mainstream Publishing, Edinburgh.

Searle, G. 2008 'The influence of mega-events on city structure under contemporary urban governance: the example of Sydney's Olympic Games', pp. 87–108, in Cashman and Hay eds.

Sereny, G. 1995 *Albert Speer: his battle with the truth*. Picador, London.

Shanghai Expo, 2010 'World Expo 2010 Shanghai China: communication & promotion plan', Shanghai: Shanghai 2010 World Expo Organising Committee. Online at: http://en.expo2010.cn/expo/expo_english/document/dc/userobject1ai48897/00000000.pdf

Shead, S. 2014a 'iCity tech hub in London's Olympic park gets renamed Here East', 26 February, *TechWorld*. Online at: www.techworld.com/news/startups/city-tech-hub-in-londons-olympic-park-gets-renamed-here-east-3504012/

Shead, S. 2014b 'Here East: the UK's largest tech centre being quietly developed in London's Olympic Park', 25 November, *TechWorld*. Online at: www.techworld.com/startups/here-east-uks-largest-tech-centre-quietly-being-developed-3588462/

Shin, H.B. 2012 'Unequal cities of spectacle and mega-events in China'. Vol. 16, 6, pp. 728–44, *City: Analysis of Urban Trends, Culture, Theory, Policy, Action*. Online at: http://dx.doi.org/10.1080/13604813.2012.734076

Shin, H.B. 2016 'China meets Korea: the Asian Games, entrepreneurial local states, and debt-driven development', ch. 11 in Gruneau and Horne eds 2016b.

Shin, H.B. and Bingqin, L. 2013 'Whose games? The costs of being "Olympic citizens" in Beijing'. Vol. 25, 2, pp. 559–76, *Environment and Urbanization*.

Silk, M. 2011 'Towards a sociological analysis of London 2012'. Vol. 45, 5, pp. 733–48, *Sociology*.

Silverman, S. 2008 'Spectacle and iragedy open Beijing Olympics', People.com. Online at: www.people.com/people/article/0,,20218095,00.html

Sklair, L. and Gherardi, L. 2012 'Iconic architecture as a hegemonic project of the transnational capitalist class'. Vol. 16, 1–2, pp. 57–73, *City: Analysis of Urban Trends, Culture, Theory, Policy, Action*. Online at: http://dx.doi.org/10.1080/13604813.2012.662366

Slater, T. and Wyly, E. eds 2010 *The gentrification reader*. Routledge, London.

SMH 2010 'Taxpayers will compensate axed Metro losers: Keneally', 21 February, *Sydney Morning Herald*, Sydney. Online at: www.smh.com.au/nsw/taxpayers-will-compensate-axed-metro-losers-Keneally-20100221.on6h.html

Smith, A. 2012 *Events and urban regeneration: the strategic use of events to revitalise cities*. Routledge, London.

Smith, M. 2003 *The social construction of ancient cities*. Smithsonian Institution, London.

Smith, N. 2002 'New globalism, new urbanism: gentrification as global urban strategy'. Vol. 34, 3, pp. 427–50, *Antipode*.

Smith, R. and Wooden, G. 2013 'FA Premier League takes the lead in battle against linking to infringing match content', EIP. Online at: www.eip.com/uk/updates/article/fa_premier_league_takes_the_lead_in_battle_against_linking_to_infringing_match_content

SOPA 2009 Sydney Olympic Master Plan 2030, Sydney Olympic Park Authority (SOPA), NSW. Online at: www.sopa.nsw.gov.au/our_park/

SOPA 2012 Sydney Olympic Park – annual report 2011–12, Sydney Olympic Park Authority (SOPA), NSW.

SOPA 2014 'Sydney Olympic Park hot property with office vacancy rate at 1.3 per cent', SOPA, NSW. Online at: http://www.sopa.nsw.gov.au/resource_centre/park_news/2014_park_news2/sydney_olympic_park_hot_property

SOPA 2015 Sydney Olympic Park information, Sydney Olympic Park Authority, NSW. Online at: www.sopa.nsw.gov.au/our_park/

South Bank London 2015 'The History of South Bank', South Bank London, London. Online: www.southbanklondon.com/history

Southbank Centre 2015 'Southbank Centre history', Southbank Centre, London. Online at: www.southbankcentre.co.uk/about-us/histry-and-archive/southbank-centre-history

Spaaij, R. 2016 'Terrorism and security at the Olympics: empirical trends and evolving research agendas'. Vol. 4, pp. 451–67, *The International Journal of the History of Sport*.

Spampinato, A. 2015 'Stadium history', World Stadiums. Online: www.worldstadiums.com/stadium_menu/architecture/historic_stadiums.shtml

Spangler, T. 2014 'IOC to launch year-round Olympics internet TV channel', 8 December *Variety*. Online at: http://variety.com/2014/digital/news/ioc-to-launch–year-round-olympics-internet-tv-channel-1201374451

Speer, A. 1970 *Inside the Third Reich*. Weidenfeld, London.

Sprackler, K. and Lamond, I. eds 2016 *Critical event studies*. Routledge, London.

Standard 2008 'Ken Livingstone admits he only bid for 2012 Olympics to "ensnare" taxpayer billions to develop East End', 24 April, *Evening Standard*, London. Online at: www.standard.co.uk/news/ken-livingstone-admits-he-only-bid-for-2012-Olympics-to-ensnare-taxpayer-billions-to-develop-East-End-790494.html

Statista 2015a 'Global Apple iPhone sales in the fiscal years 2007–2014 (in million units)', Statista. Online at: www.statista.com/statistics/276306/global-apple-iphone-sales-since-fiscal-year-2007/

Statista 2015b 'Global smartphone sales from 2009 to 2013, by operating system (in millions)', Statista. Online at: www.statista.com/statistics/276306/global-smartphone-sales-by-operating-system-since-2009/

Statista 2015c 'Number of monthly active Facebook users worldwide as of 1st quarter 201 (in millions)', Statista. Online at: www.statista.com/statistics/264810/umber-of-monthly-active-facebook-users-woldwide/

Statista 2015d 'Number of monthly active Twitter users worldwide from 1st quarter 2010 to 1st quarter 2015 (in millions)', Statista. Online at: www.statista.com/statistics/282087/number-of-monthly-active-twitter-users/

Statista 2015e 'Average number of unique You Tube users per month in 2011, by country (in millions)' Statista. Online at: www.statista.com/statistics/280685/number-of-monthly-unique-youtube-users/

Statista 2015f 'Global Google+ penetration from 2012 to 2014', Statista. Online at: www.statista.com/statistics/319714/global-google-plus-penetration/

Statista 2015g 'Number of worldwide internet users from 2000 to 2014 (in millions)', Statista. Online at: www.statista.com/statistics/273018/number-of-internet-users-worldwide/

Statista 2015h 'iPhone, iPad and iPod sales from 1st quarter 2006 to 4th quarter 2014 (in million units)', Statista. Online at: www.statista.com/statistics/253725/iphone-ipad-and-ipod-sales-comparison/

Stott, R. 2015 'Architect's reactions to Frei Otto's Pritzker Prize win', 31 March, *Arch Daily*. Online at: www.archdaily.com/615064/architects-reactions-tofrei-otto-s-pritzker-prize-win/

Strauss, K. 2013 'TV and film piracy: threatening an industry?', Forbes. Online at: www.fortbes.com/sites/karstenstrauss/2013/03/06/tv-and-film-piracy-threatening-an-industry/

Swaine, J. 2008, 'Beijing Olympics: opening ceremony watched by 15 per cent of the world's population', 12 August, *Daily Telegraph*, London. Online at: www.telegraph. co.uk/port/olympics/2545106/Beijing-Olympics-opening-ceremony-watched-by-15-per-cent-of-worlds-population.html

Sweney, M. 2008 'Beijing Olympics gets official YouTube channel', 4 August, *Guardian*, London. Online at; www.theguardian.com/media/2008/aug/04/digitalmedia. olympicsandthemedia

Sweney, M. 2012 'London 2012 Olympics digital chief warns Rio to plan for mobile', 8 September, *Guardian*, London. www.theguardian.com/media/2012/sep/28/london-2012-olympics

Tam, F. 2012a 'Shenzhen wasted billions on World University Games, audit finds', 29 December, *South China Morning Post*. Online at: http://scmp.com/print/news/china/article/1114677/shenzhen-wasted-billions-world-university-games-audit-finds

Tam, F. 2012b 'Details emerge in graft investigation into former Shenzhen vice-mayor', 4 December, *South China Morning Post*. Online at: www.scp.com/print/news/china/article/1096854/details-emerge-graft-investigation-former-Shenzhen-vice-mayor

Tatlow, D. 2014 'Xi Jinping on exceptionalism with Chinese characteristics', 14 October, *New York Times*, New York. Online at: http://sinosphere.blogs.nytimes.com/2014/10/14/xi-xinping-on-exceptionalism-with-chinese-charactersitics/?_r=0

Taylor, D. and Camayd, S. 2014 'Domain name seizures by authorities on the rise', 10 February, Hogan Lovells, World Trademark Review- Daily. Online at: www.hogan-lovells.com/domain.name.seizures-by-authorities-on-the-rise-02-10-2014/

Taylor, E. 2000 'Our green village', Australian Broadcasting Corporation (ABC). Online at: www.abc.net.au/scienceslab/olympics/

TED 2012 'TED reaches its billionth video view!', Blog, TED. Online at: http://blog.ted.com/ted-reaches-its-billionth-view/

Telegraph 2012 'London 2012: what the world thought of the opening ceremony', 28 July, *Daily Telegraph*, London. Online at: www.telegraph.co.uk/sport/olympics/london-2012/9434319/London-2012-What-the-world-thought-of-the-opening-ceremony.html

Telo, M. ed. 2001 *European union and new regionalism; regional actors and global governance in a post-hegemonic era*. Ashgate, Aldershot.

Temperton, J. 2014 'UCL to open huge tech and engineering campus', 2 December, *Wired*. Online at: www.wired.co.uk/news/archive/2014-12/02ucl-east-technology-engineering

TERA 2010 *Building a digital economy: the importance of saving jobs in the EU's creative economy*. TERA and the International Chamber of Commerce, Paris.

TF 2008 'Millions download Olympics Opening Ceremony via Bittorrent', 12 August, Torrent Freak. Online at; http://torrentfreak.com/millions-download-olympics-via-bittorrent-080812/

TF 2015 'UK blocking more than 100 pirate sites after new court order', 24 March, Torrent Freak. Online at: https://torrentfreak.com/uk-blocking-more-than-100-pirate-sites-after-new-court-order-150324

Tiffen. S. 2012 'Germany considers two-strikes online piracy law', 23 February, Deutsche Welle (DW). Online at: www.dw.com/en/germany-considers-two-strikes-online-piracy-law/a-15761430

Tilly, C. 1994 *Cities and the rise of the states in Europe AD 1000 to 1800*. Westview Press, Oxford.

Time 2014 'The not so sustainable Sochi Winter Olympics', 30 January, *Time Magazine.* Online at: http://time.com/2828/sochi-winter-olympics-environmental-damage/

TIQ 2014 'The International Quarter: key facts', TIQ Stratford City. Online at: www. tiqstratfordcity.com/about/key-facts

TNS 2014 'TV strikes back: rise of digital devices drives new viewing habits', TNS. Online at: www.tnsglobal.com/press-release/connected-life-tv-press-release

Tomlinson, A. 2002 'Theorising spectacle: beyond Debord', ch. 3 in Sugden, J. and Tomlinson, A. eds *Power Games: A critical sociology of sport.* Routledge, London.

Tomlinson, A. 2014 *FIFA: the men, the myths and the money.* Routledge, London.

Tomlinson, A. and Young, C 2006a 'Culture, politics and spectacle in the global sport event – an introduction', ch. 1 in Tomlinson and Young eds 2006b.

Tomlinson, A. and Young, C. eds 2006b *National identity and global sports events: culture, politics and spectacle in the Olympics and the Football World Cup.* State University of New York, Albany.

Tonnelat, S. 2010 'The sociology of urban public spaces', CNRS/NYU-CIRHUIS, New York. Online at: www.stephane.tonnelat.free.fr/Welcome_files/SFURP-Tonnelat.pdf

Toohey, K. 2008 'The Sydney Olympics: striving for legacies …', Vol. 25, 14, pp. 1953–71, *The International Journal of the History of Sport.*

Toohey, K. and Veal, A. 2007 *The Olympic Games: a social science perspective* (2nd edition). CABI, Wallingford.

Tremlett, G. 2009 'Prosperous Spanish city falls victim to hard times', 15 February, *Guardian*, London. Online at: www.theguardian.com/world/2009/feb/15zaragoza-spain-economy

Tribunal de Cuentas 2010 'Report on the supervision of the evolution of the assets and liabilities of ExpoAgua Zaragoza 2008 etc', *Tribunal de Cuentas*, Madrid. Online at: www.tcu.es/tribunal-de-cuentas/es/search/alfresco/index.html?

Tryhorn, C. and Johnson, B. 2009 'Murdoch plans to strip Google of news', 10 November, *Guardian*, London. Online at: www.theguardian.com/media/2009/nov/10/rupert-murdoch-google

Twombly, R. ed. 2010 *Frederick Law Olmsted: essential texts.* W.W. Norton & Company, London.

UCL 2014 'UCL has announced a second campus – UCL East – on Queen Elizabeth Olympic Park', University College Lonodn (UCL). Online at: www.ucl.ac.uk/news/news-articles/1214/021214_UCL_East_govt_funding_announcement

Ueberroth, P. 1985 *Made in America.* William Morrow & Co. Inc, New York.

UK 2010 'Digital Economy Act 2010', UK Government, London. Online at: www.statu-telaw.gov.uk/content.aspx?activeTextDocld=3699621

UKactive 2014a 'Turning the tide of inactivity', UKactive. Online at: www.ukactive.com/downloads/managed/Turning_the_tide_of_inactivity.pdf

UKactive 2014b 'Steps to solving inactivity', November, UKactive. Online at: www.ukac-tive.com/downloads/managed/Final_Final_Final_Steps_to_Report.pdf

UK Gov 2010 'Digital Economy Act 2010', UK Government, London. Online at: www. legislation.gov.uk/ukpga/2010/24/pdfs/ukpga_20100024_en.pdf

UK Gov 2011 'The English indices of deprivation 2010', Department of Communities and Local Government, UK Government, London. Online at: www.gov.uk/government/uploads/system/uploads/attachment_data/file/6871/1871208.pdf

UK Gov 2013 'Inspired by 2012: ihe legacy from the London 2012 Olympic and Paralympic Games', HM Government and Mayor of London. Online at: www.gov.uk/

government/uploads/system/uploads/attachment_data/file/224148/2901179_OlympicLegacy_acc.pdf

UN 1948 'Universal Declaration of Human Rights', United Nations, New York. Online at: www.un.org/en/documents/udhr/

UN 1976 'The International Covenant on Economic, Social and Cultural Rights', United Nations, New York. Online at: www.ochr.org/Documents/ProfessionalInterest/crescr.pdf

UN 2006 'The Convention of the Rights of Persons with Disabilities', United Nations, New York. Online at: www.un.org/disabilities/default.asp?id=290

UNDESA 2012 *Shanghai manual – a guide for sustainable urban development in the 21st century*. United Nations Department of Economic and Social Affairs (UNDESA), New York. Online at: https://sustainabledevelopment.un.org/index.php?page=view&type=400&n=633&menu=35

UNDESA 2014 'World urbanization prospects: the 2014 revision', UNDESA, New York. Online at: www.esa.un.org/unpd/wup/Highlights/WUP-Highlights.pdf

UNEP 2006 'Green score card for Winter Olympics', United Nations Environmental Programme (UNEP). Online at: www.unep.org/Documents.Multilingual/default.asp?DocumentID=5441&l=en

UNEP 2010 'UNEP environmental assessment: Expo 2010, Shanghai, China', United Nations Environmental Programme (UNEP). Online at: www.unep.org/pdf/SHANGHAI_REPORT_FullReport.pdf

UNEP 2012 'London 2012 will leave a lasting legacy for the UK and the Olympic movement: UNEP Executive Director', 26 July, United Nations Environmental Programme (UNEP). Online at: www.unep.org/NEWSCENTRE/default.aspx?DocumentId=2691&ArticleID=9239

UNESCO 2010 'World Anti-Piracy Observatory' (WAPO), 23 April, UNESCO, Paris. Online at: http://unesco.org/culture/en/antipiracy-observatory

UNESCO 2015 The World Heritage Convention, UNESCO, Paris. Online at: http://whc.unesco.org/en/convention/

UN-SF 2015 'Universal sustainable development goals: understanding the transformational challenge for developed countries', by Osborn, D., Cutter, A. and Ullah, F., Stakeholder Forum (SF), United Nations (UN), New York. Online at: http://sustainabledevelopment.un.org/index.php?page=view&type=400&nr=1684&menu=35

UN Watch 2010a 'Issue 247 – Chinese nationals protest forced evictions'. Search item 32, UN Watch. Online at http://unwatch.org/

UN Watch 2010b 'Joint NGO appeal for 18,000 victims of forced evictions by Shanghai World Expo' Search item 32, Issue 247, UN Watch. Online at www.unwatch.org/site

UNWTO 2014 'UNTWO tourism highlights, 2014 edition', UNWTO. Online at: http://mkt.unwto.org/publication/unwto-tourism-highlights-2014-edition

URLRate 2014 'firstrow1.eu is worth $5,870,880', URLRate. Online at: www.urlrate.com/www/firstrow1.eu

Urry, J. 2003 *Global complexity*. Polity, Cambridge.

Usborne, S. 2008 'After the party: what happens when the Olympics leave town', 19 August, *Independent*, London. Online at: www.independent.co.uk/sport/olympics/after-the-party-what-happens-when-the-Olympics-leave-town-901629.html

Ustinet 2008 'Sweden passes on IOC piracy complaint'. Online at: http://news.usti.net/home/newscn/?/living.entertainment.misc/2/wed/cq/Uolym-piratebay.RZMz.IaJ.html

Vainer, C. 2016 'Mega-events and the city of exception: theoretical explorations of the Brazilian experience', ch. 6 in Gruneau and Horne eds 2016b.

Vanderhoven, E. 2012 'London 2012: a social legacy for East London?', Community Links. Online at: www.community-links.org/linkswk/wp-content/PDF/London_2012_social_legacy.pdf

Verkaik, R. 2010 'Internet piracy crackdown by US studios', 1 March, *Independent*, London. Online at: www.independent.co.uk/news/media/online/internet-piracy-crackdown-by-us-studios-1913673.html

Viehoff, V. and Poynter, G. eds 2015 *Mega-event cities: urban legacies of global sport events*. Ashgate, Farnham.

Vincent, D. 2000 *The rise of mass literacy: reading and writing in modern Europe*. Polity, Cambridge.

Visit Britain 2012 'The London 2012 Olympic and Paralympic Games: our story' – Interim report, November. Online at: www.visitbritain.org/Images/VB Corporate DocLoRes_tcm29-5694.pdf

Wainwright, O. 2015 'Expo 2015: what does Milan gain by hosting this bloated global extravaganza?', 12th May, *Guardian*, London. Online at: www.theguardian.com/cities/2015/may/12expo-2015-what-does-milan-gain-by-hosting-this-bloated-global-extravaganza

Wainwright, O. 2016 'Into Orbit: my dizzying drop down the world's biggest slide', 23 June, *Guardian*, London. Online at: www.theguardian.com/artanddesign/2016/jun/23/carsten-holler-arcelormittal-orbit-slide-first-ride

Waitt, G. 2003 'Social impact of the Sydney Olympics'. Vol. 30, 1, pp. 194–215, *Annals of Tourism Research*.

Waldmeir, P. 2010 'Futuristic yet fruitful', 29 April, *Financial Times*, London. Online at: www.ft.com/cms/s/0/abbea04e-52f5-11df-813e-00144feab49a.html#axzz3bMxOecvr

Wall, R. 2014 'Special market reports: Issue 23 – Zaragoza, Spain', June, Horwath HTL. Online at: http://horwathhtlc.uk/2014/06/24/special-market-report-isssue-23-zaragoza-spain

Wallerstein, I. 2004 *World-system analysis: an introduction*. Duke University Press, Durham, NC.

Walls, M. 2009 'Parks and recreation in the United States: local park systems', Resources for the Future, Washington, DC. Online at: www.rff.org/documents/RFF-BCK-ORRG_LocalParks.pdf

Wang, D. 2008 *Rural-urban migration and policy responses in China: challenges and options*. ILO Asian Regional Programme on Governance of Labour Migration, International Labour Organization, Bangkok.

Wang, F.-L. 2007 'Brewing tensions, maintaining stabilities: the dual role of the Hukou system in contemporary China', ch. 2 in Yang ed.

WantChinaTimes 2012 'Shenzen deputy mayor latest casualty in anti-corruption efforts', 3 December, WantChinaTimes. Online at: www.wantchinatimes.com/news-subclass-cnt.aspx?id=20121203000075&cid=1101

Ward, K. 2011 'The World in 2050: Quantifying the shift in the global economy', HSBC Global Research. Online at: www2.warwickac.uk/fac/soc/csgr/green/foresight/economy/2011_hsbc_the_world_in_2050_-_quantifying_the_shift_in_the_global_economy.pdf

Washington Post 2005 'Cost of 2004 Athens Games continues to escalate', 10 August, *Washington Post*, Washington, DC. Online at: www.washingtonpost.com/wp-dyn/content/article/2005/08/09/AR200508090065.html

Wasserstrom, J. 2008 'A new kind of spectacle: how China changed the Olympics', 27 July, *Atlantic*. Online at: www.theatlantic.com/international/archive/2012/07/a-new-kindolympics/26047/

Wasserstrom, J. 2009 *Global Shanghai, 1850–2010: a history in fragments*. Routledge, London

Wasserstrom, J. 2010a *China in the 21st century*. Oxford University Press, New York

Wasserstrom, J. 2010b 'The Shanghai Expo: some things everyone needs to know', *China Daily*. Online at: http://usa.chinadaily.com.cn/thinktank/2010-04/29/content_9790628.htm

Watt, P. 2013 ' "It's not for us" – regeneration, the 2012 Olympics and the gentrification of East London'. Vol. 17, 1, 99–118, *City*. Online at: http://dx.doi.org/10.1080/1360 4813.2012.754190

WB 2014 'Ranking of the world's richest countries by GDP' (World Bank statistics formatted by Classora), Classora. Online at: http://en.classora.com/reports/t24369/general/ranking-of-the-worldsrichest-countries-bygdp?edition=1970&fields=

Webster, D. 2011 'City-building in China', ch. 13 in Birch, E. and Wachter, S. eds *Global Urbanization*. University of Pennsylvania Press, Philadelphia.

Webster, F. 2006 *Theories of the Information Society* (3rd edition). Routledge, London.

Wessels, B. 2009 *Understanding the internet*, Palgrave, London.

Wessels, B. 2014 *Exploring social change*. Palgrave, London.

Whannel, G. 1992 *Fields in vision: television sport and cultural transformation*. Routledge, London.

Wharton 2009 'From "star projects" to white elephants: the changing rule for urban development in Spain', Knowledge Wharton, University of Pennsylvania. Online at: http://knowledge.wharton.upenn.edu/article/from-star-projects-to-white-elephants-the-changing-rules-for-urban-development-in-spain/

Wheatcroft, G. 2007 *Le Tour: a history of the Tour de France*. Pocket Books, Simon and Schuster, New York.

Whyte, M. ed. 2010 *One country, two societies: rural-urban inequality in contemporary China*. Harvard University Press, London.

Wi-Fi 2015 'Who we are', Wi-Fi Alliance. Online at: www.wi-fi.org/who-we-are

Wiki 2011 '2011 Summer Universiade', Wikipedia. Online at: http://en.wikipedia.org/wiki/2011_Summer_Universiade

Wiki 2013a 'Cost of the Olympics Games', Wikipedia. Online at: http://en.wikipedia.org/wiki/Cost_of_the_Olympics_Games

Wiki 2013b 'Migration in China', Wikipedia. Online at: http://en.wikipedia.org/wiki/Migration_in_China

Wiki 2015a 'Olympic Stadium (Montreal)', Wikipedia. Online at: http://en.wikipedia.org/wiki/Olympic_Stadium_(Montreal)

Wiki 2015b '2004 Summer Olympics', Wikipedia. Online at: http://en.wikipedia.org/wiki/2004_Summer_Olympics

Wiki 2015c 'Wikipedia', Wikipedia. Online at: http://en.wikipedia.org/wiki/Wikipedia

Williams, H. 2012 'Anish Kapoor's Olympic Orbit tower unveiled', 11 May, *Independent*, London. Online at: www.independent.co.uk/arts-entertainment/art/news/anish-kapoors-olympic-orbit-tower-unveiled-7737118.html

Williams, M. 2012 'Spa and Pipa votes shelved after Congress climbs down on piracy bills', 20 January, *Guardian*. Online at: www.theguardian.com/technology/2012/jan/20/pipa-vote-shelved-harry-reid

Williams, R. 1961 *The long revolution*. Penguin Books, London.

Williams, R. 1974 *Television: technology and cultural form*. Fontana, London.

Williamson, T. 1998 *Polite landscapes: gardens and society in eighteenth century England*. Sutton Publishing Ltd, Stroud.

Wilson, D. and Purushothaman, R. 2003 'Dreaming with BRICs: the path to 2050', Goldman Sachs. Online at: www.goldmansachs.com/our-thinking/archive/archive-pdfs/brics-dream.pdf

Winter, T. ed. 2012 *Shanghai Expo: an international forum on the future of cities*. Routledge, London.

Winter, T. 2013 'Auto-exoticism: cultural display at the Shanghai Expo'. Vol. 18, 1, pp. 69–90, *Journal of Material Culture*.

WIPO 2015a 'Sport and broadcasting rights: adding value' (R. Vazquez), April, WIPO Magazine, World Intellectual Property Organization (WIPO). Online at: www.wipo.int/wipo_magazine/en/2013/02/article_0005.html

WIPO 2015b 'The Olympic Games', World Intellectual Property Organization (WIPO). Online at: www.wipo.int/ip-sport/en/olympic.html

Wolff, M. 2010 *The man who owns the news: inside the secret world of Rupert Murdoch*. Broadway Book, Random House, New York.

Wood, L. 1983 *FLO: a biography of Frederick Law Olmstead*. Johns Hopkins University Press, Baltimore.

Woodman, E. 2015 'Stratford's Olympicopolis: hung, drawn and culturally quartered', 7 January, *Architectural Review*. Online at: www.architectural-review.com/stratfords-olympicopolis-hung-drawn-and-culturally-quartered/8674318.article

Woollacott, E. 2014 'ISPs can be forced to block piracy sites, EU Court rules', Forbes. Online at: www.forbes.com/sites/emmawoollacott/2014/03/27/isps-can-be-forced-to-block-piracy-sites-eu-court-rules/

Work Foundation 2010 'A lasting legacy: how can London fully exploit the opportunities created by the Olympic Games in the recovery and to 2030?', The Work Foundation in association with Oxford Economics and the Department of Culture, Media and Sport (DCMS). Online at www.theworkfoundation.com/assets/docs/olympics 011210.pdf

World Audit 2015 'Democracy audit', World Audit.org. Online at: www.worldaudit.org/democracy.htm

WTTC 2007 'Lisbon: the impact of travel and tourism on jobs and the economy', World Travel and Tourism Council (WTTC). Online at: www.visitlisboa.com/getdoc/9b5c151b-fb28-4619-bee2-3051598145e1/Lisbon—The-Impacts-of-Travel—Tourism-on-Jobs-an.aspx

Wurtzel, A. 2012 'Olympic gold mine', 23 March, Research-Live. Online at: www.research-live.com/features/Olympic-gold-mine/4007796.article

Wurtzel, A. and Fulgoni, G. 2012 'Media consumption from the 2012 London Olympics', 1 October, LoveStats. Online at: http://lovestats.wordpress.com/2012/10/01/media-consumption-from-the-2012-london-olympics-wurtzel-from-nbc-and-fulgoni-from-comscore-amaresearch-mrx/

WWF 2014 'Living Planet report 2014', World Wildlife Fund (WWF). Online at: www.footprintnetwork.org/images/article_uploads/LPR2014_summary_low_res.pdf

Xinhua 2010 'Chinese leaders honor contributors to Shanghai Expo's success', 27 December, Xinhua News Agency. Online at: http://news.xinhuanet.com/english2010/china/2010-12/27/c_13666628.htm

Xinhua 2011 'Shenzen's pre-Universiade eviction of 80,000 "high risk" people sparks controversy', 13 April, Xinhua News Agency. Online at: http://news.xinhuanet.com/english2010/china/2011-04/13/c_13826681.htm

Xinhua 2012 'Shanghai Expo pavilions repurposed as art museums', 25 September, Xinhua News Agency. Online at: http://news.xinhuanet.com/english/china2012-09/25/c_123761307.html

Yanan, Z. 2015 'Internet industry – boom and boom', March, NewsChina Magazine. Online at: www.newschinamag.com/magazine/boom-and-boom

Yang, D. ed. 2007 *Discontented miracle: growth, conflict and institutional adaptation in China*. World Scientific, Singapore.

Yar, M. 2007 'Teenage kids or virtual villainy?', ch. 7 in Jewkes, Y. ed. *Crime online*. Willan Publishing, Cullompton.

Yiftachel, O. 2006 'Re-engaging planning theory? towards "south eastern" perspectives'. Vol. 5, 3, pp. 211–22, *Planning Theory*.

Zaragoza Ayuntamiento 2008a 'Expo Zaragoza and the transformation of the city'. Online at: www.soslogistica.org/publicpages/convegno_2008/Relazioni/Arnal_Citt_di_Zaragoza_RID.pdf

Zaragoza Ayuntamiento 2008b 'Mille digital campus'. Online at: www.milladigital.es/ingles/04_campusMilla.php

Zhen, L. 2010 'Asian Games in Guangzhou gets China gold, but sport neglected', 8 December, *Epoch Times*. Online at: www.theepochtimes.com/n2/china-news/asian-games-in-guangzhou-gets-china-gold-but-sport-neglected-47155.html

Ziakos, V. and Boukas, N. 2014 'Post-event leverage and Olympic Legacy'. Vol. 1, 2, pp. 87–101, *Athens Journal of Sports*.

Zimbalist, A. 2015 *Circus Maximus: the economic gamble behind hosting the Olympics and the World Cup*. Brookings Institutions, Washington, DC.

Zimmerman, P. 1976 'Los Angeles 1932', pp. 53–6, in Killanin and Rodda eds.

Zukin, S. 1995 *The cultures of cities*, Blackwells, Oxford.

Index